THE AMERICAN INDIAN

Past and Present

THE AMERICAN INDIAN

Past and Present

FIFTH EDITION

Edited by
ROGER L. NICHOLS
UNIVERSITY OF ARIZONA

McGraw-Hill
College

New York   St. Louis   San Francisco   Auckland   Bogotá   Caracas   Lisbon
London   Madrid   Mexico City   Milan   Montreal   New Delhi   San Juan
Singapore   Sydney   Tokyo   Toronto

McGraw-Hill College

A Division of The McGraw·Hill Companies

THE AMERICAN INDIAN: PAST AND PRESENT, FIFTH EDITION

This book is printed on acid-free paper.

1 2 3 4 5 6 7 8 9 0 QPF/QPF 9 3 2 1 0 9 8

ISBN 0-07-046600-9

Editorial director: *Jane E. Vaicunas*
Senior sponsoring editor: *Lynn Uhl*
Editorial assistant: *Rachael Morgan*
Developmental editor: *Monica Freedman*
Senior marketing manager: *Suzanne Daghlian*
Senior project manager: *Kay J. Brimeyer*
Senior production supervisor: *Sandra Hahn*
Designer: *JoAnne Schopler*
Compositor: *Carlisle Communications, Ltd.*
Typeface: *10/12 Times*
Printer: *Quebecor Printing Book Group/Fairfield, PA*

Library of Congress Cataloging-in-Publication Data

The American Indian : past and present / [edited by] Roger L. Nichols
— 5th ed.
    p.   cm.

  ISBN 0–07–046600–9
  1. Indians of North America.   I. Nichols, Roger L.
E77.2.A47   1999
973.04'97—dc21
                                                 98–27761
                                                 CIP

www.mhhe.com

ABOUT THE EDITOR

ROGER L. NICHOLS, a Wisconsin native, received his Ph.D. in American history from the University of Wisconsin. He has taught at Wisconsin State University, the University of Georgia, the University of Maryland, and, since 1969, at the University of Arizona. Currently a professor of history, he teaches courses in frontier America, Western America, and the Indians in American history. In addition to earlier editions of The American Indian, he has written or edited seven other books: General Henry Atkinson, The Missouri Expedition, Natives and Strangers, Stephen Long and American Frontier Exploration, American Frontier and Western Issues, Black Hawk and the Warrior's Path, and Indians in the United States and Canada: A Comparative History. In addition, he has written articles, chapters in multi-authored books, and essays on frontier towns, Western literature, transportation, the army, and Indian affairs. Nichols is married and has four children.

For Bradley Hawk, Matthew Hawk, and Hunter Barr

CONTENTS

PREFACE

In the past decade American public interest in minority and ethnic group issues has been limited primarily to envy of a few highly publicized successes of Indian gaming operations, to increasing concern over what is seen as a flood of undocumented aliens into the country, and to arguments over bilingual education. Occasionally an event beyond these topics related to Native American people catches media attention for a few days, but such items do not remain before the public for very long. For example in mid-January, 1998 the National Aeronautics and Space Agency (NASA) launched a rocket carrying the remains of Gene Shoemaker, a prominent planetary scientist, to the moon in tribute to his career accomplishments. That action brought an immediate negative response from Navajo Nation President Albert Hale who criticized NASA for insensitivity to Indian religious beliefs because it had defiled the moon which some Navajos consider to be sacred. Government officials apologized almost immediately, but just a few days later opinion ran strongly against Hale because of what was seen as his introduction of religion into public matters considered to be purely secular. Within a week the NASA action, Navajo protest, NASA apology, and public reactions had come and gone. It seems likely that many Americans heard little if anything about the incident. If events like this one get the headlines, it is an indication of how little serious interest the general society has in learning about minority affairs, particularly those regarding tribal peoples.

Nevertheless, minority issues continue as a central focus in American society, with the Indians representing some of the thorniest questions the nation faces. The long-standing nature and centrality of these matters has kept them before scholars continuously, resulting in a continuing flood of articles, essays, and longer studies concerning Native Americans. Because many categories and topics have received attention, no collection such as this can offer material on everything. Recognizing that these essays represent only a sample of materials from existing literature, this edition attempts to provide readings for all time periods and areas in the country. Clearly some gaps exist. For example there is little on Spanish-Indian relationships because of my inability to locate items that lend themselves to effective undergraduate teaching.

The scholarship on Indian-related topics continues to change each decade. While constitutional questions such as self-determination and tribal sovereignty occupy a smaller part of the current scholarship than previously, they have not lost their significance. Rather, many scholars have turned their interests to other matters resulting in a dramatic shift in what is being published about Indians today. As noted in the previous edition, attention to the environment, intratribal affairs, culture and religion, Indian literature, education, and comparisons with other minority groups in both American society and abroad has continued and even increased. In addition, more use of social science theory and models has characterized some of the recent writing. Topics such as world systems and their meanings for minority peoples, the Europeans' physical invasion of the Americas, and new emphases on the significance of race, class, and gender within American society may all be seen in the readings that follow.

One broad theme that runs through many of the essays is that of invasion, conquest, and domination of the Indians by the Europeans from the 1500s to the present. Clearly the military aspects of these processes have mostly disappeared, although at look at Wounded Knee, South Dakota in 1990 or at the New York-Canada border a few years later might persuade some that military or at least major police actions continue. The question of European and then Anglo-American determination to dominate and control the developing society runs through many of the essays. Whether trying to direct tribal agriculture and livestock raising in colonial New England or de-tribalizing Indian children in twentieth-century government-operated schools, the goal remained the same—to make Native Americans disappear as identifiable groups in the society.

Gradually this led to a situation where the government forced the tribes onto reservations. There, after having lost their original autonomy, they became administered peoples. Federal regulations dictated many aspects of their lives, and the allotment of tribal lands further reduced their economic base. Some of the readings address these issues directly by discussing the Navajo, reservation people in northern California, or the allotment program. When reservations came to be seen as having failed because they fostered Indian cultural pride and self identity, federal policies shifted to correct the apparent mistake of having established reservations in the first place. Thus, after World War II efforts to "terminate" the tribes, or to dismantle their reservations came to the fore. Coupled with that the bureaucrats attempted to move Indian people from the reservations to the major cities, apparently hoping to depopulate the reservations as cultural enclaves this way.

Despite the efforts to impose cultural domination on Native Americans, European and American societies and governments did not always succeed. Indians used their cultural strengths and determination to retain their independent identities and to undermine, deflect, or even actively oppose the invaders' actions. Often working through religious and cultural leaders particular groups strove to rebuff the invaders. These individuals joined forces from the days of Opechancanough in early colonial Virginia through the Lakota Ghost Dance actions at the end of the nineteenth century. In the twentieth century the Native American Church continues to serve a similar function. It provides cultural unity, religious strength, and a statement of group autonomy despite the near constant suspicion and even active opposition to its operations within the majority society.

When the first Europeans reached North America they came in tiny numbers and the native peoples outnumbered them many times over. However, virulent diseases swept across the continent destroying untold numbers as they went. In the face of such destruction, Indian superiority soon waned. Their numbers fell while those of the invaders grew steadily. Soon, in areas of mutual contact, Indians found themselves in a position of equality with their new and dangerous neighbors. Yet that too lasted only a short time, because the whites brought with them an overpowering sense of cultural superiority and ethnocentrism. Within a few years they came to see Indians as savage and backward people, and almost immediately used that perception to justify actions that led to rapid subjugation of the native peoples. In addition they were determined to reshape tribal societies and cultures in their own image and turned their attention to nearly all aspects of Indian life. Whether language, religion, clothing, eating habits, shelter, or the occupations and duties of the sexes, almost nothing escaped their determined meddling. These efforts are examined by the essays that consider Creek, Cherokee, and Navajo women directly, and by several others that discuss reservation and city life.

As a group, the essays included here attempt to trace the changing situation of Indians from their aboriginal independence through their subjugation and the gradual turnaround that has occurred in the last half of the twentieth century. Today, issues such as self-determination, the degree of sovereignty tribes exercise on the reservations, and the relationships between tribal governments, the states, and the federal government are all open for reconsideration. As the tribes, Congress, and the courts wrestle with these issues, the changes that have characterized Indian experiences appear likely to continue. In fact, since the late 1970s the federal government has developed an acknowledgement program designed to examine the claims of "forgotten" Indians for recognition and tribal status. Thus, one sees circumstances where some people want to become recognized as Indians, some are working toward what they hope will bring complete sovereignty, and others are moving into the mainstream society.

Readers seeking tales of courage, or exciting victories or of massacres and defeats will find some, but not all of those things here. Most of these readings relate little of military conflict. Yet they do discuss a variety of situations in which Indian leaders and groups did succeed in achieving their objectives. This approach to Native American issues has overshadowed the older "boots and saddles" literature because most scholars now strive to place Indians at the center of the analysis and narrative. As a unique minority in our nation's history, Indians have experienced many of the difficulties and much of the discrimination suffered by others. At the same time, however, as the original inhabitants of this land they have been overrun by military force, simple numbers, or cultural and legal pressures in ways that other ethnic and racial groups have not. Despite these experiences Indians remain an integral part of American society as the nation moves into the twenty-first century. For example, in 1998 nearly 280 Indian-owned casinos are busily separating other Americans from their money, while at least thirty-one tribally operated colleges now bring higher education and vocational training to reservation people in states across the country.

Readers having a variety of concerns should find this collection of articles interesting and useful. As previously mentioned, one basic goal of the readings is to offer material related to all parts of the country and the entire range of American history, at least from colonial Virginia to the present. Another goal is to include the most interesting articles on each of the topics being presented so that students and others will actually read this material. These essays can be used as a text or a supplement in a variety of courses in either the social sciences or the humanities. Classes in United States history, American Indian or Native American history, Native American studies, ethnic studies, and minority history will all benefit from the insights the readings offer. In compiling this anthology, every effort has been made to select items by the most competent scholars. Except for deleting the footnotes all of the articles appear in full, as their authors intended them. Brief headnotes introduce each chapter and provide background information or historical perspective for the reader.

Many people helped with the planning and preparation of this edition, and they all deserve thanks. Faculty and scholars at other colleges and universities read the proposed outline or responded to my request for items to be considered. Even though I did not accept all of their suggestions, the ideas they offered stimulated my thinking and affected my choices. Several of the students in one of my recent graduate courses made valuable recommendations. They include Albert J. McCarn, Jr., Valerie J. Phillips, and John M. Shaw. Jennifer Fish Kashay contributed both as a member of that class, and also as my research assistant in the final stages of manuscript preparation. Having the cooperation of the authors whose works are included and of the editors and permissions staff people from the journals where the articles appeared originally was essential. Thanks are also due to Lyn Uhl and the editorial and production staff at McGraw-Hill for their help, cooperation, and support.

Roger L. Nichols
University of Arizona

IMPORTANT EVENTS IN NATIVE AMERICAN HISTORY

1535	Jacques Cartier visits St. Lawrence Valley
1540	Coronado visits the New Mexico pueblos
	DeSoto visits the southeastern United States
1585	St. Augustine, Florida is founded by Spain
	English land at Roanoke Island, North Carolina
1598	Oñate brings settlers into New Mexico
1607	English found Jamestown, Virginia settlement
1608	French found Quebec settlement
1609–14	First Anglo-Powhatan War in Virginia
1616–19	Epidemics sweep through coastal tribes of New England
1620	Pilgrims found Plymouth Colony
1621	Massasoit and Pilgrims make a long-lasting treaty
1622	Opechancanough leads major Indian attack on Virginia
1637	English defeat the Pequots in New England
1642–43	Dutch defeat Hudson River Valley Tribes in New York
1644	Opechancanough is defeated and killed in last Powhatan resistance
1649	Iroquois begin destruction of Hurons
1661	Franciscans raid Pueblo kivas to destroy Indian religious items
1675–76	Metacom's (King Philip's) War is major defeat for New England tribes
1676	Bacon's Rebellion brings last major war to Virginia tribes
1680	Pueblo Revolt drives Spanish from Southwest
1691	Spanish reconquer New Mexico
1701	Iroquois Confederacy makes peace with France and Great Britain
1703–04	Slave raids against Apalachees in northern Florida
1711–12	Tuscarora War in Carolina
1715	Yamassee War in Carolina
1722	Abenaki War in Maine
1729–31	Natchez Tribe is destroyed by French in Mississippi
1751	Pima Revolt drives Spain out of Arizona

1763	Royal Proclamation Line tries to separate tribes and pioneers
	Pontiac leads a multitribal rebellion against the British
1769	Spanish settlement of California
1775–83	American Revolution
1779–81	Major smallpox epidemic among the tribes
1782	Massacre of peaceful Christian Indians at Gnanenhutten
1790	Alexander McGillavry signs Treaty of New York for Creeks
1790–94	Fighting between Indians and pioneers in Ohio River Valley
1794	Indians are defeated at Battle of Fallen Timbers
1799	Handsome Lake begins preaching a new religion among Senecas
1805	Shawnee Prophet Tenskwatawa begins religious pantribal movement
1809	Tecumseh tries to form a defensive alliance of tribes against United States
1811	Indians are defeated at Battle of Tippecanoe
1812	Ohio Valley tribes join British in War of 1812
1813	Tecumseh is killed in Battle of the Thames
1813–14	Creek, or Red Stick, War in Alabama
1819	Congress establishes Indian Civilization Fund
1821	Sequoyah develops a Cherokee syllabary
1824	War Department organizes the Office of Indian Affairs
1828	*Cherokee Phoenix,* a bilingual newspaper, is begun
1830s	Forced removal of Eastern tribes beyond the Mississippi River
1830	President Jackson signs the Indian Removal Act
1831	*Cherokee Nation* v. *Georgia* decision
1832	*Worcester* v. *Georgia* decision
	Black Hawk War in Illinois and Wisconsin
1834	Indian Trade and Intercourse Act is passed
1835–42	Second Seminole War
1837	Major smallpox epidemic hits tribes along Missouri River
1846	U.S. acquires Oregon, with border at 49th parallel
1848	Mexican Cession brings the Southwest into the United States
1847–49	Oregon and California trails bring pioneers west
1849	Office of Indian Affairs moves to newly created Interior Department
1861–65	American Civil War
1862	Sante Sioux War in Minnesota
1863–68	Navajo are forced to the Bosque Redondo
1864	Sand Creek Massacre of Cheyennes by Colorado Volunteers
1866	Fetterman Massacre

1867	Board of Indian Commissioners is established
1868	Red Cloud leads Sioux to victory; Bozeman Trail is closed
	Fourteenth Amendment to the Constitution denies Indians the vote
1869	President Grant launches his Quaker Policy
1870	Congress appropriates first money specifically for Indian education
1871	Congress ends the treaty system
1872–73	Modoc War in Oregon
1874	Red River War in Texas
1875–77	Great Sioux War; Custer is defeated in 1876
1877	Nez Perce War
1878	Funds appropriated for Indian police forces on the reservations
1879	National Indian Association is founded
	Richard Pratt founds Carlisle Indian School
1881	Sun Dance is outlawed, and tribal medicine men are arrested
1882	Indian Rights Association is founded
1883	Lake Mohonk Conferences begin
	Courts of Indian Offenses are established
1884	Beginning of modern peyotism rites
1885	Helen Hunt Jackson publishes *A Century of Dishonor*
1886	Geronimo's surrender ends the Apache Wars
1887	Dawes Severalty Act (General Allotment Act) is passed
1889	Wovoka spreads his Ghost Dance teachings
1890	Massacre of Sioux at Wounded Knee, S.D.
1896	Office of Indian Affairs orders adult males to have hair cut
1903	*Lone Wolf* v. *Hitchcock* decision
1907	Burke Act amends the Dawes Act
1911	Society of American Indians is founded
1917–18	8,000 Indians serve in World War I
1918	Native American Church incorporated in Oklahoma
1923	Committee of One Hundred investigation of Indian affairs
1924	American Indian Citizenship Act
1926	National Council of American Indians is founded
1928	Meriam Report is published
1934	Indian Reorganization Act is passed
1935	Indian Arts and Crafts Board is established
1941–45	25,000 Indians serve in World War I II
1944	National Congress of American Indians is founded
1946	Indian Claims Commission is established
1952	Public Law 280

1953	House Concurrent Resolution 108
	Congress revises liquor regulations for Indians
1957	Reservation industries program begins
1961	American Indian Chicago Conference demands self-determination
	National Indian Youth Council is founded
1964	Institute of American Indian Arts is founded at Santa Fe
1966	Navajo found Rough Rock Demonstration School
1968	Congress passes the Indian Bill of Rights
	American Indian Movement (AIM) is founded
1969	N. Scott Momaday (Kiowa) wins Pulitzer Prize for *House Made of Dawn*
	Indians occupy Alcatraz Island
1970	Taos Pueblo regains Blue Lake
1971	Alaska Native Claims Settlement Act
1972	Trail of Broken Treaties and occupation of BIA office in Washington, D.C.
1973	Sixty-seven day confrontation at Wounded Knee
1974	*United States* v. *State of Washington*—Boldt decision
1975	Indian Self-Determination and Educational Assistance Act
1978	American Indian Religious Freedom Act
	Tribally Controlled Community College Act is passed
	Federal Tribal Acknowledgement Program is established
1980	Penobscot/Passamaquoddy claims settled
1988	Indian Gaming Regulatory Act
1990	Native American Grave Protection and Repatriation Act
1990	*Employment Division* v. *Smith* decision
1991	Custer Battlefield National Monument renamed Little Bighorn Battlefield National Monument
1992	Mashantucket Pequots begin work on Foxwoods Casino in Connecticut
1994	George Gustav Heye Center of the National Museum of the American Indian opened in New York City
1998	Thirty-one tribal colleges in operation

1

FULL BLOOD, MIXED BLOOD, GENERIC, AND ERSATZ: THE PROBLEM OF INDIAN IDENTITY

WILLIAM T. HAGAN

All of the contributors to this collection assume some definition of Indianness and the nature of tribal societies. Yet the issue of just who is an Indian, who decides that, and what criteria are used has remained unclear throughout American history. Do the Indians decide? What authority should the government have in this matter? Have federal laws, administrative actions, or court decisions laid down any clear guidelines on this issue? In this essay the author suggests that few answers to these questions are clear and accepted. In general, federal officials have insisted that for a person to be considered an Indian he or she needs to have some Indian blood and a formal connection with some recognized tribal group. Just what percentage of blood and what evidence is needed to establish that fact vary widely. In addition, proof of a person's tie to an organized tribe might differ as well. Formal status as a tribal member is important because of things as varied as voting rights in the corporate activities of Alaskan native people or membership in social and religious societies in parts of the West. The author claims that during most of American history the federal government dealt with the tribes without giving much careful thought to the nature of Indian status and tribal membership. Then he traces what guidelines have come into being and the impact they have had on Native American societies down to the present.

William T. Hagan is a professor of history at the University of Oklahoma.

One of the most perplexing problems confronting American Indians today is that of identity. Who is an American Indian? The question is raised in a bewildering variety of situations. Contingent on its resolution can be the recognition of a group by the federal government, voting rights in a multimillion-dollar Alaskan corporation, or acceptance of an individual as a member of a pueblo's tightly knit society. Nor is this a question

Source: William T. Hagan, "Full Blood, Mixed Blood, Generic, and Ersatz: The Problem of Indian Identity," *Arizona and the West,* 27 (Winter 1985), pp. 309–326. © *Arizona and the West* 17 (Winter 1975). Reprinted with permission of the publisher.

which has arisen only recently. It has been a problem for individuals, tribes, and government administrators since the birth of this nation.

Four centuries to the year after Christopher Columbus began the semantic confusion over how to label the original inhabitants of this hemisphere, Commissioner of Indian Affairs Thomas Jefferson Morgan spoke to a more important issue. He devoted six pages of his 1892 annual report to the question: What is an Indian? "One would have supposed," observed Morgan, "that this question would have been considered a hundred years ago and had been adjudicated long before this." "Singularly enough, however," he continued, "it has remained in abeyance, and the Government has gone on legislating and administering law without carefully discriminating as to those over whom it has a right to exercise such control."

Nearly a century after Commissioner Morgan expressed surprise at this state of affairs (1980), the Department of Education spent $90,000 to try to establish a useful definition of the term *Indian.* Another government agency, the Branch of Federal Acknowledgement, plans (1984) to spend millions to try to determine which of nearly a hundred tribes applying for federal recognition should merit it.

The founding fathers provided little guidance in the Constitution on matters relating to Indians. They included no legal definition of the term *Indian,* and in fact mentioned the word only twice. The federal agencies responsible for the conduct of Indian affairs, first the War Department and then the Interior Department, failed to fill the gap, and it was left to the courts to grapple with the problem of Indian identity.

In a series of cases in the nineteenth century the courts dealt with the issue but never formulated a simple definition to put the issue to rest. According to Felix Cohen, author of the monumental *Handbook of Federal Indian Law* (1971), the courts did find two considerations most significant in determining Indian identity and status. These considerations were enunciated in *United States* v. *Rogers* in 1846. First, the individual must have some Indian blood; and second, those Indians with whom he/she claimed affiliation must accept him/her as a fellow tribesman.

Cohen adds that ethnological evidence also has been used in determining full-blood status. A notorious example was in a series of cases involving the inhabitants of pueblos in New Mexico. In 1869 the supreme court of New Mexico Territory held that the residents of the pueblos were not Indians, in part because they were "a peaceable, industrious, intelligent, honest, and virtuous people." Presumably, if they had been militant, indolent, stupid, dishonest, and immoral, they would have qualified as Indians. In 1912 a United States circuit court employed similar reasoning. It ruled in the case of a family dropped from the Lower Brulé Sioux tribal rolls that their having one-eighth Indian blood was evidence of "sufficient Indian blood to substantially handicap them in the struggle of existence." Therefore, the court ruled, the members of the family should be considered to have full-blood status and be reenrolled with the Lower Brulé Sioux.

In the second half of the nineteenth century the relative affluence of some tribes attracted numerous enterprising non-Indians, and the question of Indian identity assumed new significance. The Five Civilized Tribes, for example, were inundated by outsiders, many of whom sought membership in those tribes. By 1890 non-Indians made up more than seventy percent of the population of Indian Territory, the home of the Cherokees, Choctaws, Chickasaws, Creeks, and Seminoles. Some of these non-Indians were blacks who before the Civil War had been slaves owned by the tribesmen. After the war, the United States had prevailed upon three of the tribes—the Cherokees, Creeks, and Seminoles—to grant full citizenship to their ex-slaves. By 1890 the Choctaws had granted some privileges to their freedmen, but the Chickasaws were still holding out.

White men, however, constituted the great bulk of non-Indians living among the Five Civilized Tribes in the post–Civil War era. Some of these whites married Indian women, fathered mixed-blood children, and applied for tribal membership. The Cherokees, Choctaws, and Chickasaws permitted this. Many other white men, without a shadow of a legal claim, attempted to secure a place on tribal rolls in order to enjoy the economic benefits—principally access to land—of being a member of one of the Five Civilized Tribes.

The situation was further complicated for the Cherokees by the requests of Eastern Cherokees, descendants of those who had not removed to Oklahoma, to be admitted to the rolls of the Cherokee Nation. This led to a lawsuit in which the Eastern Band sued the United States and the Cherokee Nation. The finding of the U.S. Supreme Court in 1885 was a signal victory for the right of the Cherokee Nation to determine its own criteria for citizenship, and the decision would be used as a precedent to ensure the same authority for other tribes.

Within a few months after the court ruled for the Cherokee Nation, the agent for those Indians was directed to cease issuing citizenship certificates and to publicize the fact that in the future this would be a matter to be adjudicated exclusively by the Cherokee Nation. Encouraged by this ruling, the Cherokees created a three-man commission to handle claims to Cherokee citizenship. The tribe also moved to expel individuals who had filed for citizenship prior to the time the matter was removed from the agent's hands. Some of those ousted protested to the federal government that they were being forced off land after having made substantial improvements in the way of fencing and buildings. The Indian Commissioner expressed considerable sympathy for those squatters who could show some evidence of Cherokee blood, and he refused to assist the Cherokee Nation in ridding itself of these intruders. They were usually American citizens, and the federal government clearly placed their interests above those of noncitizen Indians.

The Five Civilized Tribes were not alone in suffering from non-Indians who hoped to acquire tribal membership and access to tribal property. A well-publicized example was the claim of the Murphy family to membership in the Sac and Fox band holding a reservation in Kansas. Largely because of the Indian Rights Association, the well-known organization of friends of the Indian, the Murphy claim was finally defeated, although not before it had caused the band considerable aggravation and expense over a period of about ten years.

The Murphy claim had arisen through a mixed-blood tie. In the 1870s, as a matter of charity, the Sac and Fox had adopted an elderly and impoverished visitor, a Menominee woman. After the woman died, her daughter, who had married a white man named Murphy, applied for adoption. After refusing her petition more than once, the Sac and Fox Council finally adopted her, although it specifically excluded her several mixed-blood children. Nevertheless, in 1889 the Murphy woman's offspring applied for adoption by the Sac and Fox in order to get access to the reservation in Kansas. Their petition denied, the Murphys sought help from the Indian Bureau. At considerable expense the government conducted two investigations of the Murphy claims. Both upheld the refusal of the Sac and Fox, but the complainants were undaunted.

Aided by the senators from neighboring Nebraska, the Murphys obtained a favorable ruling from an Indian commissioner and took possession of land on the Sac and Fox reservation, including a house occupied by an Indian. The Indian Rights Association intervened at this point and was able to get the Murphys removed from the property. The Murphys then took the matter to court, where they lost. They even tried to obtain recognition as members of the Sac and Fox band through a special act of Congress, only to have the bill die in committee. The ten-year-long struggle cost the Sac and Fox an estimated $10,000 in legal fees.

The Murphy claim had originated with the mixed-blood children of a woman adopted by the Sac and Fox. A common problem for all tribes was the question of rights to be accorded white men who married Indian women and the offspring of such unions. In 1888 Senator Henry L. Dawes, who the previous year had authored the celebrated severalty act, sponsored another piece of legislation. This bill prohibited a white man married to an Indian from acquiring from his wife's tribe any land or special privileges as a result of that marriage. The law, however, did not speak directly to the status of the mixed-blood children who were the product of such marriages.

Prior to the passage of this 1888 law there had been a contradiction between common law and tribal practice. Common law held that descent is patrilineal, and therefore the children of an American citizen and an Indian woman were themselves American citizens. Among most Indian tribes, however, descent is matrilineal. In discussing the problem of Indian identity in his 1892 report, Indian Commissioner Morgan stated that in the past the government had accepted tribal definitions of membership. Tribes usually had accepted mixed-bloods into full membership if their mothers were tribal members, a situation which had implications for land titles for some settlers.

A common provision of treaties negotiated by the Peace Commission of 1867–68 was a requirement that any subsequent purchase of land from the tribe involved would not be valid unless approved by three fourths of the adult males of that tribe. To meet this requirement, the government had routinely sought the signatures of mixed-bloods to validate purchases of tribal land. Under the circumstances, Commissioner Morgan advised continuing to allow tribes to accept mixed-bloods into full membership. To hold that this group were not Indians "would unsettle and endanger the titles to much of the lands that have been relinquished by Indian tribes and patented to citizens of the United States." As always, ensuring settlers' land titles took precedence over concern about the shabby tactics required to get enough Indian signatures on a sale of tribal land.

By the end of the nineteenth century the principle had been established that—barring action by Congress—the tribes were the final authority in determining their membership, even if the Indian practice of tracing descent matrilineally ran counter to common law. This tribal right was reaffirmed in 1978 in a case involving Santa Clara Pueblo, which, incidentally, traces descent patrilineally. A woman who had married outside the pueblo sought to have overturned a pueblo ruling that children born of that marriage were not members of the tribe. The woman had sued on the grounds that the pueblo's action was a violation of the 1968 Indian Civil Rights Act. The Supreme Court refused to interfere with what it regarded as the pueblo's authority to regulate its own "internal and social relations."

After the flurry of activity generated by non-Indians trying to cash in on severalty program allotments had subsided, there was a period in the early 1900s during which Indian identity was broadly defined in a generic sense by some Indian spokesmen. These years saw the emergence of what Hazel Hertzberg has described as Reform Pan-Indianism. Hertzberg detailed the problems that "Red Progressives" had in determining who qualified for membership in the organization they launched in 1911, the Society of American Indians. The society provided for three categories of membership, with the first two limited to those of Indian blood. Only members of these two categories could hold office in the organization.

As expected from a group of middle-class Americans of varying degrees of Indian ancestry, the founders of the society did not confine membership to just those who held tribal memberships. For example, the self-styled Seneca Arthur Parker, a founding father of the organization, was three-quarters white. Of even more importance, his mother was not Seneca—which meant that within that matrilineal tribe he was not considered truly Seneca. The best he could claim was adoption by the tribe. Thus, to qualify for one of the two memberships reserved for Indians in the society, a person needed to be only one-sixteenth Indian, if not on a tribal roll. An even smaller blood quantum was required if the applicant was on a tribal roll.

During the 1920s new leadership in the society turned away from the pan-Indianism of the founders and began to emphasize tribal affiliation and tribal cultures. Factional struggles within the organization caused a shrinking membership and a diminution of its influences. By the end of the decade the best-known Indian to the general public was not a leader in the Society of American Indians, but Sylvester Long Lance, whose claim to be Indian was debatable.

Long Lance was the 1920s version of today's Jamake Highwater, the self-proclaimed Blackfoot who in recent years has parlayed his declarations of Indian heritage into publishing and television contracts. Both Sylvester Long Lance and Highwater had roots among the remnants of Southeastern tribes who lived a troubled existence sandwiched between the much larger white and black populations. Sylvester Long, as he was known as a child, had been born into a North Carolina family of mixed black-Indian ancestry, a family which white North Carolinians designated Negro. Long, however, was admitted to Carlisle Indian School as a Cherokee. After service in the Canadian Army during World War I he settled in western Canada, where he was known as Sylvester Long Lance. In 1922 he was adopted by the Blackfoot tribe and given the status of an honorary chief and a new name, Buffalo Child. By the late 1920s Long Lance had published his life story—considerably embellished—entitled *Autobiography of a Blackfoot Indian Chief.* Reprinted twice, the book, together with articles Long Lance wrote on Indian life for *Cosmopolitan, Good Housekeeping,* and other popular magazines of the day, made him a celebrity.

While Sylvester Long Lance capitalized on his Indian roots, however remote, Congress continued to wrestle with the proper definition of *Indian.* In 1931 it restricted membership in the Eastern Cherokee Band to those at least one-sixteenth Cherokee. Three years later the Wheeler-Howard Indian Reorganization Act, which inaugurated the Indian New Deal, defined three categories of people:

1. All persons of Indian descent who were members of a recognized tribe under federal jurisdiction.
2. All persons who were descendants of such members who on June 1, 1934, were residing within the present boundaries of an Indian reservation.
3. All other persons of one-half or more Indian blood.

Clearly membership in a federally recognized tribe was the easiest and only sure way to prove eligibility for government programs under the Wheeler-Howard Act.

Besides furnishing its own definition of Indian, the act also encouraged tribes to compile membership rolls and in the process define membership criteria. These have varied widely. A common criterion required one-quarter blood in a particular tribe, although one-half was sometimes demanded. No degree of blood of the tribe concerned was specified in a few cases. And it grew complicated in some instances. The Osages, for example, developed three categories of tribal membership. One qualified the individual, as the holder of a headright or a portion of a headright, to share in certain tribal income. Then there was the general membership roll, a place on which qualified the holder to vote in tribal elections. The third membership category related to officeholding and was restricted to those with at least one-quarter Indian blood, regardless of tribe, as long as the individual was on the Osage rolls.

By the late 1960s and early 1970s new forces again focused on the issue of Indian identity. One was the rising popularity of Indianness. The activism of Red Power militants had inspired new pride among Native Americans, while at the same time the Indian image profited from their portrayal in television commercials and popular writing as the first conservationists. The remarkable increase the 1980 census showed in the number of Americans who chose to identify themselves as Indians reflected this new perception of Indians by the public.

This led to the appearance of more ersatz Indians, as they were described in 1974 in a Philadelphia newspaper article reprinted in *Wassaja,* a publication of the Indian Historical Society. The individual who inspired this reporting was one Lightfoot Talking Eagle. Talking Eagle's claim to be a Susquehannock "sun priest" had been denounced by the American Indian Society of Pennsylvania. Nevertheless, Talking Eagle had appeared on television and had delivered public lectures in his role as a sun priest. The article in the Philadelphia paper went on to denounce others who fraudulently claimed Indian ancestry to qualify for student aid reserved for Indians, to help merchandise their handicrafts, or simply to satisfy their yearning for identification with a group enjoying, at least temporarily, considerable public acceptance.

The enterprising reporter who uncovered this story even contacted *Wassaja*'s editor, Rupert Costo, for his comment on Talking Eagle. Costo, an enrolled Cahuilla, acknowledged the problem but neatly sidestepped offering a definition of *Indian,* maintaining that tribesmen were learning to cope with the problem and that in time it would be overcome. The president of the American Indian Society of Pennsylvania was less optimistic: "It is apparent the $2.00 head band and the Hong Kong medallion, with a self declaration, is going to be a method . . . by which the Indian population is going to boom."

And there were other incentives for discovering Indian ancestry. These included the well-publicized, multimillion-dollar judgments being awarded tribes in land claims cases. Every announcement of a large judgment seemed to trigger the memories of some Americans that their family trees included an Indian, usually a chief's daughter, a princess. Another incentive was the rapid increase in federal assistance programs available to Indians. This growth had its origin in President Lyndon Johnson's war on poverty, and the programs continued to proliferate under his successors. By 1980 there were over seventy programs, administered by many different government agencies, which could be tapped by Indians.

Eligibility for these federal programs, most of which were administered by offices other than the Bureau of Indian Affairs, varied from agency to agency. The Indian Health Service tended to be more flexible in its interpretation of eligibility, giving considerable latitude to the Indian communities to identify those meriting health services. In contrast, the Bureau of Indian Affairs reserved the exclusive right to determine who participated in the programs it administered. In Oklahoma, for example, in an effort to reduce the cost of the program, the bureau has an "informal agreement" with the state that the federal government will provide welfare payments only for those Cherokees with at least one-quarter Indian blood, with Oklahoma responsible for all others on the tribal roll.

Other agencies had their own definitions of *Indian*. School boards, anxious to collect subsidies from the federal government for educating Indian children, were first told by the Department of Health, Education, and Welfare that the child must be at least one-quarter Indian blood to merit assistance. That requirement was relaxed by the 1972 Education Act, which was passed at the full flood of the nation's concern for minorities and the disadvantaged. The new law more broadly defined *Indian* and provided for grants to local agencies for a wide range of projects to improve the educational opportunities of Native American children. The intent, as the report of the Senate committee handling the bill made clear, was to help remedy "the consequences of past Federal policies and programs." The policies and programs referred to were the termination and relocation efforts of the 1950s and 1960s, with their resultant "impoverishment and educational deprivation of many of the so-called non-federal Indians."

With so much government assistance and community status riding on being identified as Indian, and with tribal membership being the most frequently employed criterion, tribal affiliation assumed new significance. This was highlighted in two articles in the *American Indian Journal* in 1980. The first was by Jamake Highwater, who appeared on the membership rolls of no tribe, but maintained that both of his parents were mixed-bloods. He attacked the "exclusivity and cultural snobbery" of those tribal members who tended to look down upon individuals of Indian ancestry with no tribal status (the so-called generic Indians). According to Highwater, the "grand climax" of his "professional and personal life" came when he was adopted by Blackfeet in Canada, the same people who had extended honorary membership to Sylvester Long Lance a half-century earlier. Highwater used the term "professional and personal life" advisedly because he had used his Indian ancestry to advance himself professionally as an author and TV producer.

The companion article to Highwater's was designed to show another side of the issue. It was written by Ron Andrade, an official of the National Congress of American Indians. Andrade defended the conservatism of tribal enrollment practices. He identified the desire to share in supposed tribal wealth as the principal motivation of those seeking tribal membership and labeled them the "Indians of convenience." However, Andrade cited other possible motivations, such as living out childhood fantasies of Indian life and the desire to associate with a culture which might offer more stability than what characterized American society in the 1970s.

Andrade was concerned that, by relaxing their standards for membership, tribes would lose things more valuable than money. He feared that tribal cultures and traditions would be dangerously diluted by an influx of strangers who would "jeopardize the entire future of the tribe." Other Indians feared a more massive dilution from another quarter.

Just as there have been thousands of individuals in the last twenty-five years desiring admission to the rolls of federally recognized tribes, there were nearly a hundred groups seeking federal recognition as tribes. In the early 1960s these ranged from tribes recently terminated to groups that had preserved some kind of tribal identity but had never enjoyed federal recognition, with all the psychological and financial advantages that go with it.

Further variations in status were discernible on close examination. Some tribes had federal recognition but no access to federal assistance programs. Some were recognized by the states in which they lived but could participate in only selected federal programs. Other tribes were recognized by states but enjoyed no federal services. There were many tribes, particularly in the East, which were recognized by neither state nor federal government.

A refinement in the art of categorizing tribes was illustrated by the Coushatta case in Louisiana. The Coushattas have lived in the lower Mississippi Valley for hundreds of years. As late as the 1950s, before they fell victims to termination, the Coushattas had received limited education and health services from the federal government. In the Indian renaissance of the early 1970s the Coushattas began to agitate for state and federal recognition. First, Louisiana offered recognition, and then the federal government accepted them as eligible for the partial services available to the "landless tribes" category. To be qualified for the full range of federal programs, however, the Coushattas needed a land base. This technicality was taken care of with the assistance of the Association on American Indian Affairs, which purchased fifteen acres and deeded it to the Coushattas for a reservation. The Coushattas then turned over their newly acquired homeland to be held in trust, finally meeting all criteria for recognition as wards of the United States.

While the Coushattas were winning their battle, other tribes and bands that had been terminated in the 1950s and early 1960s were actively seeking restoration of recognition. As political entities they no longer enjoyed a special relationship with the federal government, although their individual members were still eligible for aid programs, particularly in the health and education fields.

The termination plan for the Utes of the Unitah and Ouray Reservation had been particularly unfortunate. It has created two classes, according to blood quantum. Those over one-half Ute were classified as full-bloods and remained wards of the federal government. Those one-half or less were classified as mixed-bloods, given a share of tribal assets proportional to their numbers, and terminated. The arrangements, however, did not take into consideration hunting and fishing rights on the million-acre Ute reservation. This arbitrary division of the Ute people has, in the thirty years it has been in force, produced real tension between the two groups and spawned lawsuits and near violence.

Restoring federal recognition to the Utes and Coushattas inspired little opposition, as contrasted to the resistance met by those groups seeking federal recognition for the first time. Nevertheless, beginning in 1956 with the Lumbees of North Carolina, a number of tribes, who never previously enjoyed it, have managed to secure the status of wards of the federal government. For the Lumbees the victory initially was tempered by the provision that their federal recognition carried with it no federal services.

In the 1960s the combination of greater pride in Indianness, the millions of dollars available in Indian programs, and the publicity accorded the land claims cases led to first a trickle and then a flood of applications for federal recognition. The American Indian

Policy Review Commission, created by Congress in 1970, estimated in its 1977 report that more than a hundred tribes, comprising over 100,000 Indians, were being denied the "protection and privileges of the Federal-Indian relationship." By the end of 1983 nearly one hundred petitions for recognition had been received by the Bureau of Indian Affairs.

The report of the Policy Review Commission had concluded: "Every Indian tribal group which seeks recognition must be recognized; every determination that a group is not an Indian tribal group must be justified soundly on the failure of that group to meet any of the factors which would indicate Indian tribal existence." The commission also proposed that the government aid tribes financially in the expensive task of researching their history in order to meet government criteria.

Nevertheless, there were forces opposed to the federal government recognizing any more tribes. The Interior Department was not sure it even had the legal right to unilaterally grant recognition. As a result, the department was not prepared to push for recognition of particular tribes until Congress took action, either in individual cases, as it had done with the Lumbees, or by authorizing a formal recognition procedure for all applicants. Members of Congress, for their part, were not anxious to rush into a policy which could result in land being removed from local tax rolls and thousands being added to eligibility lists for federal aid programs.

Nor were the already recognized tribes eager to share the federal pie. In 1978 Veronica Murdock, then president of the National Congress of American Indians, appeared before the Senate Select Committee on Indian Affairs, which was considering guidelines for recognition. Murdock expressed concern that "indiscriminate recognition . . . could have adverse impact on all Indian tribes." It would, she argued, "diminish the significance of tribal claims to sovereign rights" and, unless appropriations increased proportionately, "mean slicing the 'Federal funding pie' too thin."

As early as 1969 a bill had been introduced into Congress to extend recognition to all organized tribes in the United States. However, not until 1977, when Congress was asked to restore some of the tribes terminated in the 1950s, did the need for recognition procedures attract much attention. By that time nearly twenty-five applicants were in line.

To meet the need, the Bureau of Indian Affairs prepared an addition to the Code of Federal Regulations. After the initial draft had been circulated and amended, in June of 1978 new procedures for recognition of Indian tribes were published in the *Federal Register.* In general, their objective was to acknowledge those groups which had "maintained their political, ethnic and cultural identity."

To implement the new procedures, a Branch of Federal Acknowledgment was created within the Bureau of Indian Affairs. But this was only one of three methods available to a tribe seeking federal recognition. Congressional action remained an option. Another possibility was to take the expensive and possibly protracted route through the federal courts. Between 1970 and 1983 eleven tribes won recognition through the administrative procedure, five were acknowledged by act of Congress, and three were beneficiaries of court action. In the same period three groups were denied recognition.

The Mashantucket Pequot was one of the tribes that achieved federal recognition by an act of Congress, and its experience offered hope to every small cluster of Native Americans with aspirations for federal status. In 1974 the Pequot tribe consisted of a paltry fifty-five members, whose only common possession was 212 acres of land in Connecticut. Under the leadership of a dynamic young chairman, the Pequots incorporated and began aggressively seeking support, first from Connecticut, and then the federal government. Winning state recognition facilitated the Pequot request for federal funds, even though they still lacked federal recognition. In what must be some sort of record for grantsmanship, the tiny Pequot tribe was able to secure HUD, CETA, and other funds, culminating in a grant of over $1 million for fifteen units of housing.

Meanwhile, with the aid of an anthropologist employed from a grant by the Indian Rights Association, the Pequots prepared a petition for federal recognition. They also publicized plans to sue local landowners for property the tribe had lost in the nineteenth century. In 1983 this case was resolved by an out-of-court settlement, endorsed by Congress, by which the federal government granted recognition to the Pequot tribe and provided $900,000 for the purchase of eight hundred acres to add to their reservation. For its part Connecticut turned over to the tribe twenty acres, including a cemetery containing the graves of Pequots, and spent $200,000 on reservation roads. The tribe has ambitious plans for more housing, a museum, and a gift shop. In these and other projects state and federal aid figured prominently. Most recently the Pequots have received one federal grant of $128,750 for the purchase of a pizza restaurant and $300,000 to help launch a bingo operation.

Given the cornucopia of grants and awards that had enriched the Pequots in ten years, it is not surprising that the tribe's population has risen six-fold, from the fifty-five of 1974 to more than 350. If history tells us anything, it is just a matter of time until this booming tribal population will be torn by dissension over just who is a Pequot and entitled to share in the bonanza.

Indian identity remains a serious question for several constituencies. From the standpoint of the acknowledged tribes, there hopefully will come a time when no new tribes will be recognized. Otherwise, assuming that the U.S. Treasury is not bottomless, the size of the slices of the federal pie must shrink as more share it. Many taxpayers also would subscribe to the view that the time must come when no more individuals or groups will be given federal recognition and access to the federal trough. Moreover, as Ron Andrade pointed out, tribal members have to be concerned that continuing to admit new members to tribes can result in dilution of the cultural heritage. But can we ignore the desires of the individuals and tribes seeking acknowledgment of their Indianness? At stake for these people is a recognition which is important to them for psychological as well as economic reasons. Clearly, Indian identity is a complex and persisting problem. It has been a serious issue for Indians and the federal government for over 150 years and shows every indication of being around for many more.

Readings for William T. Hagan:

Issues of Indian identity are discussed briefly in several places, but full-length studies are rare. The most recent is Joane Nagel, *American Indian Ethnic Renewal* (New York: Oxford, 1996). See also Alvin M. Josephy, Jr., *Now that the Buffalo's Gone* (New York: Knopf, 1982); Joan Weibel-Orlando, *Indian Country, L.A.: Maintaining Ethnic Community in Complex Society* (Champlain: University of Illinois Press, 1991); and Richard D. Alba, *Ethnic Identity: The Transformation of White America* (New Haven: Yale University Press, 1990).

2

OPECHANCANOUGH: INDIAN RESISTANCE LEADER

J. FREDERICK FAUSZ

As the field of Native American history continues to mature, scholars have begun to analyze individual leaders for insights into the motivations of tribal peoples. A biographic focus allows some writers to dispel at least a few of the ethnocentric ideas that remain current about Indians. For example, many people still seem to think that Native Americans treated the Europeans who stumbled ashore near their villages as gods or magical creatures with immense power. Although the invaders did possess firearms, the wheel, and domesticated animals, frequently the native peoples dealt with the local situation in more effective ways. This reading shows that the Virginia tribal leaders Powhatan and his brother Opechancanough recognized clearly both the dangers and the opportunities the English colonists presented. After Powhatan's death, Opechancanough strove to keep the colonists from taking tribal lands for tobacco production. Throughout his several decades of leadership the forceful chief showed his skill as a diplomat, an inspirational leader, and a military planner. The author demonstrates Opechancanough's efforts to use Indian religious beliefs and traditions to generate a backlash against English incursions. In analyzing the Indian's motivations and actions, this essay shows how much can be learned about the internal workings of a tribal society. Biography can not answer all of the questions historians want to raise, but in this case it shows how both the English and the native people tried to manipulate the local situation to their own advantage. It also presents the depth of Indian cultural pride and the ethnocentrism of both whites and Indians alike.

J. Frederick Fausz is a dean at the Pierre LeClede Honors College, University of Missouri, St. Louis.

In May 1607, as the loblolly pines swayed in the spring breeze and the sturgeon were beginning their spawning runs up the broad tidal rivers, a determined band of 105

Source: J. Frederick Fausz, "Opechancanough: Indian Resistence Leader," in David Sweet; Gary Nash. *Struggle and Survival in Colonial America,* pages 21–37 (text only). Copyright © 1981 The Regents of the University of California.

Englishmen established an invasion beachhead among the fertile meadows and marshy lowlands of Indian Virginia. Only four decades later, with their once-meager numbers now swelled to some fifteen thousand persons, the invaders had made themselves the masters of tidewater Virginia.

The possessors of this rich land—the people the English defeated, displaced, and nearly annihilated in creating the first successful colony in British America—were Algonquian Indians, known collectively as the Powhatans. Because they lost and because historians of the United States have been the political descendants of the victorious English invaders, there have been few attempts to comprehend the personalities or motivations of the Virginia Indians. The legends and tales that abound about the romantic Pocahontas and her father, the "Emperor" Powhatan, have remained popular primarily because they symbolize the so-called superiority and strength of the English conquerors. Pocahontas was a "good Indian" because she renounced her culture and became a converted Englishwoman, while Powhatan confirmed the myths of Indian weakness by capitulating to the whites within a few years after 1607.

While it is true that Pocahontas and Powhatan dealt with the English presence as they saw fit, there was a more characteristic manner of responding to invaders in the context of Powhatan cultural traditions. This was the way represented by Opechancanough (O-puh-can´-can-ō), kinsman of Pocahontas and Powhatan and the much-vilified architect of the bloody Indian uprisings of 1622 and 1644.

Who was this man who has been referred to as the cruel leader of the "perfidious and inhumane" Powhatans, the "unflinching enemy . . . of the Saxon race," and a chieftain "of large Stature, noble Presence, and extraordinary Parts" who "was perfectly skill'd in the Art of Governing"? Although few details are known about his early life or background, Opechancanough—or Mangopeesomon, as he was later called by his people—was trained from boyhood to be a leader of the Powhatans in war and in peace.

When the English arrived in Virginia, they reported that Opechancanough was linked by blood and alliance to Powhatan, the supreme chieftain (*Mamanatowick*), who had constructed a proud and strong tidewater Indian empire in the last quarter of the sixteenth century. By 1607 Powhatan ruled the largest, most politically complex and culturally unified chiefdom in Virginia. Called Tsenacommacah (Sen-ah-com´-ma-cah)—meaning "densely inhabited land"—this Indian chiefdom had a total population of some twelve thousand persons. Forged by conquest, based on efficient administration and common defense, and maintained by force of arms, tribute, religious beliefs, and the authoritarian personality of a determined ruler, Tsenacommacah was a sovereign and extensive political domain. Powhatan was regarded as the great lord of an integrated kinship society administered by carefully selected local chiefs, or governors, of much power and wealth. These tribal leaders were called *werowances* ("he who is rich"), and among them there was none stronger than Opechancanough.

From a cluster of villages located near the present West Point, Virginia, where tributaries form the York River, Opechancanough ruled over the important Pamunkey tribe. The largest single tribe in Powhatan's domain, the Pamunkeys around 1607 had a population of some twelve hundred, including over three hundred warriors. Their territory—called Opechancheno, after their leader—abounded in fresh water, deer-filled forests, large villages, and acres of planted corn, tobacco, beans, and squash. The Pamunkeys' homeland was also rich in copper and in pearls from freshwater mussels, and Opechancanough's influence derived at least partially from his monopoly of the latter commodity.

The most important source of Opechancanough's power, and a significant factor in explaining many of his later actions, was undoubtedly his role as chief of the most fearsome band of Powhatan warriors. The English often spoke of how disciplined and fierce the Pamunkeys were and reported that Opechancanough was able to mobilize a thousand bowmen in two days' time. His warriors joined battle armed with skillfully made longbows, four-foot arrows, and wooden clubs; their faces and shoulders were smeared with scarlet pigment, and they were adorned with mussel shells, beads, copper medallions, feathers, bird talons, and fox fur.

Despite his considerable power and influence, in 1607 Opechancanough was still subordinate to Powhatan. Although second to his kinsman, Opitchapam, in the line of succession to the title of *Mamanatowick,* he was forced to do the great chief's bidding, just as was any other tribesman less endowed with talent and status. Powhatan had no rivals in tidewater Virginia. As long as he lived, all the *werowances,* including Opechancanough, owed him deference and paid him tribute from the tribes under their control.

In May 1607, only two weeks after the English landed at Jamestown, the *Mamanatowick* mobilized his *werowances* and decided to test the white men by force of arms. It was Opechancanough's duty to keep the more important English leaders distracted some miles upriver from the settlement while other *werowances* attacked James Fort. This assault by several hundred warriors failed to dislodge the English garrison, however, and within days Powhatan altered his strategy. He now decided to offer hospitality to the invaders, and again Opechancanough followed his lead by sending presents of food and overtures of peace to Jamestown.

Similarly, when in December 1607 the *Mamanatowick* desired his first audience with an Englishman, Opechancanough was dispatched to capture Captain John Smith, the most conspicuous leader at Jamestown, and to conduct him safely to Werowocomoco, Powhatan's capital. This Opechancanough did, although some of his own Pamunkey tribesmen called for the death of the white captain.

Opechancanough's inferior position was further emphasized in the February–March 1608 negotiations for a joint Anglo-Powhatan expedition against the Monacan Indians to the west. It was decided that Powhatan and Captain Christopher Newport, "being great Werowances," would not personally lead their forces into battle but would leave the military details to lesser war chiefs: John Smith and Opechancanough.

Although there is no evidence that Opechancanough was ever disloyal to Powhatan in these years, he was an ambitious man who doubtless resented his subordinate status under the *Mamanatowick.* His position became increasingly undesirable after 1608, since while trying to preserve the tenuous peace advocated by Powhatan, he was forced to endure insufferable aggressions by the English. After September 1608 John Smith initiated a purposeful campaign of intimidation, using both threats and force to put Powhatan's people on the defensive. On one occasion Smith captured and imprisoned two Indian warriors, and Opechancanough was obliged to humble himself and negotiate for their release. He sent his own shooting glove and wrist guard to Smith as a token of goodwill and entreated the captain to free the hostages "for his sake." The prisoners were eventually released, but the fact that Opechancanough had been forced to beg meant that the cost in pride had been high.

It was only a matter of time before the brash Smith took still further advantage of his reputed ability to intimidate Indian leaders. In January 1609 he brazenly led a contingent of armed Englishmen into Opechancanough's Pamunkey enclave in search of food. When the warriors refused to supply corn to the English, an enraged Smith grabbed Opechancanough by the hair and held a loaded pistol to his chest. He threatened the frightened *werowance* in front of the Pamunkeys and forced the tribesmen "to cast downe their armes, little dreaming anie durst in that manner have used their king." Smith demanded pledges of good behavior and a regular corn tribute from Opechancanough's people and vowed to load his ship with their "dead carkasses" if they ever again crossed him. In addition, soon after this incident Smith physically assaulted a son of Opechancanough and "spurned [him] like a dogge."

Such harsh and shockingly disrespectful treatment of a Pamunkey leader was unprecedented, and Opechancanough's credibility as a war chief and status as a "royal" *werowance* were jeopardized by such incidents. Perhaps as a result of this, sometime between 1608 and 1612 Opechancanough was humiliated by a fellow *werowance* named Pipsco. Pipsco brazenly stole away one of Opechancanough's favorite wives and flaunted his relationship with the woman for years afterward. In the light of such events, how was the Pamunkey chieftain to cope with his own declining status as well as with the larger threat that the increasingly aggressive English invaders posed to all of Indian Virginia?

Matters soon got worse for the Powhatans in general, although Opechancanough's particular position gradually improved after 1609. John Smith's policy of intimidation with limited bloodshed was succeeded in 1609 by a chaotic period during which short-sighted Englishmen senselessly robbed and murdered Indians. Violent retaliation by the Powhatans quickly escalated into full-scale warfare between 1609 and 1614. Although many Englishmen were killed at first, their overall position was eventually strengthened by increased financial and moral support from London, by large supplies of arms, and by the arrival in Virginia of several dozen fighting men under experienced military commanders.

This First Anglo-Powhatan War proved disastrous for the Powhatans. In a series of sharp and brutal engagements, armored English musketeers attacked tribe after tribe until they gained control of the James River from Chesapeake Bay to the fall line. Powhatan, the aging chief, was unable to halt the English advance, but Opechancanough and his Pamunkeys fared better. In November 1609 they decimated an English force that had come to steal corn, and the result was that the leaders of the colony cautiously waited until 1613 before they felt confident enough to invade the Pamunkeys' territory again. Because of their strength in arms and the placement of their villages at some distance from the area of most active fighting along the James River, the Pamunkeys were spared the worst ravages of the war. Relative to Powhatan's declining power and the losses sustained by other area tribes, the Pamunkeys under Opechancanough became ever stronger.

Powhatan, the once-awesome ruler of tidewater Virginia, spent the war years largely in seclusion. The repeated English onslaughts had taken their toll on the energy and abilities of the *Mamanatowick,* already in his late sixties. By this time Powhatan "delighted in security, and pleasure, and . . . peace" and desired to be "quietly settled amongst his owne." He had tired of conflict. "I am old," he told the English, "and ere long must die. . . . I knowe it is better to eat good meat, lie well, and sleep with my women and children, laugh and be merrie . . . then [to] bee forced to flie . . . and be hunted." Powhatan's favorite daughter, Pocahontas, was captured by the English in 1613. In the next year she renounced her heritage, accepted the Anglican faith, and prepared to marry an English planter, John Rolfe. But Powhatan stubbornly refused to capitulate to the English until the Pamunkeys under Opechancanough were attacked by a large force of armed musketeers. Now a broken man, Powhatan meekly accepted a humiliating peace treaty in the spring of 1614. He who might have crushed the English in 1607 found himself, only seven years later, pathetically entreating his enemies for a shaving knife, bone combs, fishhooks, a dog, and cat.

While Powhatan contented himself with making ceremonial tours throughout his domain after 1614, Opechancanough boldly stepped into the power vacuum created by the war. In the year of the peace, Indian informants told colony leaders that whatever Opechancanough "agreed upon and did, the great King [Powhatan] would confirm." The English noted that Opechancanough was the Powhatans' "chief Captaine, and one that can as soone (if not sooner) as Powhatan commande the men." And in 1615 it was reported that Opechancanough "hath already the commawnd of all the people." Finally, in the summer of 1617, Powhatan, grief-stricken upon learning of Pocahontas's death in England, allegedly "left the Government of his Kingdom to Opachanko [Opechancanough] and his other brother [Opitchapam]" and sought refuge among the Patawomeke tribe along the Potomac River.

Powhatan's abdication in 1617 revealed a power struggle among the tidewater Indian *werowances*. At the center of this contest was Opechancanough, who deftly used the English to increase his authority over the area tribes. In 1616 he convinced the proud and quick-tempered governor of the colony, George Yeardley, that the independent Chickahominy tribe had been killing English livestock. This carefully planted information resulted in an English attack during which some forty Chickahominies were treacherously murdered. It was no coincidence that Opechancanough was nearby to witness the slaughter and that he quickly stepped forward to comfort the bloodied and frightened Chickahominies. That tribe then declared Opechancanough their king, gave him their allegiance, and agreed to pay him tribute. As John Smith later explained these events, Opechancanough had succeeded in his plan "for the subjecting of those people, that neither hee nor Powhatan could ever [before] bring to their obedience."

Such maneuvers clearly demonstrated Opechancanough's ambition, and upon Powhatan's death in April 1618 the wily Pamunkey *werowance* became the effective overlord of the tidewater tribes. Opechancanough was finally the "great Kinge," and as "a great Captaine" who "did always fight," he was called upon to use his talents and status in an active, dangerous struggle against the English. But his lust for political control was not only a personal one; it was also an unselfish and desperate attempt to prevent the total collapse of a weakened and threatened Tsenacommacah. Between 1618 and 1622 Opechancanough's priorities were clearly focused on strengthening and revitalizing his people.

The challenges he faced were immense. In the years immediately following the First Anglo-Powhatan War, the English had dispossessed the Indians of much of their best land. This was especially true after 1618, when a boom in tobacco prices sharpened English land appetites, and famine and disease wracked the once-strong Powhatans. Poor harvests made the Indians dependent on their hated enemies for food, while epidemics devastated the Powhatans and even the deer in their forests between 1617 and 1619. Although disease attacked all the tidewater tribes, Opechancanough's Pamunkeys may have suffered proportionately less than other Powhatans because their territory lay at some distance from the English settlements.

In the wake of these tragedies the Powhatans were pitiable but not pitied. Their English enemies regarded the debilitated, depopulated, and seemingly unthreatening Indians more as defeated and downtrodden pawns than as proud and fierce warriors. Complacent in the peace of 1614 and temporarily less dependent on the Indians for food, the English considered the Powhatans merely impotent and troublesome obstacles to the exploitation of Virginia's lands and resources. It was in these exceedingly adverse circumstances that Opechancanough began his methodical consolidation of the remnants of Powhatan's once-united chiefdom, along with the recruitment of tribes like the Chickahominies who had never been a part of Tsenacommacah. It was ironic that although Opechancanough had often displayed his potential for leadership, it was only the harsh presence of the English that brought him to the fore.

Opechancanough's plan depended on manipulating two intertwined social pressures: the desire of the Indians to procure the colonists' muskets and the attempts of the English to convert and "civilize" the Powhatans. The Virginia Company of London, the joint-stock corporation in charge of colony affairs, was sincerely interested in Christianizing and educating Indian youths, and colonial officials approached Opechancanough many times in an effort to borrow or even buy Powhatan children for this purpose. But the chief refused to allow any Indians to live among the English unless they were permitted the use of muskets. Ever since 1607 the Powhatans had been attempting to obtain firearms from the English. Recognizing that this single technological advantage was the key to English domination, Opechancanough was determined somehow to alter the colonists' monopoly of muskets. Faced with his refusal to provide children for Christianization and under unceasing pressure from missionary idealists among the company's investors in London, the Virginia leaders finally allowed some Powhatans to be trained in the use of firearms.

Thus, while the colonists were preoccupied with growing tobacco and were complacent about the Indians' reputed powerlessness, Opechancanough's men were becoming competent marksmen. By 1618 Englishmen were occasionally being killed by Indians using muskets, and it was reported that the Powhatans would be "boulde . . . to assault" white settlements whenever they concluded that English firearms were "sicke and not to be used" against them.

By 1622 Opechancanough's leadership had made the tidewater tribes stronger than at any other time since 1607. The English judged the chief's own stronghold so defensible that three hundred musketeers—more men than had been drawn together in a single force during the First Anglo-Powhatan War—would be required to launch an attack against the Pamunkeys. This was a far cry from the English assessment of a decade before that the Indians were incapable of inflicting harm.

Opechancanough had succeeded in engineering this military renaissance and the psychological revitalization of his people in large part through the efforts of Nemattanew (Ne-mat´-ten-ū), a mysterious prophet, war captain, and advisor, who was himself one of the first Powhatans to become an able marksman with English muskets. Called "Jack of the Feathers" by the colonists, Nemattanew always went about attired in elaborate and unique feather garments, "as thowghe he meant to flye." He was respected by the Powhatans, and by Opechancanough especially, as a charismatic and talented policymaker, while the English called him a "very cunning fellow" who "took great Pride in preserving and increasing . . . [the Indians'] Superstition concerning him, affecting every thing that was odd and prodigious to work upon their Admiration." Significantly, Nemattanew told his people that he was immortal, that he was therefore invulnerable to English bullets, and that he possessed "an Ointment" and special powers "that could secure them" from bullets as well.

By the spring of 1621, as Nemattanew's revitalizing influence grew among the Powhatans, Opechancanough made plans to annihilate the hated English. His first step was to conclude a firm peace with the colony so that the whites would confidently put aside their muskets for plows and allow the Powhatans to move freely among their plantations. Then, further to lure the English into complacency, Opechancanough decided to tell his adversaries what they wanted to hear concerning the religious and cultural conversion of his people.

He was able to accomplish his goals because in 1620–21 the Virginia Company had sent two naive and optimistic reformers to the colony to implement its program for the "civilization" of the Indians. These men were Sir Francis Wyatt, Jamestown's new governor, and George Thorpe, an idealistic proselytizer. They tried to win over Opechancanough's people with lavish gifts, English clothes, and kind words. Wyatt and especially Thorpe set out to undermine Powhatan religion and traditions and to alienate Indian youths from their elders by promoting English customs and Christianity among them. This energetic new campaign seemed especially dangerous to Opechancanough, but he acted coolly and resourcefully in the face of it.

Late in 1621 Opechancanough met with the zealous Thorpe, who had been trying to convert him for months, and to the astonishment of everyone renounced the major teachings of Powhatan religion. He promised to allow English families to live among the Pamunkeys and gave his permission for the colonists to take any lands not actually occupied by the Powhatans! These startling announcements would have amounted to heresy had they been made sincerely, but Opechancanough was purposefully deceptive in initiating the final chapter in his consolidation of power. By lulling Thorpe, Wyatt, and the other Englishmen into complacency, Opechancanough was forging a strategy more subtle in its execution, more ethnocentric in its foundation, and more revolutionary in its potential impact than Thorpe's.

Thanks to the efforts of Opechancanough and Nemattanew, the Powhatans were by this time more strongly committed to their own culture than ever. Opechancanough saw clearly that there could be no Anglo-Powhatan relations based on peace. Every tragedy that could have befallen the Indians had occurred, and the English had brought destruction to the tribes as readily in times of peace as in times of war. A prolonged peace could only result in more seizures of Indian corn and territory and in further attempts to destroy his people's culture. What did the Powhatans have to gain by keeping the peace? What could they lose by breaking it?

From Opechancanough's personal standpoint, everything the English had done before 1621 had served to increase his power and leverage in Powhatan politics; anything they might do from that time forward was likely to weaken his position. The chief's bold strategy with Thorpe nevertheless revealed confidence in the Indians' future rather than despair. Opechancanough had no intention of leading the Powhatans into physical or cultural suicide; his statements and actions reflected strength and pride, not weakness or desperation.

Opechancanough's plans were suddenly put in jeopardy when in early March 1622 some Englishmen "accidentally" murdered the "immortal" Nemattanew under suspicious circumstances. But Powhatan resiliency and Opechancanough's resolve were confirmed only two weeks later when, as spring breezes once again replaced winter's chill among the pines, an impressive Indian alliance suddenly attacked the English settlements along the entire length of the James River. In this famous uprising of March 22, 1622, Opechancanough's warriors infiltrated white homesteads without arousing suspicion and managed to kill some 330 people before the colony mobilized its forces. Shocked and frightened by this bold and bloody stroke, the English grudgingly recognized Opechancanough's skill as the "Great generall of the Salvages."

The 1622 uprising touched off a ten-year war, and for a brief time Powhatan warriors outdid their enemies, using muskets made in England. Distraught whites reported that the Indians became "verie bold, and can use peeces [muskets] . . . as well or better than an Englishman." With the Powhatans well armed with captured weapons, the colonists feared that they would "brave our countrymen at their verie doors."

This Second Anglo-Powhatan War reached its peak in autumn 1624, when an intertribal force of eight hundred warriors, dominated by Pamunkeys, fought English musketeers in a fierce, two-day battle in open field. In this unusual engagement waged in Pamunkey territory, Opechancanough's warriors fought to defend their homeland and to preserve their excellent reputation among other area tribes. Although the Pamunkeys were eventually forced to retreat, never before had the Indians demonstrated such tenacity under fire. Even Governor Wyatt had to admit that this battle "shewed what the Indyans could doe."

Recognizing Opechancanough's importance to the Indians' courage and persistence, Jamestown officials placed a bounty on his head. The English came close to killing him in 1623 by means of an elaborate plot to ambush and poison several parleying chiefs. Opechancanough was almost certainly present at the meeting, where many Indian leaders died, but somehow he managed to escape the English trap.

The war continued, but by 1625 both sides had come to the realization that the annihilation of their enemies was impossible. For almost three years Governor Wyatt and his commanders had "used their uttermost and Christian endeavours in prosequtinge revenge against the bloody Salvadges" without making Opechancanough or his people submit. The Pamunkey *werowance* had proved a better "generall" than Powhatan, and in 1625 the fatigued English soldiers decided to suspend their twice-yearly campaigns against him. Choosing to plant tobacco rather than to pursue the utter destruction of the Powhatans, the colonists had, in Governor Wyatt's words, "worne owt the Skarrs of the Massacre."

Although the Second Anglo-Powhatan War did not end officially until 1632, the early years of the conflict were the most significant in demonstrating that the Indians' pride had not been extinguished by a decade and a half of disruptive and frequently brutal contact with the Englishmen. By war's end it might be said that Opechancanough had won a qualified victory. If he had not succeeded in annihilating the colonists, he had at least ended the threat of enforced culture change. His people had willingly risked death rather than adopt the Christian religion and English manners. Although many Powhatans did die, their traditions were for the time being preserved.

After peace was agreed to in 1632, there followed a decade of tenuous coexistence between the Powhatans and the English. The Indians had been weakened by the war, and they welcomed an opportunity to tend their fields in peace. In the long run, however, the period after 1632 proved more damaging to the Powhatans than the war years. The

Virginia colony developed so rapidly that the Indians' territorial and cultural foundations were quickly and irrevocably eroded. After a dozen years, with nowhere to go and with a smaller and smaller amount of land on which to preserve their traditions and to raise their children, the Powhatans once again chose the desperate option of war.

In the spring of 1644, as the sturgeon and the meadows again experienced nature's season of renewal, the tireless Opechancanough mobilized a new generation of warriors for an even more desperate rebellion. As in 1622, the Powhatans struck at the English plantations without warning and killed some five hundred of the land-hungry colonists. But this uprising proved futile, for by this time the odds against success were overwhelming. In 1646, after almost two years of brutal warfare, the by now infirm but indefatigable Pamunkey chief, who had seen some eighty winters, was captured and murdered by the English.

Opechancanough's death ended a talented and tempestuous career of leadership that spanned four eventful decades. He had known and warred with an entire generation of Englishmen, long since dead. The Virginia governor who captured him in 1646 had been a mere babe in the cradle when Jamestown was founded.

The last of the "true" Powhatans, Opechancanough had symbolized the precontact glory of Tsenacommacah, while adapting to the postcontact exigencies of cultural survival. He had demonstrated resiliency and political resolve in his magnificent effort to save the Powhatan way of life, and he had in fact succeeded in the difficult task of rebuilding and enlarging Powhatan's domain after the first peace with the English in 1614. The Pamunkeys' resort to arms in two bloody wars between 1622 and 1646 reveal that Opechancanough had managed to reinstill pride and purpose in his people.

Opechancanough coped as best he knew how with the strange and aggressive forces of European colonization. Although his indomitable courage and unyielding fight against foreign domination failed to prevent the eventual subjugation of the Powhatans, Opechancanough's refusal to submit was a reassertion of the proud warrior traditions of his culture. He led his people in a struggle for survival while trying to preserve their self-respect. When the Powhatans had to choose between cultural survival and individual sacrifice, they proudly chose death over enslavement. Victory or defeat mattered less to them than the act of resistance.

In this the "Great generall" set a strong personal example. Even as a captive in 1646, the exhausted Opechancanough displayed pride and dignity until the end. Just before he was treacherously shot in the back by an English guard, the aged Pamunkey *werowance*— "so decrepit that he was not able to walk alone," with "Eye-lids . . . so heavy that he could not see"—was protesting the fact that he had been placed on public exhibition like a caged animal. For such a man and such a culture in such an era, the ability to cope was the ability to fight bravely against overwhelming odds and to die with dignity and purpose.

Readings for Frederick Fausz:

The peoples of early Virginia are treated in Helen C. Rountree, *The Powhatan Indians of Virginia: Their Traditional Culture* (Norman: University of Oklahoma Press, 1989), and Peter H. Wood, Gregory A. Waselkov, and M. Thomas Hatley, eds., *Powhatan's Mantle: Indians in the Colonial Southeast* (Lincoln: University of Nebraska Press, 1989). For a broader range of issues see Peter C. Hoffer, ed., *Indians and Europeans: Selected Articles on Indian-White Relations in Colonial North America* (New York: Garland Publishing, 1988).

3

KING PHILIP'S HERDS: INDIANS, COLONISTS, AND THE PROBLEM OF LIVESTOCK IN EARLY NEW ENGLAND

VIRGINIA DEJOHN ANDERSON

When examining the relationships between the intruding English and their Indian neighbors, one expects to find disputes over the land. After all, the Indians had occupied and used it long before the Europeans arrived, and the newcomers wanted to use it. That alone was enough to cause trouble. However, this essay examines disputes that went far beyond the basic quarrels over land by focusing on the roles domestic animals played in seventeenth-century colonial society. Unlike today, the farmers rarely bothered to fence the livestock securely. In fact often they encouraged their animals to graze freely, to wander through the forests and to trample the crops of nearby Indian villages. This essay presents the livestock as an unexpected cause of friction between the Indians and the English.

After several decades of objecting to depredations caused by the colonists' cattle and hogs, some Indians began to raise those animals themselves. Rather than being pleased that the tribal people had adopted their agricultural practices, the English complained that the Indians failed to keep their animals under firm control in order to prevent the destruction of the colonists' crops. This discussion demonstrates the centrality of differing cultural and economic practices as one of the factors separating the races, and also as one of several eventual causes for war.

Virginia DeJohn Anderson is an associate professor of history at the University of Colorado.

On a late spring day in 1669, the ambitious younger son of a prominent Rhode Island family received a letter from the town clerk of Portsmouth. Like many of his neighbors, the young man raised livestock and followed the common practice of placing his pigs on a nearby island where they could forage safe from predators. But that was what brought

Source: Virginia DeJohn Anderson, "King Philip's Herds: Indians, Colonists, and the Problem of Livestock in Early New England," *William and Mary Quarterly,* 3d Ser., 51, October 1994, 601–24. Reprinted with permission of the author and the Omohundro Institute of Early American History and Culture.

him to the attention of Portsmouth's inhabitants, who ordered the clerk to reprimand him for "intrudeinge on" the town's rights when he ferried his beasts to "Hog-Island." The townsmen insisted that he remove "Such Swine or other Catle" as he had put there, on pain of legal action. They took the unusual step of instructing the clerk to make two copies of the letter and retain the duplicate—in effect preparing their legal case even before the recipient contested their action.

It was by no means unusual for seventeenth-century New Englanders to find themselves in trouble with local officials, particularly when their search for gain conflicted with the rights of the community. But this case was different. We can only wonder what Metacom, whom the English called King Philip, made of the peremptory directive from the Portsmouth town clerk—for indeed it was to him, son of Massasoit and now sachem of the Wampanoags himself, that the letter was addressed. Because the records (which directed no comparable order to any English swine owner) do not mention the outcome of the dispute, we may suppose that Philip complied with the town's demand. The episode was thus brief, but it was no less important for that, because it involved the man whose name would soon be associated with what was, in proportion to the populations involved, the most destructive war in American history.

For three centuries, historians have depicted Philip in many ways—as a savage chieftain, an implacable foe of innocent Christian settlers, and a doomed victim of European aggressors—but never as a keeper of swine. Although the Hog Island episode may seem unrelated to the subsequent horrors of King Philip's War, the two events were in fact linked. Philip resorted to violence in 1675 because of mounting frustrations with colonists, and no problem vexed relations between settlers and Indians more frequently in the years before the war than the control of livestock. English colonists imported thousands of cattle, swine, sheep, and horses (none of which is native to North America) because they considered livestock essential to their survival, never supposing that the beasts would become objectionable to the Indians. But the animals exacerbated a host of problems related to subsistence practices, land use, property rights and, ultimately, political authority. Throughout the 1660s, Philip found himself caught in the middle, trying to defend Indian rights even as he adapted to the English presence. The snub delivered by Portsmouth's inhabitants showed him the limits of English flexibility, indicating that the colonists ultimately valued their livestock more than good relations with his people. When Philip recognized that fact, he took a critical step on the path that led him from livestock keeper to war leader.

Successful colonization of New England depended heavily on domestic animals. Nowhere is this better seen than in the early history of Plymouth Colony. Not until 1624—four years after the *Mayflower*'s arrival—did Edward Winslow bring from England "three heifers and a bull, the first beginning of any cattle of that kind in the land." This date, not coincidentally, marked the end of the Pilgrims' "starving times" as dairy products and meat began to supplement their diet. By 1627, natural increase and further importations brought the Plymouth herd to at least fifteen animals, whose muscle power increased agricultural productivity. The leaders of Massachusetts Bay Colony, perhaps learning from Plymouth's experience, brought animals from the start. John Winthrop regularly noted the arrival of settlers and livestock during the 1630s, often recording levels of shipboard mortality among animals as well as people. Edward Johnson estimated that participants in the Great Migration spent £12,000 to transport livestock across the ocean, not counting the original cost of the animals.

Early descriptions often focused on the land's ability to support livestock. John Smith noted that in New England there was "grasse plenty, though very long and thicke stalked, which being neither mowne nor eaten, is very ranke, yet all their cattell like and prosper well therewith." Francis Higginson informed English friends that the "fertility of the soil is to be admired at, as appeareth in the abundance of grass that groweth every-where." "It is scarce to be believed," he added, "how our kine and goats, horses, and hogs do thrive and prosper here and like well of this country." Colonists preferred to set-tle in areas with ample natural forage. Salt marshes attracted settlers to Hampton, New Hampshire, and Sudbury's founders valued their town's riverside fresh meadow. Haver-hill's settlers negotiated with the colony government for a large tract for their town in order to satisfy their "over-weaning desire . . . after Medow land." Most inland clearings bore mute witness to recent habitation by Indians, whose periodic burnings kept the ar-eas from reverting to forest.

The size of a town's herds soon became an important measure of its prosperity. As early as 1634, William Wood noted that Dorchester, Roxbury, and Cambridge were par-ticularly "well stored" with cattle. Other commentators added to the list of towns with burgeoning herds. In 1651, Edward Johnson tallied the human and livestock populations for several communities as a measure of divine favor. His enumeration revealed that towns with three or four dozen families also contained several hundred head of live-stock. Like Old Testament patriarchs, New England farmers counted their blessings as they surveyed their herds.

Their interest in livestock grew in part from their English experience. Many set-tlers came from England's wood-pasture region, where they had engaged in a mixed hus-bandry of cattle and grain. In New England, the balance in that agrarian equation tipped toward livestock because the region's chronic labor shortage made raising cattle a par-ticularly efficient use of resources. Selectmen usually hired one or two town herdsmen, freeing other livestock owners to clear fields, till crops, and construct buildings and fences. Until settlers managed to plant English hay, livestock foraged on the abundant, though less nutritious, native grasses, converting otherwise worthless herbage into milk and meat for consumption and sale. Livestock were so important to survival that New Englanders reversed the usual English fencing practices. English law required farmers to protect their crops by confining livestock within fenced or hedged pastures, but New England farmers were enjoined to construct and maintain sufficiently sturdy fences around cornfields to keep their peripatetic beasts out.

Raising livestock had cultural as well as economic ramifications. For colonists, the absence of indigenous domestic animals underscored the region's essential wildness. "The country is yet raw," wrote Robert Cushman in 1621, "the land untilled; the cities not builded; the cattle not settled." The English saw a disturbing symmetry between the sav-agery of the land and its human and animal inhabitants. America, noted Cushman, "is spa-cious and void," and the Indians "do but run over the grass, as do also the foxes and wild beasts." Such evaluations ultimately fueled colonists' own claims to the land. The "sav-age people," argued John Winthrop, held no legitimate title "for they inclose no ground, neither have they cattell to maintayne it, but remove their dwellings as they have occa-sion." Winthrop's objection to the Indians' seminomadic habits stemmed from a cultural assumption that equated civilization with sedentarism, a way of life that he linked to the keeping of domesticated animals. Drawing on biblical history, Winthrop argued that a "civil" right to the earth resulted when, "as men and cattell increased, they appropriated some parcells of ground by enclosing and peculiar manurance." Subduing—indeed, domesticating—the wilderness with English people and English beasts thus became a cultural imperative. New England could become a new Canaan, a land of milk and honey, only if, Thomas Morton wryly observed, "the Milke came by the industry" of its civilizing immigrants and their imported livestock.

Accordingly, only those Indians who submitted to "domestication" could live in the New England Canaan. They had to accept Christianity, of course; in addition, colonists insisted that they adopt English ways entirely, including the keeping of domestic animals. Roger Williams urged natives to move "from Barbarism to Civilitie, in forsaking their filthy nakednes, in keeping some kind of Cattell." John Eliot offered livestock, among other material incentives, to entice Indians to become civilized. He admonished one native audience: "if you were more wise to know God, and obey his Commands, you would work more then [sic] you do." Labor six days a week, as God commanded and the English did, and, Eliot promised, "you should have cloths, houses, cattle, riches as they have. God would give you them."

To assist Indians in making this transformation, Puritan officials established fourteen "praying towns" where they could proceed toward conversion as they earned the material rewards Providence would bestow. The inhabitants of these communities not only would learn to worship God as the English did but also would wear English clothes, live in English framed houses, and farm with English animals. Among the goods sent from England to support this civilizing program were seven bells for oxen, to be distributed to Indian farmers who exchanged their traditional hoe agriculture for the plow. Soon the increase in livestock became as much a hallmark of the success of the praying towns as it was of English communities. Daniel Gookin reported in 1674 that the praying town of Hassanamesitt (Grafton) was "an apt place for keeping of cattle and swine; in which respect this people are the best stored of any Indian town of their size." He went on to observe, however, that though these natives "do as well, or rather better, than any other Indians" in raising crops and animals, they "are very far short of the English both in diligence and providence."

Praying Indians raised livestock as participants in what may be called an experiment in acculturation. By moving to places such as Natick or Hassanamesitt, they announced their intention to follow English ways—including animal husbandry—in hopes of finding favor with the Christian God. But the praying towns never contained more than a tiny minority of the native population; most Indians rejected the invitation to exchange their ways for English ones. For the vast majority, the cattle and swine that served as emblems of the praying Indians' transformation had a very different meaning. They became instead a source of friction, revealing profound differences between Indians and colonists.

As Indians encountered these unfamiliar animals, they had to decide what to call them. Williams reported that the Narragansetts first looked for similarities in appearance and behavior between an indigenous animal and one of the new beasts and simply used the name of the known beast for both animals. Thus *ockqutchaun-nug,* the name of a "wild beast of a reddish haire about the bignesse of a Pig, and rooting like a Pig," was used for English swine. Finding no suitable parallels for most domestic animals, however, the Narragansetts resorted to neologisms such as "cowsnuck," "goatesuck," and eventually "hogsuck" or "pigsuck." The "termination *suck,* is common in their language," Williams explained, "and therefore they adde it to our English Cattell, not else knowing what names to give them."

Giving these animals Indian names in no way implied that most Indians wanted to own livestock. In fact, contact with domestic animals initially produced the opposite reaction, because livestock husbandry did not fit easily with native practices. Indians could hardly undertake winter hunting expeditions accompanied by herds of cattle that required shelter and fodder to survive the cold weather. Swine would compete with their owners for nuts, berries, and roots, and the presence of livestock of any kind tended to drive away deer. Moreover, the Indians, for whom most beasts were literally fair game, struggled with the very notion of property in animals. They assumed that one could own only dead animals, which hunters shared with their families.

Further, the adoption of livestock would alter women's lives in crucial ways by affecting the traditional gender-based division of labor. Would women, who were mainly responsible for agricultural production, assume new duties of animal husbandry? If not, how would men's involvement with livestock rearing alter women's powerful role as the primary suppliers of food? Who would protect women's crops from the animals? How would the very different temporal cycle of livestock reproduction and care be reconciled with an Indian calendar that identified the months according to stages in the planting cycle?

Animal husbandry also challenged native spiritual beliefs and practices. Because their mental universe assumed no rigid distinction between human and animal beings, the Indians' hunting rituals aimed to appease the spirits of creatures that were not so much inferior to, as different from, their human killers. Such beliefs helped to make sense of a world in which animals were deemed equally rightful occupants of the forest and whose killing required an intimate knowledge of their habits. Would Indians be able to apply these ideas about animals as *manitous,* or other-than-human persons, to domestic beasts as well? Or would those beasts' English provenance and dependence on human owners prohibit their incorporation into the spiritual world with bears, deer, and beaver?

Finally, a decision to keep livestock ran counter to a powerful hostility toward domestic animals that dated from the earliest years of English settlement. Because colonists often established towns on the sites of former Indian villages depopulated by the epidemics that preceded their arrival, no line of demarcation separated English from Indian habitation. Native villages and colonial towns could be quite close together, and the accident of propinquity made for tense relations. At least at first, friction between these unlikely neighbors grew less from the very different ideas that informed Indian and English concepts of property than from the behavior of livestock. Let loose to forage in the woods, the animals wandered away from English towns into Indian cornfields, ate their fill, and moved on.

Indians, who had never had to build fences to protect their fields, were unprepared for the onslaught. Even their underground storage pits proved vulnerable, as swine "found a way to unhinge their barn doors and rob their garners," prompting native women to "implore their husbands' help to roll the bodies of trees" over the pits to prevent further damage. Hogs attacked another important food source when they "watch[ed] the low water (as the Indian women do)" along the shoreline and rooted for clams, making themselves "most hatefull to all Natives," who called them "filthy cut throats, &c." In Plymouth Colony, settlers in Rehoboth and their Indian neighbors engaged in a long-running dispute over damages from trespassing animals. At first, in 1653, the colonists claimed to "know nothing of" the Indian complaints. By 1656, settlers had erected a fence along the town boundary, but because a stream—across which livestock were "apte to swime"—also separated English and native lands, the animals still made their way into Indian cornfields. Four years later, Philip's older brother Wamsutta, known to the English as Alexander, was still bringing the Indians' complaints to the attention of Plymouth authorities.

English livestock also proved to be a nuisance as they roamed through the woods. Cattle and swine walked into deer traps, and the English held the Indians liable for any injuries they sustained. Similarly, in 1638, when William Hathorne of Salem found one of his cows stuck with an arrow, he insisted on restitution. Salem officials demanded the exorbitant sum of £100 from local Indians at a time when a cow was generally valued at about £20. Roger Williams pleaded the natives' case with John Winthrop, explaining that the colonists had charged the wrong Indians and that the sachems were outraged because the English held them personally responsible for the fine levied for their subjects' purported offense. "Nor doe they believe that the English Magistrates doe so practice," Williams reported, "and therefore they hope that what is Righteous amongst our Selves we will accept of from them."

Williams went on to observe that "the Busines is ravelld and needes a patient and gentle hand to rectifie Misunderstanding of Each other and misprisions." He foresaw that endless recriminations would flow from colonists' attempts to raise livestock in the same space where Indians hunted. Native leaders, finding Williams a sympathetic listener, informed him of the "feares of their Men in hunting or travelling," for they had reason to believe they would be held responsible for every domestic animal found hurt or dead in the woods. Williams urged Winthrop to work with the Indians to contrive an equitable procedure to be followed in similar cases so that Indian hunters would not feel so much at risk from the rigors of a judicial system that appeared biased against them.

Instead of recognizing the fundamental incompatibility of English and Indian subsistence regimes, colonial authorities repeatedly permitted joint use of land. In so doing, they assumed that Indians would agree that the colonists' livestock had, in effect, use rights to the woods and fields too. Indians could hunt on lands claimed by the English only if they accepted certain restrictions on their activities. Indians who set traps within the town of Barnstable, for instance, had "fully and dilligenttly" to visit their traps daily to check for ensnared livestock and, if any were found, "thaye shall speedyli lett them out." The Connecticut government imposed stricter limits on Indian hunters when the town of Pequot was founded in 1649. Uncas, the Mohegan sachem, was instructed "that no trapps [should] bee sett by him or any of his men" within the town, although colonial officials saw no reason completely "to prohibitt and restraine Uncus and his men from hunting and fishing" unless they did so on the Sabbath. Connecticut authorities acquired meadow land from the Tunxis Indians in 1650 and similarly recognized native rights of hunting, fishing, and fowling on the property so long as such activities "be not dun to the breach of any orders in the country to hurt cattle." As late as 1676, in the aftermath of King Philip's War, Connecticut officials allowed "friendly" Indians "to hunt in the conquered lands in the Narrogancett Country, provided they sett not traps to prejudice English cattell."

Joint use was doomed to failure, not by Indian unwillingness to comply with English conditions, but by the insurmountable problems that arose from grazing livestock on hunting lands. Accidental injuries were bound to occur and to disturb colonists, while Indians resented the damage done by domestic animals wandering out of the woods and into their cornfields. The behavior of livestock—creatures as indispensable to the English as they were obnoxious to the Indians—undermined the efforts of each group to get along with the other. Attempts to resolve disputes stemming from trespassing livestock led only to mutual frustration.

The Indians were doubtless the first to recognize the difficulties inherent in the joint use of land and the unrestricted foraging of colonists' animals. One Connecticut sachem actually attempted to restrict the *settlers'* use of land that he was willing to grant them outright. When Pyamikee, who lived near Stamford, negotiated with town officials, he tried to make the English agree not to put their livestock on the tract, for he knew that "the English hoggs would be ready to spoyle their [the Indians'] corne" in an adjacent field," and that the cattell, in case they came over the said five mile river," would do likewise. But the colonists would only assure Pyamikee that livestock would always travel under the supervision of a keeper.

In another case, in 1648 in Rhode Island, an unfortunate Shawomet Indian spent five days chasing swine from his cornfields, only to be confronted by an Englishman, armed with a cudgel, who "asked the Indian in a rage whie he drove out the Swine." When he replied, "because they dide eate the Corne," the Englishman "ran upon the Indian," and a melee ensued among the disputants' companions. An attempt to adjudicate the case led to further complications, for the Englishmen involved were Rhode Islanders whereas the land where the incident occurred was claimed by Plymouth. Skeptical of his chances for a fair hearing in the Plymouth court, Pumham, a Shawomet sachem acting on behalf of the aggrieved Indians, asked to have the case tried in Massachusetts.

It might seem remarkable that Pumham trusted the English judicial system at all. Yet like Pumham, many Indians used colonial courts to seek redress for damage caused by trespassing livestock. English authorities, in turn, often recognized the legitimacy of such complaints and granted restitution, as in 1632 when the Massachusetts General Court ordered Sir Richard Saltonstall to "give Saggamore John a hogshead of corne for the hurt his cattell did him in his corne." Trespass complaints were so frequent, however, that colonial governments instructed individual towns to establish procedures for local arbitration lest the courts be overwhelmed. In Plymouth Colony, the task of reviewing such cases fell either to town selectmen or to ad hoc committees. If the livestock owner ignored their orders to pay damages, the aggrieved Indian could "repaire to some Majestrate for a warrant to recover such award by distraint." Massachusetts and Connecticut adopted similar measures.

But the colonists were less accommodating than they seemed. They insisted that Indians resort to an English court system that was foreign to them, the proceedings of which were conducted in an incomprehensible language necessitating the use of not-always reliable translators. (In the case described above, one of Pumham's objections to using the Plymouth court was his mistrust of the court interpreters.) Moreover, the English soon required Indians to fence their cornfields before they could seek reparations. As early as 1632, Sagamore John, who received the award of damages from Saltonstall, had to promise "against the next yeare, & soe ever after" to fence his fields. In 1640 Massachusetts law required settlers to help their Indian neighbors "in felling of Trees, Ryving & sharpning railes, and holing of posts" for fences, but this friendly gesture was coupled with stern provisos. Any Indian who refused to fence his fields after such help was offered forfeited his right to sue for damages. In addition, Indian complainants had to identify which beasts had trampled their corn—an impossible task if the animals had come and gone before the damage was discovered. Beginning in the 1650s, Plymouth magistrates allowed Indians to impound offending beasts, but this meant either that they had to drive the animals to the nearest English pound or construct one on their own land and walk to the nearest town to give "speedy notice" of any animals so confined.

Even if they complied with English conditions, Indians could not depend on the equitable enforcement of animal trespass laws. The coercive power of colonial governments was limited—magistrates could hardly march off to view every downed fence and ruined field—and reliance on local adjudication meant that townsmen had to police themselves. New England colonists were notoriously litigious, but it was one thing to defend against the charges of an English neighbor and quite another to judge impartially an Indian's accusations of trespass. When problems arose near the centers of colonial government, Indians could generally get a fair hearing, as did Sagamore John near Boston. But the enforcement of animal trespass laws became more haphazard toward the edges of settlement. Indians in the praying town of Okommakamesit (Marlborough)— thirty miles from Boston—abandoned a 150-acre tract with an apple orchard for "it brings little or no profit to them, nor is ever like to do; because the Englishmen's cattle, &c. devour all in it, because it lies open and unfenced," and they clearly expected no redress. Along the disputed border between Rhode Island and Plymouth, settlers could scarcely agree among themselves who was in charge. Under such circumstances, as Pumham and his fellow Shawomets discovered, cudgel-wielding Englishmen all too easily took the law into their own hands. Farther away—in Maine, for example—even the pretense of due process could vanish. In 1636, Saco commissioners empowered one of their number to "excecut any Indians that ar proved to have killed any swyne of the Inglishe" and ordered all settlers summarily to "apprehend, execut or kill any Indian that hath binne known to murder any English, kill ther Cattell or any waie spoyle ther goods or doe them violence."

Given the deficiencies of the colonial legal system, it is not surprising that many Indians dealt with intrusive livestock according to their own notions of justice. Indians who stole or killed livestock probably committed such deeds less as acts of wanton mischief, as the English assumed, than in retribution for damages suffered. In their loosely knit village bands, Indians placed a premium on loyalty to kin rather than to the larger social group. The strength of these kinship bonds at once limited the authority of sachems (a point lost on the magistrates who had ordered sachems to pay for Hathorne's cow) and sanctioned acts of violence undertaken in revenge for wrongs done to family members. English authorities did not bother to inquire into Indian motives for theft and violence toward animals. But when, for instance, Pumham and other Shawomets—who had previously encountered irascible colonists and ineffective courts—were later charged with "killing cattle, and forceable entry" on settlers' lands, it takes little imagination to suspect that they were exacting their own retributive justice.

Once they took matters into their own hands, Indians could be charged with theft and destruction of property with the full force of English law turned against them. The penalties for such offenses further corroded relations between the groups. Unable to pay the requisite fines—often levied in English money—Indians found themselves imprisoned or sentenced to corporal punishment. Thus their options shrank even as livestock populations grew. Retaliation against the animals brought severe sanctions from the English, while efforts to accommodate the beasts on English terms required unacceptable alterations in Indian agriculture and the virtual abandonment of hunting. By the middle of the seventeenth century it was clear to the Indians that the English and their troublesome animals would not go away. The English, for their part, assumed that the solution was for Indians to abandon their ways and become livestock keepers themselves.

Some Indians—most notably King Philip—adopted livestock husbandry, though not in capitulation to English example and exhortation. Their adaptation was not a step, either intentional or inadvertent, toward acculturation, for they refused to make the complete transformation advocated by Englishmen who linked animal husbandry to the acquisition of civilized ways. The natives' decision instead fit into a broader pattern of intercultural borrowing that formed an important theme in Anglo-Indian relations during the first decades of contact. Much as settlers incorporated native crops and farming techniques into their agricultural system, Indians selected from an array of English manufactures such items as guns, cloth, and iron pots that were more efficient substitutes for bows and arrows, animal skins, and earthenware. Neither group forfeited its cultural identity in so doing, and when some Indians began to raise livestock—again largely for practical considerations—they deliberately selected the English beast that would least disrupt their accustomed routines.

Indians who raised livestock overwhelmingly preferred hogs. More than any other imported creatures, swine resembled dogs, the one domesticated animal that Indians already had. Both species scavenged for food and ate scraps from their owners' meals. Although hogs also competed with humans for wild plants and shellfish and could damage native cornfields, these disadvantages were offset by the meat they supplied and the fact that Indians could deal with their own swine however they wished. Like dogs, swine aggressively fended off predators, such as wolves. Roger Williams recorded an instance of "two English Swine, big with Pig," driving a wolf from a freshly killed deer and devouring the prey themselves. Hogs could also be trained like dogs to come when called, a useful trait in an animal that foraged for itself in the woods.

Swine keeping required relatively few adjustments to native subsistence routines—far fewer than cattle rearing would have involved. It made minimal demands on labor, rendering moot the issue of who—men or women—would bear primary responsibility for their care. Keeping cattle would have either dramatically increased women's work loads or involved men in new types of labor tying them more closely to the village site. Cattle needed nightly feeding, and cows had to be milked daily. Most male calves would have had to be castrated, and the few bulls required careful handling. Since cattle needed fodder and shelter during the winter, Indians would have had to gather and dry hay and build and clean barns—activities that infringed on their mobility during the hunting season. Some members of each village would have had to become herdsmen. Losing a cow in the woods was a more serious matter than losing a pig, for pigs had a far higher rate of reproduction.

In return for a limited investment in labor, native hog keepers acquired a year-round supply of protein that replaced the meat they could no longer get from a dwindling deer population. These Indians may in fact have enjoyed an improved diet, avoiding the seasonal malnutrition resulting from their former dependence on corn and game. Swine also provided products that replaced items formerly obtained from wild animals. Gookin noted in 1674 that Indians "used to oil their skins and hair with bear's grease heretofore, but now with swine's fat." And in at least one instance, Indians fashioned moccasins from "green hogs skinns" in place of deerskin. Settlers, in contrast, valued cattle for reasons that had little appeal for Indians. They plowed with oxen, but Indians who farmed with hoes did not need them. Colonists also prized the meat and dairy products supplied by their herds; although Indians would eat beef, most native adults were physiologically unable to digest lactose except in tiny amounts and would have learned to avoid milk products.

Settlers raised hogs and ate pork, but they did not share the Indians' preference for swine over cattle. Cattle were docile and, to the English mind, superior beasts. Swine, on the contrary, were slovenly creatures that wallowed in mud, gobbled up garbage, and were rumored to kill unwary children. Colonists named their cows Brindle and Sparke and Velvet; no one named pigs. The English kept swine as if on sufferance, tolerating their obnoxious behavior in order to eat salt pork, ham, and bacon. Most of all, swine keeping did not promote hard work and regular habits so well as cattle rearing did. Writers who extolled the civilizing benefits of livestock husbandry doubtless envisioned sedentary Indian farmers peacefully gathering hay and tending herds of cattle alongside their English neighbors, but the reality was hardly so bucolic.

Settlers instead encountered Indians who lived much as they always had, but who now had swine wandering across their lands—and occasionally into English cornfields. The colonists recognized only grudgingly the Indians' property in animals and usually assumed that the natives' hogs were stolen. In 1672, Bay Colony officials insisted that Indians pilfered swine although they acknowledged that "it be very difficult to proove" that they had done so. Other explanations—that the Indians had captured feral animals or had purchased hogs from settlers—were seldom advanced. The fact that "the English, especially in the inland plantations, . . . loose many swine" and that Indians had hogs invited suspicion.

To discourage the theft of animals among themselves and to identify strays, settlers used earmarks. Each owner had a distinctive mark that was entered in the town records, to be checked when an animal was reported stolen or a stray was found. The proliferation of town and colony orders requiring earmarks, as well as the increasing intricacy of the marks themselves—a mixture of crops, slits, "forks," "half-pennies," and so on—provides as good a measure as any of the growing livestock population. The earmark itself became a form of property handed down from one generation to the next. Instead of assigning earmarks to native owners, however, magistrates ordered that "no Indians shall give any ear mark to their Swine, upon the penalty of the forfeiture" of the animal. An Indian who wished to sell a hog had to bring it with its ears intact; if he sold pork, he had to produce the unmarked ears from the carcass. This practice made native purchases of English hogs problematic, for the animals would already have marked ears. Should the

Indian subsequently desire to sell such an animal, he could be required to "bring good Testimonies that he honestly obtained such Swine so marked, of some English." Moreover, Indian owners were at the mercy of unscrupulous settlers who might steal their animals and mark them as their own. Colonists did not prohibit Indian ownership of swine, but they denied Indians the acknowledged symbol of legitimate possession.

The Indians' selective involvement with animal husbandry scarcely improved relations between natives and colonists. To the previous list of problems new and equally vexing issues were added, including trespasses by Indian animals, theft, and difficulties with proving ownership of animal property. For settlers, probably the least welcome change appeared when enterprising Indians started selling swine and pork in competition with English producers of the same commodities. Many orders pertaining to earmarks begin with a preamble that assumes that native competition went hand in hand with native dishonesty. In the Bay Colony, there was "ground to suspect that some of the Indians doe steale & sell the English mens swine;" in Plymouth, settlers complained "of Indians stealing of live Hogs from the English, and selling them." Thus magistrates urged colonists to mark their animals to protect their property from native thieves. In fact, the charges of theft were not substantiated; the real problem was commercial, not criminal. Earmark regulations aimed at least as much to make Indian sales difficult as to make Indians honest.

Competition with Indians was more than colonists had bargained for. In 1669— just six years before the start of King Philip's War—the Plymouth General Court proposed to license certain colonists "to trade powder, shott, guns, and mony (now under prohibition) with the Indians" as a means of discouraging the local Indians' pork trade. The magistrates complained that "a greate parte of the porke that is now carryed by the Indians to Boston" was "sold there at an under rate," hurting Plymouth pork sellers. The court felt no need to make explicit connections between its proposal to sell arms and its complaint about competition, but the likeliest explanation is that Plymouth Indians were using the proceeds of their Boston pork sales to purchase guns from licensed Bay Colony sellers, tapping into an arms trade that the Massachusetts General Court had established in the previous year. If the Indians could obtain arms from Plymouth suppliers, they presumably would cede the Boston pork trade to Old Colony producers. The court expressed no particular interest in helping out Boston consumers who spurned the wares of their fellow Englishmen in order to buy cheaper meat; its explicit aim was to ensure that the pork trade would "fall into the hands of some of our people, and soe the prise may be kept up."

The Plymouth government's concern in this instance testifies to a remarkable set of native adaptations. If the Indians indeed brought pork and not live animals to the Bay Colony, they had learned to preserve meat in a way that appealed to English consumers. Some colonists, noting native ignorance of salting techniques, had assumed that Indians did not know how to preserve food. We do not know whether Plymouth Indians had learned to salt as well as to sell pork, but there is no doubt that they had identified Boston as New England's most lucrative food market. Almost from the start, Boston merchants and shopkeepers vied with farmers over the relatively scarce amount of land on the small peninsula occupied by the town. As early as 1636, officials prohibited families from grazing more than two cows on the peninsula itself, and in 1647, the town herd was fixed at seventy beasts. By 1658, swine had become such a public nuisance that Boston officials required owners to keep them "in their owne ground," effectively limiting the number of hogs each family could maintain. Given these restrictions, many Bostonians apparently gave up raising animals and bought meat from livestock producers in nearby towns, who were also raising stock for the West Indies market. Did the Plymouth Indians know this when they went to Boston? Their business acumen should not be underestimated. Although he did not refer specifically to the meat trade, Williams noticed that Indian traders "will beate all markets and try all places, and runne twenty thirty, yea forty mile, and more, and lodge in the Woods, to save six pence." Ironically, native enterprise met with suspicion rather than approbation from colonists who liked the Indians less the more like the English they became.

The extent of native livestock husbandry is difficult to measure because colonial records mainly preserve instances in which animals became a source of conflict. The evidence does suggest that Indians residing near English settlements had a greater tendency to raise domestic animals than did those farther away. The Wampanoags, living in the Mount Hope area between Plymouth Colony and Rhode Island, apparently began to raise hogs by the middle of the seventeenth century, after some thirty years of contact with English settlers. The location and timing of their adaptation were scarcely accidental.

The Wampanoags had close contact with settlers and, accordingly, a greater need for livestock than did native peoples living elsewhere. The ecological changes caused by English settlers steadily converting woodland into fenced fields and open meadows around Mount Hope reduced the deer population on which the Wampanoags depended; their swine keeping substituted one form of protein for another. Their trade in hogs and pork may also have been intended to offer a new commodity to settlers as other trade items disappeared or diminished in value. By the 1660s, the New England fur trade had ended with the virtual extinction of beaver. At the same time, English demand for wampum sharply declined as an improving overseas trade brought in more hard currency and colonies ceased accepting wampum as legal tender. But hogs and pork failed as substitutes for furs and wampum. Most colonists owned swine themselves and—as the response of the Plymouth magistrates in 1669 suggests—evidently preferred to limit the market in animals to English producers.

Wampanoag swine keeping also contributed to growing tensions with colonists over land, creating disputes that were even harder to resolve than those concerning trade. Land that diminished in usefulness to Indians as it ceased to support familiar subsistence activities regained value for raising hogs; indeed, such places as offshore islands held a special attraction to keepers of swine. The Wampanoags' desire to retain their land awakened precisely when settlers evinced an interest in acquiring it. By the 1660s, a younger generation of settlers had reached maturity and needed farms. In Plymouth Colony, bounded on the north by the more powerful Bay Colony and on the west by an obstreperous Rhode Island, aggressive settlers eyed the lands of their Wampanoag neighbors. During the 1660s, new villages were formed at Dartmouth, Swansea, and Middleborough, while established towns such as Rehoboth and Taunton enlarged their holdings—and in effect blockaded the Wampanoags on Mount Hope peninsula.

No man was harder pressed by these developments than King Philip. As sachem of the Wampanoags since 1662, he had tried to protect his people and preserve their independence in the face of English intrusion. Over time, his tasks became far more difficult. The number of occasions when the interests of Indians and settlers came into conflict grew as his ability to mediate diminished. Since Wampanoag land bordered on Massachusetts, Rhode Island, and Plymouth, Philip had to contend at various times with three, often competing, colonial governments. Even more problematic were his relations with neighboring towns, whose inhabitants pursued their economic advantage with little fear of intervention from any colony government and no regard for how their actions would affect Indian welfare.

Philip confronted the implications of New England localism most directly in cases of trespass. Colonial governments ordered towns to address Indian grievances but could not or would not enforce compliance. For six years, beginning in the mid-1650s, Rehoboth's inhabitants virtually ignored complaints from nearby Indians about damage from livestock, despite orders from the Plymouth court to solve the problem. In 1664, more than a decade after the issue first arose, Philip himself appeared at court—this time to complain about Rehoboth men trespassing on Wampanoag land to cut timber—and even then he may have hoped for a favorable outcome. But if he did, the court soon compounded his problems by deciding to refer trespass cases to the selectmen of the towns involved. From then on, Philip and his people would have to seek justice at the hands of the very people who might well own the offending beasts.

The Wampanoag leader's problems in dealing with townsmen whose attitudes ranged from unsympathetic to hostile worsened after the colony government declared its hands-off policy on trespass and reached a low point in 1671, when Plymouth officials charged Philip with stockpiling arms and conspiring with other Indian groups to attack the colonists. He denied the charges and appealed to Bay Colony magistrates to confirm his innocence. But Plymouth threatened coercion if he did not submit to its authority, and Philip signed a compact that further eroded his ability to safeguard Wampanoag interests. This agreement compelled him to seek Plymouth's approval before he disposed of any native territory, but colony officials were not similarly constrained by the need for Philip's permission before they approached Indians to purchase land. He also agreed that differences between natives and settlers would be referred to the colony government for resolution, although the magistrates' record in dealing even with straightforward cases of trespass gave little cause for optimism.

The Plymouth court intended to subvert Philip's authority over his people in order to facilitate the acquisition of Wampanoag land by a new generation of colonists who would, in turn, raise new generations of livestock. As early as 1632, William Bradford recognized that settlers who owned animals required a lot of land to support their beasts. He complained when families abandoned Plymouth to form new towns where meadow was available, but he could not stop them. Instead, he could only lament that "no man now thought he could live except he had cattle and a great deal of ground to keep them." Expansion accelerated during the 1660s and early 1670s, once again fueled by a burgeoning livestock population. During the two decades before King Philip's War, Plymouth officials approached local Indians at least twenty-three times to purchase land, often mentioning a specific need for pasture. Sometimes they only wanted "some small parcells"; on other occasions they desired "all such lands as the Indians can well spare."

The need to sustain their herds drove the English to seek Indian land, and their expansionary moves collided with an urgent Wampanoag need to preserve what remained of their territory. Joint use of land, although fraught with problems, at least recognized mutual subsistence needs; by the 1660s, however, the practice had greatly diminished.

Now the English not only wanted more land but demanded exclusive use of it. They asserted their property rights even in situations when accommodating Indian interests would have presented little threat. Allowing Philip to put his swine on Hog Island probably would not have harmed Portsmouth's inhabitants and might have improved relations between Indians and settlers. But what was Philip to think of the townsmen's summary refusal to share land, even when he proposed to use it for precisely the same purpose as they did? In that spring of 1669, Philip personally experienced the same English intransigence that he encountered as the representative of his people. After the Hog Island episode, and even more after his forced submission to Plymouth in 1671, he could not fail to see that while the colonists insisted that he yield to them, they would not yield in any way to him.

In an atmosphere of increasing tension, trespass assumed new significance. As colonists moved closer to native villages, the chances that livestock would stray onto Indian lands multiplied. With both groups competing for a limited supply of land, colonists did not restrain their animals from grazing wherever they could, while Indians grew ever more sensitive to such intrusions. Whenever livestock were concerned, the English ignored the Indians' property rights, while demanding that the natives recognize English rights. Indians resented encroachment by beasts that usually presaged the approach of Englishmen requesting formal ownership of land that their animals had already informally appropriated. Faced with the manifest inability—or unwillingness—of New England towns to solve the problem of trespass, and discouraged from seeking help from colony governments, Indians often resorted to their own means of animal control; they killed the offending beasts. This response would once have landed Indians in court, but by 1671 they faced far more serious consequences.

In that year, a group of angry colonists living near Natick very nearly attacked the Wampanoags of Mount Hope for killing livestock that had trespassed on Indian land. Interceding on behalf of the Indians, the Bay Colony's Indian commissioner, Daniel Gookin, begged for forbearance from the settlers, arguing that it was not worth *"fighting with Indians about horses and hogs,* as matters too low to shed blood." He urged the settlers to keep their animals on their own land; if any strayed into native territory and were killed, the owners should make a record of the fact, presumably to facilitate legal recovery. War was averted, but this incident nonetheless showed that tension over livestock had reached dangerously high levels.

Both sides now understood that disputes over trespassing animals epitomized differences so profound as to defy peaceful solution. Whenever Indians killed livestock that had damaged their cornfields, colonists denounced such acts as willful violations of English property rights—rights that some settlers wanted to defend by force of arms. For Indians, trespassing animals constituted an intolerable violation of *their* sovereign rights over their land. The problem intensified by the early 1670s, for the English were determined to deprive Philip of all means of ensuring the integrity of the shrinking tracts of Wampanoag land, even as they refused effectively to control their beasts. The issue of trespassing livestock generated such tension precisely because it could not be separated from fundamental questions of property rights and authority.

When war broke out in 1675, the Indians attacked first, but the underlying causes resembled those that had provoked English belligerence four years earlier. John Easton, a Rhode Island Quaker, sought out Philip early in the conflict to ask why he fought the colonists; Philip's response indicated that intermingled concerns about sovereignty, land, and animals had made war inevitable. He supplied Easton with a litany of grievances that recalled past confrontations with the English and particularly stressed intractable problems over land and animals. He complained that when Indian leaders agreed to sell land, "the English wold say it was more than thay agred to and a writing must be prove [proof] against all them." If any sachem opposed such sales, the English would "make a nother king that wold give or seell them there land, that now thay had no hopes left to kepe ani land." Even after they sold land, Indians suffered from English encroachments, for "the English Catell and horses still incresed that when thay removed 30 mill from wher English had anithing to do"—impossible for the native inhabitants of Mount Hope—"thay Could not kepe ther coren from being spoyled." The Indians had expected that "when the English boft [bought] land of them that thay wold have kept ther Catell upone ther owne land."

Because livestock had come to symbolize the relentless advance of English settlement, the animals were special targets of native enmity during the war. Colonel Benjamin Church, who led colonial forces in several campaigns, reported that Indians "began their hostilities with plundering and destroying cattle." In an attack near Brookfield, Indians burned dwellings and "made great spoyle of the cattel belonging to the inhabitants." At Rehoboth "they drove away many cattell & h[ors]es"; at Providence they "killd neer an hundered cattell"; in the Narragansett country they took away "at the least a thousand horses & it is like two thousan Cattell And many Sheep." As the human toll also mounted in the summer of 1675, English forces failed to stop Philip from slipping away from Mount Hope and only managed to capture "six, eight, or ten young Pigs of King Philip's Herds."

The livestock on which colonists depended exposed them to ambush. Early in the war, Indians attacked "five Men coming from Road-Island, to look up their Cattel upon Pocasset Neck." Settlers sought refuse in garrison houses and secured their cattle in palisaded yards but could not provide enough hay to sustain them for long. Sooner or later they had to drive the creatures out to pasture or bring in more hay. Philip and his forces—who had a keen understanding of the voraciousness of English livestock—would be waiting. Near Groton in March 1676 "a Parcel of Indians . . . laid an Ambush for two Carts, which went from the Garison to fetch in some Hay." At about the same time at Concord, "two men going for Hay, one of them was killed." Settlers counted themselves lucky when they escaped, even if their animals fell victim. When Hatfield inhabitants let their livestock out to graze in May 1676, they lost the entire herd of seventy cattle and horses to Indians who had anticipated the move.

The Indians seized and killed cattle mainly to deprive the colonists of food, but some of their depredations also suggest an intense animosity toward the animals themselves. One contemporary reported that "what cattle they took they seldom killed outright: or if they did, would eat but little of the flesh, but rather cut their bellies, and letting them go several days, trailing their guts after them, putting out their eyes, or cutting off one leg, &c." Increase Mather described an incident near Chelmsford when Indians "took a Cow, knocked off one of her horns, cut out her tongue, and so left the poor creature in great misery." Such mutilations recalled the tortures more often inflicted on human victims and perhaps similarly served a ritual purpose. Certainly when Indians—who found a use for nearly every scrap of dead game animals—killed cattle "& let them ly & did neither eat them nor carry them away," they did so deliberately to send a message of terror to their enemies.

Symbolic expressions of enmity, however, were a luxury that the Indians generally could not afford. As the war progressed, with cornfields ruined and hunting interrupted, Indians often needed captured livestock for food. When Church and his troops came upon an abandoned Indian encampment in an orchard, they found the apples gone and evidence of "the flesh of swine, which they had killed that day." At another site, colonial forces "found some of the English Beef boiling" in Indian kettles. In Maine, where fighting dragged on for months after Philip's death in August 1676, the "English took much Plunder from the Indians, about a thousand Weight of dried Beef, with other Things." Edward Randolph, sent by the crown to investigate New England affairs in the summer of 1676, reported to the Council of Trade on the devastation caused by the war. He estimated that the settlers had lost "eight thousand head of Cattle great and small"— a tremendous reduction in the livestock population but not enough to starve the colonists into defeat or sustain the Indians to victory.

The presence of livestock in New England was not the sole cause of the deterioration in relations between Indians and settlers. But because of their ubiquity and steady increase, domestic animals played a critical role in the larger, tragic human drama. The settlers had never been able to live without livestock, but as the animal population grew, Indians found it increasingly difficult to live with them. Both sides threatened violence over the issue of livestock—the English in 1671 and the Indians, who made good on the threat, in 1675. The cultural divide separating Indians and colonists would have existed without the importation to America of domestic animals. But the presence of livestock brought differences into focus, created innumerable occasions for friction, tested the limits of cooperation—and led, in the end, to war.

Readings for Virginia DeJohn Anderson:

The best examination of early New England Indian-White relations is Neal Salisbury, *Manitou and Providence: Indians, Europeans, and the Making of New England, 1500–1643* (New York: Oxford, 1982). William Cronon, *Changes in the Land: Indians, Colonists, and the Ecology of New England* (New York: Hill and Wang, 1983) focuses more on the environmental changes that occurred during the colonial era. The early portions of Howard S. Russell, *A Long, Deep Furrow: Three Centuries of Farming in New England* (Hanover, NH: University Press of New England, 1976) consider the impact of agriculture in the region, while a later example of misunderstandings over livestock is found in Rebecca Kugel, "Of Missionaries and Their Cattle: Ojibwa Perceptions of a Missionary as Evil Shaman," *Ethnohistory*, 41:2 (Spring 1994), pp. 227–44.

4

THE BEWITCHING TYRANNY OF CUSTOM: THE SOCIAL COSTS OF INDIAN DRINKING IN COLONIAL AMERICA

PETER C. MANCALL

Alcohol, firearms, and disease all brought widespread destruction to Native American societies after their introduction into North America. Of the three, it is likely that alcohol use has remained the most damaging for Indians down to the present. Its continued use has produced the stereotype of the drunken Indian and claims that Native Americans are more susceptable to its effects than are Anglo-Americans. While scientific evidence has long disproved that idea it remains firmly in place.

Usually scholars have addressed alcohol-related issues in the context of the fur trade and its role in disrupting tribal social and economic practices. That certainly occurred, and many of the village societies proved unable to avoid the destruction its use brought. In this essay the author moves well beyond the fur trade to examine a variety of roles drinking played in Indian societies. He demonstrates that in some cases individual tribal members used liquor for existing social and religious practices. The narrative also shows that both Indians and whites recognized the potential dangers of excessive drinking, and it examines the steps taken to avoid those by all concerned. In presenting a variety of drinking patterns and other responses to liquor, the author shows that the Indians worked consciously to confront and manage alcohol-related matters. The essay highlights the centrality of liquor in colonial-era Indian-white relations and how tribal peoples dealt with it.

Peter C. Mancall is an associate professor of history at the University of Kansas.

Alcohol abuse has been the most significant ongoing health problem American Indians have experienced since the mid-seventeenth century. The social costs of Indian drinking in modern society are staggering: Deaths related to alcoholism (including cirrhosis) remain four times higher for Indians than for the general population; alcohol plays a role

Source: Peter C. Mancall, " 'The Bewitching Tyranny of Custom': The Social Costs of Indian Drinking in Colonial America," pp. 15–42. Reprinted from the *American Indian Culture and Research Journal,* volume 17, number 2, by permission of the American Indian Studies Center, UCLA. © Regents of the University of California, 1993.

in perhaps 90 percent of all homicides involving Indians; inebriated Indians die while walking along roads, either hit by cars or succumbing to hypothermia; 70 percent of all treatment provided by Indian Health Service physicians is for alcohol-related disease or trauma. Alcohol abuse at times appears among Indian children by age thirteen; most seek complete intoxication. There is even one reported case of delirium tremens in a nine-year-old boy in northern New Mexico, himself the son of an alcoholic father. Maternal drinking has contributed to the growing incidence of fetal alcohol syndrome and has led also to an increased rate of other neonatal problems. So intense is the desire to become intoxicated among some Indians today, especially on reservations in the West, that they mix cleaning solvents with other fluids in order to produce what is now known as "Montana Gin," a concoction that can cause profound somatic disorders, including aspiration pneumonia and organic brain syndrome, which can lead to death. These social and clinical problems have occurred in spite of the fact that North American Indians, so far as clinicians and medical researchers can tell, are no more susceptible physiologically to abusing alcohol than other Americans.

Yet in spite of the myriad problems associated with drinking, Indians' early use and abuse of alcohol have not been described in much depth. Some researchers, notably Nancy O. Lurie, Craig MacAndrew, and Roger Edgerton, have attempted to demonstrate the ways in which Indians have structured their drinking practices, but they have not focused on the social costs of the alcohol trade for Indians in early America. Historians, often following the documentary evidence, have recognized the catastrophic consequences of drinking; most today accept the fact that alcohol contributed to problems, particularly violence, in early Indian communities. Russell Thornton has even suggested that alcohol abuse contributed directly to mortality and thus to the depopulation of many groups. Historians have made these assertions because colonial sources make one indisputable point: From Canada to West Florida and from the Atlantic to the western margins of British America in the Mississippi Valley, alcohol reached diverse groups of Indians during the seventeenth and eighteenth centuries, and most of the Indians who became involved in the liquor trade ultimately suffered as a result.

But, although historians have recognized the outlines of the problem, virtually no substantial studies exist of alcohol use among the Indians who inhabited colonial British America. Such an absence is particularly noticeable given the existing work on Indians and alcohol in other parts of the Western Hemisphere, notably New France (Canada) and New Spain (Mexico). This work draws on the extensive documentation available for drinking practices in these Catholic colonies, much of it left by missionaries or church officials. Together, these studies describe, in more than general terms, the precise uses and costs of drinking in Indian communities in the colonies created by Europeans in the early modern period.

This essay attempts to fill the gap by describing the ways that alcohol destabilized Indian communities in British America, the territory between the Atlantic and the Mississippi Valley from the mid-seventeenth century to the late eighteenth century. The sources for such study are vast; evidence of Indian drinking and the problems it created appear in colonial statutes, travelers' accounts, traders' ledgers, missionaries' diaries, and treaty negotiations, to name only the most prominent locations. Though abundant, the surviving accounts are not, in themselves, necessarily the surest evidence of abusive drinking among Indians. Most important, colonial descriptions of Indian drinking appear to conform to certain formulae; the dominant image of the drunken Indian often seems more a projection of ubiquitous colonial anxieties than an accurate assessment of Indian drinking practices. Further, colonial sources emphasize the consumption of alcohol by hunters, typically young men, but reports of children drinking, women selling liquor as well as consuming it, and older men imbibing along with others suggest that drinking was not limited to trading sessions where hunters met with liquor purveyors. Finally, colonists who wrote about Indian drinking often ignored the many Indians who abstained, thus giving the mistaken impression that all Indians drank. Still, the surviving evidence, however flawed, points unambiguously toward one conclusion: In the opinion of many colonists, Indians suffered from the alcohol trade.

Significantly, Indians agreed with colonists that liquor brought problems, but they drew their own conclusions about how alcohol changed their lives and who was responsible for liquor-related troubles. There are, to be sure, problems in interpreting Indian testimony, too. It has survived in documents written primarily by colonists and thus no doubt was constructed through certain culturally defined parameters. Further, colonists were not always aware that many Indians believed in the benefits of alcohol; in eastern North America, alcohol helped some to achieve highly valued dreamlike states of mind, and many Indians also incorporated alcohol into hospitality and mourning rites, marriages, and ceremonial dances.

But although Indians throughout eastern North America often organized their drinking in culturally approved ways, many came to believe that liquor created tension and animosity in their villages, dangerously reoriented the economies of their communities, led to domestic violence, and further facilitated the conquest of eastern North America by colonists. Most important, while some Indians blamed other Indians for the ill effects of drinking, many placed the responsibility for their problems with colonists who either participated in the trade directly or allowed it to continue in spite of mounting evidence of its enormous costs. In the end, as many Indians discovered, the alcohol trade became perhaps the most insidious aspect of European colonialism in North America.

"A Peculiar Kind of Insobriety"

Europeans first provided liquor to Indians in the sixteenth century, and, over time, alcohol became increasingly prominent in intercultural trade in British America. Hundreds of references to Indian drinking appear in the extant documents from the colonial period. Colonial accounts provide unambiguous evidence that spirits, particularly rum, threatened groups of Indians and thus made their survival, already at risk because of the spread of Old World pathogens, ever more precarious. Given the apparent impact of alcohol on Indians and the persistent colonial fears about the threats represented by disorderly Indians, it is not surprising that colonists often wrote about the destructive impact of liquor on Indians. These observations contain more than information about the consumption of alcohol. Taken together, they represent what colonists intended to be a devastating critique of Indian society. Yet, in spite of their cultural blinders, colonists left ample testimony about the social costs of alcohol for Indians, especially the way that drinking led to violence, accidents, community disruptions, poverty, and, on occasion, death. The diffusion of such information throughout the colonies had little impact on the trade.

Colonists were so eager to trade with the indigenous peoples of America that they maintained the commerce in spite of its devastating impact on Indian communities.

The liquor trade developed and grew over time, because traders believed they could always sell liquor to Indians; unlike durable manufactured goods, it was depleted when used. Unfortunately, the paucity of exact information about the population history of Indians in eastern North America and the even less accessible information regarding the numbers of Indians who actually consumed alcohol when it was available make estimates of per capita consumption exceedingly vague and limited; the best that exist relate to local areas only and pertain to episodic drinking bouts.

Still, it is possible to estimate the extent of the trade, at least for the eighteenth century. In the northern reaches of European colonization, Hudson's Bay Company traders made brandy a staple of their fur trade. Although they sold only seventy gallons to Indians in 1700 from their post at Fort Albany-Eastmain, the volume increased to just over two thousand gallons of brandy sold each year from the four posts they operated in the late 1750s, and the trade continued well beyond the colonial period. Further south, the trade was far more extensive, at least by the 1760s and 1770s, when the best evidence is available. In spite of problems associated with overland and water carriage of liquor from the coast across the Appalachian Mountains, George Morgan, a partner in the prominent Philadelphia trading firm of Baynton, Wharton, and Morgan, had almost eight thousand gallons of alcohol, most of it distilled spirits from the West Indies, at his trading post at Kaskaskia in the Illinois country in December 1767; he intended to sell most (if not all) of it to Indians. Traders brought at least sixty-five hundred gallons of rum to Fort Pitt in 1767, and Alexander McKee, the local commissary of Indian affairs at the post, believed that "double that Quantity is brought here by them exclusive of large Quantities brought up by Sutlers and others." According to Jehu Hay, the Detroit commissary of Indian affairs, traders brought over twenty-four thousand gallons of rum to that post in 1767. As both McKee and Hay informed Sir William Johnson, the fur trade prospered at both posts, with traders receiving more than 300,000 skins that year. Johnson was already well aware of the extent of the rum trade: In 1764, he estimated that traders sold fifty thousand gallons of rum to Indians in the territory under the auspices of the northern department of the superintendent of Indian affairs.

Although it seems unlikely that there was sufficient liquor to allow any Indian who wanted alcohol to be constantly inebriated if he or she so chose, the available rum did allow for fairly regular drinking bouts. Colonial observers often attended Indian drinking sessions, although they did not quite know what to make of the Indians' drinking practices. Missionaries and colonial officials generally believed that drinking led to the decay of Indian communities and that sexual excess, violent death, domestic strife, and poverty all followed in the wake of drinking. Some colonists particularly lamented the impact of alcohol on their efforts to convert Indians to Christianity.

Colonial descriptions of Indian drinking sprees began with the premise that intoxicated Indians followed a predictable pattern. François Vachon de Belmont, who became a missionary in the Sulpician Order in the early 1680s and traveled from France to New France to convert Indians to Christianity, observed drinking practices among Indians who inhabited the Northeast and wrote the most extensive critique of Indian drinking patterns. Liquor, he argued, caused three basic changes in Indians: First, he wrote, it "enlivens their natural sluggishness, dispels their timidity, their sense of shame and inferiority, which their dull nature gives them." Second, liquor prompted Indians "to undertake with vigor and bravado almost any evil action such as anger, vengeance, or impurity." Third, drunkenness provided Indians with "a valid excuse for any evil which they might commit in such a condition." These changes were unique to Indians, or so he thought when he wrote that "this is a peculiar kind of insobriety."

Indians "imbibe only to become drunk," Belmont declared. This was most evident when there was a limited amount of alcohol available to a particular group. Rather than share the liquor equally, presumably as Europeans would do in such circumstances, the Indians chose one of their number to consume all of the liquor and thereby become inebriated, while the others remained completely sober. There was, he wrote, "only one degree of drunkenness worthwhile, the sort which they call 'Gannontiouaratonseri,' complete insobriety. And when they begin to feel the effects of the brandy they rejoice shouting, 'Good, good, my head is reeling.' " Most of those who drank in this fashion were young men "who are professedly given to bravado, whose pride urges them to seek notoriety whereby they may receive attention for some deed or other." The Reverend John Clayton, rector of the parish at James City, Virginia, during the mid-1680s offered a similar view of the reasons Indians drank as they did. "[T]hey will allways drink to excess if they can possibly get [spirits]," he wrote in 1697, "but do not much care for them unless they can have enough to make them drunk. I have heard it said that they wonder much of the English for purchasing wine at so dear a rate when Rum is much cheaper & will make them sooner drunk."

Along with the other horrors, Indian drinking proved particularly frustrating to clerics because drunkenness impeded conversion to Christianity. Inebriated Indians could not, they believed, make the rational choice to convert; made senseless by liquor, Indians were unable to realize the full import of the missionaries' teachings. Such views were common among Catholic missionaries in Canada, and British colonists had similar thoughts. At times, missionaries themselves came under fire for allegedly taking liquor to Indians and thus compromising the effort to spread Christianity. In a sermon published in Boston in 1704, Cotton Mather attacked an "Indian-Preacher" who possessed both scripture and liquor. "But he minded his Bottel more than his *Bible,*" Mather declared, and thus weakened his ability to convert Indians to Christian ways.

The colonists' critique of Indian drinking also included a great interest in the role liquor played in releasing Indians from their sexual inhibitions. Inebriated Indians' sexual behavior particularly fascinated natural historians. Nicholas Denys, during his travels in Acadia, and Bernard Romans, during his sojourn in East and West Florida, noted that consumption of alcohol had an immediate impact on Indians' sexual mores. So did William Bartram, who, while touring the Southeast in the early 1770s, found a rapid change in a group of Creeks near Mount Royal, in Georgia, after they had returned from St. Augustine with "a very liberal supply of spirituous liquors, about twenty kegs, each containing five gallons." Once they began to drink, they continued for ten days." In a few days this festival exhibited one of the most ludicrous bacchanalian scenes that is possible to be conceived," Bartram wrote. "White and red men and women without distinction, passed the day merrily with these jovial, amorous topers, and the nights in convivial songs, dances, and sacrifices to Venus, as long as they could stand or move; for in these frolics both sexes take such liberties with each other, and act, without constraint or shame, such scenes as they would abhor when sober or in their senses; and would endanger their ears and even their lives." Soon, however, the liquor ran out. Most of the

Creeks, Bartram noted, were "sick through intoxication," and, when they became more sober, "the dejected lifeless sots would pawn every thing they were in possession of, for a mouthful of spirits to settle their stomachs, as they termed it."

While some colonists came to lament the way that liquor led to sexual license and thus interfered with the civilizing of Indians, most had more mundane concerns, especially related to the violent consequences of Indian drinking for both colonists and Indians. For this reason, colonists had feared Indian drunkenness from the start. On the eve of settlement, the governor and deputy of the New England Company forbade colonists going to Massachusetts Bay from selling liquor to Indians. "Wee pray you endeavor," they wrote, "though there be much strong water sent for sale, yett so to order it as that the salvages may not for lucre sake bee induced to the excessive use, or rather abuse of it, and of any hand take care or people give noe ill example." William Bradford, ever wary of disorder that could threaten Plymouth, acted swiftly to limit what he believed were the dangerous excesses of Thomas Morton's antics at Merrymount. Among Morton's sins, along with providing the Indians with firearms and scrawling salacious verse on a maypole, was his apparent provision of liquor to Indians.

Over the course of the seventeenth century, New England colonists repeatedly tried to limit the sale of alcohol to Indians. As early as July 1633, provincial officials in Massachusetts Bay ordered that "noe man shall sell or (being in a course of tradeing) give any stronge water to any Indean." Although the colony relaxed its statutes when it allowed Indians who brought in the head of a wolf to receive three quarts of wine for their reward and even allowed some traders to sell wine to Indians, problems of Indian intemperance prompted provincial officials in the late 1650s to stop the trade. Since the General Court lamented its failure to limit "excessive drinkinge & drunkenes among the Indians" and noted that "the fruits whereof are murther & other outrages," the elimination of the liquor trade was not surprising. Fearing the disorder that accompanied Indian drinking, provincial officials detailed severe fines and corporal punishment for Indians found inebriated and for colonists who provided them with liquor.

Nonetheless, over time the use of liquor spread throughout British America and led to violence, at least in the opinion of colonial witnesses who were quick to describe what they believed were the savage aspects of Indians' lives. Explorer and author John Lawson wrote in his widely reprinted account of early eighteenth-century Carolina that Indians "will part with the dearest Thing they have" to buy rum, "and when they have got a little in their Heads, are the impatients Creatures living, 'till they have enough to make 'em quite drunk; and the most miserable Spectacles when they are so, some falling into the Fires, burn their Legs or Arms, contracting the Sinews, and become Cripples all their Life-time; others from Precipices break their Bones and Joints, with abundance of Instance, yet none are so great to deter them from that accurs'd Practice of Drunkenness, though sensible how many of them (are by it) hurry'd into the other World before their Time, as themselves oftentimes confess." Lawson noted that "[m]ost of the Savages are addicted to Drunkenness," and that it contributed directly to the decline of southern Indians; combined with smallpox, rum "made such a Destruction amongst them, that, on good grounds, I do believe, there is not the sixth Savage living within two hundred Miles of all our Settlements, as there were fifty Years ago."

The violence attending Indian drinking sessions troubled colonists throughout British America. "Drunkenness hath occasioned some *Indians* to be burnt to Death in their little Houses," declared Samuel Danforth, preaching at Bristol, Rhode Island, in October 1709 at the execution of two Indians who had committed murder while intoxicated. "Other *Indians* by their being drowned first in Drink, have been exposed to a second drowning in Water. Nor are these the first (who now stand in the midst of this great Assembly) who have committed Murder, when overcome with Drink, and have been Executed for it." Charles Stuart, brother of the southern superintendent of Indian affairs John Stuart and an agent to the Choctaw, believed that liquor constituted four-fifths of the trade goods purchased by those Indians in 1770. Traveling among their settlements a few years later, he wrote that he "saw nothing but rum Drinking and Women Crying over the Dead bodies of their relations who have died by Rum." Liquor, he believed, fundamentally disrupted the social order because of the violence it seemingly released; it was "the cause of their killing each other daily" and the "[c]ause of every disturbance in the nation." Stuart was not the only one in the southern Indian administration concerned with the violence committed by drunken Indians; the emissary to the Creek in 1771, David Taitt, often encountered intoxicated Indians seemingly always on the verge of attacking him or someone nearby. Taitt, like agents throughout the South, knew well that rum had become a staple of the skin trade in the Southeast in spite of the troubles it brought.

According to colonial observers, drinking often led Indians to injure or kill each other. Some colonists speculated that Indians feigned drunkenness in order to attack other Indians and not suffer any consequences. Others described less deliberate assaults. The sale of rum by unlicensed traders throughout the South endangered "the general Peace and Tranquility" of southern Indians, agent Thomas Bosworth wrote in December 1752; a "general Peace and Quietness reigns among them," another agent wrote to South Carolina Governor Glen in August 1754, "excepting what Disturbance is occasioned by immoderate Quantities of Rum brought among them, which if a Stop put to, would very much contribute towards a good Harmoney among the Indians." Trader and historian James Adair, writing on the eve of the Revolution, also noted decidedly self-destructive behavior. "By some fatality," he wrote in a description of the Catawba, "they are much addicted to excessive drinking, and spirituous liquors distract them so exceedingly, that they will even eat live coals of fire." William Byrd joined the chorus as well. "The trade [the Indians] have had the misfortune to drive with the English," he wrote in his *History of the Dividing Line betwixt Virginia and North Carolina,* "has furnished them constantly with rum, which they have used so immoderately that, what with the distempers and what with the quarrels it begat amongst them, it has proved a double destruction."

The violence brought on by alcohol, combined with an apparent decline in the health of drinkers, led some observers to make direct links between the trade and Indian mortality. Drinking, familiar to the Powhatan Indians of the Chesapeake region by the 1680s, prompted the governor of Maryland to speculate that "the Indians of these parts decrease very much, partly owing to smallpox, but the great cause of all is their being so devilishly given to drink." Almost a century later, Guy Johnson, who briefly served as superintendent of Indian affairs in the northern colonies after the death in 1774 of his uncle, Sir William Johnson, also believed that alcohol contributed to Indian population decline. "The State of Population is greatest where there is the least Intercourse with the Europeans," he wrote, in part because alcohol was "peculiarly fatal to their Constitutions, & to their Increase," especially when combined with smallpox. Benjamin Franklin agreed. "[I]f it be the Design of Providence to extirpate these Savages in order to make room for Cultivators of the Earth," he wrote in his autobiography, "it seems not improbable that Rum may be the appointed Means. It has already annihilated all the Tribes who formerly inhabited the Sea-Coast."

Though such statements demonstrated concern on the part of colonists for the apparent plight of Indians, other colonists had more mundane concerns: They feared Indian drinking because of the potential for violence by inebriated Indians against colonists. Concerns about Indian assaults led numerous colonial officials to pass laws banning the sale of alcohol to Indians in virtually every British North American colony, although some of these statutes were short-lived.

But, even when these laws were in force, traders quickly discovered ways to circumvent them, and some inebriated Indians acted exactly as colonists feared. At times, colonists caused the trouble, but more often, in the opinion of colonial leaders, Indians were to blame. Indians in Maine, purportedly inebriated, traveled to a colonial settlement and threatened to attack colonists and their livestock; other colonists apprehended them before they had done much damage, and the colonist who had provided them with rum subsequently found himself facing a magistrate in Boston, charged with violating laws prohibiting the sale of liquor to Indians. John Toby, a Nanticoke in Pennsylvania, purportedly sexually assaulted an eight-year-old colonial girl. According to the complaint of the girl's father, recorded in a deposition, Toby responded to the allegation by saying "that he had been drunk and did not Remember what he did with the girl." Three colonists then took him off to jail to await a trial. Readers of the first edition of *The American Magazine, or a Monthly View of the Political State of the British Colonies,* published in Philadelphia in January 1741, could read about a murder committed by a drunken Indian. "The *Indians* who live nearer the *English,* and, by Reason of that Vicinity, have more frequent Opportunities of intoxicating themselves with strong Liquors," the magazine reported, "are indeed more dangerous: so that it happen'd once in about fifty Years, that one of them, in a drunken Fit slew an *Englishman.*" The murderer was, the readers were reassured, subsequently hanged, and "[h]is Country-men, instead of murmuring at, highly approved of that Act of Justice." For missionaries living among Indians, the risks seemed even more immediate, as the Protestant missionary Gideon Hawley discovered during a 1753 trip to Oquaga, a community of Indians from various tribes located alongside the Susquehanna River; there he encountered a number of inebriated Indians, one of whom, apparently by accident, nearly shot his head off. After his experiences with Indian drinking, it was no wonder that he refused to establish a mission in any community where Indians allowed alcohol.

Violence, however, proved only the most obvious risk of Indian drinking; the long-term economic consequences of the liquor trade appeared, to numerous colonial observers, just as devastating to Indians and, ultimately, to colonists also. In spite of a 1711 law in South Carolina forbidding the sale of rum by unlicensed traders, Indians there continued to fall into debt to liquor purveyors. The problem so exasperated southern colonial officials that they periodically forgave the debt of the Indians. Yet the problems remained. Thomas Bosomworth, an agent to the Creek, noted in his journal that liquor continued to impoverish Indians. "Nothing worthy of Notice during our Stay here," he wrote in October 1752 in a discussion of a meeting of provincial agents with the lower Creek, "though I could not help remarking the extream Poverty and Nakedness of those Indians that are contiguous to the French Fort [where] they are supplied with Liquor for those Goods they purchase from our Traders. The fatal Effects of which the Indians themselves are sencible off." Northern commentators agreed. New England Indians "will part with all they have to their bare skins" to purchase rum, naturalist John Josselyn wrote in the mid-1670s, "being perpetually drunk with it, as long as it is to be had, it hath killed many of them, especially old women who have dyed when dead drunk."

By the mid-eighteenth century, the problems associated with the illegal rum trade, especially the economic plight of Indians apparently defrauded by liquor dealers, greatly troubled some colonists involved in the transatlantic skin trades. Charleston merchant Edmund Atkin, who became the southern superintendent of Indian affairs in 1755, believed that alcohol undermined the trade network and had disastrous consequences for the English. Rum traders working out of Augusta were particularly troublesome. These nefarious dealers placed "themselves near the Towns, in the way of the Hunters returning home with their deer Skins," he wrote. "The poor Indians in a manner fascinated, are unable to resist the Bait; and when Drunk are easily cheated. After parting with the fruit of three or four Months Toil, they find themselves at home, without the means of buying the necessary Clothing for themselves or their Families." In such a state, they were "dispose[d] for Mischief"; a "licentiousness hath crept in among [the young] men, beyond the Power of the Head Men to Remedy." Even the quality of the deerskins declined in such circumstances, since the rum peddlers needed to deal quickly and then leave with their wares, and Indians accustomed to trading lower quality skins for liquor proved to be less cooperative commercial partners: "[T]he Indians require the other Traders in their Towns to take [deerskins] in the same Condition." Drunken Indians, Atkin warned, became embittered when liquor was used to purchase their land, as he claimed it was among the Chickasaw on the Savannah River, and inebriated Indians proved easy prey to colonists who wished to murder Indians. Northern officials also believed that colonists threatened the entire system of intercultural trade when they deceived Indians with alcohol.

Faced with a growing body of evidence that drunken Indians threatened colonists, as well as other Indians, in a number of ways, some observers looked for the source of the problem. Many blamed selfish traders for undermining efforts to convert Indians and for supplying Indians with liquor. "While the present ill adapted measures are continued," Adair wrote in a plea for better organization of the Indian trade, "nothing less than the miraculous power of deity can possibly effect the Indians' reformation; many of the present traders are abandoned, reprobate white savages. Instead of showing good examples of moral conduct, besides their other part of life, they instruct the unknowing and imitating savages in many diabolical lessons of obscenity and blasphemy." It would have been impossible for colonial commentators to imagine a worse group of people to be in constant contact with Indians.

Many colonists believed that Indians were ultimately accountable for their own behavior. Although high-ranking colonial officials periodically sought to limit the trade by passing laws making it illegal, they also repeatedly excoriated Indians for their drinking; their efforts to stop Indian drinking often seem little more than criticism of particular Indians' ways of life, especially their inability to control their appetites. Governor George Johnstone of West Florida, addressing a group of Chickasaw and Choctaw at a treaty in Mobile in March 1765, feared that liquor-bearing traders created animosity among the Indians. To prevent trouble, he urged Indians not to drink, stressing the economic and social plight that resulted from drinking. But, although the governor cast blame on the traders (those "Guilty of carrying that Liquor amongst you ought to be

Considered as your real Enemies much more than if they lifted the Hatchet against you," he stated) he tried to shame Indians into avoiding liquor. "He who dies in War, his Time shall be remembered," he declared, "but he who is destroyed by Drunkenness shall be forgott like the Hog who has perished in the swamp."

Few expressed criticism of Indian life as effectively as Sir William Johnson, perhaps the best-informed colonial official in regards to the rum trade because of his many years living in the New York hinterland, where he was first a trader and then superintendent of Indian affairs for the northern colonies. Although he, like others, blamed traders for carrying rum into the backcountry, he ultimately believed it was the Indians' inability to resist liquor that caused their problems. "The Indians in general are so devoted to & so debauched by Rum," he wrote to James Abercromby in May 1758, "that all Business with them is thrown into confusion by it & my transactions with them unspeakably impeeded. The Mohock Castles in particular are become scenes of perpetual riot, and the Indians selling the necessaries they receive from the Crown thro me for Rum, to the infinite detriment of His Majestys service & the increase of Indian Expences." But what, he wondered, could he do about the problem. "Provincial penal Laws have been made, but to no purpose," he averred. "I have done all in my power against this universal Enemy, to indeed His Majestys service in general, but it is too subtle & too powerful a one for me to reduce within proper bounds as to the Indians."

Nine years later, after he had defended the economic utility of the liquor trade in a report to the Lords of Trade, Johnson clarified his views further when he told a group of Indians who claimed they had been unable to control their desire for liquor that "[t]he best Medicine I can think of to prevent your falling into your former Vice of drinking is to embrace Christianity" and that they should follow the example of other sober Indians. Johnson, it should be noted, was at the same time sending his own trading agents into the woods, often supplying them with little else but rum for trade with the Indians.

The reports of colonial observers, despite their biases, reveal certain similarities. Young men drank more often than other members of most communities, no doubt because they had the most frequent interactions with traders, especially liquor purveyors who worked beyond the bounds of legal trading posts. Further, in all likelihood, the costs of drinking, whether borne by the young hunters or the entire community, differed somewhat by season; mortality rates due to accidents were higher in winter when inebriated Indians ran a greater risk of exposure, especially in northern climates. In addition, regardless of the gender or age of the person who died as a result of an alcohol-related accident, Indian families suffered profoundly; the loss of family members disrupted the domestic economy and had a shattering impact on those who remained after the tragedy.

In the end, many colonial descriptions of Indian drinking reveal that liquor played a key role in the effort to colonize British America. In the seventeenth and eighteenth centuries, missionaries, traders, and government officials were engaged in a campaign, not always successful, to convert Indians to European ways. Indians needed to trade, colonizers argued, to become civilized. And even though the liquor trade was destructive, it had to be maintained. Without it, Johnson informed the Board of Trade in October 1764, in a moment of remarkable frankness, "the Indians can purchase their cloathing with half the quantity of Skins, which will make them indolent, and lessen the fur trade." Legislators who tried to ban the liquor trade because they believed that Indians were unable to control their thirst for alcohol took a different approach, to be sure. But their inability to stop the commerce revealed that many other colonists believed the trade should continue, and these commercial interests prevailed. However diverse the existing views on the liquor trade, colonial observers shared one belief: Indians needed colonists to guide them in a world seemingly awash in liquor. Many Indians saw the situation quite differently.

"The Accursed Use We Make of Rum"

Despite some colonists' fears, Indians suffered more than colonists did from drinking and from the alcohol trade. The survival of their testimony on the subject leaves little doubt that the social problems observed by colonists—including poverty, domestic violence, and even fatalities—were far more desperate than colonists could understand. But, although Indians who have left records of their beliefs about alcohol did not always agree with one another, they also did not necessarily agree with colonial commentators. While many acknowledged that they could not control alcohol consumption and thus needed assistance in their battle against liquor, they also believed that colonists bore ultimate responsibility for the havoc alcohol brought to their communities. Colonists, not Indians, had initiated what an anonymous author, purported to be a Creek Indian, termed "the bewitching Tyranny of Custom." Such logic led many Indians to condemn the alcohol trade and those colonists who let it continue.

To be sure, some Indians, perhaps following the lead of colonial leaders, blamed themselves for the ill effects of drinking. "[W]hen we drink it, it makes us mad," declared several leaders of Delaware Valley Indians in the late seventeenth century. "[W]e do not know what we do, we then abuse one another; we throw each other into the Fire, Seven Score of our People have been killed, by reason of the drinking of it, since the time it was first sold us." Alcohol, some Indians believed, eroded the ties needed to maintain communities. A group of Chickasaw informed a colonial official in 1725 that they were unable to keep members of their village under control because "if the Young Men were drunk and Mad," they "could not help it," but they would do their best to minimize the problems.

In what became the most famous printed assault of any Indian on the liquor trade, Samson Occom, a Mohegan who became a missionary and who himself purportedly had problems with liquor, exhorted his "Indian Brethren" to stop drinking. Occom's attack on Indian intemperance clearly shows the influence of his Christian teachings. Writing in response to the execution of Moses Paul, a Christian Indian who, when drunk, had murdered Moses Cook, Occom wrote a broadside in 1772 warning of the dangers of alcohol. "My kindred Indians, pray attend and hear," he wrote in verse form, "With great attention and with godly fear;/This day I warn you of that cursed sin, That poor, despised Indians wallow in." The sin was drunkenness, and it led to a host of social problems in addition to this particular murder.

> Mean are our houses, and we are kept low,
> And almost naked, shivering we go;
> Pinch'd for food and almost starv'd we are,
> And many times put up with stinking fare. . . .
> Our little children hovering round us weep,
> Most starv'd to death we've nought for them to eat;
> All this distress is justly on us come,
> For the accursed use we make of rum."

Occom continued his attack on liquor in sixteen verses, most often noting the social costs of drinking: Drunken Indians, he wrote, were unable to "go, stand, speak, or sit"; they risked increased chances for being defrauded and scorned; children and women also became inebriated; Indians who drank descended to a lower order of existence, "On level with the beasts and far below / Are we when with strong drink we reeling go." Not surprisingly, Occom concluded his remarks with an appeal that Indians convert to Christianity and thus presumably shed the barbarous traits that had led to drunkenness in the first place. His sermon on the subject covered these points in greater depth, often echoing the tone of Puritan assaults on excessive drinking; it proved so popular that it was published in a ninth edition by 1774. As Occom no doubt knew well, however, even Indians who converted to Christianity occasionally stumbled into intemperance.

Indians living in communities with missionaries also blamed themselves for alcohol-related maladies. They thought that members of their towns who were thirsty for rum threatened the economies of backcountry villages by concentrating their efforts on hunting instead of agriculture, since pelts, not corn, purchased liquor. Not coincidentally, Indians in these communities also overhunted indigenous furbearing animals, thereby endangering the fur trade. Some men, village residents complained, spent so much time hunting that they neglected their crops, with devastating implications for the survival of their communities. "It is quite evident that there are now so few Indians, when they had been so numerous formerly," several Nanticokes told two Moravian missionaries visiting Onondaga, the meeting place of the Iroquois tribes in central New York, in July 1754. "The cause of this falling off is their use of too much rum. Let the Indians try to do without rum for but four years even, and they will be astonished at the increase of the population, and at the decrease of diseases and early death. All this is the result of rum drinking, which is also the primary cause of famine among them, caused by their not planting their crops at the proper time."

Although some Indians accepted responsibility for the troubles brought by drinking, others looked outward for the source of their distress. They decided to act on their beliefs by demanding that colonial officials end the liquor trade because of its disastrous effects on the economies of their villages. Time and again, Indians claimed that colonists had repudiated earlier agreements to stop the flow of alcohol into the hinterland. Charles Thomson recounted numerous Indian complaints about the alcohol trade, and he publicized his views in *An Enquiry into the Causes of the Alienation of the Delaware and Shawnee Indians from the British Interest,* printed in London in 1759. At a treaty council between leaders of the Mingo, Shawnee, and Conoy at Conestoga in 1722, the Indians, according to Thomson, urged Governor Keith of Pennsylvania to stop the trade." At this Treaty the *Indians* complain of the Damage they receive by strong Liquor being brought among them," he wrote. "They say, 'The *Indians* could live contentedly and grow rich, if it were not for the Quantities of Rum that is suffered to come amongst them, contrary to what *William Penn* promised.' " At other sessions, Indians in Pennsylvania complained that traders brought little else but rum with them to trading sessions, instead of the goods, such as shot and powder, that the Indians needed. Many Indians sold their clothing for liquor, the Conestoga chief Tawenna noted at a meeting in Philadelphia in 1729, " 'and are much impoverished thereby.' "

Indians throughout the hinterland joined the effort to stop the liquor trade. In August 1731, two Indian leaders, the Delaware sachem Sassoonan and the Iroquois Shickellamy, pleaded with Pennsylvania officials to stop rum sellers traveling to Indian villages because, as Sassoonan declared, " 'tis to be feared by means of Rum Quarrels may happen between them & Murther ensue, which may tend to dissolve that Union & loosen the Tye" between British colonists and Indians; to prevent problems, these Indians wanted rum to be available for sale only in colonial settlements. Later, Indians became more strident in their requests. In the late 1760s and early 1770s, Sir William Johnson received reports or heard complaints from groups of Miami, Shawnee, Delaware, and Oneida who wanted the alcohol trade stopped. "[I]t is You that Make the liquor," a Shawnee spokesman informed a colonial official at Fort Pitt in 1771, "and to you we must look to Stop it." The Indians wanted help immediately. "[I]f no Method can be fallen upon to prevent their bringing Rum into the Country, the Consequences must be dreadful; All the Western Nations fear it as well as us, and we all know well that it is in your great Men's Power to Stop it, and make us happy, if they thought it worth the Trouble."

Indians battled the liquor trade because the commerce could, on occasion, lead to profoundly destructive tensions within their communities; on occasion, it created trouble between men and women in backcountry villages. A group of Delaware Indians told Charles Beatty, who was traveling through the Ohio country in 1766 on an exploratory venture for the Presbyterian church, that they wanted to complain about the participation of Indian women in the trade. "[T]here are some that do at times hire some of our Squaws to goe to Bed with them & give them rum for it," they declared; "this thing is very Bad, & the Squaws again selling the Rum to our People make them Drunk." Although intercultural sexual relations were not new in the region, these Indians found the inclusion of rum in the relationship wholly inappropriate. "[W]e Beseech you," they concluded, "to advise our Brothers against this thing & do what you can to have it stopped."

More devastating still was the alcohol-related poverty that led some Indians to contemplate putting an end to the fur trade. When Pennsylvania trader and provincial negotiator Conrad Weiser traveled through the backcountry of the middle colonies in March 1737, he found Indians at Otsiningo battling the alcohol trade. He had been to the town of the Onondaga and Shawnee along the Susquehanna River twelve years earlier and now discovered that this village was experiencing hard times. In his journal, he noted that the Indians were "short of provisions" and that "their children looked like dead persons and suffered much from hunger." Local Indians then presented what must have been a devastating omen. They told Weiser that they had difficulty finding game and that "the Lord and Creator of the world was resolved to destroy the Indians." They explained that one of their seers had "seen a vision of God," who declared that Indians killed game "for the sake of the skins, which you give for strong liquor and drown your senses, and kill one another, and carry on a dreadful debauchery. Therefore have I driven the wild animals out of the country, for they are mine. If you will do good and cease from your sins, I will bring them back; if not, I will destroy you from off the earth." The Indians, according to Weiser, believed the seer's story. "Time will show, said they, what is to happen to us," he wrote. "[Rum] will kill us and leave the land clear for the Europeans without strife or purchase." Contained within the vision was an unambiguous message. If Indians halted the fur trade, they would no longer suffer from the liquor trade; the hunters' sins could be erased and the community purged of its debauchery.

To many Indians, the social costs of the liquor trade were ubiquitous, especially the violence drinking caused. Colonists mistreated Indians when they were drunk, declared a group of Maine Indians in 1677. "[W]e love yo," their petition declared, "but when we are dronk you will take away our cot & throw us out of dore." Further, mean-spirited colonists sometimes gave Indians liquor "& wen we were drunk killed us." Dutch traveler Jaspar Danckaerts, journeying through New York near the end of the seventeenth century, encountered an Indian who explained, quite clearly, that although drinking weakened Indian communities, the fault lay entirely with those who sold alcohol to the Indians. The Indian, named Jasper, noted that divine spirits governed life on earth and punished those "who do evil and drink themselves drunk," yet he also freely admitted that he drank to excess and did not have to fear retribution. Asked by colonists why he drank, Jasper replied, "I had rather not, but my heart is so inclined that it causes me to do it, although I know it is wrong. The Christians taught it to us, and give us or sell us the drink, and drink themselves drunk." Apparently annoyed at his answer, the colonists responded that if they lived near the Indians, the Indians would never see them inebriated nor would they provide liquor to the Indians. "That," he replied, according to Danckaerts, "would be good."

In some important ways, Indian beliefs differed markedly from those of colonists. Indians did not share the view that drinking led to bacchanalian orgies, although some felt that drinking threatened relations between men and women in Indian communities. Most Indians did not believe that liquor impeded their religious lives but some certainly thought that the trade did threaten their customary relations with the animals they hunted. Indians in eastern North America had many reasons to consume alcohol, and they did not believe their drunken comportment indicated, as some colonists apparently believed, that they were culturally inferior to colonists.

Alcohol and Colonialism

For all their differences, the testimony of Indians and colonists agrees on one point: The alcohol that came from trade with colonists destabilized many Indian communities. Although it was not clear to early Americans, it now seems evident that the liquor trade promoted British imperial expansion in North America. While some colonists and Indians might have exaggerated the role played by alcohol in the decline of Indian populations, abundant evidence confirms that the liquor trade impoverished Indians and threatened their families. Since Indians throughout most of the colonial period had to cope with the continuing inroads of epidemic disease as well as colonists' seemingly insatiable hunger for land, alcohol apparently played a key role in the social decline and eventual disappearance of many villages. The desire to become intoxicated did not, in itself, force Indians into desperate circumstances, but the poverty caused by the liquor trade could have contributed to the decision of many Indians to sell their lands to colonists and migrate westward in search of greater opportunity.

Further, the liquor trade and Indian responses to it reinforced the cultural chasm separating the peoples of North America. To colonists, Indians' inability to control their drinking—to drink, that is, as colonists did—seemed a sign that Indians remained a people apart, perhaps forever inferior and savage. Although colonists often recognized the problems brought by liquor—as early as September 1673, the General Assembly of Rhode Island condemned the "abominable filthynes" of selling alcohol to Indians—colonial officials proved either unable or unwilling to halt the trade. Economic logic dictated that the trade continue lest the English receive fewer skins, a prospect even those intimately familiar with the costs of Indian drinking chose to avoid. Stopping this commerce, even if it was possible, would also have meant repudiating a longstanding effort, dating to the sixteenth century, to turn Indians into trade partners.

Although alcohol contributed to the spread of the empire by weakening the social structure and economic basis of Indian communities, it simultaneously created resentment among Indians that gave them added determination to battle the expansion of colonial settlements. It is thus not surprising that Indian prophets who led revitalization movements in the late colonial period made temperance one of their primary goals. It is also quite likely that whatever success these prophets enjoyed stemmed, at least in part, from earlier Indian efforts to resist the tide of colonization by battling the liquor trade.

Whatever the social costs of the alcohol trade, liquor remained a staple of Indian-colonist trade in the American hinterland. The commerce survived because it apparently was profitable to colonists involved in the business, and because it represented a valuable enterprise in the mercantile empire. Few, if any, colonists celebrated the troubles Indians experienced because of the liquor trade. But even when Indians made the social costs known, colonists too easily ascribed the Indians' sufferings to faults of the Indians themselves. In an age when many other Americans were working relentlessly to overthrow the imperial tyrant who, they believed, threatened their freedom, many Indians found the liquor trade, and the empire it represented, another kind of tyranny that threatened to destroy their world.

Readings for Peter C. Mancall:

A fuller treatment of alcohol use may be found in Peter C. Mancall, *Deadly Medicine: Indians and Alcohol in Early America* (Ithaca, NY: Cornell University Press, 1995). For discussions of this issue in other areas and times see Margaret Anne Kennedy, *The Whiskey Trade on the Northwest Plains: A Multidisciplinary Study* (New York: P. Lang, 1993); and George Harwood Phillips, "Indians in Los Angeles, 1781–1875: Economic Integration, Social Disintegration," *Pacific Historical Review,* 49:3 (August, 1980), pp. 427–51.

5

GUARDIANS OF TRADITION AND HANDMAIDENS TO CHANGE: WOMEN'S ROLES IN CREEK ECONOMIC AND SOCIAL LIFE DURING THE EIGHTEENTH CENTURY

KATHRYN E. HOLLAND BRAUND

In the past several decades, scholars have focused increasing attention on the internal workings of tribal societies. This has brought more attention to the duties and action of Indian women within the villages. Early studies of Muscogulge or Creek women built upon theories of economic dependency, portraying Indian societies as being caught up in the ever-increasing demands of the international fur trade. Some presented the era prior to the trade as a sort of golden age for Indian women as they lived in peace and comfort. This essay questions such ideas as the author examines the relationships between growing Creek economic dependency on the European traders and their goods and the social and cultural changes that took place during the eighteenth century.

The author analyzes ways in which Creek women dealt with the demands of the deerskin trade and the changes that enterprise brought to Creek village life. Because women held a central place in cultural retention, their ideas and actions are evidence for understanding Indian responses to the trade. The narrative discusses the adaptive techniques Creek women tried as they attempted to retain their cultural practices. The discussion presents Creek women as discerning and effective at protecting their heritage and society.

Kathryn E. Holland Braun is an independent scholar.

Muscogulge or Creek women were members of the largest Indian nation in the southeast. The Creeks claimed most of the territory encompassed by the states of Georgia,

Source: Kathryn E. Holland Braund, "Guardians of Tradition and Handmaidens to Change: Women's Roles in Creek Economic and Social Life During the Eighteenth Century," pp. 239–58. Reprinted from *American Indian Quarterly,* volume 14, number 3 by permission of the University of Nebraska Press. Copyright © 1990 by the University of Nebraska Press.

Alabama, and northern Florida, but most of the population was concentrated in interior settlements along major rivers. By the late eighteenth century, Creek population stood at twenty thousand persons. The loosely structured confederacy had two geopolitical divisions comprised of many different ethnic groups. The Upper Towns, in modern north-central Alabama, were peopled by Alabamas, Tallapoosas, and Abeikas. Cowetas dominated the Lower Towns, which were scattered along the Chattahoochee River, though there was much ethnic diversity. Altogether, there were sixty-two major Creek towns.

Beginning in the late seventeenth century, the Creek towns established trade relations with the Europeans who had settled around them in Carolina and Florida. By the middle of the eighteenth century, most Creek commerce was conducted by traders from Augusta, Georgia. The barter of deerskins for European goods was the single most powerful force in Creek history during the eighteenth and early nineteenth centuries. Though they were dependent on foreign goods for their survival, the Creeks were able to retain their most cherished beliefs and social systems. Although most historians have overlooked women in their discussions of Creek life during this period, Creek women were central elements in a complicated cycle of cultural adaptation, change, and persistence that dominated Creek history in the late eighteenth century.

There are several difficulties associated with the study of Creek women. Most importantly, the written sources are entirely European and exclusively male in origin. White male traders, travelers, and employees of the British, French, Spanish, and American governments left general descriptions of these women and their place in Indian society. But, white European males were denied access to many feminine activities. And even when they married Creek women, European males were excluded from many aspects of their wives' social lives. Moreover, they often did not record information available to them that would be valuable to Creek scholars today. Sometimes, they drew the wrong conclusion from what they recorded. For example, only a few ever acquired a working knowledge of Creek kinship. Nevertheless, it is possible to understand women's role in tribal life from the accounts left by the white men who lived and traveled among the Creek towns during the eighteenth and nineteenth centuries.

Anglo-American visitors were impressed by the quiet dignity, hard work, and sensual beauty of Creek women. The Quaker naturalist William Bartram noted that "The Muscogulge women, though remarkably short of stature, are well formed; their visage round, features regular and beautiful; the brow high and arched; the eye large, black, and languishing, expressive of modesty, diffidence, and bashfulness; they are . . . loving and affectionate. James Adair, Chickasaw trader, historian, and husband of a Chickasaw woman, tells us that the native women of the southeast were "mild, amiable, [and of] soft disposition: exceedingly modest in their behaviour, and very seldom noisy, either in the single, or married state."

During the sultry southern summers, women wore only a lightweight skirt which reached to mid-calf. In winter, they added a short cloth or deerskin jacket decorated with beads and lace. Like the men, women adorned their bodies with elaborate tattoos. European traders had much admiration for their hair, which they wore in long, plaited braids "fastened on the crown, with a silver broach, forming a wreathed top-knot, decorated with an incredible quantity of silk ribbands."

Creek society was matrilineal, which meant that children traced their family descent through their mother's line. Since Creeks always married people outside their own clans, a man's clan affiliation was always different from that of his wife and children. Those who claimed a common (and known) ancestress constituted a matrilineage, which was the most important family unit in Creek society. Clans were comprised of matrilineages which had a common, though distant and usually mythical, ancestor. Most clans were represented by animal totems, such as Bear, Eagle, and Tiger. Clan elders oversaw the distribution of crop land, approved marriages, were responsible for training of young men who would be eligible for holding offices which the clan was entitled, and sought retribution for crimes committed against fellow clansmen.

During the eighteenth century, the nuclear family, having a husband, wife, and offspring, was the basic economic unit in Creek life. A young woman was allowed to express her personal preference regarding prospective mates, but clan elders had to approve her choice. It was not uncommon for clan elders to arrange a suitable marriage for a girl at an early age. But, even then, a young woman could not be forced to take a husband against her will. The young man, or his female relatives, presented a marriage proposal to the elder women of his intended bride's matrilineage. Once a woman and her clan accepted a proposal of marriage, the man had to prove that he was a good provider. According to one late eighteenth century account, the "bridegroom then gets together a blanket, and such other articles of clothing as he is able to do, and sends them by the women [of his clan] to the females of the family [clan] of the bride. If they accept of them the match is made and the man may then go to her house as soon as he chooses. And when he has built a house, made his crop and gathered it in, then made his hunt and brought home the meat and put all this in possession of his wife, the ceremony ends. They are married, or as they express it, the woman is bound." Though divorce was acceptable, it was uncommon after the birth of children. This was no doubt due to the fact that the father was still responsible for the maintenance of the young children and their mother until she married again. Polygamy was also allowed in Creek society, but few men took more than one wife since only the best hunters could manage the burden of supporting more than one wife and set of children. Men who did take more than one wife had to obtain their first wife's consent, and additional wives were usually sisters or other close relatives of the primary wife.

After marriage, the husband took up residence in his wife's town, or in the section of his own town where his wife's clan had their residences. A woman always lived in the same vicinity as the other women of her lineage. One observer noted "These houses stand in clusters of four, five, six, seven and eight together, irregularly distributed up and down the banks of rivers or small streams each cluster of houses contains a clan, or family of relations, who eat and live in common." The extended matrilineal household would have included a variety of age groups, including mature women with their husbands, their unmarried children, married daughters and sons-in-law, grandchildren, and elderly male relatives and other dependents. Creek women had power and authority in their own sphere, and they enjoyed companionship and a built-in support network of female relatives. A Creek woman's husband built her dwelling and storage buildings and prepared the corn fields belonging to her matrilineage, but the land and improvements remained the property of her family. And while a father and son had a natural affection, a boy's maternal uncles were his nearest male relatives. It was a boy's uncle, or an elder of high status within his own clan, who was responsible for a young man's education and a male gained status from the position he inherited through his mother's lineage.

Creek men and women conformed to very clear-cut gender roles. The main male occupations were hunting and warfare. Warfare was episodic, and undertaken for the protection of the town or to gain retribution for wrongs against fellow clan members by an enemy. Hunting was for the sole benefit of a man's immediate family. The hunting season lasted intermittently from late October until February or March. During the early spring, men were responsible for the preparation and planting of the large communal village corn fields. If a man failed to labor in the corn fields of his wife's family, he forfeited the right to punish his spouse should she commit adultery. Men also participated in the harvest of the corn crop. Fishing was primarily a male activity, and Creek men used a variety of techniques, including shooting fish with bow and arrows and using plant intoxicants, baskets, and nets to harvest fish from nearby rivers and streams. Ball play, an important amusement as well as training for warfare, occupied considerable time, as did other ceremonies. Men built houses, storage sheds, public buildings, and facilities as need dictated. They also produced canoes, tools, musical instruments, equipment for ball play, ceremonial implements, pipes, and other items.

Men gathered daily in the town square, from which women were excluded, to discuss matters of importance to the town and confederacy. The surviving record does not make it clear how much input women had in political matters, but they must have had considerable impact on public policy. For government was by consensus, and women influenced public opinion by such private means as tears, ridicule, and other methods to persuade husbands, brothers, uncles, and sons. This was especially true in matters of war and peace. Women would call for an end to war when they believed their dead relatives had been properly avenged. Conversely, women were often responsible for raising war fervor against enemies, and war captives were often tortured in a most heinous manner by vengeful Creek women. While there are brief references in the surviving historic record of Creek Beloved Women, their exact role in Creek political life remains a mystery.

Women's primary duties were child rearing and food cultivation, collection, preparation, and preservation. Corn was the most important crop, and it was grown in large communal fields. Men tilled and prepared the fields and helped with the planting while women and children tended the crop from planting until the last harvest in August. Each woman cultivated a smaller family vegetable patch near her dwelling. After harvest, women processed corn into a variety of products, including parched corn, meal, and hominy. With their children, they collected wild fruits, nuts, berries, and roots, and processed them into food items for storage and later use. From bark, leaves, roots and herbs they concocted medicine and remedies for a variety of ailments. Much of their labor was heavy and burdensome, including collecting and hauling firewood and water. During the winter, most women accompanied their husbands on extended hunting expeditions, and they smoked the meat and processed deerskins and other hides into usable materials for clothing and shelter. Women fashioned clothing, blankets, shoes, and a variety of personal ornaments and decoration from tanned deerskins and other hides and furs. In the days before European textiles were available, women produced textiles from buffalo and opossum hair, feathers, grasses and other plant and tree fibers. Women were responsible for the manufacture of pottery, baskets, and other household items.

Though their employment also followed a seasonal cycle, women spent much of their time separated from the men in their family. John R. Swanton related that one of his best Creek informants noted that "In ancient times men and women were almost like two distinct people." While women were primarily occupied in their homes and fields, men tended to spend most of their time in the town square and other public places. An American army officer reported that "Every family has two huts or cabins; one is the man's, and the other belongs to his wife, where she stays and does her work, seldom or ever coming into the man's house, unless to bring him victuals, or on other errands."

Concepts of purity were paramount in Creek ceremonialism and everyday life. Purity—the absence of pollution—was achieved by the separation of opposites, including men and women. Thus, at certain times, men and women were completely separated from each other. This was especially true during a woman's menstrual cycle: "They oblige their women in their lunar retreats, to build small huts, at as considerable a distance from their dwelling-houses, as they imagine may be out of the enemies reach; where, during the space of that period, they are obliged to stay at the risque of their lives. Should they be known to violate that ancient law, they must answer for every misfortune that befalls any of the people." Childbearing meant further separation. Anthropologist Charles Hudson has noted "As with women, the men were ritually isolated when they were most completely men." Accordingly, men abstained from contact with their wives both before and following warfare and during certain ceremonial events, ball play, and during ritual purification prior to hunting. While the lives of Creek men and women were strictly regulated by social customs and taboos, they were nonetheless intricately linked by affection and economic cooperation.

The deerskin trade was the most important influence on Creek history during the eighteenth century. By the early part of the eighteenth century, the Creeks had become commercial hunters of the white-tailed deer and other fur-bearing animals. They eagerly exchanged their hides for a variety of technologically advanced tools, textiles, and trinkets. By the last quarter of the eighteenth century, they had become dependent on goods of European manufacture. Subsistence agriculture remained an important economic activity, but hunting stressed the importance of male economic pursuits. Women's lives were especially changed by the influx of European goods. Previously, they had manufactured their own textiles, pottery and agricultural tools. Now they became dependent, not simply on foreign goods, but dependent on their hunter husbands for cotton and woolen textiles and metal agricultural tools.

While it is natural to assume Creek men—the hunters—were the primary participants in the deerskin trade, it is incorrect. Hunters were accompanied by their wives and children on long, extended expeditions. Creek villages became virtual ghost towns during the winter months as townspeople established hunting camps throughout the Creek domain. All except the elderly and "those unable to bear the fatigue of traveling," deserted the comforts of home for the hunting ranges. There was one practical advantage to leaving established town sites during winter. After decades of occupation, firewood was scarce near Creek towns. It was easier to find firewood in the hunting ranges.

Commercial hunting became a joint economic venture for Creek men and women. Men stalked and killed the deer and skinned the carcass. Creek women then processed or dressed many of the skins for use as clothing. This complex process involved carefully scraping the flesh from the skin, which was then stretched on frames and dried. Later, many of these skins were soaked and the hair removed by scraping it with a knife. These skins were then treated with deer brains, smoked, and later dyed. The result was a soft and supple leather. Those deerskins destined for market were not subjected to such elaborate preparations, but were simply cleaned and scraped. This was done either in their hunting camps or their towns. Minimally processed deerskins, variously called "skins in the hair," "raw," or "green skins," were less valuable than "half-dressed" hides, which had the hair removed. This is very evident from the price lists and trade regulations negotiated between the Creeks and the British trading establishment. Thus, the women who dressed deerskins contributed in a very real way to Creek productivity.

The exchange prices for European goods were high, and even the most successful hunters had to work hard to obtain basic clothing and tools for their families. In exchange for their deerskins and furs, the Creeks received guns, an astounding variety of cloth, blankets, hoes, axes, knives, rum, and occasional luxuries such as hair ribbons, mirrors, and other adornments. Needles, scissors, and thimbles were highly prized trade goods. Ready-made garments, such as men's shirts, were also available, but were more expensive than cloth. The introduction of textiles and metal sewing implements eased the tremendous burden of fashioning clothing and blankets from leather and plant fibers and revolutionized Creek costume. Creek women took up European needles and scissors with skill and imagination, transforming Creek fashion into an exotic mix of native and European materials and styles.

Manufactured goods were expensive and Creeks paid dearly for imported items. Fabric prices ranged from one pound of leather for a yard of the cheapest material to eight pounds of leather for two yards of heavy woolen cloth. Wool blankets could be obtained for eight pounds of dressed leather while prices for men's shirts varied from three to eight pounds of leather depending on the quality of the shirt. Tool prices were generally lower: hoes were traded for three to four pounds of leather, hatchets from one to three pounds, common knives for one pound of leather.

So all-consuming was the need to procure deerskins for the trade that Creek men and women often spent up to six months of the year in stalking deer on their hunting ranges. Usually, the Creeks broke into small hunting groups, sometimes limited to a single nuclear family. This meant a woman's duties intensified since she was deprived of the assistance of members of her extended matrilineal household. Besides dressing deerskins and smoking deer meat, there were the ever-present tasks of cooking, looking after children, and daily procurement of water and firewood. Since men hunted in the lands that traditionally belonged to their clans, hunting temporarily disrupted the pattern of matrilocal residence, accentuated the influence of a woman's husband on her family, and tended to loosen the authority of the matrilineal clan system.

Several other factors associated with the deerskin trade disrupted traditional Creek lifeways. The very nature of Creek society encouraged potential young warriors to be adventurous and bold; even reckless. During the eighteenth century, numerous wars and border skirmishes with neighboring Indian tribes and colonies combined with availability of rum and the pressures of commercial hunting to effectively shape a generation of "restless" young Creek men. Haughty and heedless of their cooler-headed elders, they were volatile and often absent from their towns, away from the watchful eyes of Creek headmen. In addition, the adoption of guns and metal tools resulted in the abandonment of native handicrafts. As a result, much high-quality interaction time between young men and their elders disappeared as old skills and manufacturing techniques fell into disrepute and were not passed to succeeding generations. Conversely, traditional female activities were accentuated by the trade, including the preparation of deerskins, the manufacture of clothing, and the continued reliance on native pottery as opposed to imported ceramic ware. The continued importance of subsistence agriculture also reinforced female roles and strengthened the bond between generations of Creek women. Creek females, left to the care of their clanswomen and elder male relatives, noticed less disruption in their lives. The stability of the female role helped offset the ill effects of the trade and white contact on young Creek men and bolstered traditional social institutions.

There were ways other than hunting to procure European trade goods. And those who could not hunt—women, widows, the elderly, the disabled, and orphans—often traded venison, honey, wild foods, fresh vegetables, and processed food items such as hickory nut oil, to the traders or settlers in Georgia or the Floridas. The Creek people knew the value of their produce well, and there were loud complaints from Creek traders about the "exorbitant" prices they were forced to pay for fresh vegetables. Moreover, traders were not allowed to use slaves and plows to raise their own food in the Creek towns, since this would have deprived widows and the elderly of their "support and maintenance."

A less savory method of obtaining goods was horse theft. Horses owned by traders and white settlers along the Creek-Anglo boundary were the primary targets, but thieves also took horses properly branded by their Indian owners. Stolen horses were taken to plantations and settlements in the Floridas, where there were many eager buyers. The practice reached epidemic proportions by the last quarter of the eighteenth century. Like many Indian men, Creek women found horse theft a rewarding activity. In 1765, a leading Upper Creek chief complained that many women were forced to steal and barter horses to obtain European goods. He suggested to the British that they distribute presents of trade goods to Creek women as well as Creek men in order to minimize the practice.

The great evil of the Creek-Anglo trade was rum. By the 1760s, unrestrained consumption of rum had resulted in a soaring crime rate, disrupted relationships between husbands and wives, and meant poverty for those who bartered their deerskins for rum instead of essential goods. Edmund Atkin, the first British Superintendent of Indian Affairs for the Southern Department, described the situation that existed when a hunter fell victim to unscrupulous peddlers of "that bewitching Liquor": "After parting with the fruit of three or four Months Toil, they find themselves at home, without the means of buying the necessary Clothing for themselves or their Families. Their Domestick and inward Quiet being broke, Reflection sours them, and disposes them for mischief."

Unmarried women or those women whose husbands traded their deerskins for rum occasionally used their feminine talents for economic gain. That respectable prude William Bartram was shocked by a "ludicrous bacchanalian" scene he observed in the early 1770s. A war party of about forty Lower Creek [Seminole] warriors had obtained twenty kegs, approximately one hundred gallons, of rum. Inebriated warriors begged the women who accompanied them to join their celebration. A sober Bartram observed:

"But the modest fair, veiling her face in a mantle, refuses, at the beginning of the frolick; but he presses and at last insists. She being furnished with an empty bottle, concealed in her mantle, at last consents, and taking a good long draught, blushes, drops her pretty face on her bosom, and artfully discharges the rum into her bottle, and by repeating this artifice soon fills it; this she privately conveys to her secret store, and then returns to the jovial game, and so on during the festival; and when the comic farce is over, the wench retails this precious cordial to them at her own price."

Some Creek women resorted to sex to earn trade goods and rum. Creek sexual standards were very different from those of the Europeans in their midst. Unmarried Creek women suffered no disgrace for casual sexual encounters. Creeks were forbidden to have sexual relations with members of their own clans and members of their father's clan. But beyond that, an unmarried woman's body was deemed her property to use as she wished. Surveyor and historian Bernard Romans noted "They will never scruple to sell the use of their bodies when they can do it in private; a person who wishes to be accommodated here can generally be supplied for payment, and the savages think a young woman nothing the worse for making use of her body, as they term it; but it is a great falsehood which has been related of these savages, that they exhort their young women to cohabitation with white men." By providing an avenue to obtain trade goods, casual sexual liaisons between Creek women and European men became more common during the late eighteenth century. Despite the harsh penalties for adultery, many married women also had sexual relations with traders in order to obtain goods. This resulted in considerable unrest, as the traders were then guilty of adultery and likely to suffer at the hands of the offended husband and his clan. The Creek penalty for such illicit conduct involved public beating, hair cropping, and mutilation of the ears and nose. The traders themselves propositioned married women so frequently that leading headmen credited many disturbances in Creek towns to their indiscretions. Traders were said to be "very guilty with women that have husbands, if a woman brings anything to the house of a white man, let him pay her and let her go again or if a single woman chuses to live with a white man, we have nothing to say against it, but many white men are very impudent and occasion uneasiness."

Some Creek women painted their bodies in a particular manner to be easily identified by those wishing to engage in sex-for-trade goods exchanges. These women were most certainly unmarried. It seems likely they had been responsible for some indiscretion, such as adultery or violation of a taboo, and had become outcasts from honorable Creek society and saw this as a way to support themselves. These women would have been regarded very differently from young single women who were given considerable sexual license before marriage.

One important result of Creek participation in the world economy was the large number of marriages, according to Indian custom, between Creek women and white traders. When white traders first appeared among the Creeks, the village headman often cemented his friendship with the trader by arranging a marriage to his niece or other female relative. Coosaponokeesa, better known as Mary Musgrove Matthews Bosomworth, is a prime example of this practice. Mary was the niece of Brims of Coweta, headman of the most powerful Lower Creek town. Mary was of mixed blood, and is reported to have been the daughter of Henry Woodward, who in 1685 established the first English trading store in the Creek country. Coosaponokeesa received instruction in the Christian faith, and spoke English as well as Muskogee. She was a woman of very high status, and her three marriages to white Georgians were as important to the Lower Creeks as they were to early Georgia. With her husbands, she operated a substantial trading establishment that supplied the Lower Creek towns. She served Oglethorpe's Georgia as an interpreter and peacemaker in addition to providing the colony with goods and supplies.

Virtually every major eighteenth-century trader had an Indian wife and raised a mixed-blood family. The Creeks did not oppose these unions and certainly preferred them to the adulterous conduct that many lesser traders were well known for. There were advantages for those traders who took a Creek wife. At the most basic level, marriage to a Creek woman linked the outsiders to specific clans that supported them, protected them and guaranteed a certain number of customers from the clan network. At a more intimate level, Creek women provided companionship, served as interpreters, and helped their husbands learn the language and customs of their people faster. Undoubtedly, they facilitated debt collection, dressed and tanned deerskins procured through the trade, kept their husbands informed of tribal temperament, and warned them when there was danger. When their husbands were away from their stores, Creek wives, and their male relatives, protected the trading establishment and looked after the traders' interests. It is no surprise that many leading eighteenth-century headmen became known by such appellations as Duvall's Landlord or McBean's Friend.

One eighteenth-century observer recorded that "the traders are fully sensible how greatly it is to their advantage to gain their [Creek women's] affections and friendship in matters of trade and commerce; and if their love and esteem for each other is sincere, and upon principles of reciprocity, there are but few instances of their neglecting or betraying the interests and views of their temporary husbands; they labor and watch constantly to promote their private interests, and detect and prevent any plots or evil designs which may threaten their persons, or operate against their trade or business." For their part, Creek women stood to gain status, power, and economic security from their relationships with white men.

Some Creek wives were so devoted that they assisted their husbands in a variety of unsavory business practices, including trading in rum and stolen horses. Such was the case with Francis Lewis, an employee of George Galphin, who engaged in a common scam. Lewis provided his Creek companion with rum. She then used the rum to "purchase back the goods from the Indians which he [Lewis] has sold or trusted them with, so that he is obliged to fit them out a second time on credit which greatly increases their debts to his employer but is a great profit to himself as the skins that he purchases with rum or goods bought with it he claims as his own."

But many Creek wives received high praise from both their husbands and visitors to Creek towns. Many of these relationships were stable and long-lived, as was the marriage of Nicholas White, a Frenchman, and his wife from Fusihatchee. White entered the Creek trade in the mid-1760s, and in 1796, Benjamin Hawkins noted that "He lives comfortable, has stables, and a kitchen and his wife appears, tho' old, healthy, industrious and pretty cleanly." Of their four children, three had married Creeks. William Bartram noted that the wife of James Germany was "of a very amiable and worthy character and disposition, industrious, prudent and affectionate." Germany was a forthright and honest trader of long standing in the Creek country. With the help of his wife and her relatives, Germany managed to acquire a "pretty fortune." If Mrs. White and Mrs. Germany were sterling examples of Creek womanhood, the beautiful and beguiling daughter of the Lower Creek chief the White Captain was not. She had married a "stout genteel well-bred" North Carolinian who had built up a large trade with the Lower Creeks in Florida. William Bartram claimed that "this little charmer" had "drained [her husband] of all his possessions, which she dishonestly distributes amongst her savage relations." Her husband was suicidal and White Captain was sympathetic, but unable to do anything more than condemn her "dishonesty and cruel conduct."

An important and obvious result of these marriages and informal liaisons between Creek women and white traders was the sizable number of mixed-blood offspring. Prominent Augusta trader Lachlan McGillivray married Sehoy Marchand, the mixed-blood daughter of a French officer who had been stationed at Fort Toulouse. From that union came the best-known Creek of the eighteenth century: Alexander McGillivray. By European reckoning, Alexander McGillivray was only one-fourth Creek. The Creek people made no such distinction. To his mother's people, he was a Tallassee of the Wind Clan. Alexander McGillivray had scores of contemporaries who could also claim English, Scotch, or Irish ancestry. David Cornell, also known as the Dog Warrior, was the son of trader Joseph Cornell and a Tuckabatchee woman. He served as an interpreter for the Creek treaty delegation to New York in 1790. Other well-known mixed bloods include Oche Finceco, alias Charles Cornells, the son of colonial trader James Cornells; Timpoochee Barnard, son of pre-Revolutionary trader Timothy Barnard and an Uchee woman; Richard Bailey, whose father, of the same name, was a prominent Augusta trader; and David Tate, the son of Alexander McGillivray's sister and David Taitt, the last British commissary to the Creeks.

Under Creek custom, it was the right of the mother's male relatives (her elder brothers or uncles) to educate her male children. Creek women were often adamant that their families be raised according to traditional methods. On the other hand, white fathers wanted control of their sons' education and expected them to inherit their property and at least some of their cultural orientation. But "Children always fall to the woman's lot," related one early historian, so that "it even seems impossible for the Christians to get their children." James Germany could not convince his Tallapoosa wife to allow his children to go to Savannah or Charleston for an education. Young Alexander McGillivray's mother gave her approval; his Charleston education was an important factor in his later success. In 1797, the Creek wife of trader Timothy Barnard sought to marry her daughter to Benjamin Hawkins. Hawkins, who served as the chief representative of the American government to the Creeks from 1796 until 1816, told Mrs. Barnard he would take her mixed-blood daughter for his wife on the condition that he be allowed to supervise the upbringing of any children. Mrs. Barnard refused to consider the possibility, and Hawkins was forced to seek conjugal pleasures elsewhere. In the end, Hawkins was forced to concede that Creek women would not change their attitudes. In early 1799, he noted "that a white man by marrying an Indian woman of the Creek nation so far from bettering his condition becomes a slave of her family." Therefore, he forbade employees in the Indian Department to marry Indian women.

In the period after the American Revolution, the children of these mixed marriages reached maturity. Though they were often less traditional than other Creeks, most embraced their cultural heritage, including participation in Creek ceremonial and political life and adherence to social customs. At the same time, many mixed-blood males used their cross-cultural backgrounds to their own advantage. William C. Sturtevant has noted that these men were "intermediaries or cultural brokers . . . [who could] facilitate and exploit the interaction between the two societies." They often had survival skills that the new times demanded, and which many of their contemporaries lacked: a knowledge of English or Spanish, literacy, and knowledge of white culture. Females of mixed blood were given fewer opportunities for formal schooling and cross-cultural experiences than their brothers. Traders usually showed less interest in their female issue, and young women were more secluded than their male counterparts. Even the most acculturated Creek women remained traditionalists at heart. Alexander McGillivray's sisters provide an excellent example of this. They too spoke English. Following the death of their brother, they maintained, at least for a time, trade ties with the Pensacola trading firm of Panton, Leslie and Company. While they supported formal English educations for their male children and were amenable to new economic endeavors, their actions regarding the disposition of Wind Clan property at their brother's death indicate firm adherence to Muscogulge kinship and inheritance patterns and social norms.

By the end of the eighteenth century, the deer population of the southeast had been drastically thinned by overhunting. In 1789, Benjamin Hawkins observed that "the Traveller in passing through a country as extensive and wild as this, and so much in a state of nature, expects to see game in abundance. I believe the whole of the Creek claims, the Seminoles included, cover 300 miles square; and it is difficult for a good hunter in passing through in any directions to obtain enough for his support." To compound the problem, the prices for deerskins had dropped on European markets. It seemed clear to many that new economic endeavors needed to be introduced or promoted to revive the devastated Creek trading economy. The 1790 Treaty of New York between the United States and the Creek towns had outlined a "Civilization Program" designed to restructure the Creek economy. In the treaty, the United States agreed to "furnish gratuitously . . . domestic animals and implements of husbandry" so that the Creeks could be "led to a greater degree of civilization, and to become herdsmen and cultivators, instead of remaining in a state of hunters." The treaty also provided for the appointment of agents to supervise and direct the economic transformation. In one of the treaty's secret articles, the federal government agreed to "educate and clothe such of the Creek youth as shall be agreed upon, not exceeding four in number at any one time." It was understood that the youths would be of mixed blood. Thus, an educated elite would help lead the Creeks to civilization and finally, incorporation into the larger white culture. Benjamin Hawkins, who was appointed as the federal representative to the Creeks in 1796, became responsible for the implementation of the program. Meanwhile, in the Creek towns, many retired deerskin traders, and their mixed-blood offspring, had already turned to commercial agriculture and stock raising. Hawkins, upon his arrival in the nation, noted their prosperous farms and he hoped to use these men, their wives and children, in his effort to "civilize" the more traditional Creeks.

The success of the civilization program depended on the widespread adoption of individual self-sufficient farms. In the words of one mixed-blood Creek, the government's plan sought "to improve their morals and reform their customs." No longer would healthy Creek men be allowed to avoid agricultural labor and engage in such "leisure" activities as hunting, fishing, and ball play while Creek women chopped wood and toted water. For their part, women would be taught better morals, proper manners, and the duties of a good farm wife. In reality, the American government's civilization policy was an assault against traditional Creek social and economic organization. It promoted private farms as opposed to communal fields controlled by matrilineal clans, encouraged the demise of traditional residence and inheritance patterns, and sought to introduce a new division of labor between the sexes. The American government was not motivated by humanitarian considerations in promoting the "civilization" program. Since settled farmers needed less land than commercial hunters, the government assumed once the

Creeks had embraced commercial agriculture, they would be willing to part with significant tracts of Creek hunting land.

The program did offer many new economic opportunities for both men and women. Weaving cloth, stock raising, and commercial agriculture all had their proponents and practitioners. Slaves and iron plows became more common, as did fences and cattle. Hawkins approached several of the mixed-blood Creek women with free cotton cards, spinning wheels, and looms, and they "adopted this part of the plan with spirit." The manufacture of cloth was no doubt appealing since it brought new technology to an old and highly regarded task. Even so, some jealous husbands worried that their wives might soon become independent and be able to clothe themselves. Only a few Creek men welcomed the prospect. Yet as Hawkins was forced to admit, his plan was not the success he had envisioned. The absence of adequate markets for Creek produce and adherence to traditional agricultural practices and gender roles hindered the transition to commercial agriculture. Some of those who adopted the new economic endeavors were able to cultivate a new cultural viewpoint and began to think and live like white people. But the majority of Creeks found it difficult to abandon their past. In 1798, they plainly told the agent "they did not understand the plan, they could not work, they did not want ploughs, it did not comport with the ways of the red people, who were determined to persevere in the ways of their ancestors." As time passed, the differences between those who were "civilized" and those who were not became more pronounced. These distinctions between traditionalists and those who embraced the new materialism became the major force in Creek history in the nineteenth century. Yet even the most acculturated Creeks retained much of their traditional culture.

To many it might seem that the eighteenth-century Creeks were colossal failures. Economically dependent on foreign supplies, they suffered from material poverty, alcoholism, conflict with whites, repeated land cessions, and misguided attempts by outsiders to transform their economy. The nineteenth century brought a civil war in 1813, and more land cessions. Eventually, the Creeks were overpowered militarily and forced from their homeland. Yet Creek culture endured the hardships. That the Creek people survived is a testament to the strength of their traditional values. Creek social organization, despite heavy pressures from without and within, remained stable. Matrilineal kinship patterns, matrilocal residence, town organization, the ceremonial year, and other traditional institutions continued as central features of Creek life well after Removal. Most Creeks who resettled in the Indian Territory were married, raised their children, and were buried according to old customs. This was due in great measure to the determination and influence of Creek wives and mothers who during the eighteenth century were indeed guardians of tradition and handmaidens to change.

Readings for Kathryn E. Holland Braund:

This same author offers a more detailed analysis of Creek Indian life and economics in her *Deerskins and Duffels: The Creek Indian Trade with Anglo-America, 1685–1815* (Lincoln: University of Nebraska Press, 1993). For an examination of the Creeks' neighbors see Theda Perdue, *Slavery and the Evolution of Cherokee Society, 1540–1886* (Knoxville: University of Tennessee Press, 1979). Nancy Shoemaker, ed., *Negotiators of Change: Historical Perspectives of Native American Women* (New York: Routledge, 1995) offers a more general look at related issues.

6

THE INDIANS' NEW WORLD: THE CATAWBA EXPERIENCE

JAMES H. MERRELL

Many discussions of the European discovery and early settlement of the Western Hemisphere refer to North and South America as the New World. Certainly for the tens of thousands of Europeans and Africans who crossed the Atlantic, labeling this region as "new" was accurate. For the resident Native American peoples, however, the flood of invaders into their homeland soon changed their entire existence so drastically that the author claims that they also faced a New World. In making this assertion, he examines both place and process as important factors. Tracing the experiences of coastal groups from Virginia south through the Carolinas, he demonstrates how the spreading of European activities and settlement all affected the local tribes adversely. Not only did the invasion hurt the Native American societies, but it brought fundamental changes in the ways those peoples dealt with each other and with their physical environment. Social forms, demographic patterns, economic practices, technology, and even locations all changed because of the European intrusion. Gradually these changes altered tribal existence. The author's discussion shows how and why these trends occurred, while placing the Indian experiences in the Southeast within the broader context of European colonial actions in North America. This essay considers the story not just from the tribal side but from within the local villages and small groups whenever possible. Its analysis presents Indians as acting in their own interests, not merely as responding to the invading Europeans.

James H. Merrell is a professor of history at Vassar College.

In August 1608 John Smith and his band of explorers captured an Indian named Amoroleck during a skirmish along the Rappahannock River. Asked why his men—a hunting party from towns upstream—had attacked the English, Amoroleck replied that they had heard the strangers "were a people come from under the world, to take their world from them." Smith's prisoner grasped a simple yet important truth that students

Source: James H. Merrell, "The Indians' New World: The Catawba Experience," *William & Mary Quarterly,* 3 ser. 41 (October 1984), pp. 537–65. Reprinted by permission.

of colonial America have overlooked: After 1492 Native Americans lived in a world every bit as new as that confronting transplanted Africans or Europeans.

The failure to explore the Indians' new world helps explain why, despite many excellent studies of the Native American past, colonial history often remains, "a history of those men and women—English, European, and African—who transformed America from a geographical expression into a new nation." One reason Indians generally are left out may be the apparent inability to fit them into the new-world theme, a theme that exerts a powerful hold on our historical imagination and runs throughout our efforts to interpret American development. From Frederick Jackson Turner to David Grayson Allen, from Melville J. Herskovits to Daniel C. Littlefield, scholars have analyzed encounters between peoples from the Old World and conditions in the New, studying the complex interplay between Europeans or African cultural patterns and the American environment. Indians crossed no ocean, peopled no faraway land. It might seem logical to exclude them.

The natives' segregation persists, in no small degree, because historians still tend to think only of the new world as the New World, a geographic entity bounded by the Atlantic Ocean on the one side and the Pacific on the other. Recent research suggests that process was as important as place. Many settlers in New England re-created familiar forms with such success that they did not really face an alien environment until long after their arrival. Africans, on the other hand, were struck by the shock of the new at the moment of their enslavement well before they stepped on board ship or set foot on American soil. If the Atlantic was not a barrier between one world and another, if what happened to people was more a matter of subtle cultural processes than mere physical displacements, perhaps we should set aside the maps and think instead of a "world" as the physical and cultural milieu within which people live and a "new world" as a dramatically different milieu demanding basic changes in ways of life. Considered in these terms, the experience of natives was more closely akin to that of immigrants and slaves, and the idea of an encounter between worlds can—indeed, must—include the aboriginal inhabitants of America.

For American Indians a new order arrived in three distinct yet overlapping stages. First, alien microbes killed vast numbers of natives, sometimes before the victims had seen a white or black face. Next came traders who exchanged European technology for Indian products and brought natives into the developing world market. In time traders gave way to settlers eager to develop the land according to their own lights. These three intrusions combined to transform native existence, disrupting established cultural habits and requiring creative responses to drastically altered conditions. Like their new neighbors, then, Indians were forced to blend old and new in ways that would permit them to survive in the present without forsaking their past. By the close of the colonial era Native Americans as well as whites and blacks had created new societies, each similar to, yet very different from, its parent culture.

The range of native societies produced by this mingling of ingredients probably exceeded the variety of social forms Europeans and Africans developed. Rather than survey the broad spectrum of Indian adaptations, this article considers in some depth the response of natives in one area, the southern piedmont (see map on page 68). Avoiding extinction and eschewing retreat, the Indians of the piedmont have been in continuous contact with the invaders from across the sea almost since the beginning of the colonial period, thus permitting a thorough analysis of cultural intercourse. Moreover, a regional approach embracing groups from South Carolina to Virginia can transcend narrow (and still poorly understood) ethnic or "tribal" boundaries without sacrificing the richness of detail a focused study provides.

Indeed, piedmont peoples had so much in common that a regional perspective is almost imperative. No formal political ties bound them at the onset of European contact, but a similar environment shaped their lives, and their adjustment to this environment fostered cultural uniformity. Perhaps even more important, these groups shared a single history once Europeans and Africans arrived on the scene. Drawn together by their cultural affinities and their common plight, after 1700 they migrated to the Catawba Nation, a cluster of villages along the border between the Carolinas that became the focus of native life in the region. Tracing the experience of these upland communities both before and after they joined the Catawbas can illustrate the consequences of contact and illuminate the process by which natives learned to survive in their own new world.

For centuries ancestors of the Catawbas had lived astride important aboriginal trade routes and straddled the boundary between two cultural traditions, a position that involved them in a far-flung network of contacts and affected everything from potting techniques to burial practices. Nonetheless, Africans and Europeans were utterly unlike any earlier foreign visitors to the piedmont. Their arrival meant more than merely another encounter with outsiders; it marked an important turning point in Indian history. Once these newcomers disembarked and began to feel their way across the continent, they forever altered the course and pace of native development.

Bacteria brought the most profound disturbances to upcountry villages. When Hernando de Soto led the first Europeans into the area in 1540, he found large towns already "grown up in grass" because "there had been a pest in the land" two years before, a malady probably brought inland by natives who had visited distant Spanish posts. The sources are silent about other "pests" over the next century, but soon after the English began colonizing Carolina in 1670 the disease pattern became all too clear. Major epidemics struck the region at least once every generation—in 1698, 1718, 1738, and 1759—and a variety of less virulent illnesses almost never left native settlements.

Indians were not the only inhabitants of colonial America living—and dying—in a new disease environment. The swamps and lowlands of the Chesapeake were a deathtrap for Europeans, and sickness obliged colonists to discard or rearrange many of the social forms brought from England. Among native peoples long isolated from the rest of the world and therefore lacking immunity to pathogens introduced by the intruders, the devastation was even more severe. John Lawson, who visited the Carolina upcountry in 1701, when perhaps ten thousand Indians were still there, estimated that "there is not the sixth Savage living within two hundred Miles of all our Settlements, as there were fifty Years ago." The recent smallpox epidemic "destroy'd whole Towns," he remarked, "without leaving one *Indian* alive in the Village." Resistance to disease developed with painful slowness; colonists reported that the outbreak of smallpox in 1759 wiped out 60 percent of the natives, and, according to one source, "the woods were offensive with the dead bodies of the Indians; and dogs, wolves, and vultures were . . . busy for months in banqueting on them."

Survivors of these horrors were thrust into a situation no less alien than what European immigrants and African slaves found. The collected wisdom of generations could vanish in a matter of days if sickness struck older members of a community who kept

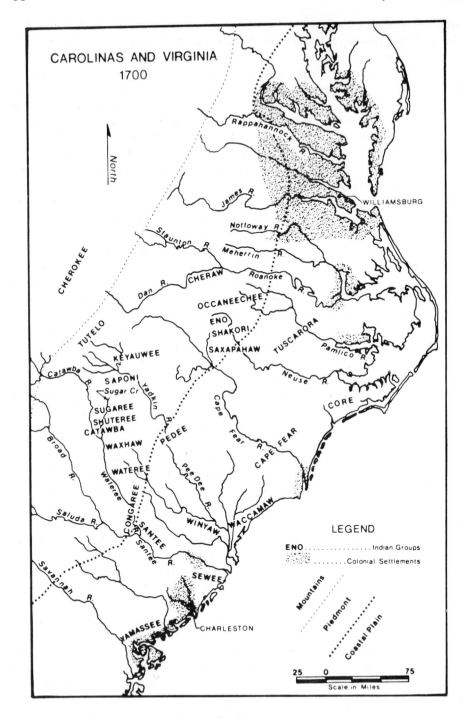

CAROLINAS AND VIRGINIA
1700

North

CHEROKEE

Rappahannock R.

James R.

WILLIAMSBURG

Nottoway R.

Staunton R.

Meherrin R.

CHERAW

Roanoke R.

Dan R.

OCCANEECHEE

ENO
SHAKORI

TUTELO

KEYAUWEE

SAXAPAHAW

TUSCARORA

Pamlico R.

Catawba R.

SAPONI

Sugar Cr

Yadkin R.

Neuse R.

SUGAREE
SHUTEREE
CATAWBA

WAXHAW

PEDEE

Cape Fear R.

CORE

CAPE FEAR

Broad R.

WATEREE

Wateree R.

Pee Dee R.

Saluda R.

CONGAREE

SANTEE

WINYAW

WACCAMAW

Savannah R.

Santee R.

SEWEE

YAMASSEE

CHARLESTON

LEGEND

ENO . . . . Indian Groups
. . . . Colonial Settlements

Mountains

Piedmont

Coastal Plain

25   0   75

Scale in Miles

sacred traditions and taught special skills. When many of the elders succumbed at once, the deep pools of collective memory grew shallow and some dried up altogether. In 1710 Indians near Charleston told a settler that "they have forgot most of their traditions since the Establishment of this Colony, they keep their Festivals and can tell but little of the reasons: their Old Men are dead." Impoverishment of a rich cultural heritage followed the spread of disease. Nearly a century later a South Carolinian exaggerated but captured the general trend when he noted that Catawbas "have forgotten their ancient rites, cere-monies, and manufactures."

The same diseases that robbed a piedmont town of some of its most precious re-sources also stripped it of the population necessary to maintain an independent exis-tence. In order to survive, groups were compelled to construct new societies from the splintered remnants of the old. The result was a kaleidoscopic array of migrations from ancient territories and mergers with nearby peoples. While such behavior was not un-heard of in aboriginal times, population levels fell so precipitously after contact that sur-vivors endured disruptions unlike anything previously known.

The dislocations of the Saponi Indians illustrate the common course of events. In 1670 they lived on the Staunton River in Virginia and were closely affiliated with a group called Nahyssans. A decade later Saponis moved toward the coast and built a town near the Occaneechees. When John Lawson came upon them along the Yadkin River in 1701, they were on the verge of banding together in a single village with Tutelos and Keyauwees. Soon thereafter Saponis applied to Virginia officials for permission to move to the Meherrin River, where Occaneechees, Tutelos, and others joined them. In 1714, at the urging of Virginia's Lt. Gov. Alexander Spotswood, these groups settled at Fort Chris-tanna farther up the Meherrin. Their friendship with Virginia soured during the 1720s, and most of the "Christanna Indians" moved to the Catawba Nation. For some reason this arrangement did not satisfy them, and many returned to Virginia in 1732, remaining there for a decade before choosing to migrate north and accept the protection of the Iroquois.

Saponis were unusual only in their decision to leave the Catawbas. Enos, Occa-neechees, Waterees, Keyauwees, Cheraws, and others have their own stories to tell, sim-ilar in outline if not in detail. With the exception of the towns near the confluence of Sugar Creek and the Catawba River that composed the heart of the Catawba Nation, piedmont communities decimated by disease lived through a common round of catas-trophes, shifting from place to place and group to group in search of a safe haven. Most eventually ended up in the Nation, and during the opening decades of the eighteenth cen-tury the villages scattered across the southern upcountry were abandoned as people drifted into the Catawba orbit.

No mere catalog of migrations and mergers can begin to convey how profoundly unsettling this experience was for those swept up in it. While upcountry Indians did not sail away to some distant land, they, too, were among the uprooted, leaving their ances-tral homes to try to make a new life elsewhere. The peripatetic existence of Saponis and others proved deeply disruptive. A village and its surrounding territory were important elements of personal and collective identity, physical links in a chain binding a group to its past and making a locality sacred. Colonists, convinced that Indians were by Nature "a shifting, wandring People," were oblivious to this, but Lawson offered a glimpse of the reasons for native attachment to a particular locale. "In our way," he wrote on leav-ing an Eno-Shakori town in 1701, "there stood a great Stone about the Size of a large

Oven, and hollow; this the *Indians* took great Notice of, putting some Tobacco into the Concavity, and spitting after it. I ask'd them the Reason of their so doing, but they made me no Answer." Natives throughout the interior honored similar places—graves of ancestors, monuments of stones commemorating important events—that could not be left behind without some cost.

The toll could be physical as well as spiritual, for even the most uneventful of moves interrupted the established cycle of subsistence. Belongings had to be packed and unpacked, dwellings constructed, palisades raised. Once migrants had completed the business of settling in, the still more arduous task of exploiting new terrain awaited them. Living in one place year after year endowed a people with intimate knowledge of the area. The richest soils, the best hunting grounds, the choicest sites for gathering nuts or berries—none could be learned without years of experience, tested by time and passed down from one generation to the next. Small wonder that Carolina Indians worried about being "driven to some unknown Country, to live, hunt, and get our Bread in."

Some displaced groups tried to leave "unknown Country" behind and make their way back home. In 1716 Enos asked Virginia's permission to settle at "Enoe Town" on the North Carolina frontier, their location in Lawson's day. Seventeen years later William Byrd II came upon an abandoned Cheraw village on a tributary of the upper Roanoke River and remarked how "it must have been a great misfortune to them to be obliged to abandon so beautiful a dwelling." The Indians apparently agreed: In 1717 the Virginia Council received "Divers applications" from the Cheraws (now living along the Pee Dee River) "for Liberty to Seat themselves on the head of Roanoke River." Few natives managed to return permanently to their homelands. But their efforts to retrace their steps hint at a profound sense of loss and testify to the powerful hold of ancient sites.

Compounding the trauma of leaving familiar territories was the necessity of abandoning customary relationships. Casting their lot with others traditionally considered foreign compelled Indians to rearrange basic ways of ordering their existence. Despite frequent contacts among peoples, native life had always centered in kin and town. The consequences of this deep-seated localism were evident even to a newcomer like John Lawson, who in 1701 found striking differences in language, dress, and physical appearance among Carolina Indians living only a few miles apart. Rules governing behavior also drew sharp distinctions between outsiders and one's own "Country-Folks." Indians were "very kind, and charitable to one another," Lawson reported, "but more especially to those of their own Nation." A visitor desiring a liaison with a local woman was required to approach her relatives and the village headman. On the other hand, "if it be an *Indian* of their own Town or Neighbourhood, that wants a Mistress, he comes to none but the Girl." Lawson seemed unperturbed by this barrier until he discovered that a "Thief [is] held in Disgrace, that steals from any of his Country-Folks," "but to steal from the *English* [or any other foreigners] they reckon no Harm."

Communities unable to continue on their own had to revise these rules and reweave the social fabric into new designs. What language would be spoken? How would fields be laid out, hunting territories divided, houses built? How would decisions be reached, offenders punished, ceremonies performed? When Lawson remarked that "now adays" the Indians must seek mates "amongst Strangers," he unwittingly characterized life in native Carolina. Those who managed to withstand the ravages of disease had to redefine the meaning of the term *stranger* and transform outsiders into insiders.

The need to harmonize discordant peoples, an unpleasant fact of life for all Native Americans, was no less common among black and white inhabitants of America during these years. Africans from a host of different groups were thrown into slavery together and forced to seek some common cultural ground, to blend or set aside clashing habits and beliefs. Europeans who came to America also met unexpected and unwelcome ethnic, religious, and linguistic diversity. The roots of the problem were quite different; the problem itself was much the same. In each case people from different backgrounds had to forge a common culture and a common future.

Indians in the southern uplands customarily combined with others like themselves in an attempt to solve the dilemma. Following the "principle of least effort," shattered communities cushioned the blows inflicted by disease and depopulation by joining a kindred society known through generations of trade and alliances. Thus, Saponis coalesced with Occaneechees and Tutelos—nearby groups "speaking much the same language"—and Catawbas became a sanctuary for culturally related refugees from throughout the region. Even after moving in with friends and neighbors, however, natives tended to cling to ethnic boundaries in order to ease the transition. In 1715 Spotswood noticed that the Saponis and others gathered at Fort Christanna were "confederated together, tho' still preserving their different Rules." Indians entering the Catawba Nation were equally conservative. As late as 1743 a visitor could hear more than twenty dialects spoken by peoples living there, and some bands continued to reside in separate towns under their own leaders.

Time inevitably sapped the strength of ethnic feeling, allowing a more unified Nation to emerge from the collection of Indian communities that occupied the valleys of the Catawba River and its tributaries. By the mid-eighteenth century, the authority of village headmen was waning and leaders from the host population had begun to take responsibility for the actions of constituent groups. The babel of different tongues fell silent as "Kàtahba," the Nation's "standard, or court-dialect," slowly drowned out all others. Eventually entire peoples followed their languages and their leaders into oblivion, leaving only personal names like Santee Jemmy, Cheraw George, Congaree Jamie, Saponey Johnny, and Eno Jemmy as reminders of the Nation's diverse heritage.

No European observer recorded the means by which nations became mere names and a congeries of groups forged itself into one people. No doubt the colonists' habit of ignoring ethnic distinctions and lumping confederated entities together under the Catawba rubric encouraged amalgamation. But Anglo-American efforts to create a society by proclamation were invariably unsuccessful; consolidation had to come from within. In the absence of evidence, it seems reasonable to conclude that years of contacts paved the way for a closer relationship. Once a group moved to the Nation, intermarriages blurred ancient kinship networks, joint war parties or hunting expeditions brought young men together, and elders met in a council that gave everyone some say by including "all the Indian Chiefs or Head Men of that [Catawba] Nation and the several Tribes amongst them together." The concentration of settlements within a day's walk of one another facilitated contact and communication. From their close proximity, common experience, and shared concerns, people developed ceremonies and myths that compensated for those lost to disease and gave the Nation a stronger collective consciousness. Associations evolved that balanced traditional narrow ethnic allegiance with a new, broader, "national" identity, a balance that tilted steadily toward the latter. Ethnic differences died hard, but the peoples of the Catawba Nation learned to speak with a single voice.

Muskets and kettles came to the piedmont more slowly than smallpox and measles. Spanish explorers distributed a few gifts to local headmen, but inhabitants of the interior did not enjoy their first real taste of the fruits of European technology until Englishmen began venturing inland after 1650. Indians these traders met in upcountry towns were glad to barter for the more efficient tools, more lethal weapons, and more durable clothing that colonists offered. Spurred on by eager natives, men from Virginia and Carolina quickly flooded the region with the material trappings of European culture. In 1701 John Lawson considered the Wateree Chickanees "very poor in *English* Effects" because a few of them lacked muskets.

Slower to arrive, trade goods were also less obvious agents of change. The Indians' ability to absorb foreign artifacts into established modes of existence hid the revolutionary consequences of trade for some time. Natives leaped the technological gulf with ease in part because they were discriminating shoppers. If hoes were too small, beads too large, or cloth the wrong color, Indian traders refused them. Items they did select fit smoothly into existing ways. Waxhaws tied horse bells around their ankles at ceremonial dances, and some of the traditional stone pipes passed among the spectators at these dances had been shaped by metal files. Those who could not afford a European weapon fashioned arrows from broken glass. Those who could went to great lengths to "set [a new musket] streight, sometimes shooting away above 100 Loads of Ammunition, before they bring the Gun to shoot according to their Mind."

Not every piece of merchandise hauled into the upcountry on a trader's packhorse could be "set streight" so easily. Liquor, for example, proved both impossible to resist and extraordinarily destructive. Indians "have no Power to refrain this Enemy," Lawson observed, "though sensible how many of them (are by it) hurry'd into the other World before their Time." And yet even here, natives aware of the risks sought to control alcohol by incorporating it into their ceremonial life as a device for achieving a different level of consciousness. Consumption was usually restricted to men, who "go as solemnly about it, as if it were part of their Religion," preferring to drink only at night and only in quantities sufficient to stupefy them. When ritual could not confine liquor to safe channels, Indians went still further and excused the excesses of overindulgence by refusing to hold an intoxicated person responsible for his actions. "They never call any Man to account for what he did, when he was drunk," wrote Lawson, "but say, it was the Drink that caused his Misbehaviour, therefore he ought to be forgiven."

Working to absorb even the most dangerous commodities acquired from their new neighbors, aboriginal inhabitants of the uplands, like African slaves in the lowlands, made themselves at home in a different technological environment. Indians became convinced that "Guns, and Ammunition, besides a great many other Necessaries, . . . are helpful to Man" and eagerly searched for the key that would unlock the secret of their production. At first many were confident that the *"Quera,* or good Spirit," would teach them to make these commodities "when that good Spirit sees fit." Later they decided to help their deity along by approaching the colonists. In 1757 Catawbas asked Gov. Arthur Dobbs of North Carolina "to send us Smiths and other Tradesmen to teach our Children."

It was not the new products themselves but the Indians' failure to learn the mysteries of manufacture from either Dobbs or the *Quera* that marked the real revolution wrought by trade. During the seventeenth and eighteenth centuries everyone in eastern North America—masters and slaves, farmers near the coast and Indians near the mountains—became producers of raw materials for foreign markets and found themselves caught up in an international economic network. Piedmont natives were part of this larger process, but their adjustment was more difficult because the contrast with previous ways was so pronounced. Before European contact, the localism characteristic of life in the uplands had been sustained by a remarkable degree of self-sufficiency. Trade among peoples, while common, was conducted primarily in commodities such as copper, mica, and shells, items that, exchanged with the appropriate ceremony, initiated or confirmed friendships among groups. Few, if any, villages relied on outsiders for goods essential to daily life.

Intercultural exchange eroded this traditional independence and entangled natives in a web of commercial relations few of them understood and none controlled. In 1670 the explorer John Lederer observed a striking disparity in the trading habits of Indians living near Virginia and those deep in the interior. The "remoter Indians," still operating within a precontact framework, were content with ornamental items such as mirrors, beads, "and all manner of gaudy toys and knacks for children." "Neighbour-Indians," on the other hand, habitually traded with colonists for cloth, metal tools, and weapons. Before long, towns near and far were demanding the entire range of European wares and were growing accustomed—even addicted—to them. "They say we English are fools for . . . not always going with a gun," one Virginia colonist familiar with piedmont Indians wrote in the early 1690s, "for they think themselves undrest and not fit to walk abroad, unless they have their gun on their shoulder, and their shot-bag by their side." Such an enthusiastic conversion to the new technology eroded ancient craft skills and hastened complete dependence on substitutes only colonists could supply.

By forcing Indians to look beyond their own territories for certain indispensable products, Anglo-American traders inserted new variables into the aboriginal equation of exchange. Colonists sought two commodities from Indians—human beings and deerskins—and both undermined established relationships among native groups. While the demand for slaves encouraged piedmont peoples to expand their traditional warfare, the demand for peltry may have fostered conflicts over hunting territories. Those who did not fight each other for slaves or deerskins fought each other for the European products these could bring. As firearms, cloth, and other items became increasingly important to native existence, competition replaced comity at the foundation of trade encounters as villages scrambled for the cargoes of merchandise. Some were in a better position to profit than others. In the early 1670s Occaneechees living on an island in the Roanoke River enjoyed power out of all proportion to their numbers because they controlled an important ford on the trading path from Virginia to the interior, and they resorted to threats, and even to force, to retain their advantage. In Lawson's day Tuscaroras did the same, "hating that any of these Westward *Indians* should have any Commerce with the *English,* which would prove a Hinderance to their Gains."

Competition among native groups was only the beginning of the transformation brought about by new forms of exchange. Inhabitants of the piedmont might bypass the native middleman, but they could not break free from a perilous dependence on colonial sources of supply. The danger may not have been immediately apparent to Indians caught up in the excitement of acquiring new and wonderful things. For years they managed to dictate the terms of trade, compelling visitors from Carolina and Virginia to abide by aboriginal codes of conduct and playing one colony's traders against the other to ensure an abundance of goods at favorable rates. But the natives' influence over the protocol of exchange combined with their skill at incorporating alien products to mask a loss of control over their own destiny. The mask came off when, in 1715, the traders—and the trade goods—suddenly disappeared during the Yamassee War.

The conflict's origins lay in a growing colonial awareness of the Indians' need for regular supplies of European merchandise. In 1701 Lawson pronounced the Santees "very tractable" because of their close connections with South Carolina. Eight years later he was convinced that the colonial officials in Charleston "are absolute Masters over the *Indians* . . . within the Circle of their Trade." Carolina traders who shared this conviction quite naturally felt less and less constrained to obey native rules governing proper behavior. Abuses against Indians mounted until some men were literally getting away with murder. When repeated appeals to colonial officials failed, natives throughout Carolina began to consider war. Persuaded by Yamassee ambassadors that the conspiracy was widespread, and convinced by years of ruthless commercial competition between Virginia and Carolina that an attack on one colony would not affect relations with the other, in the spring of 1715 Catawbas and their neighbors joined the invasion of South Carolina.

The decision to fight was disastrous. Colonists everywhere shut off the flow of goods to the interior, and after some initial successes Carolina's native enemies soon plumbed the depths of their dependence. In a matter of months refugees holed up in Charleston noticed that "the Indians want ammunition and are not able to mend their Arms." The peace negotiations that ensued revealed a desperate thirst for fresh supplies of European wares. Ambassadors from piedmont towns invariably spoke in a single breath of restoring "a Peace and a free Trade," and one delegation even admitted that its people "cannot live without the assistance of the English."

Natives unable to live without the English henceforth tried to live with them. No upcountry group mounted a direct challenge to Anglo-America after 1715. Trade quickly resumed, and the piedmont Indians, now concentrated almost exclusively in the Catawba valley, briefly enjoyed a regular supply of necessary products sold by men willing once again to deal according to the old rules. By mid-century, however, deer were scarce and fresh sources of slaves almost impossible to find. Anglo-American traders took their business elsewhere, leaving inhabitants of the Nation with another material crisis of different but equally dangerous dimensions.

Indians casting about for an alternative means of procuring the commodities they craved looked to imperial officials. During the 1740s and 1750s native dependence shifted from colonial traders to colonial authorities as Catawba leaders repeatedly visited provincial capitals to request goods. These delegations came not to beg but to bargain. Catawbas were still of enormous value to the English as allies and frontier guards, especially at a time when Anglo-America felt threatened by the French and their Indian auxiliaries. The Nation's position within reach of Virginia and both Carolinas enhanced its value by enabling headmen to approach all three colonies and offer their people's services to the highest bidder.

The strategy yielded Indians an arsenal of ammunition and a variety of other merchandise that helped offset the declining trade. Crown officials were especially generous when the Nation managed to play one colony off against another. In 1746 a rumor that the Catawbas were about to move to Virginia was enough to garner them a large shipment of powder and lead from officials in Charleston concerned about losing this "valuable people." A decade later, while the two Carolinas fought for the honor of constructing a fort in the Nation, the Indians encouraged (and received) gifts symbolizing good will from both colonies without reaching an agreement with either. Surveying the tangled thicket of promises and presents, the Crown's superintendent of Indian affairs, Edmond Atkin, ruefully admitted that "the People of both Provinces . . . have I believe [*sic*] tampered too much on both sides with those Indians, who seem to understand well how to make their Advantage of it."

By the end of the colonial period delicate negotiations across cultural boundaries were as familiar to Catawbas as the strouds they wore and the muskets they carried. But no matter how shrewdly the headmen loosened provincial purse strings to extract vital merchandise, they could not escape the simple fact that they no longer held the purse containing everything needed for their daily existence. In the space of a century the Indians had become thoroughly embedded in an alien economy, denizens of a new material world. The ancient self-sufficiency was only a dim memory in the minds of the Nation's elders.

The Catawba peoples were veterans of countless campaigns against disease and masters of the arts of trade long before the third major element of their new world, white planters, became an integral part of their life. Settlement of the Carolina uplands did not begin until the 1730s, but once underway it spread with frightening speed. In November 1752 concerned Catawbas reminded South Carolina governor James Glen how they had "complained already . . . that the white People were settled too near us." Two years later five hundred families lived within thirty miles of the Nation and surveyors were running their lines into the middle of native towns. "[T]hose Indians are now in a fair way to be surrounded by White People," one observer concluded.

Settlers' attitudes were as alarming as their numbers. Unlike traders who profited from them or colonial officials who deployed them as allies, ordinary colonists had little use for Indians. Natives made poor servants and worse slaves; they obstructed settlement; they attracted enemy warriors to the area. Even men who respected Indians and earned a living by trading with them admitted that they made unpleasant neighbors. "We may observe of them as of the fire," wrote the South Carolina trader James Adair after considering the Catawbas' situation on the eve of the American Revolution, " 'it is safe and useful, cherished at proper distance; but if too near us, it becomes dangerous, and will scorch if not consume us.' "

A common fondness for alcohol increased the likelihood of intercultural hostilities. Catawba leaders acknowledged that the Indians "get very Drunk with [liquor] this is the Very Cause that they oftentimes Commit those Crimes that is offencive to You and us." Colonists were equally prone to bouts of drunkenness. In the 1760s the itinerant Anglican minister, Charles Woodmason, was shocked to find the citizens of one South Carolina upcountry community "continually drunk." More appalling still, after attending church services "one half of them got drunk before they went home." Indians sometimes suffered at the hands of intoxicated farmers. In 1760 a Catawba woman was murdered when she happened by a tavern shortly after four of its patrons "swore they would kill the first Indian they should meet with."

Even when sober, natives and newcomers found many reasons to quarrel. Catawbas were outraged if colonists built farms on the Indians' doorstep or tramped across ancient burial grounds. Planters, ignorant of (or indifferent to) native rules of hospitality, considered Indians who requested food nothing more than beggars and angrily drove them away. Other disputes arose when the Nation's young men went looking for trouble. As hunting, warfare, and other traditional avenues for achieving status narrowed, Catawba youths transferred older patterns of behavior into a new arena by raiding nearby farms and hunting cattle or horses.

Contrasting images of the piedmont landscape quite unintentionally generated still more friction. Colonists determined to tame what they considered a wilderness were in fact erasing a native signature on the land and scrawling their own. Bridges, buildings, fences, roads, crops, and other "improvements" made the area comfortable and familiar to colonists but uncomfortable and unfamiliar to Indians. "The Country side wear[s] a New face," proclaimed Woodmason proudly; to the original inhabitants, it was a grim face indeed. "His Land was spoiled," one Catawba headman told British officials in 1763. "They have spoiled him 100 Miles every way." Under these circumstances, even a settler with no wish to fight Indians met opposition to his fences, his outbuildings, his very presence. Similarly, a Catawba on a routine foray into traditional hunting territories had his weapon destroyed, his goods confiscated, his life threatened by men with different notions of the proper use of the land.

To make matters worse, the importance both cultures attached to personal independence hampered efforts by authorities on either side to resolve conflicts. Piedmont settlers along the border between the Carolinas were "people of desperate fortune," a frightened North Carolina official reported after visiting the area. "[N]o officer of Justice from either Province dare meddle with them." Woodmason, who spent even more time in the region, came to the same conclusion. "We are without any Law, or Order," he complained; the inhabitants' "Impudence is so very high, as to be past bearing." Catawba leaders could have sympathized. Headmen informed colonists that the Nation's people "are oftentimes Cautioned from . . . ill Doings altho' to no purpose for we Cannot be present at all times to Look after them." "What they have done I could not prevent," one chief explained.

Unruly, angry, intoxicated—Catawbas and Carolinians were constantly at odds during the middle decades of the eighteenth century. Planters who considered Indians "proud and deveilish" were themselves accused by natives of being "very bad and quarrelsome." Warriors made a habit of "going into the Settlements, robbing and stealing where ever they get an Oppertunity." Complaints generally brought no satisfaction— "they laugh and makes their Game of it, and says it is what they will"—leading some settlers to "whip [Indians] about the head, beat and abuse them." "The white People . . . and the Cuttahbaws, are Continually at varience," a visitor to the Nation fretted in June 1759, "and Dayly New Animositys Doth a rise Between them which In my Humble oppion will be of Bad Consequence In a Short time, Both Partys Being obstinate."

The litany of intercultural crimes committed by each side disguised a fundamental shift in the balance of physical and cultural power. In the early years of colonization of the interior the least disturbance by Indians sent scattered planters into a panic. Soon, however, Catawbas were few, colonists many, and it was the natives who now lived in fear. "[T]he white men [who] Lives Near the Neation is Contenuely asembleing and goes In the [Indian] towns In Bodys . . . ," worried another observer during the tense summer of 1759. "[T]he[y] tretton the[y] will Kill all the Cattabues."

The Indians would have to find some way to get along with these unpleasant neighbors if the Nation was to survive. As Catawba population fell below five hundred after the smallpox epidemic of 1759 and the number of colonists continued to climb, natives gradually came to recognize the futility of violent resistance. During the last decades of the eighteenth century they drew on years of experience in dealing with Europeans at a distance and sought to overturn the common conviction that Indian neighbors were frightening and useless.

This process was not the result of some clever plan; Catawbas had no strategy for survival. A headman could warn them that "the White people were now seated all round them and by that means had them entirely in their power." He could not command them to submit peacefully to the invasion of their homeland. The Nation's continued existence required countless individual decisions, made in a host of diverse circumstances, to complain rather than retaliate, to accept a subordinate place in a land that once was theirs. Few of the choices made survive in the record. But it is clear that, like the response to disease and to technology, the adaptation to white settlement was both painful and prolonged.

Catawbas took one of the first steps along the road to accommodation in the early 1760s, when they used their influence with colonial officials to acquire a reservation encompassing the heart of their ancient territories. This grant gave the Indians a land base, grounded in Anglo-American law, that prevented farmers from shouldering them aside. Equally important, Catawbas now had a commodity to exchange with nearby settlers. These men wanted land, the natives had plenty, and shortly before the Revolution the Nation was renting tracts to planters for cash, livestock, and manufactured goods.

Important as it was, land was not the only item Catawbas began trading to their neighbors. Some Indians put their skills as hunters and woodsmen to a different use, picking up stray horses and escaped slaves for a reward. Others bartered their pottery, baskets, and table mats. Still others traveled through the upcountry, demonstrating their prowess with the bow and arrow before appreciative audiences. The exchange of these goods and services for European merchandise marked an important adjustment to the settlers' arrival. In the past, natives had acquired essential items by trading peltry and slaves or requesting gifts from representatives of the Crown. But piedmont planters frowned on hunting and warfare, while provincial authorities—finding Catawbas less useful as the Nation's population declined and the French threat disappeared—discouraged formal visits and handed out fewer presents. Hence the Indians had to develop new avenues of exchange that would enable them to obtain goods in ways less objectionable to their neighbors. Pots, baskets, and acres proved harmless substitutes for earlier methods of earning an income.

Quite apart from its economic benefits, trade had a profound impact on the character of Catawba-settler relations. Through countless repetitions of the same simple procedure at homesteads scattered across the Carolinas, a new form of intercourse arose, based not on suspicion and an expectation of conflict but on trust and a measure of friendship. When a farmer looked out his window and saw Indians approaching, his reaction more commonly became to pick up money or a jug of whiskey rather than a musket or an axe.

The natives now appeared, the settler knew, not to plunder or kill, but to peddle their wares or collect their rents.

The development of new trade forms could not bury all of the differences between Catawba and colonist overnight. But in the latter half of the eighteenth century the beleaguered Indians learned to rely on peaceful means of resolving intercultural conflicts that did arise. Drawing a sharp distinction between "the good men that have rented Lands from us" and "the bad People [who] has frequently imposed upon us," Catawbas called on the former to protect the Nation from the latter. In 1771 they met with the prominent Camden storekeeper, Joseph Kershaw, to request that he "represent us when [we are] a grieved." After the Revolution the position became more formal. Catawbas informed the South Carolina government that, being "destitute of a man to take care of, and assist us in our affairs," they had chosen one Robert Patten "to take charge of our affairs, and to act and do for us."

Neither Patten nor any other intermediary could have protected the Nation had it not joined the patriot side during the Revolutionary War. Though one scholar has termed the Indians' contribution to the cause "rather negligible," they fought in battles throughout the southeast and supplied rebel forces with food from time to time. These actions made the Catawbas heroes and laid a foundation for their popular renown as staunch patriots. In 1781 their old friend Kershaw told Catawba leaders how he welcomed the end of "this Long and Bloody War, in which You have taken so Noble a part and have fought and Bled with your white Brothers of America." Grateful Carolinians would not soon forget the Nation's service. Shortly after the Civil War an elderly settler whose father had served with the Indians in the Revolution echoed Kershaw's sentiments, recalling that "his father never communicated much to him [about the Catawbas], except that all the tribe . . . served the entire war . . . and fought most heroically."

Catawbas rose even higher in their neighbors' esteem when they began calling their chiefs "General" instead of "King" and stressed that these men were elected by the people. The change reflected little if any real shift in the Nation's political forms, but it delighted the victorious Revolutionaries. In 1794 the Charleston *City Gazette* reported that during the war "King" Frow had abdicated and the Indians chose "General" New River in his stead. "What a pity," the paper concluded, "certain people on a certain island have not as good optics as the Catawbas!" In the same year, the citizens of Camden celebrated the anniversary of the fall of the Bastille by raising their glasses to toast "King Prow [*sic*]—may all kings who will not follow his example follow that of Louis XVI." Like tales of Indian patriots, the story proved durable. Nearly a century after the Revolution one nearby planter wrote that "the Catawbas, emulating the examples of their white brethren, threw off regal government."

The Indians' new image as republicans and patriots, added to their trade with whites and their willingness to resolve conflicts peacefully, brought settlers to view Catawbas in a different light. By 1800 the natives were no longer violent and dangerous strangers but what one visitor termed an "inoffensive" people and one group of planters called "harmless and friendly" neighbors. They had become traders of pottery but not deerskins, experts with a bow and arrow but not hunters, ferocious warriors against runaway slaves or tories but not against settlers. In these ways Catawbas could be distinctively Indian yet reassuringly harmless at the same time.

The Nation's separate identity rested on such obvious aboriginal traits. But its survival ultimately depended on a more general conformity with the surrounding society. During the nineteenth century both settlers and Indians owned or rented land. Both spoke proudly of their Revolutionary heritage and their republican forms of government. Both drank to excess. Even the fact that Catawbas were not Christians failed to differentiate them sharply from nearby white settlements, where, one visitor noted in 1822, "little attention is paid to the sabbath, or religeon."

In retrospect it is clear that these similarities were as superficial as they were essential. For all the changes generated by contacts with vital Euro-American and Afro-American cultures, the Nation was never torn loose from its cultural moorings. Well after the Revolution Indians maintained a distinctive way of life rich in tradition and meaningful to those it embraced. Ceremonies conducted by headmen and folk tales told by relatives continued to transmit traditional values and skills from one generation to the next. Catawba children grew up speaking the native language, making bows and arrows or pottery, and otherwise following patterns of belief and behavior derived from the past. The Indians' physical appearance and the meandering paths that set Catawba settlements off from neighboring communities served to reinforce this cultural isolation.

The natives' utter indifference to missionary efforts after 1800 testified to the enduring power of established ways. Several clergymen stopped at the reservation in the first years of the nineteenth century; some stayed a year or two; none enjoyed any success. As one white South Carolinian noted in 1826, Catawbas were "Indians still." Outward conformity made it easier for them to blend into the changed landscape. Beneath the surface lay a more complex story.

Those few outsiders who tried to piece together that story generally found it difficult to learn much from the Indians. A people shrewd enough to discard the title of "King" was shrewd enough to understand that some things were better left unsaid and unseen. Catawbas kept their Indian names, and sometimes their language, a secret from prying visitors. They echoed the racist attitudes of their white neighbors and even owned a few slaves, all the time trading with blacks and hiring them to work in the Nation, where the laborers "enjoyed considerable freedom" among the natives. Like Afro-Americans on the plantation who adopted a happy, childlike demeanor to placate suspicious whites, Indians on the reservation learned that a "harmless and friendly" posture revealing little of life in the Nation was best suited to conditions in post-Revolutionary South Carolina.

Success in clinging to their cultural identity and at least a fraction of their ancient lands cannot obscure the cost Catawba peoples paid. From the time the first European arrived, the deck was stacked against them. They played the hand dealt them well enough to survive, but they could never win. An incident that took place at the end of the eighteenth century helps shed light on the consequences of compromise. When the Catawba headman, General New River, accidentally injured the horse he had borrowed from a nearby planter named Thomas Spratt, Spratt responded by "banging old New River with a pole all over the yard." This episode provided the settler with a colorful tale for his grandchildren; its effect on New River and his descendants can only be imagined. Catawbas did succeed in the sense that they adjusted to a hostile and different world, becoming trusted friends instead of feared enemies. Had they been any less successful, they would not have survived the eighteenth century. But poverty and oppression have plagued the Nation from New River's day to our own. For a people who had once been proprietors of the piedmont, the pain of learning new rules was very great, the price of success very high.

On that August day in 1608 when Amoroleck feared the loss of his world, John Smith assured him that the English "came to them in peace, and to seeke their loves." Events soon proved Amoroleck right and his captor wrong. Over the course of the next three centuries not only Amoroleck and other piedmont Indians but natives throughout North America had their world stolen and another put in its place. Though this occurred at different times and in different ways, no Indians escaped the explosive mixture of deadly bacteria, material riches, and alien peoples that was the invasion of America. Those in the southern piedmont who survived the onslaught were ensconced in their new world by the end of the eighteenth century. Population levels stabilized as the Catawba peoples developed immunities to once-lethal diseases. Rents, sales of pottery, and other economic activities proved adequate to support the Nation at a stable (if low) level of material life. Finally, the Indians' image as "inoffensive" neighbors gave them a place in South Carolina society and continues to sustain them today.

Vast differences separated Catawbas and other natives from their colonial contemporaries. Europeans were the colonizers, Africans the enslaved, Indians the dispossessed: From these distinct positions came distinct histories. Yet once we acknowledge the differences, instructive similarities remain that help to integrate natives more thoroughly into the story of early America. By carving a niche for themselves in response to drastically different conditions, the peoples who composed the Catawba Nation shared in the most fundamental of American experiences. Like Afro-Americans, these Indians were compelled to accept a subordinate position in American life yet did not altogether lose their cultural integrity. Like settlers of the Chesapeake, aboriginal inhabitants of the uplands adjusted to appalling mortality rates and wrestled with the difficult task of "living with death." Like inhabitants of the Middle Colonies, piedmont groups learned to cope with unprecedented ethnic diversity by balancing the pull of traditional loyalties with the demands of a new social order. Like Puritans in New England, Catawbas found that a new world did not arrive all at once and that localism, self-sufficiency, and the power of old ways were only gradually eroded by conditions in colonial America. More hints of a comparable heritage could be added to this list, but by now it should be clear that Indians belong on the colonial stage as important actors in the unfolding American drama rather than bit players, props, or spectators. For they, too, lived in a new world.

Readings for James H. Merrell:

Merrell gives a fuller description of the issues surrounding tribal survival and adaptation in colonial America in his *The Indians' New World: Catawbas and their Neighbors from European Contact through the Era of Removal* (Chapel Hill: University of North Carolina Press, 1989). For the experiences of other southeastern tribes see Richard White, *The Roots of Dependency: Subsistence, Environment, and Social Change among the Choctaws, Pawnees, and Navajos* (Lincoln: University of Nebraska Press, 1983); Tom Hatley, *The Dividing Paths: Cherokees and South Carolinians through the Era of Revolution* (New York: Oxford University Press, 1995); and J. Leitch Wright, Jr., *Creeks and Seminoles: The Destruction and Regeneration of the Muscogulge People* (Lincoln: University of Nebraska Press, 1986).

7

THINKING AND BELIEVING: NATIVISM AND UNITY IN THE AGES OF PONTIAC AND TECUMSEH

GREGORY E. DOWD

For Indians living near the Great Lakes, the 1760–1815 era brought rapid, continuing, and often catastrophic changes. The British defeated and removed the French as an active force in that region. Then the colonists rebelled, drove out the British and established a new nation, the United States. These events each brought a host of related changes as trade patterns shifted dramatically, pioneers stormed west over the Appalachian Mountains, and tribal populations plummeted. While the balance of power shifted away from the tribes, British and then American authorities sought to force a degree of acculturation on the villagers, mostly through the efforts of Christian missionaries. That set the stage for a series of Indian cultural, political, military, and religious revitalization movements to counter the unwelcome changes that seemed to engulf them. These movements aimed at returning to a past way of life in which the villagers would retake control of the decisions that most shaped their lives.

In studying these movements scholars have identified the elements that highlighted each. At the same time they depicted the revivals as clearly religious-cultural, or as political-military movements. This essay suggests that such distinctions may confuse the issues. In addition, Dowd notes that the prophets Neolin and Tenskwatawa, although separated by nearly a half century, appear to have shared some ideas. His study examines the revitalization movements between 1760 and 1815, and he finds striking similarities in how the Indians thought and acted.

Gregory E. Dowd is an associate professor of history at the University of Notre Dame.

Source: Gregory E. Dowd, "Thinking and Believing: Nativism and Unity in the Ages of Pontiac and Tecumseh," pp. 309–35. Reprinted from *American Indian Quarterly,* volume 16, number 3 by permission of the University of Nebraska Press. Copyright © 1992 by the University of Nebraska Press.

If we think seriously about belief, if we take Indian religion seriously, we will have to revise a stock interpretation of two early movements for pan-Indian unity. The first movement, dated roughly from 1760 to 1765, we associate with the Ottawa warrior Pontiac and the Delaware Prophet Neolin. The second movement, dated roughly from 1805–1813, we associate with the Shawnee diplomat and warrior Tecumseh and his brother, the Shawnee Prophet, Tenskwatawa.

Histories of the two movements for intertribal unity resonate with a distinction between the sacred and the profane. Each of the two movements has been keenly subdivided in our book-length histories into its religious and its secular dimensions. Each dimension is, in turn, personified in our histories by a leader. The two Prophets—separated by a half century—dream, traverse the heavens, and stir souls as atavistic, charismatic leaders. The two warriors—Pontiac and Tecumseh—stand, negotiate, and fight as great, even pragmatic, Americans. Several works from the age of Francis Parkman to our own day have explicitly placed the Prophets in one camp and the war leaders in another, claiming that the Delaware Prophet "may serve as a counterpart to the famous Shawnee Prophet," that Tecumseh "took Pontiac for his model."

The distinction between the sacred and the secular, between the believer and the thinker, a distinction that goes far beyond that between the priest and the soldier, cannot be maintained. Perhaps this distinction results from the paradoxical product of Christian hostility toward native belief and of secular hostility toward belief in general. If so, then this interpretive framework should be dismantled. In this paper I will argue that the prophets and the military leaders drew inspiration from the same sources. My hypothesis implies that figures at opposite corners of the standard interpretation, for instance the Shawnee Prophet of the 1800s and the Ottawa Pontiac of the 1760s, shared visions and strategies, and shared them with their compatriots. This implication, I should add, does not originate with me. It was first suggested by the Shawnee Prophet himself, who in 1810 "boasted that he would follow in the footsteps of the Great Pontiac." Declaring himself an heir to a figure that scholars have mistakenly isolated with Tecumseh as a pragmatist, even as a nonbeliever, the Prophet was creating good history.

Militant Foundations

Let us first briefly investigate the relationship between Pontiac and Neolin. It is worth noting that our most extensive report of the Delaware Prophet's visions comes to us through Pontiac's voice. According to most analyses of the relationship between the two leaders, the pragmatic Pontiac found Neolin's spiritual message useful, altering it for his political ends. A fresh look at the record strongly suggests that Pontiac got Neolin's message right after all, and got it in the heart.

The interpretation that isolates Pontiac from Neolin hinges upon their differing perceptions of the French. Versions of Neolin's message recorded in the Delawares' and Shawnees' Upper Ohio Country reveal no concern for the French, yet Pontiac's version of the Delaware prophecy has the Master of Life proclaiming of the French that "I love them," while for the Master the English "are my enemies, and the enemies of your [French] brothers." Scholars have understandably, though unconvincingly, concluded that Pontiac, out of a desire to win over Detroit's *habitants,* revised Neolin's message to suit his own ends.

Neolin may, however, have spoken as favorably of the French as did Pontiac. A party of Ohioan Delawares and Shawnees, visiting Pontiac when his siege was already six weeks old, insisted, in the Great Spirit's name, that care be taken of Detroit's French inhabitants. Denouncing Pontiac's seizure of the local French people's arms and ammunition, a spokesman for the Delawares chided, presumably with Neolin in mind, that "the Master of Life . . . forbade us to attack our brothers the French." Pontiac, it appears, did not twist Delaware words, but reported what he believed he had heard—reported, to put it simply, what he believed.

He behaved like a believer. Visiting Fort Chartres, Illinois, in an abortive effort to secure French aid, he attempted to persuade French officers to take the messianic movement seriously. It was, he argued in 1764, the Master of Life who "put Arms in our hands, and it is he who has ordered us to fight against this bad meat that would come and infest our lands. . . . Think then my Father that thou goest against the Master of life and that all the red Men conform to his will." It is difficult to read a cynic into these lines, spoken to Christians who would not find them automatically persuasive. It is, of course, possible that Pontiac sought to impress his Indian listeners, but such speculation only underscores the hypothetical nature of the standard assessment of Pontiac's spirituality.

Pontiac, in short, belongs among his people. While he did indeed seek to wage what Howard Peckham and Wilbur Jacobs have called an "Indian war of Independence," he sought to do it in Indian ways; he did not have to depart from, or worse, to rise above his people's way of thinking to come up with the notion. The idea of Indian unity, fostered by a long history of native interaction, most recently by widespread intertribal cooperation during the Seven Years' War, had been circulating among the peoples since the withdrawal of the French from the Lakes. Pontiac did not develop the notion single-handedly, nor did he develop it devoid of its spiritual content. He could both think and believe. In the same spirit, let us turn to Tecumseh and his brother, the Shawnee Prophet Tenskwatawa, and because their movement drew heavily upon the earlier movement's thought, we will not leave Pontiac and Neolin behind.

Interpreting the Shawnee Brothers

Histories of Tecumseh and Tenskwatawa, far more than of Pontiac and Neolin, place a barrier between religion and realpolitik. The dramatic effect is to raise tensions, for not only does religion confront reason, but brother battles brother. In creating this distinction, the histories portray Tecumseh not only as a great man, but also as an exceptional Indian, thinking beyond the traditions of his people. Tecumseh did *not*, however, differ from his followers in culture or in vision any more than did Pontiac, nor was it a lack of traditional tribal identity that blocked his success. His most recent biographer credits Tecumseh with having "conceived of a plan for uniting the red people," but Tecumseh did not conceive of the plan from scratch. Indeed, he drew upon traditions of nativism and well-established networks of intertribal relations that had long been vibrant throughout the trans-Appalachian borderlands, reaching back into the past far beyond the time of Pontiac. With Tecumseh, also drawing from this legacy, stood the Shawnee Prophet.

Tenskwatawa, like the Delaware Prophet before him, did not possess a strictly "tribal" identity. In fact, his first visions occurred while living among Delawares, not

Shawnees. The Delaware Prophet, forty years earlier, had similarly displayed his trans-tribal identity by dwelling among the Shawnees in the final months of Delaware in-volvement in Pontiac's War. Such mingling among Indians was hardly exceptional in the turbulent late eighteenth-century Old Northwest. More striking was Tenskwatawa's in-vitation in 1806 to all Indian peoples to join him in settling a new, deliberately polyglot town at Greenville, Ohio. The Shawnee Prophet made the move in clear symbolic defi-ance of the 1795 Treaty of Greenville, which had imposed a massive land cession upon the Indians and had firmly established the annuity system in the Old Northwest. He re-peated the gesture by establishing his town at Tippecanoe (1808–12), in outright defi-ance of the Miami Little Turtle, who claimed tribal authority over that land, and who had negotiated several recent treaties with the United States. Plans for the Tippecanoe set-tlement, Tenskwatawa declared, had been "layed by all the Indians in America." He in-formed the Miami leader that Indian unity alone would end Indian poverty and defend Indian land. Before Tecumseh entered the historical record, then, the Prophet had demonstrated that he could think beyond the boundaries of tribe.

That Indians were conscious of Tenskwatawa's participation in a tradition of pan-Indian militancy is indicated by the actions of a band of Wyandots. Joining the Shawnee Prophet in 1810, they bound the movement to earlier decades by bringing with them "the Great Belt which was the Symbol of Union between the Tribes in their late war with the United States." Consciously reviving the pan-Indianism of their recent past, these Wyan-dots, in the Shawnee Prophet's words, could not "sit still and see the property of all the Indians usurped."

The Separate Creation and Indian Unity

To support his intertribal call, the Shawnee Prophet had at his disposal a concept of In-dian identity that had been developing since at least the middle of the eighteenth cen-tury, a concept embodied in the notion of the separate creation of Anglo-Americans and Indians. As early as 1751 a Presbyterian encountered the notion among Delawares on the Susquehanna River in Pennsylvania, and in the 1760s Neolin employed separation theology in forming his movement. The idea was taken up by other lesser-known Delawares and Shawnees in the late 1760s and early 1770s, the years of Tenskwatawa's youth. The notion, however, did not lead directly to nativism; it was so widespread that even such federally recognized chiefs as Black Hoof and the Wyandot Tahre expressed the view at the turn of the nineteenth century. But leaders seeking accommodation with the United States could never turn the notion of separate creation to their advantage with the dexterity of their nativistic opponents, for in its logical conclusion, the doctrine meant an Indian rejection of American domination. The Great Spirit warned the Shawnee Prophet to be wary, for the "white man was not made by himself but by an-other spirit who made and governed the whites and over whom he had no control."

The separate, even evil, nature of American citizens emerged also in Indian inter-pretations of Christianity. The line here also derives from at least as far back as Neolin's mid-eighteenth century, when some Indians turned Christianity against Christians to demonstrate the depth of the missionaries' abomination. One Delaware contemporary of Neolin's claimed that he had read the Bible cover to cover, but nowhere in it could he find it written that Indians "should live like the white people." A Mingo in the same period listened to a sermon about the crucifixion of Jesus, then quipped, "If it is true, the Indians are not to blame for his death, but the white man." At the crucifixion, he argued, Europeans had killed their own God. In the early militant phase of the Seneca movement under Handsome Lake (1798–1802), his half-brother Cornplanter, who "liked some ways of the white people," told the Quaker missionary Henry Simmons, "It was the white people who kill'd our Saviour." Simmons countered, "It was the Jews," and then tried to drive the point home by dragging out the already hackneyed argument that Indians were members of the lost tribes of Israel: "Indians were their descendants, for many of their habits were similar to the Jews, in former days." We don't know what Cornplanter made of that contention—perhaps he was simply at a loss for words—but twentieth-century practitioners of the Handsome Lake Religion make no mention of it and still consider the crucifixion a deed performed by whites. They learn that the Seneca Prophet, in his early visions, met Jesus, who described himself as "a man upon the earth who was slain by his own people." Furthermore, Jesus had ordered Handsome Lake to "tell your people that they will become lost when they follow the ways of the white people." Among the literally surrounded Senecas the notion did not lead to a complete break with the United States, nor did it prevent their exploration of Anglo-American culture. But the more militant, and still more autonomous, Old Northwestern peoples leaned more heavily on the argument.

Responding to a Moravian missionary in 1806, one of Tenskwatawa's followers said of the crucifixion, "Granted that what you say is true, He did not die in Indian land but among the white people." In 1810, Tecumseh himself revealed his own concerns for spiritual things, asking Indiana Territory's governor William Henry Harrison in pointed terms, "How can we have confidence in the white people [?] when Jesus Christ came upon the earth you kill'd and nail'd him on a cross." Given the Shawnee warrior's nativistic assumptions, his participation in a way of thinking common among his people, it was a logical question.

If, as the Shawnee Prophet said, Americans were inimical to Indians, if "the Great Spirit did not mean that the white and red people should live near each other [because the newcomers] poison'd the land," and if all Indians came from a common creation different from others, then it made sense that only Indians should unite against the American threat. It seems likely that, as in Pontiac's day, the threat was not felt from Canada (however British it was now), but from the Americans alone. Room for the British is explicitly written into at least one report of militant nativism during the age of Tecumseh: in the midst of the War of 1812, Potowatomis received news from the Lake Erie theatre that "a Prophet had arisen in England, [who told the King that] the Great Spirit was much displeased with the Americans." The Great Spirit ordered the King to "assist all the Indians to drive the Americans out." Leaving room, perhaps, for cooperation from British Canada, Indian militants emphasized their spiritual separation from the Americans, giving sacred sanction to Native American unity.

Overhunting

Neolin and Tenskwatawa shared a material concern over changes in the environment that also meshed with their spiritual concerns. According to Pontiac, the Great Spirit explained to Neolin that "I led the wild animals into the depths of the forests so that ye had to depend on your brothers to feed and shelter you. Ye have only to become good again and do what I wish, and I will send back the animals for your food." Forty-five years later Tenskwatawa knew that the Indians' gross overhunting of game for the peltry trade had led to a decline in deer stocks. Moravian missionaries reported that the Great Spirit "had shown him the deer were half a trees' length under the ground and that these would soon appear again on the earth if the Indians did what he told them to do, and then there would be an abundance of deer once more." Tenskwatawa would allow trade with Anglo-Americans, as long as it was on terms that the Indians deemed just. He proposed that a one-for-one trade be instituted: one shirt for one raccoon skin and one blanket for one deerskin. The call for such a trade, albeit impossible given the Indians' complete lack of influence on an overseas market upset by the Napoleonic Wars, stood as an open challenge to Anglo-American economic authority. Tenskwatawa sought isolation far less than he sought to free Indians from the outside control that in his view was ensnaring the Indians of the borderlands.

Both Neolin in the wake of the Seven Years' War and Tenskwatawa on the eve of the War of 1812 addressed economic and political issues. And though proceeding from a theological base, they played the politics of Indian autonomy and unity. The standard assessment of Pontiac, that he "possessed the ability to channel red resentment toward meaningful goals," as if the Delaware Prophet and his believing disciples lacked worthy objectives, is in need of revision. An even stronger case for revision should be made regarding the history surrounding Tenskwatawa and Tecumseh. With these two leaders the historians' division of the sacred from the profane has been given not only a pair of names but a pair of dates: 1809, the year of the Treaty of Fort Wayne, and 1811, the year of the scrap at Tippecanoe. To understand fully both these events and the origins of the conventional wisdom, we must investigate, as Daniel Richter suggests, the issue of factionalism.

Factions

By the winter of 1805–06, when the Shawnee Prophet began to prophesy, several men had secured recognition by the United States as the leaders of their "tribes" in areas now known as Ohio and Indiana. Most of these men had built distinguished military careers in the wars against the Anglo-Americans; each of them had ended those wars by signing the Treaty of Greenville. Their military reputations gave them widespread support among their peoples; their cooperation with the United States following the wars gave them the confidence of American officialdom. By 1804 they had fashioned themselves into the chief conduits for the passage of the United States' annuities to Indians. Of them, Little Turtle of the Miamis and Black Hoof of the Shawnees became useful foils for the nativist movement. In fact, "annuity chiefs," leaders with both a native base and federal support, provided the anvil upon which the prophets forged this early nineteenth-century phase of the struggle for Indian unity.

During the first decade of the nineteenth century, Little Turtle gathered a great deal of power in the Old Northwest. His influence was so strong that the Secretary of War, Dearborn, informed Harrison that "the neighboring Indians are . . . extremely jealous of the Little Turtle." His influence may be partially attributed to his success in winning an unusually large annuity for the Miamis at the Treaty of Greenville. He accomplished this feat by insisting that the Eel River Indians were a separate tribe, confederated under his authority. Partly too, he basked in the former glory of his reportedly brilliant leadership in the victories over Harmar and St. Clair (1790 and 1791, respectively). In general, however, he retained power through his effective management of the Miami annuity: his refusal to indulge in luxuries, his generosity toward his Miami people, and his hospitality to whites. Once in power, he handled himself with such skill that animosities toward him often worked in his favor. For example, the federal agents opposed "those jealousies" with "all the fair means in [their] power." "All the fair means" tended to translate into "all means fair or foul." This was demonstrated in the Miami leader's partnership with William Wells, the federal government's agent at Fort Wayne.

Wells, who knew several Indian languages as a result of his childhood captivity among the Northwesterners, worked closely with Little Turtle in attempting to manage Indian-American relations in his quarter; so closely, in fact, that by 1809 charges of misconduct led to his demotion from agent to translator. This demotion, despite his impressive skills and connections, makes little sense when viewed in the light of accusations, leveled in 1807, that he had mistranslated speeches to advance his own and Little Turtle's interests. Whatever the logic of his demotion, he was suspected in 1809 of both deliberately exaggerating the Prophet's friendship for the British, and, more seriously as far as the federal government was concerned, of embezzling Delaware annuities.

Wells and Little Turtle had also interfered with the federal and Quaker effort to "civilize" the Shawnees. They intended to prevent rival Old Northwestern leaders, including Black Hoof, from rising to prominence in relations with the federal government. Throughout the first decade of the nineteenth century, Little Turtle had managed to secure annuities for his Miamis at almost every cession of land, often by challenging the claims made by other peoples. He wanted no contenders to threaten his hold on the disposition of what he came to view as the Miamis' most precious commodity.

But in Little Turtle's efforts against the Shawnee annuity chief, he misspent energies better devoted toward those who would become more serious opponents: those who hoped to prevent land from ever being traded as a commodity again. For the true threat to Little Turtle came not from his accommodating rivals, but from the resurgence of militant pan-Indian nativism under the direction of the prophets. Not until the Shawnee Prophet threw down the gauntlet by settling among the Miamis in 1808 did Little Turtle and Wells move strongly against him, and even then, it was Wells, not Little Turtle, who dealt the telling blows. So hostile was Wells to Tenskwatawa that in 1809, when groups of starving nativists appeared at Vincennes, Harrison reported to the Secretary of War that the Indian agent "was for having me starve all." And in the months following the Battle of Tippecanoe (1811), Wells boasted: "Yes sir I would of [sic] destroyed this scoundrel 4 years ago had I not of [sic] been prevented by my superiors." By 1809, Wells and Little Turtle sought to combat the resurgence of militant nativism and all challenges from other accommodating leaders (their earlier efforts were directed mainly against the latter). Little Turtle played the part of tribal Chief, and put his Miamis' interests before those of other peoples.

Black Hoof, Little Turtle's rival among the faction of Shawnees eager to accommodate the United States, also dispensed government annuities. Like the Miami, Black Hoof carried a good record as a warrior and defender of his people. As an elderly though still active man in the early nineteenth century, he was reported to be among those who surprised Braddock in 1755; it is certain that he had fought valorously in the wars of the 1780s and 1790s. Balancing his youthful show of military zeal was his more mature posture of warmth for the Americans. The moment when youth and age balanced was in 1795, after devastating Northwestern defeats, when Black Hoof put his mark on the Greenville cession. For the next two decades he cooperated with the federal government.

Little Turtle and Black Hoof did not simply cede land, accept annuities, and redistribute the proceeds among their people. They too had designs for the future. To carry them out, they actively cooperated with the Quaker bearers of the civilizing mission. These missionaries of religion and culture sought to establish "demonstration farms" to be used to persuade Indian men to replace hunting with agriculture and Indian women to abandon agriculture for domestic pursuits. The Friends received federal support and cooperation.

In 1804—in accordance with an agreement among Quaker delegates, Little Turtle, and the Potawatomi Five Medals—Quaker Philip Dennis planted his twenty-acre farm about forty miles southwest of Fort Wayne, on rich soil beside the Wabash. There, argued Little Turtle, both the Potawatomis and the Miamis could benefit by observing Dennis' progress, but Dennis was clearly in the heartland of the Miamis.

In 1807, Black Hoof likewise allowed the Quaker William Kirk to set up a demonstration farm near the Shawnee town of Wapakoneta, within reach of the Wyandots at Sandusky. Black Hoof's support enabled Kirk to enclose one hundred acres of land and to plant a full two hundred acres in corn. By April 1808, Kirk reported progress: several of the Shawnees operated private farms; the people as a whole possessed "a good stock of Cattle and Hogs." The Wyandots' "improvements," he claimed, were similar. A year later Indian agent John Johnson noted that Black Hoof's people had both a saw mill and a grist mill under construction; many lived in log houses with chimneys; their village, overall, bore "the marks of industry." However, despite these developments and petitions on Kirk's behalf, the war department (apparently because of Kirk's poor record keeping) withdrew its support from the mission in late 1808. It is worth noting that Little Turtle and Wells, seeking to prevent potential rivals, had stood against Kirk's arrangement with the Shawnees and Wyandots. The brief history of Kirk's agency demonstrated, and this is the critical point, that the Quakers, the federal government, the Indian agents, and the government chiefs—all the main advocates of accommodation in the Old Northwest—were seriously divided, often for the most petty of reasons. This division gave rise to a strong nativist movement that challenged these scattered projects.

The Quaker missionaries faced obstacles more difficult to negotiate than factionalism among the forces of accommodation. For one thing, they had underestimated the difficulties of their mission. For example, they clearly intended to alter the gender division of labor among the Indians they observed. Philip Dennis actively attempted to dissuade the young Indian women who "wished to work in preparing the ground and in tending the corn," by hiring a white woman to teach them spinning and knitting. The Quakers, arguing against Indian tradition, claimed that women "are less then Men, they are not as strong as Men, they are not as able to endure fatigue and toil as men." Rather, women should "be employed in our houses, to keep them clean, to sew, knit, and weave; to dress food for themselves and [their] families." Such an arrangement practically reversed the contemporary production arrangements among Indians, for the men obtained clothing through hunting and trade, while women raised the crops and vegetables. Quite apart from the cosmological consequences Indians would fear in such a transformation, the material demands of the Friends' proposal were enormous: among the Indians, women alone possessed the knowledge of field work. If carried out, then, the proposed gender reversal might have resulted in a dangerous drain of horticultural skills.

Therefore, even proponents of accommodation could support the role reversal with little more than words. When the Quakers arrived, Little Turtle claimed that he "and some others of my brother Chiefs have been endeavouring to turn the minds of our People [men] towards the Cultivation of the Earth," but he admitted no success. The Quakers would not do much better. For the moment then, this aspect of the mission proved a failure in the Northwest.

The Shawnee Prophet, who emerged as the chief opponent of the civilizing mission, clearly preferred traditional gender roles to those sponsored by the Quakers. According to William Wells, the Prophet declared Kirk to be a "Master" imposed over the Indians by the President, "from which circumstance it was evident that the President intended making women of the Indians—but when the Indians was [sic] all united they would be respected by the President as men."

The Prophet's concern with the civilizing mission, and the gender revolution it would have entailed, grew out of both the very earthly grounds that it robbed from the Indians, their political independence, and the cosmological proposition that robbed the Indians of their sacred powers. He and other opponents of the mission directed their most searing attacks at its Indian sponsors, whom they believed were undermining the strength of the Indian peoples.

In 1805, shortly after his first visions, the Shawnee Prophet directly challenged the authority of the annuity chiefs. The Prophet spoke openly against those "chiefs who were very wicked, would not believe, and tried to keep the people from believing, and encouraged them on in their former wicked ways." Black Hoof, the Prophet's strong Shawnee opponent, maintained the loyalties of many Shawnees, despite the Prophet's vigorous denunciations. In order for the Prophet to gain independence from Black Hoof and his followers, as well as to challenge the Greenville Treaty upon which Black Hoof's authority partially rested, "the Great Spirit told" Tenskwatawa "to separate from these wicked chiefs and their people and showed him particularly where to come, towards the big ford where the peace was concluded with the Americans; and there [to] make provision to receive and instruct all from the different tribes that were willing to be good."

A realignment of Indian loyalties resulted. While Black Hoof and Little Turtle each worked against the other, lobbying with their particular American allies to secure their influence within the federal government, Tenskwatawa sought intertribal support for both a rebellion against these government chiefs and a posture of defiance toward American expansion. Thus, Tenskwatawa's effort was against both domestic and foreign authority. The moment for domestic success, moreover, was opportune. His Indian opponents, as we have seen, were divided among themselves.

The struggle for the control of Indian councils manifested itself most violently in the Shawnee Prophet's witch hunt, a hunt for witches who bore little resemblance to those of earlier Anglo-colonial society: the first accused were often powerful men. Opposition to witchcraft, a long-standing feature of nativism, lay at the center, not the periphery, of the Prophet's code. Tenskwatawa began preaching, one source has it, on the death of Pengahshega (Change of Feathers), a powerful Shawnee opponent of witches.

What's more, witch hunts had bedeviled Indian communities during the nativistic up-heavals of the 1750s, 1760s, and early 1770s.

Tenskwatawa claimed that the Great Spirit had given him the power to discover witches, even among powerful leaders of the community. To find the guilty parties, the Prophet stood the villagers in a circle about him, and "after a great many ceremonies," he pointed to the evil beings. Tenskwatawa's witch hunt initially hit the Delawares with the greatest severity. The Prophet had been living among the Delawares when he expe-rienced his first visions. By the late winter of 1805–1806, strong parties of Delawares sought "to destroy all the reputed witches, . . . as well as those who had poison among them. They resolved to use fire to bring about the confessions of those whom the Schawano would accuse." All of the known condemned Delawares had close ties with the Americans and with the civilizing mission. Two of the condemned, Tedapachsit and Hackingpomska, were chiefs, and they had both signed the Greenville Treaty of 1795 and had ceded land to the United States at the Delaware Treaty of 1804, agreeing that the new annuities would be "exclusively appropriated to the purpose of ameliorating their condition and promoting their civilization." Tedapachsit, killed by the Prophet's followers, had openly supported the activities of Christian missionaries. Hackingpom-ska, though taken prisoner, was not executed, perhaps because he yielded momentarily to the growing opposition to the white missions, by joining a Delaware Council in fa-voring native prophets over American ministers. An old woman, baptized by the Mora-vians, fell victim to the charge; so did the Indian "Brother Joshua," who not only had converted to Christianity, but who had been, as the militants suspected, an active spy for the United States during the American Revolution. Tenskwatawa's Delaware targets ac-cepted and cultivated direct American intervention in Indian government, religion, and society. For the nativists, such cultivation was tantamount to sorcery.

By mid-summer, internal Delaware opposition to the killings led many to recoil from the witch hunt and to turn their suspicions against the hunters, leaving the Delawares deeply divided over killings that had so clearly reflected political and cultural conflict. As one Moravian missionary put it while he fled Delaware country, "The Indi-ans hate each other with a bitter hatred, which may flame forth at the slightest provoca-tion." (Note that this hatred was not tribal.) Here, Delaware followers of a Shawnee at-tacked one another.

Among the Shawnees, two of Black Hoof's followers, accused of using "bad Me-disin [sic]," lost their lives to the Prophet's assassins in the spring of 1807. Not surpris-ingly, in light of the nativists' hostility toward leaders who cooperated with the Ameri-cans, Tenskwatawa had even discovered Black Hoof to be a witch, along with chiefs Black Snake and Butler. None of them was killed, but it is worth noting that the three accused supported the federally sponsored Quaker mission.

Recriminations between Black Hoof's and the Prophet's parties flew so furiously that the federal government temporarily treated the nativist movement as a strictly in-ternal Shawnee affair. In early August 1807, while anti-British passions over the *Chesa-peake-Leopard* naval affair boiled in the United States, President Thomas Jefferson de-clined to relate Indian matters to British maritime policy. With "respect to the Prophet," he informed his Secretary of War, "if [the chiefs] who are in danger from him would set-tle it their own way, it would be their affair. But we should do nothing towards it." Noth-ing, in Jefferson's curious usage, meant a little judicious peddling of influence: "The best conduct we can pursue to countervail these movements among the Indians is to confirm our friends by redoubled acts of justice and favor."

Throughout 1807, beating against the winds of continued federal favor for annuity chiefs, the nativists' notions slipped deeper into the Upper Great Lakes region. In the spring, Michigan Territorial Governor William Hull advertised the intent of the federal government to purchase some lands from the Ottawas. As a result, Tenskwatawa's messianic Ottawa ally, the Trout, launched a more stringent brand of nativism, though he did so in the Shawnee's name. By September, Michigan's traders felt the first force of the Ottawa revival. One merchant wrote, "All the Ottawas from L'arbe au Croche adhere strictly to the Shawney Prophets advice they do not wear Hats, Drink, or Conjure." These Ottawas planned on spending the autumn at the Prophet's Town and refused liquor even when offered it free of charge. The traders lamented, "Rum is a Drug [on the market]. . . . Indians do not purchase One Gall[11] [*sic*] per month."

By the spring of 1808, when the Prophet gathered his followers for a move to the Wabash River, near Tippecanoe Creek, on lands claimed by the Miamis, the Miami chief Little Turtle finally took serious notice of the Prophet. With the Potawatomi Five Medals, Little Turtle threatened to kill Tenskwatawa if he made the proposed move. In response, Tenskwatawa loudly condemned all government chiefs who had "sold all the Indian land to the United States" and who had asked the President to "appoint masters over them to make them work."

If the nativists opposed the accommodating chiefs for their advocacy of the civilizing mission and for their role in land sales, it was the latter role they most vocally condemned. Between 1804 and the end of 1808 the governors of the Indiana and Michigan Territories had negotiated a half dozen treaties with the annuity chiefs. According to these treaties, the United States had obtained a large chunk of southeastern Michigan, large cessions in southern Indiana and Illinois, and most of the land that had been left to the Indians in Ohio. The United States had also gained the right to build and use a road running through a portion of what remained of Indian territory. Washington paid for these grants with increased annuities, to be distributed through the leaders it recognized. To opponents of the annuity chiefs, the payments reeked of bribery.

The Treaty of Fort Wayne

In 1809, the annuity chiefs unwittingly, even negligently, galvanized the nativists with another land cession, embodied in the Treaty of Fort Wayne. The treaty has long been recognized as a milestone on the road to the battle of Tippecanoe, a transforming event that took a religious movement and made it political. The treaty, concluded between the United States and the federally recognized leaders of the Delaware, "Eel River," Miami, and Potawatomi Indians, gained for the states "upwards of two milions [*sic*] and a half of acres" at the cost of "less than two cents per acre." From the Treaty forward, according to several histories on the eve of the War of 1812, Tenskwatawa's brother, Tecumseh, fashioned and led the pan-Indian movement, while the Prophet himself receded. The Prophet, however, lost no authority following the treaty. More power to Tecumseh did not, by some law of finite volume, mean less power for the Prophet: the two were brothers, allies, and believers. It is a mistake to assign them relative weights with reference to their peoples' affairs; they were too closely intertwined in the struggle for autonomy and power, albeit playing different roles, to be separated without doing both men injury.

Tenskwatawa's preaching continued to exhibit both the political overtones and material concerns that political and social historians find worth in understanding. Like Tecumseh, Tenskwatawa spoke out vigorously against both the Fort Wayne cession and the Indians who had agreed to it. In the spring and summer of 1810, half a year after the signing of the treaty, the Prophet informed an uncovered American spy that his people were "much exasperated at the cession of Lands made last winter" and that they had "agreed that the Tract on the N. west side of the Wabash should not be surveyed." His disciples followed up this declaration by successfully opposing a surveying party in September.

Tippecanoe (and Toto Too?): A Revision

The second date assigned to the demise of the Prophet's authority is November 7, 1811, at the battle of Tippecanoe. Tenskwatawa's career, already eclipsed by Tecumseh's meteoric rise in the traditional account, here described a pitiful coda. According to conventional knowledge, the Shawnee Prophet had promised his followers a marvelous victory on the battle's eve. After his defeat and the abandonment of his village, the Prophet met massive dissent among his erstwhile disciples, and was placed under Winnebago bondage, blamed for Indian losses, and finally threatened with death. Tecumseh, the tale continues, upon his return to the North from his southern mission sometime in the middle of January 1812, exploded in rage before his brother, taking him by the hair and chastising him for having precipitously attacked the Americans. The historians who so argue have not done so without evidence. Even if we screen out the memoirs written by those who had always been hostile to the Prophet and stick mainly to the contemporary documents, we find some evidence to support the standard narrative. But we also see serious, overwhelming, reason for doubt.

Two arguments will be challenged here. First, that Tenskwatawa was abandoned by his followers following the Battle of Tippecanoe. There is sufficient evidence in the record to contradict the standard description, which has Harrison play the part of Dorothy's dog Toto, exposing the Shawnee as just another "very bad Wizard," an ordinary man behind the curtain, no longer worthy of attention. The most extravagant contemporary rumors that spread among Americans had the Shawnees surrender the Prophet to the jailkeepers of Vincennes, but such vapors dissipated quickly, and fortunately did not infect our histories. Other stories, however, found a host in the full body of writing on the subject. They were passed into the histories through the medium of a storm of euphoric correspondence brewed in the confusion that followed William Henry Harrison's victory. This correspondence, however, proves to be deeply flawed as evidence, for its very writers would soon revise their precipitous claims about the Prophet's fall, as they came to recognize his continuing power.

In one early and influential passage, for instance, Captain Josiah Snelling, commanding Fort Harrison, notified Harrison that the Indians were "reproaching the Prophet in bitter terms for the defeat he had brought on them." The Winnebagos, Snelling had heard, charged the Prophet with fraud, "bound him with cords, and it was the opinion of Little Eyes [Snelling's Miami informant] they would sacrifice him." Snelling concluded that "all the confederated tribes had abandoned their faith in the Prophet except about forty Shawanoes who still adhered to him." The letter, written in late November, was supplemented by others that described widespread distrust of the Prophet, the refusal of villages to allow him to join them, and the general abandonment of his movement. From this letter springs the standard interpretation that the Prophet fell after Tippecanoe. Missing, however, are the letters' notes of caution: "I cannot say sir how much of the above may be depended on," or, "It is however pretty certain that the Winnebagos have not returned home as the Kickapoos asserted."

Correction soon supplemented caution. Within seven weeks of Snelling's first letter, Americans found reason to revise their information. Snelling told Harrison that

> he was informed confidentially by a Wea Indian that the Disposition of the Kickapoos and Winnebagos was by no means such as they wished us to believe. That many of them still retained their confidence in the Prophet, who had assured them that his want of success in the late action was caused by an accident of an uncommon kind. . . . That many of them believed that they would all die as soon as the Prophet was put to death.

Harrison soon came to doubt the sincerity of Snelling's original informant, Little Eyes, who, Harrison decided, had "long been in the interest of the Prophet." Snelling himself had noted that Little Eyes committed robberies against American settlers, supporting Harrison's suspicions and casting into question any word this militant Miami gave to his American enemies. In another two weeks Snelling learned that "it was the determination of all the Indians to go to War with the United States."

In the months after Tippecanoe, evidence continued to accumulate suggesting that the Prophet still commanded a following, and that the militants among the Indians, as the *National Intelligencer* put it in February, "will generally attach themselves to the Prophet and his measures." Thomas Forsyth at Peoria summed up the results of the Battle of Tippecanoe as the following: "the Prophet's party was dispersed only for a moment." Such evidence finds occasional contradiction, even including the renewal of open warfare in the summer of 1812. It is worth noting that by May, possibly as early as January, the Prophet's village of Tippecanoe, the scene of his supposed demise, had repopulated with "about 300 winebagoes [*sic*] and about 200 of other tribes and that he [that is, the Prophet] was daily gaining strength." By June Harrison noted that the militants' force at Tippecanoe was "equal to that which they commanded last summer." When the Prophet's village was again destroyed by American troops in the fall of 1812, it and the adjoining and allied Kickapoo village supported some 200 cabins and huts, a considerable settlement by the region's standards. The Indians, dejected according to the standard interpretation, had rebounded after the first attack on Tippecanoe, and had prepared to resist the continued expansion of the United States. As Governor Ninian Edwards of the Illinois Territory had worried with the approach of the post-Tippecanoe spring, "the Prophet is regaining his influence." So much was this the case that Harrison had sought to have "the Prophet or Tecumseh or both" visit the President of the United States. Still conceiving of the Prophet as worthy of special attention, Harrison, by the late winter of 1812, shaped a policy around the equal consideration of the brothers. Tenskwatawa remained indispensable.

The second argument of the standard interpretation, that Tecumseh rejected his brother after Tippecanoe, is more difficult to assess, for it involves the personal beliefs of an individual who left us no writings. A violent scene—which includes Tecumseh's shock at the defeat at Tippecanoe, his furious manhandling of the Prophet, charging him with a premature assault on the Americans—has repeatedly been reconstituted to suggest that Tecumseh's involvement in the movement was largely secular; that Tecumseh was at heart indifferent to prophecy, and went along with it only as long as it met his higher purpose: the formation of his confederacy. The interpretation originates with Anthony Shane, a Shawnee-metis employee of the federal government, a man long hostile to the Prophet, interviewed by historian Benjamin Drake ten years after the fact. Shane claimed that Tecumseh, always silently cognizant of his brother's fraud, was twice on the verge of killing Tenskwatawa, the second time after the Tippecanoe fiasco. Shane's Tecumseh had opposed Tenskwatawa's religion at its very beginning, but had later realized that "as a matter of policy" he might wield it "to further his own designs." Others who knew the two men recalled events differently, but there is some evidence from the period itself to support Shane's story. Strikingly similar to tales of Pontiac's manipulation of Neolin's message, the story of Tecumseh's falling out with his brother bears examination.

The best piece of evidence to support the Shane thesis comes from the pen of William Claus, British commander at Amherstburg, who received it from Isidor Chaine, a Wyandot culture broker. Claus wrote that "Teekumthie was much dissatisfied with his Brother [*sic*] for engaging Governor Harrison, last fall, as their plans were not sufficiently matured." A less direct but good piece of evidence describes Tecumseh "much exasperated against his brother." Still, these letters and similar rumors in American soldiers' journals and memoirs cannot support the weight they now bear, the hefty loads not merely of Tecumseh's disappointment at the results of the confrontation at Tippecanoe, a limited point that is quite plausible, but, far less plausibly, of his final overthrow of his brother. The contemporary documents simply do not address Tecumseh's devotion, nor do they suggest, as Shane's memoir and subsequent histories have, that Tecumseh either defrocked his brother or was on the verge of putting the Prophet to death. What they do tell us is that Tecumseh was "much dissatisfied," even "exasperated," at the Prophet for his failure to prevent the battle. These words cannot be stretched to suggest that Tecumseh contemplated even apostasy, much less his brother's assassination.

Three interrelated questions must be addressed: Did Tecumseh blame his brother for the Indians' losses at Tippecanoe? Did he think the losses were significant? And did he abandon his brother's convictions? The traditional interpretation's affirmative answer to each question, supported by the Shane memoir and the letters, finds contradiction elsewhere in more direct records.

On May 15, 1812, for example, Tecumseh spoke to a council of Indians from a dozen peoples, militant and non-militant alike. Tecumseh claimed, as the traditional interpretation would have it, that the battle would not have occurred had he been at Tippecanoe to prevent it. But nowhere did Tecumseh blame his brother. Among Indians, he blamed only "a few of our younger men," a description that could not, in terms of either age or occupation, apply to Tenskwatawa. Indeed, the quotation throws into question Tenskwatawa's role at Tippecanoe. Was it the Prophet who ordered the fight? We have no uncontradicted contemporary evidence. British agent Matthew Elliot's mid-January battle report to Major Brock removed the blame from Tenskwatawa; Elliot described the incidents leading to the battle as haphazard and unpredictable. The Indians wisely placed pickets around Harrison's camp, but "Two young Winibiegoes, no doubt out of curiosity," went too near the American sentinels and were fired on, precipitating an unintended battle." In a later report by Elliot, Tecumseh himself, though calling the Prophet's village in his absence "a poor set of people," again absolves his brother, declaring at the battle of Tippecanoe that "You cannot blame Your Younger Brothers the Shawanoes." Instead he charged Potawatomis with precipitating the crisis.

But Tecumseh placed the bulk of the blame, during the Indian Council of May 15, 1812, on the Americans. He said, "Governor Harrison made war on my people in my absence." The traditional interpretation, by emphasizing Tecumseh's anger at his brother, implies that he charged Tenskwatawa with attempting to defend the village against Americans who, in Tecumseh's words, came "to our village with the intention of destroying us." Nor was the Prophet's brother alone in charging the Americans with aggression. The Kickapoo Permoratome explained that the widespread Indian disaffection with the Americans in the spring of 1812 was due to "the army that went last fall against the Shawanoe Prophet," a victim of aggression for whom Permoratome had no harsh words. The standard depiction, in other words, displays Tecumseh as a man who, while devoting his life to his peoples' defense, rose in anger at his brother's attempt to defend his people. This is not plausible.

On the significance of the battle, there is also room for doubting the validity of the traditional story. First, as early as January 1812, the early expectation that peace would reside along the borderlands had evaporated. Doubts as to the decisiveness of Tippecanoe had, as we have seen, already emerged among its very celebrants in the United States. Second, the British and the Indians did not see the battle as decisive. Indeed, Elliot wrote only two months after the battle that "The Prophet and his people do not appear as a vanquished enemy; they re-occupy their former ground." Then in June 1812, Tecumseh referred to the battle as simply "a struggle between little children who only scratch each others faces." That description, though contrary to the standard narrative, may in fact describe the general attitude at Tippecanoe as the village repopulated with Winnebagoes, Kickapoos, and other militants. Again, Tecumseh's image removes Tenskwatawa, neither a child nor a young man, from the picture.

Finally, there is the vexing question of Tecumseh's belief in his brother's religion. While we cannot enter his soul, we do see him defend his brother against Potawatomi government chiefs at the Indian council of May 15, 1812. These Potawatomis, chastising the militants whom they had long opposed, twice refer to Tenskwatawa as a *pretended prophet.*" In his rejoinder, Tecumseh attacks the *pretended chiefs of the Potawatomis and others, who have been in the habit of selling land to the white people that did not belong to them.*" It is a cutting response, turning about the charge of fraud. As to a second charge levied by the government chiefs that the Prophet and Tecumseh had been giving evil counsel to young men of the different tribes, Tecumseh, speaking for both himself and his brother, admits only that "it is true, we have endeavored to give all our brothers *good advice;* and if they have not listened to it, we are sorry for it. We defy any living creature to say we ever advised any one, directly or indirectly, to make war on our white brothers." Tecumseh and his brother continued, in short, to speak in one voice, to act in union, and to command support. As William Wells reported when Tecumseh had only just returned from his southern journey, the two men had together pledged their lives against further encroachments by the United States: "they both say they will consent to be put to Death if Governor Harrison will pledge himself to the Indians that the United States will neither buy nor take any more land from the Indians."

Tenskwatawa's loss of power following the battle of Tippecanoe has been, at best, exaggerated and selectively extracted from contradictory evidence. We do not know that Tenskwatawa was responsible for the Indians' defeat in 1811, and we do not know that Tecumseh or other militant Indians held him responsible, nor is it clear that militants saw the battle as critical. An alternative is both plausible and supported by much of the contemporary evidence: Tenskwatawa remained an important spiritual leader of a movement that continued to animate its participants, Tecumseh included, with a quest for power, sacred and profane. Indeed, for over a year following the Battle of Tippecanoe, a year that saw the outbreak of full-scale war and the consequent rise to military fame of Tecumseh, references abound in the documents to the "Prophet's Party," the "Prophet's town," the "followers of the Prophet," the "Prophet's interest," the "Prophet's Army," and even the "Prophet's confederacy," denominations which, along with others, render Tenskwatawa as a commander of persistent, militant loyalties. Tecumseh is often cited as the true military leader, but never, before his death, is the movement given his name. The standard interpretation, however correct in assigning different attributes to each brother, is in error in driving a wedge between them. In rendering one a falling priest and the other a rising statesman, it overexposes the differences between the two, underestimating the strength, resilience, and credibility of their shared beliefs.

Diplomatic Missionary

It might be argued that Tecumseh's southern journey in the late summer and fall of 1811 demonstrates a vision grander than all others, but even here, Tecumseh traveled with others and in others' footsteps. There is tantalizing evidence that Shawnees and other northwestern Indians carried the Shawnee Prophet's message to the Creeks *before* Tecumseh's famous southward journey. As early as July 1807, when Tecumseh had not yet entered the historical record, Harrison informed his superiors that, on the basis of "information which cannot be doubted," he knew "that war belts have been passing through all the Tribes from the Gulf of Florida to the lakes. The Shawnees are the bearers of these belts and they have never been our friends." In June 1810, a Potawatomi government chief informed Harrison that the Shawnee Prophet "will now endeavor to raise the southern Indians, the Choctaws and the Creeks particularly (the Prophet's mother was a Creek)." One year later, Tecumseh fulfilled the Potawatomi's predictions.

Visits in the other direction, from the south to the north, also prepared Tecumseh's way. In 1807, while the Secretary of War, Henry Dearborn, worried about Tenskwatawa's movement, he recommended that a "banditti of Creeks" should "be driven out of" Indiana Territory. In 1810, twenty to thirty Creeks were reportedly visiting the Prophet at Tippecanoe. Dissident Cherokees also maintained their presence in the Northwest. In July 1805, a Cherokee family that maintained contact with its southeastern kin annoyed the Moravian mission to the Delawares at White River, Indiana, preparing "a heathen sacrificial feast . . . and [inviting] to it a large number." This event may have had no direct connection with the Prophet's similar activities toward the end of the year, but it does indicate an anti-Christian Cherokee presence in his very neighborhood. Five years later a Cherokee at Black Hoof's Shawnee town informed John Norton, a

Mohawk who was at the time returning from a visit with the Cherokee Nation, that "many" Cherokees "were at the Village of the Prophet." Cherokees, then, may have joined the militant followers of the Shawnee Prophet before Tecumseh's renowned tour; both Cherokees and Creeks were certainly acquainted with the Northern movement.

Tecumseh was as much one of his people as was his brother. This was true in diplomacy as in other endeavors. Scholars wishing to distinguish between the pragmatic Tecumseh and his religious brother have dwelt on the "statesman's" diplomacy. Tecumseh's journey, however, had another, inextricably related object: he sought to spread religion, to spread the call for a restoration of sacred power. To that end, he traveled with another Shawnee prophet, a religious leader who remained among the Southerners and fought with the Red Sticks in the Creek War.

None of the versions of Tecumseh's speeches to Southern Indians are very trustworthy, but the American reports of his address to the Creeks are nonetheless packed with revealing assumptions. Creeks and Americans in the Southeast describe Tecumseh as a religious extremist, a holy warrior; indeed both Benjamin Hawkins, who knew the Creeks better than any government official of his day, and Alexander Cornells, one of Hawkins's Creek allies, thought Tecumseh *was* the Shawnee Prophet. The Creeks' identification of Tecumseh with religion long survived him. In the late nineteenth century, Creeks continued to remember Tecumseh as a mystic. Similarly, among emigrant peoples from Tecumseh's homeland, miraculous tales surrounded the story of his death, and modern Shawnees have called him a "saint." So it has also been said of Pontiac. An Ojibwa Indian in the mid-nineteenth century informed Francis Parkman that Pontiac had been the member of a religious society, a memory that renders a sacred aura to his calls for war against the English.

Historians might pay more attention to such memories, for they bear a closer relation to the four nativists' understandings of power than do the popular biographies of the brothers and the professional histories of their movements. The four men did not divide themselves neatly into the charismatic and the pragmatic, for none believed that power could be gained without attention to spirits and to ceremony. As their peoples remembered them, attending to the teachings and achievements of their fellow militants, both were participants in what amounted to a half-century of struggle for Indian unity, autonomy, and sacred power.

Readings for Gregory E. Dowd:

Dowd expands on his ideas in *A Spirited Resistance: The North American Indian Struggle for Unity, 1745–1815* (Baltimore: The Johns Hopkins University Press, 1992). More information on this topic may be found in R. David Edmunds, *The Shawnee Prophet* (Lincoln: University of Nebraska Press, 1983) and Joseph B. Herring, *Kenekuk, the Kickapoo Prophet* (Lawrence: University Press of Kansas, 1988). An older but still excellent treatment of Indian revitalization movements is Anthony F. C. Wallace, *The Death and Rebirth of the Seneca* (New York: Vintage Books, 1969).

8

BACKDROP FOR DISASTER: CAUSES OF THE ARIKARA WAR OF 1823

ROGER L. NICHOLS

Issues related to interracial trade and warfare continue to attract scholars' attention. The Arikara War of 1823 provides a good example of how intratribal as well as intertribal factors might combine to bring violence as often as Indian-white difficulties did. A culmination of many factors, the process leading to military confrontation proved more important than the eventual fighting. In this case the Missouri River fur trade had brought the tribe into close social and economic contact with the whites for some decades. Despite the disruption of village economic patterns, the introduction of epidemic disease, and considerable ecological devastation, these Indians remained at peace with the white traders. In fact, when war did occur in 1823, it came about at least as much because of factors within the tribe and disputes with other tribes as because of basic disputes with traders. Competition with the nearby Sioux and Mandan peoples, as well as misunderstandings of American diplomatic activities in the region, set the stage for trouble. When the fighting began, it caught both traders and government officials by surprise. Neither group understood the complexities of the situation nor had any idea of why the Arikara had attacked. As this narrative indicates, the Indians acted as they did because they understood their own economic decline as well as the personal motivations of village leaders as they competed with each other. The tribal people had understandable and rational reasons for their attack on the traders. Contemporary whites characterized the tribe as treacherous and undependable only because they failed to understand the local situation.

Roger L. Nichols is a professor of history at the University of Arizona and the editor of this book.

Source: Roger L. Nichols, "Backdrop for Disaster: Causes of the Arikara War of 1823," *South Dakota History,* 14 (Summer 1984), pp. 93–113. Reprinted by permission from *South Dakota History.* © 1984 by the South Dakota State Historical Society.

99

Rays from the setting sun illuminated the Saint Louis waterfront as the keelboats *Rocky Mountains* and *Yellowstone Packet* pulled away from shore and headed north into the Mississippi River current. With sails in place, flags flying, and hired musicians serenading spectators who lined the riverbank, William Ashley's party of seventy mountain men began its journey on 10 March 1823, heading north and west toward the Rocky Mountains. Weeks passed uneventfully as they toiled up the Missouri River. By late May they were traveling through present-day South Dakota, where events shattered their comfortable routine. Stopping briefly to trade for horses, the whites provoked a fight with the unpredictable Arikara Indians, who were then occupying two villages along the Missouri near the mouth of the Grand River. This incident, labeled "the worst disaster in western fur trade history," coupled with the retaliatory expedition against the villagers led by Col. Henry Leavenworth later that summer, came to be known as the Arikara War.

The conflict paralleled many early nineteenth century Indian wars in which, for what at the time seemed unclear reasons, Indian Americans attacked intruding white Americans. With surprise on their side, the Indians won the initial skirmish, driving the trappers from the scene. Once the frontiersmen recovered from their shock, however, an overwhelming force invaded the Indian country to punish the tribesmen. This counterattack succeeded. The Arikara fled, leaving the enraged whites to burn their abandoned villages.

Students of South Dakota history undoubtedly recall these events well. Nevertheless, a few details of the incident may clarify the situation and help to explain how and why this war occurred. Hurrying up the Missouri toward the Rockies, Ashley had not expected to visit the Arikara. In fact, reports of their hostility that spring convinced him that they should be avoided. Just south of the Indian towns, however, he learned that his partners in the mountains needed another forty or fifty horses for use that coming season. Thus, despite misgivings and with little advance thought, Ashley decided to halt. He hoped that the ninety-man party of trappers and boatman was large enough to persuade the Indians to trade rather than fight. After a short parley on 30 May the chiefs agreed to trade the next morning. On 31 May the trappers and Indians began their barter, but with limited success. Far from other sources of horses, the Arikara demanded top prices for their animals. Because Ashley had not anticipated this trading session, his stock of trade items may not have been adequate. When the trading ended that day, the whites had only nineteen horses and the Indians had balked at the amount and quality of the whites' trade goods.

Continuing signs of Indian discontent convinced Ashley that he should move quickly upriver with the few horses he had obtained. Unfortunately, bad weather made it impossible to travel the next morning. The whites were forced to remain, some guarding the animals on the beach while the rest huddled aboard the boats waiting for the storm to pass. At dawn the following day, 2 June, the Arikara warriors attacked. In a few minutes their musket balls and arrows destroyed the horses and killed or wounded most of the trappers on the beach. Caught by surprise and defeated soundly, Ashley's remaining men scrambled aboard the keelboats and fled downstream.

News of the Arikara attack reached Fort Atkinson, just north of present-day Omaha, Nebraska, and set into motion a combination rescue effort and retaliatory expedition. Col. Henry Leavenworth rushed six companies of United States infantrymen upriver, while Saint Louis trader Joshua Pilcher joined the troops with a force of nearly sixty trappers and fur company employees. Along the way, this so-called Missouri Legion recruited a force of nearly 750 Sioux allies. By early August 1823 the mixed group of soldiers, trappers, and Indians arrived at the Arikara villages, where the mounted Sioux auxiliaries swept ahead of the foot soldiers and launched a preliminary attack on their long-time foes. A stream of Arikara warriors poured out of the villages to meet them. After spirited fighting, the Arikara saw the regular troops moving up and fled back behind the village palisades.

The next morning, 10 August, Colonel Leavenworth ordered his artillery to shell the villages, but, through ineptitude or carelessness, the soldiers sent most of their shots whistling harmlessly overhead. Seeing this, the colonel ordered an infantry attack on the upper village. Although the soldiers fought bravely, the Indian defenders refused to budge. At that point, fearing both a possible heavy loss of his men and perhaps even the total destruction of the Indian towns, Leavenworth chose to negotiate an end to the fighting. Late that afternoon the whites persuaded several Arikara chiefs to join them for peace talks. Although divided and bickering acrimoniously among themselves, the invading forces concluded a treaty with the Indians the next day, but the wary Arikara abandoned their villages during the following night. On 15 August Leavenworth led his force back down the river to Fort Atkinson. No sooner had the soldiers left than several fur company employees burned the villages to the ground. As a result of this campaign, the Arikara scattered. Many of them moved away from their traditional home for more than a decade.

There is little dispute about these events. Yet both Indian and white motivations remain murky. To reach an understanding of the forces that led to the Arikara War, several factors have to be considered. The nature of Arikara village life and society provides one clue to the reasons behind the Arikaras' actions. The villagers' pattern of dealing with other American Indian groups in the Missouri Valley likewise offers some insights into their behavior toward all outsiders. Obviously these Indians had developed a bitter hostility toward the white traders, or they would not have risked an all-out war with them, and the growth of antiwhite attitudes needs to be examined. At the same time, white ideas about the Arikara and the traders' responses to the villagers provide the other necessary threads in the pattern. When taken together, the Indian and white motivations offer the basis for a clear perception of the conflict. Historical accounts of Indian wars often focus chiefly on white actions. In this circumstance, however, the Indian motivations, attitudes, and actions proved more important than those of the whites in shaping the course of events. The following discussion, therefore, focuses more attention on Arikara actions than on those of Ashley or the Leavenworth Expedition.

Among the developments that propelled the Arikara toward their 1823 encounter with Ashley's trappers were several long-term trends within the villagers' society that played increasingly important roles. A Caddoan people related to, or perhaps part of, the Skidi Pawnee, the Arikara lived in nearly permanent towns on the banks of the Missouri River throughout most of the eighteenth century. There, between the White and Cheyenne rivers in central South Dakota, they fished in the Missouri, farmed its banks and bottom lands, hunted on the nearby plains to the west, and participated in the existing Indian trade network. The most important long-term trends in their society resulted from their growing role as traders. In that capacity they increased their corn production and exchanged their surplus harvest with the nearby hunting peoples for meat, hides, and leather goods. This activity tied the villagers into trade patterns that connected aboriginal peoples from central Canada to the borders of Mexico, and from the Rocky Mountains to the Mississippi River and beyond.

In the mid-eighteenth century, or earlier, the Arikara traders added European goods to their traditional wares. People from the southern plains offered horses to the Missouri Valley dwellers, while manufactured goods and guns filtered south and west from Canada. Before long, European traders followed their goods into the Indians towns, forever altering aboriginal life. As the century drew to a close, the Arikara economy had undergone fundamental changes. Their earlier trade had been a matter of choice—an exchange of surplus goods with other tribal people. Now they shaped their economy to reflect their dependence on trading. True, they still hunted, but in most years their catch did not provide enough meat or hides to meet their needs. Nor did exchange of their surplus corn by itself supply these necessities any longer. Increasingly their aboriginal customers demanded guns, ammunition, and manufactured goods in addition to foodstuffs. By accident or design the villagers became ever more dependent on their white trading partners for survival.

Within most Indian communities "trade was embedded in a network of social relations" so that few individuals gained new status because of it. Direct trade with Europeans, however, brought opportunities for increased wealth within many tribes and bands. Before the fur-and-hide trade, clan chiefs and other village leaders maintained a superior status because of their social functions. Direct trading with whites meant that individual hunters might acquire more wealth than was possible under the aboriginal system. Chiefs might still take a share of this new wealth, but a growing individual participation in the trade with the whites produced new economic pressures within many Indian societies. There is little direct evidence that this pattern was of major importance in the Arikara villages, but the lack of evidence may reflect the inability of white traders, who provided the early accounts of the Arikara, to perceive their own impact on the villagers. This pattern seems to have occurred repeatedly among other aboriginal groups, and there is little reason to dismiss it as a factor among the Arikara.

While such changes reshaped the villagers' economic life, even more disruptive events rent the fabric of Arikara society. Soon after the first meetings between European traders and the Arikara, a series of major smallpox epidemics swept across the Missouri Valley and out onto the northern plains. Although the chronology and severity of these epidemics remain shrouded in antiquity, the combined results unquestionably proved disastrous. Modern scholars and eighteenth-century observers agree that the epidemics destroyed nearly three quarters of all the Indians in South Dakota. The disease struck the Arikara and other sedentary agricultural tribes a devastating blow, one from which they never fully recovered. As the pox swept through their villages, it killed or terrorized most of the inhabitants. Village, band, clan, and even family organization crumbled as aboriginal healers failed to halt the plagues. The result was catastrophic, and by 1795 most of the Indians had died. In that year a resident trader reported: "In ancient times the Ricara nation was very large; it counted thirty-two populous villages, now depopulated and almost entirely destroyed by the smallpox. . . . A few families only, from each of the villages, escaped; these united and formed the two villages now here." When Lewis and Clark visited the tribe in late 1804, they learned that the existing three villages, located near the mouth of the Grand River, included the survivors of some eighteen earlier towns along both sides of the Missouri.

While the smallpox epidemics killed most of the Indians and disrupted or destroyed their social cohesion, the consolidation of survivors in two or three villages also brought unforeseen and continuing problems. Individuals from at least ten distinct bands, each with different leaders and varying customs, as well as major linguistic differences, huddled together in their new settlements. A higher percentage of band leaders and chiefs survived than did the population as a whole. Pierre-Antoine Tabeau reported that there were more than forty-two chiefs living in the three villages in 1804. Each of the many chiefs, Tabeau noted, "wishes at least to have followers and tolerates no form of dependence" on others. This situation brought nearly incessant wrangling among contending leaders as their factions disrupted village life with "internal and destructive quarrels."

Not only did these pressures on the Arikara affect the nature and operation of their society, but they also had direct impact on their dealings with other Indians. In particular, their divided and quarreling leadership caused problems and made other situations worse than they needed to be, especially in relationships with the neighboring Mandan, Hidatsa, and Sioux. The Sioux, largest of these Indian groups, threatened all three agricultural village tribes. Although the Mandan, Hidatsa, and Arikara shared a similar function as middlemen in the area trade network and suffered alike at the hands of Sioux raiders, they quarreled and even fought with one another rather than presenting a united front in response to Sioux aggression. Not only did the Sioux "pursue a system of preventing trade to all [Indian] nations up the Upper Missouri," but they also raided the villagers' crops and horse herds repeatedly.

In the Arikara's case, the lack of clear leadership in their fractured society made it difficult for them to pursue any consistent policy toward their neighbors. In fact, it created an instability that caused other groups to see the tribe as dangerous and unpredictable. The Frenchman Tabeau complained that the splintered nature of Arikara village leadership led to endless conflicts as the chiefs and their followers robbed each other and threatened to fight others in their own communities. What was worse, in his opinion, was the Arikara's continuing inability to settle disputes with the Mandan and Hidatsa so that the three agricultural tribes could unite to defend themselves against the Sioux. Tabeau felt certain that Arikara leaders realized that it was imperative to ally themselves with the Mandans, yet they could not do so. He noted that all their efforts to make peace with that tribe failed because of "individual jealousy" within the villages. Divided leadership or a lack of unity, then, destroyed "all the plans which tend to bring about peace" with their natural allies.

The situation also made their response to direct Sioux aggression ineffective much of the time. All the roots of the conflict between these two tribes are not clear, but certainly the Sioux looked down upon their sedentary neighbors, treating the Arikara as inferior beings who farmed and did other such women's chores for their benefit. Sioux arrogance grew steadily more intolerable, and by the early nineteenth century they acted as if they were the masters rather than the equals of their trading partners. When they came to trade, Sioux visitors did little bargaining over prices. Instead, they took what they wanted and gave the villagers whatever amount of skins and meat they deemed adequate. To amuse themselves and show disdain for the Arikara, they often pillaged and trampled gardens, beat and insulted Arikara women, and ran off the villagers' horses. Outnumbered, divided, and often leaderless, the Arikara seemed unable to respond effectively to Sioux assaults.

Customs related to wealth and status among the upper Missouri Valley tribes also kept their intertribal relationships in turmoil. For young men, status within the village resulted from acts of bravery. Usually such acts included either stealing horses or fighting men from the surrounding tribes. Once a raid took place, the victims often retaliated, and a cycle of violent competition and warfare continued for generations. The warriors had strong social and economic motivations for their actions, and with village controls weakened among the Arikara, there were few restraints to curb raids against erstwhile allies or friends. Not only did these attacks and counterattacks prevent any lasting peace, but practices related to success and failure on these expeditions also worsened the situation. If raiders returned home without success, the warriors would "'cast their robes' . . . and vow to kill the first person they meet, provided he be not of their own nation." This custom explains many incidents that otherwise make little sense—particularly when the Indians visited their wrath on white traders passing through their country. Thus, the situation among the tribes of the upper Missouri region by 1800 was one of uneasy peace and bitter economic rivalry, punctuated by recurring raids and warfare.

As long as the Missouri Valley Indians dealt only with each other, matters remained relatively simple, but once white traders and trappers entered the scene, the situation became more complicated. Prior to the 1790s the Arikara had encountered few whites, but the next several decades brought increasing numbers of Euro-Americans into the region. The presence of white traders aggravated existing stresses and violence among the Indians by accident, and perhaps by design as well. For example, the incident in which Teton Sioux threatened Lewis and Clark during the summer of 1804 resulted directly from the efforts of those Indians to close the upper Missouri to white traders. The Sioux assumed that the explorers carried commercial goods and that the village people would get some of those trade items. In a series of stalling actions and near skirmishes they tried to prevent the whites from traveling further upstream. At the same time, the Arikara, Mandan, and Hidatsa lived in fear that their downriver rivals would restrict their sources of manufactured goods. Therefore, the village tribes did whatever they could to keep their trade channels open and reacted violently when they thought the whites had cooperated with their enemies or had pursued policies that might hurt them. These intertribal rivalries became so bitter that often the warriors' treatment of whites depended upon whether the traders had dealt with their Indian competitors.

Examples of this attitude abound. After Lewis and Clark ran the Sioux blockade of the Missouri in 1804, the Arikara welcomed them enthusiastically. The explorers spent five pleasant days among the villagers and reported that these people "were all friendly & Glad to See us." Nevertheless, the explorers' actions while they were with the Arikara triggered a major incident a few years later. Following their orders, Lewis and Clark persuaded Arikara leader Ankedoucharo to join a delegation of Missouri Valley chiefs going east to Washington, D.C. The Indians reached the capital in 1806, and while there, Ankedoucharo and several other chiefs died. It took until the spring of 1807 for the government to inform the uneasy villagers of their chief's death. The Indians had no way of knowing what had happened and suspected the whites of having killed their chief.

Angered by what they saw as American treachery, the villagers turned violently against the whites along the Missouri in 1807. Saint Louis trader Manuel Lisa encountered their hostility first in late summer, when several hundred armed warriors confronted his party near the villages. The Indians fired a few shots over the boats and ordered the whites ashore, but Lisa relieved the tension and escaped without a fight. At this point the United States government blundered onto the scene in its efforts to return the Mandan chief Shahaka to his North Dakota home. Shahaka had been among the group of Indian leaders taken east a year earlier, and in May 1807 Ensign Nathaniel Pryor started up the Missouri to escort him home. After an uneventful trip, the whites reached the Arikara towns in September, completely unaware of the Indians' anger or the earlier incident with Lisa's party. Pryor found the Arikara sullen and angry. At the upper village warriors attacked, and after a brief exchange of shots the unprepared whites retreated downstream. The government officials who dispatched the escort assumed that the Arikara had received news of their own chief's death peacefully, and they ignored or failed to realize that the Arikara and Mandan were at war with each other that summer.

It is not surprising that the Arikara met the whites with hostility. The government had only recently notified them of Ankedoucharo's death, and the Americans now arrived escorting an enemy chief past their towns. The Arikara's hostile response gave them an early reputation as a dangerous and unpredictable people. They were, after all, the only regional tribe to fight with United States troops up to that time. Their attack persuaded federal officials that they needed a strong force when they next tried to return the Mandan chief to his home village. Two years later an escort of militiamen under the command of Pierre Chouteau awed the Arikara enough that they apologized and promised to remain at peace.

Although no other major incidents occurred during the next few years, little happened to change American ideas about the Arikara either. Most traders treated them gingerly, remembering the attack on Pryor and his men. In 1811, however, the villagers appeared as protectors, not attackers, of two large expeditions of whites traveling through their country. That summer groups of traders led by Wilson P. Hunt and Manuel Lisa raced each other up the Missouri, both hoping to avoid the hostile Sioux. Neither succeeded, but both got past them without bloodshed. Less than a week later the traders met a combined Arikara, Mandan, and Hidatsa war party of nearly three hundred men. At first the whites feared that the Indians would attack, but to their relief the warriors escorted them north toward their home villages.

Once again the bitter rivalries between the agricultural trading villagers and the Sioux hunters explain much of this apparent dramatic shift in behavior. For a change the Arikara and their northern neighbors had put aside their differences to form a defensive alliance against the Sioux. They welcomed the traders because the whites carried a crucial supply of manufactured trade items, especially weapons and ammunition. The Indians seemed apprehensive that without the safety their escort offered, the traders might be frightened enough to turn back downstream, as the Crooks and McClellan party had done just two years earlier after an encounter with the Sioux. Arikara actions in this incident reflected their determination to protect their economic status through continued trade with the whites. Their actions may also have indicated a growing Indian awareness of their dependence on the whites for the manufactured goods that had come to play such an important role in the upper Missouri trade patterns.

Bitter rivalries and divisions among the chiefs, however, continued to disrupt the Arikara towns and often kept visiting whites uncertain of how to approach these people. In August 1812, for example, Manuel Lisa again had trouble with them. A few days before

Lisa and his men reached the Arikara settlements, Le Gauche, "The Left-Handed," a hereditary chief, met them near the river. He visited for a short time—just long enough for Lisa to give him a few small gifts—before returning to the village. Lisa's presents to Le Gauche infuriated rival chiefs, and when the whites arrived at the village, they encountered silence and obvious anger. Lisa demanded to know what had happened. Once the disgruntled chiefs explained, he offered enough presents to soothe their hurt feelings. While this incident illustrated the continuing importance of internal village divisions in shaping Indian responses to outsiders, the Arikara's lack of violence in this case showed something else. By this time they seem to have realized that because they had few furs or hides to offer the whites, they had to remain on their best behavior in order to retain a local trading post. Without such a post, they had no reliable source of white goods.

During the war of 1812 and the confused years after that conflict, few Americans penetrated the upper Missouri region. In fact, before 1818 there seems to have been little regular commerce between the villagers and the Saint Louis merchants. From 1820 on, relations between Americans and the Arikara deteriorated steadily. Time and lack of documentation shroud many of the circumstances, and Indian motivations during that era must remain uncertain. Nevertheless, some patterns continued. By 1820 the Saint Louis traders had moved north to the Big Bend of the Missouri, where they had established a trading post among the Sioux, about 150 miles south of the Arikara towns. From that location the whites provided arms, munitions, and other trade items to the hunting bands of the region. The Arikara responded to the new trading activity with violence. In 1820 a large war party attacked and robbed two trading posts along the Missouri. Here one must assume that the villagers struck the whites out of frustration and jealousy. They had no dependable source of manufactured goods, while their Sioux enemies had several.

By the early 1820s even the most obtuse company trader should have been able to discern the relationships among the Arikara, their Indian competitors, and the white traders. The villagers' actions toward the Americans varied from vicious attacks, through strained relations, to enthusiastic friendship, depending on the internal social pressures on the tribe and the success or failure of their dealings with the Sioux. Instead of acknowledging these pressures, the traders seemed both uninformed and uncaring. Either attitude seems strange because their livelihood and their lives depended upon their ability to understand the situation clearly. Without any firm basis for their picture of the Arikara, most traders seem to have accepted the negative descriptions current about these Indians. Certainly, intermittent violence by the tribesmen colored the whites' perceptions of them, but it seems likely that the negative reports of their customs and appearance fed the traders' fear and loathing of these people. Revulsion at their practice of incest and high incidence of venereal disease, grumbling about the expense of having to maintain an unprofitable trading post in their vicinity, and the confusion and violence resulting from their shattered village society all helped to persuade the traders that the Arikara were indeed troublesome and dangerous. Before the 1823 incidents they had acquired a reputation as the most unpredictable and hostile tribe along the Missouri.

It is only with this understanding of the Indian situation and actions that the Arikara War of 1823 can be understood. The local, or short-range, causes of that conflict began in 1822, when William Ashley and Andrew Henry led a group of white trappers into the northern Rocky Mountains. There they went into direct competition with both Indian trappers and traders, a move guaranteed to disrupt earlier patterns of

Indian trade. The logical result would be that white traders and trappers would supplant Indians in those activities. In the fall of 1822, however, that possibility remained in the future. Ashley's expedition stopped at the Arikara villages in early September to trade for horses. The chiefs welcomed the white men and probably made their usual request—that a trading post be established for them. Ashley, of course, had little interest in beginning an unprofitable trading post, for he planned to avoid stationary trading facilities and, by bringing his men directly to the mountains, to bypass Indian hunters altogether. Nevertheless, as part of his effort to tell the Missouri Valley tribes whatever he "thought most likely to secure and continue their friendship," he promised to supply the goods they wanted from Saint Louis the next spring. Ashley failed to recognize the significance of his promise to the village leaders and would pay dearly for breaking it. When no trader moved into their vicinity the next year, the Arikara must have realized that the whites had not meant what they said.

Had that been the only issue between the village chiefs and Ashley, the 1823 violence might have been avoided. Other problems existed, however. A major cause for Arikara hostility in the summer of 1823 grew out of an incident with some Missouri Fur Company employees. In March of that year a group of Arikara hunters had met some of these traders riding near Cedar Fort, a trading post established for the Sioux near the Big Bend of the Missouri. The traders were carrying hides to the nearby post, and the Arikara demanded that the whites surrender the goods to them, but the traders refused. Outraged, the Arikara robbed and beat them. Their anger grew out of seeing the traders helping the hated Sioux rather than from any general antiwhite feelings. The assault may also have resulted from Arikara frustration over their continuing inability to persuade the whites to keep a permanent trading post open near their villages, an ongoing source of friction between the Arikara and Saint Louis merchants.

Only a few days after the fight with the traders another and larger party of Arikara unsuccessfully attacked Cedar Fort, the Missouri Fur Company post. This time two of the Indians died and several others were wounded. One of those killed was the son of Grey Eyes, a prominent Arikara chief. Reports of the incident indicated that the Indians' failure to defeat the traders and plunder their goods had infuriated and humiliated the warriors and that they were not likely to be discriminating in their vengeance against whites. Unfortunately for Ashley's men, they ventured up the Missouri just in time to bear the brunt of this anger and frustration.

Ashley's actions toward the villagers almost certainly played some part in bringing about the Indian attack as well. As mentioned earlier, he had, in 1822, pledged to give the Arikara what they wanted most from the whites—undoubtedly a resident trader and thus a dependable supply of manufactured goods. Clearly he had little intention of keeping his promise. At the same time, he had tried to assure them that his own trappers posed no competitive threat to their efforts as Indian traders. The mountain men would gather and transport the furs themselves, but because the villagers usually traded buffalo hides rather than the pelts of smaller, fur-bearing animals, he hoped that no problems would result.

Before the ninety trappers and boatmen reached the Arikara towns in late May of 1823, Ashley had learned of the Indians' attack on Cedar Fort, and he reported taking "all the precaution in my power for some days before I reached their towns." Once there he anchored the keelboats in midstream and rowed ashore in a small skiff to meet Indian leaders and get their assurances of peaceful trade. Dissension between the two villages and among Arikara leaders was apparent as the village leaders came down to the shore, for they agreed to talk only "after a long consultation among themselves." The trader invited two chiefs, Little Soldier and Grey Eyes, aboard his skiff, and, to his surprise, the latter agreed. Grey Eyes was reputed to be the most antiwhite of the Arikara leaders and had also lost a son in the abortive raid at Cedar Fort that spring. His cooperation calmed Ashley's fears somewhat. The Indian leaders returned to their villages, and later that evening Grey Eyes reported that the Indians would be ready to open trade in the morning.

On 31 May the barter began, with the Indians bringing horses and buffalo robes to exchange for guns, ammunition, and other trade items. Business moved slowly, and when the whites had nineteen of the forty horses they needed, a dispute arose. Some Indians objected to the number and kinds of guns and the limited amount of powder the whites displayed. It is unclear whether they thought that Ashley's party offered too little for the horses or whether the Arikara merely wanted more guns and powder to use in their own trade with the plains tribes. In either case barter ceased for the day, and Ashley decided to take the animals they had already acquired and leave the next morning. Bad weather prevented this plan, and the mountain men had little choice but to remain. They could not move upstream against the strong wind and current, and to retreat downstream would only postpone the need to pass the villages. While they waited for the storm to pass, Chief Bear of the upper village invited Ashley to his lodge. The Indians assured the visitors of their friendship, and Little Soldier even warned of a possible attack by other elements in the tribe. His warning proved to be correct. At sunrise on 2 June a hail of arrows and musket balls drove the trappers back downstream.

Clearly, divided leadership and conflicting desires within the Indian towns contributed to the attack. By this time no formal Arikara tribe existed. The villages consisted of survivors of many earlier communities, and the Indians had never managed to restructure their society so that it functioned in an integrated manner. Ashley and his party noted confusion among the Indians over whether to trade or fight, but the traders seemed ignorant of how splintered Arikara society had become or how much danger this represented for them. The chiefs Grey Eyes, Little Soldier, and Bear all reacted differently to the whites' presence. The first was friendly and then became hostile. The second was aloof but later warned of danger, while the third remained friendly throughout the visit. The attitude of each town toward its guests was also different. The murder of one of Ashley's men took place in the lower village, and it was from there that Grey Eyes and his followers launched their dawn attack on the trappers. In the upper village, however, Bear and his followers vehemently denied responsibility for the fighting. Later that summer Colonel Leavenworth reported that "the people of the upper village would not give up their horses to pay for the mischief which the Chief Grey Eyes of the lower village had done."

The Leavenworth Expedition later in the summer failed to defeat the Arikara, but it ushered in a period of difficulty for the Indians. Once the invading white army left, the bands separated. Some fled north up the Missouri. A few people remained near the now burned villages and gradually resettled there. Others moved south and west into Nebraska to live with the Pawnee for a time. One band even traveled to eastern Wyoming. In 1837, after more than a decade, the bands reunited on the Missouri, just in time to be further decimated by the smallpox epidemic that swept up the valley that summer. Thus, these people, who had survived continuing warfare with Indian neighbors and sporadic fighting with the whites, succumbed instead to disease.

Many accounts of their role in the early history of South Dakota and the fur trade stress the Arikara's treacherous nature and the danger they posed to peacefully inclined traders. Certainly they killed and robbed enough white trappers and traders along the Missouri and on the nearby plains during the first third of the nineteenth century to deserve the negative reputation they acquired among whites. Yet, except for the two famous attacks—the first against Ensign Pryor in 1807 and the second against Ashley's men in 1823—their record appears to be little more violent or unpredictable than that of the Pawnee, Sioux, or Blackfeet during the same decades. In the Arikara's case, a bitter newspaper war of charges and countercharges between Henry Leavenworth and Joshua Pilcher, growing out of the 1823 campaign, helped spread the denunciations of the tribe. In the 1830s travelers, artists, and traders continued to add to the list of negative images fastened on the Arikara.

When all is said and done, however, the Arikara appear to have had some clear motivations for their actions. They remained friendly and at peace as long as the whites traded fairly and until they finally perceived the fur companies to be a major threat to their own economic well-being. They responded violently when whites aided their enemies, either their sometimes competitors the Mandans or their bitter foes the Sioux. The villagers assumed that it hurt them when the whites traded with their enemies. It is not surprising, then, that white traders were often in danger of retaliation. The Arikara strove repeatedly to keep a resident trader at or near their villages. When whites promised to locate a trader or post in their vicinity and then failed to do so, the Indians interpreted this failure as an unfriendly act and sometimes responded violently. It is also possible, of course, that certain Arikara chiefs used the divisions and confusions within their society for selfish purposes, or even that evil men fomented trouble for narrow local reasons. Whether this happened or not, the Arikara War of 1823 was not unique. It resembled other Indian wars and incidents in many ways. It was unplanned, unnecessary, and a disaster for the tribal people. There were no heroes, stirring slogans, or major accomplishments. Instead, the survivors of a once powerful tribe struck out at their perceived enemies and suffered adverse consequences. Their actions, whether we of the modern world believe them to be rational or not, made at least some sense to them at the time. In the long run, the white man's diseases, not his guns, resolved the issue. The survivors of the smallpox epidemic of 1837 eventually settled among the Mandan and Hidatsa in North Dakota, where most of their descendants remain today.

Readings for Roger L. Nichols:

The Arikara story is told best in Roy W. Meyer, *The Village Indians of the Upper Missouri* (Lincoln: University of Nebraska Press, 1977). For the role of fur traders in this incident see Richard M. Clokey, *William H. Ashley: Enterprise and Politics in the Trans-Mississippi West* (Norman: University of Oklahoma Press, 1980). Those interested in reading the letters and reports of the participants should check Doane Robinson, ed., "Official Correspondence of the Leavenworth Expedition of 1823 into South Dakota for the Conquest of the Ree Indians," *South Dakota Historical Collections,* Vol. 1 (August, 1902). Another brief discussion of this campaign is in Roger L. Nichols, *General Henry Atkinson: A Western Military Career* (Norman: University of Oklahoma Press, 1965).

9

CHEROKEE WOMEN AND THE TRAIL OF TEARS

THEDA PERDUE

Power relationships within traditional tribal societies differed widely from those accepted by Anglo-Americans during the eighteenth and nineteenth centuries. This selection shows that Cherokee culture was both matrilineal and matrilocal—that is, property, inheritance, and place of homesite all depended on the female side of the family. Under those circumstances, Perdue claims Cherokee women enjoyed substantial personal freedom as well as exercising some economic and political power. She posits a sort of aboriginal golden age in which women had considerable power because they held the land, raised the crops, and controlled all or most of the family food supply. Although some feminist scholars disagree with the notion of gender equality in the dim past, this reading tends to support that view. Perdue sees the situation as changing because of increasing contacts with the English and Americans on the frontier. She traces a gradual shift in which tribal people came to accept or have forced upon them Anglo-American ideas about gender divisions of labor and power. She sees this as a gradual decline of the authority of Indian women, in particular by the early nineteenth century, and gives examples of how the process worked. In her view the government officials, teachers, and missionaries did the most to upset traditional Cherokee sex roles, and by the removal era of the 1830s tribal leaders had adopted nontribal ideas about the role of women in their society. The removal experience brought the process to a close because frustration and family violence ended any significant authority the women may have exercised previously.

Theda Perdue is a professor of history at the University of Kentucky.

The Treaty of New Echota by which the Cherokee Nation relinquished its territory in the Southeast was signed by men. Women were present at the rump council that negotiated the treaty, but they did not participate in the proceedings. They may have met in their

Source: Theda Perdue, "Cherokee Women and the Trail of Tears," *Journal of Women's History*, 1 (1989), pp. 14–30. Reprinted with permission from the *Journal of Women's History.*

own council—precedents for women's councils exist—but if they did, no record remains. Instead, they probably cooked meals and cared for children while their husbands discussed treaty terms with the United States commissioner. The failure of women to join in the negotiation and signing of the Treaty of New Echota does not necessarily mean that women were not interested in the disposition of tribal land, but it does indicate that the role of women had changed dramatically in the preceding century.

Traditionally women had a voice in Cherokee government. They spoke freely in council, and the War Woman (or Beloved Woman) decided the fate of captives. As late as 1787 a Cherokee woman wrote Benjamin Franklin that she had delivered an address to her people urging them to maintain peace with the new American nation. She had filled the peace pipe for the warriors, and she enclosed some of the same tobacco for the United States Congress in order to unite symbolically her people and his in peace. She continued:

> I am in hopes that if you Rightly consider that woman is the mother of All—and the Woman does not pull Children out of Trees or Stumps nor out of old Logs, but out of their Bodies, so that they ought to mind what a woman says.

The political influence of women, therefore, rested at least in part on their maternal biological role in procreation and their maternal role in Cherokee society, which assumed particular importance in the Cherokee's matrilineal kinship system. In this way of reckoning kin, children belonged to the clan of their mother and their only relatives were those who could be traced through her.

The Cherokees were not only matrilineal, they also were matrilocal. That is, a man lived with his wife in a house which belonged to her, or perhaps more accurately, to her family. According to the naturalist William Bartram, "Marriage gives no right to the husband over the property of his wife; and when they part she keeps the children and property belonging to them." The "property" that women kept included agricultural produce—corn, squash, beans, sunflowers, and pumpkins—stored in the household's crib. Produce belonged to women because they were the principal farmers. This economic role was ritualized at the Green Corn Ceremony every summer when an old woman presented the new corn crop. Furthermore, eighteenth-century travelers and traders normally purchased corn from women instead of men, and in the 1750s the garrison at Fort Loudoun, in present-day eastern Tennessee, actually employed a female purchasing agent to procure corn. Similarly, the fields belonged to the women who tended them, or rather to the women's lineages. Bartram observed that their fields are divided by proper marks and their harvest is gathered separately." While the Cherokees technically held land in common and anyone could use unoccupied land, improved fields belonged to specific matrilineal households.

Perhaps this explains why women signed early deeds conveying land titles to the Proprietors of Carolina. Agents who made these transactions offered little explanation for the signatures of women on these documents. By the early twentieth century a historian speculated that they represented a "renunciation of dower," but it may have been that the women were simply parting with what was recognized as theirs, or they may have been representing their lineages in the negotiations.

As late as 1785 women still played some role in the negotiation of land transactions. Nancy Ward, the Beloved Woman of Chota, spoke to the treaty conference held at

Hopewell, South Carolina to clarify and extend land cessions stemming from Cherokee support of the British in the American Revolution. She addressed the assembly as the "mother of warriors" and promoted a peaceful resolution to land disputes between the Cherokees and the United States. Under the terms of the Treaty of Hopewell, the Cherokees ceded large tracts of land south of the Cumberland River in Tennessee and Kentucky and west of the Blue Ridge Mountains in North Carolina. Nancy Ward and the other Cherokee delegates to the conference agreed to the cession not because they believed it to be just but because the United States dictated the terms of the treaty.

The conference at Hopewell was the last treaty negotiation in which women played an official role, and Nancy Ward's participation in that conference was somewhat anachronistic. In the eighteenth century the English as well as other Europeans had dealt politically and commercially with men since men were the hunters and warriors in Cherokee society and Europeans were interested primarily in military alliances and deerskins. As relations with the English grew increasingly important to tribal welfare, women became less significant in the Cherokee economy and government. Conditions in the Cherokee Nation following the American Revolution accelerated the trend. In their defeat the Cherokees had to cope with the destruction of villages, fields, corncribs, and orchards which had occurred during the war and the cession of hunting grounds which accompanied the peace. In desperation they turned to the United States government, which proposed to convert the Cherokees into replicas of white pioneer farmers in the anticipation that they would then cede additional territory (presumably hunting grounds they no longer needed). While the government's so-called "civilization" program brought some economic relief, it also helped produce a transformation of gender roles and social organization. The society envisioned for the Cherokees, one which government agents and Protestant missionaries zealously tried to implement, was one in which a man farmed and headed a household composed only of his wife and children. The men who gained power in eighteenth-century Cherokee society—hunters, warriors, and descendants of traders—took immediate advantage of this program in order to maintain their status in the face of a declining deerskin trade and pacification and then diverted their energy, ambition, and aggression into economic channels. As agriculture became more commercially viable, these men began to farm or to acquire African slaves to cultivate their fields for them. They also began to dominate Cherokee society, and by example and legislation they altered fundamental relationships.

In 1808 a Council of headmen (there is no evidence of women participating) from Cherokee towns established a national police force to safeguard a person's holdings during life and "to give protection to children as heirs to their father's property, and to the widow's share," thereby changing inheritance patterns and officially recognizing the patriarchal family as the norm. Two years later a council representing all seven matrilineal clans, but once again apparently including no women, abolished the practice of blood vengeance. This action ended one of the major functions of clans and shifted the responsibility for punishing wrongdoers to the national police force and tribal courts. Matrilineal kinship clearly did not have a place in the new Cherokee order.

We have no record of women objecting to such legislation. In fact, we know very little about most Cherokee women because written documents reflect the attitudes and concerns of a male Indian elite or of government agents and missionaries. The only women about whom we know very much are those who conformed to expectations.

Nancy Ward, the Beloved Woman who favored peace with the United States, appears in the historical records while other less cooperative Beloved Women are merely unnamed, shadowy figures. Women such as Catherine Brown, a model of Christian virtue, gained the admiration of missionaries, and we have a memoir of Brown's life; other women who removed their children from mission schools incurred the missionaries' wrath, and they merit only brief mention in mission diaries. The comments of government agents usually focused on those native women who demonstrated considerable industry by raising cotton and producing cloth (in this case, Indian men suffered by comparison), not those who grew corn in the matrilineage's fields. In addition to being biased and reflecting only one segment of the female population, the information from these sources is second-hand; rarely did Indian women, particularly traditionalists, speak for themselves.

The one subject on which women did speak on two occasions was land. In 1817 the United States sought a large cession of Cherokee territory and removal of those who lived on the land in question. A group of Indian women met in their own council, and thirteen of them signed a message which was delivered to the National Council. They advised the Council:

> The Cherokee ladys now being present at the meeting of the Chiefs and warriors in council have thought it their duties as mothers to address their beloved Chiefs and warriors now assembled.

> Our beloved children and head men of the Cherokee nation we address you warriors in council [.W]e have raised all of you on the land which we now have, which God gave us to inhabit and raise provisions [.W]e know that our country has once been extensive but by repeated sales has become circumscribed to a small tract and never have thought it our duty to interfere in the disposition of it till now, if a father or mother was to sell all their lands which they had to depend on [,] which their children had to raise their living on [,] which would be bad indeed and to be removed to another country [.W]e do not wish to go to an unknown country which we have understood some of our children wish to go over the Mississippi but this act of our children would be like destroying your mothers. Your mother and sisters ask and beg of you not to part with any more of our lands.

The next year, the National Council met again to discuss the possibility of allotting Cherokee land to individuals, an action the United States government encouraged as a preliminary step to removal. Once again Cherokee women reacted:

> We have heard with painful feelings that the bounds of the land we now possess are to be drawn into very narrow limits. The land was given to us by the Great Spirit above as our common right, to raise our children upon, & to make support for our rising generations. We therefore humbly petition our beloved children, the head men and warriors, to hold out to the last in support of our common rights, as the Cherokee nation has been the first settlers of this land; we therefore claim the right of the soil. . . . We therefore unanimously join in our meeting to hold our country in common as hitherto.

Common ownership of land meant in theory that the United States government had to obtain cessions from recognized, elected Cherokee officials who represented the wishes of the people. Many whites favored allotment because private citizens then could obtain individually owned tracts of land through purchase, fraud, or seizure. Most Cherokees recognized this danger and objected to allotment for that reason. The women, however, had an additional incentive for opposing allotment. Under the laws of the states in which the Cherokees lived and of which they would become citizens if land were allotted, married women had few property rights. A married woman's property, even property she held prior to her marriage, belonged legally to her husband. Cherokee women and martilineal households would have ceased to be property owners.

The implications for women became apparent in the 1830s, when Georgia claimed its law was in effect in the Cherokee country. Conflicts over property arose because of uncertainty over which legal system prevailed. For example, a white man, James Vaught, married the Cherokee Catherine Gunter. She inherited several slaves from her father, and Vaught sold two of them to General Isaac Wellborn. His wife had not consented to the sale and so she reclaimed her property and took them with her when the family moved west. General Wellborn tried to seize the slaves just as they were about to embark, but a soldier, apparently recognizing her claim under Cherokee law, prevented him from doing so. After removal the General appealed to Principal Chief John Ross for aid in recovering the slaves, but Ross refused. He informed Wellborn: "By the laws of the Cherokee Nation, the property of husband and wife remain separate and apart and neither of these can sell or dispose of the property of the other." Had the Cherokees accepted allotment and come under Georgia law, Wellborn would have won.

The effects of the women's protests in 1817 and 1818 are difficult to determine. In 1817 the Cherokees ceded tracts of land in Georgia, Alabama, and Tennessee, and in 1819 they made an even larger cession. Nevertheless, they rejected individual allotments and strengthened restrictions on alienation of improvements. Furthermore, the Cherokee Nation gave notice that they would negotiate no additional cessions—a resolution so strongly supported that the United States ultimately had to turn to a small unauthorized faction in order to obtain the minority treaty of 1835.

The political organization which existed in the Cherokee Nation in 1817–18 had made it possible for women to voice their opinion. Traditionally, Cherokee towns were politically independent of one another, and each town governed itself through a council in which all adults could speak. In the eighteenth century, however, the Cherokees began centralizing their government in order to restrain bellicose warriors whose raids jeopardized the entire nation and to negotiate as a single unit with whites. Nevertheless, town councils remained important, and representatives of traditional towns formed the early National Council. This National Council resembled the town councils in that anyone could address the body. Although legislation passed in 1817 created an Executive Committee, power still rested with the Council which reviewed all Committee acts.

The protests of the women to the National Council in 1817 and 1818 were, however, the last time women presented a collective position to the Cherokee governing body. Structural changes in Cherokee government more narrowly defined participation in the National Council. In 1820 the Council provided that representatives be chosen from eight districts rather than from traditional towns, and in 1823 the Committee acquired a right of review over acts of the Council. The more formalized political organization made it less likely that a group could make its views known to the national government.

As the Cherokee government became more centralized, political and economic power rested increasingly in the hands of a few elite men who adopted the planter lifestyle of the white antebellum South. A significant part of the ideological basis for this lifestyle was the cult of domesticity in which the ideal woman confined herself to home and hearth while men contended with the corrupt world of government and business.

The elite adopted the tenets of the cult of domesticity, particularly after 1817, when the number of Protestant missionaries, major proponents of this feminine ideal, increased significantly and their influence on Cherokee society broadened.

The extent to which a man's wife and daughters conformed to the idea quickly came to be one measure of his status. In 1818 Charles Hicks, who later served as Principal Chief, described the most prominent men in the Nation as "those who have for the last 10 or 20 years been pursuing agriculture & kept their women & children at home & in comfortable circumstances." Eight years later John Ridge, one of the first generation of Cherokees to have been educated from childhood in mission schools, discussed a Cherokee law which protected the property rights of a married woman and observed that "in many respects she has exclusive & distinct control over her own, particularly among the less civilized." The more "civilized" presumably left such matters to men. Then Ridge described suitable activities for women: "They sew, they weave, they spin, they cook our meals and act well the duties assigned them by Nature as mothers." Proper women did not enter business or politics.

Despite the attitudes of men such as Hicks and Ridge, women did in fact continue as heads of households and as businesswomen. In 1828 the *Cherokee Phoenix* published the obituary of Oo-dah-less, who had accumulated a sizeable estate through agriculture and commerce. She was "the support of a large family," and she bequeathed her property "to an only daughter and three grandchildren." Oo-dah-less was not unique. At least one third of the heads of household listed on the removal roll of 1835 were women. Most of these were not as prosperous as Oo-dah-less, but some were even more successful economically. Nineteen owned slaves (190 men were slaveholders), and two held over twenty slaves and operated substantial farms.

Nevertheless, these women had ceased to have a direct voice in Cherokee government. In 1826 the Council called a constitutional convention to draw up a governing document for the Nation. According to legislation which provided for election of delegates to the convention, "No person but a free male citizen who is full grown shall be entitled to vote." The convention met and drafted a constitution patterned after that of the United States. Not surprisingly, the constitution which male Cherokees ratified in 1827 restricted the franchise to "free male citizens" and stipulated that "no person shall be eligible to a seat in the General Council, but a free Cherokee male, who shall have attained the age of twenty-five." Unlike the United States Constitution, the Cherokee document clearly excluded women, perhaps as a precaution against women who might assert their traditional right to participate in politics instead of remaining in the domestic sphere.

The exclusion of women from politics certainly did not produce the removal crisis, but it did mean that a group traditionally opposed to land cession could no longer be heard on the issue. How women would have voted is also unclear. Certainly by 1835 many Cherokee women, particularly those educated in mission schools, believed that men were better suited to deal with political issues than women, and a number of women voluntarily enrolled their households to go west before the forcible removal of 1838–39. Even if women had united in active opposition to removal, it is unlikely that the United States and aggressive state governments would have paid any more attention to them than they did to the elected officials of the nation who opposed removal or the 15,000 Cherokees, including women (and perhaps children), who petitioned the United States Senate to reject the Treaty of New Echota. While Cherokee legislation may have made women powerless, federal authority rendered the whole Nation impotent.

In 1828 Georgia had extended state law over the Cherokee Nation and white intruders who invaded its territory. Georgia law prohibited Indians, both men and women, from testifying in court against white assailants, and so they simply had to endure attacks on person and property. Delegates from the Nation complained to Secretary of War John H. Eaton about the lawless behavior of white intruders:

> Too many there are who think it an act of trifling consequence to oust an Indian family from the quiet enjoyment of all the comforts of their own firesides, and to drive off before their faces the stock that gave nourishment to the children and support to the aged, and appropriate it to the satisfaction to avarice.

Elias Boudinot, editor of the bilingual *Cherokee Phoenix*, even accused the government of encouraging the intruders in order to force the Indians off their lands, and he published the following account:

> A few days since two of these white men came to a Cherokee house, for the purpose, they pretended, of buying provisions. There was no person about the house but one old woman of whom they inquired for some corn, beans &c. The woman told them she had nothing to sell. They then went off in the direction of the field belonging to this Cherokee family. They had not gone but a few minutes when the woman of the house saw a heavy smoke rising from that direction. She immediately hastened to the field and found the villains had set the woods on fire but a few rods from the fences, which she found already in a full blaze. There being a very heavy wind that day, the fire spread so fast, that her efforts to extinguish it proved utterly useless. The entire fence was therefore consumed in a short time. It is said that during her efforts to save the fence the men who had done the mischief were within sight, and were laughing heartily at her!

The Georgia Guard, established by the state to enforce its law in the Cherokee country, offered no protection and, in fact, contributed to the lawlessness. The *Phoenix* printed the following notice under the title "Cherokee Women, Beware":

> It is said that the Georgia Guard have received orders, from the Governor we suppose, to inflict corporeal punishment on such females as shall hereafter be guilty of insulting them. We presume they are to be the judges of what constitutes *insult*.

Despite harassment from intruders and the Guard, most Cherokees had no intention of going west, and in the spring of 1838 they began to plant their crops as usual. Then United States soldiers arrived, began to round up the Cherokees, and imprisoned them in stockades in preparation for deportation. In 1932 Rebecca Neugin, who was nearly one hundred years old, shared her childhood memory and family tradition about removal with historian Grant Foreman:

> When the soldier came to our house my father wanted to fight, but my mother told him that the soldiers would kill him if he did and we surrendered without a fight. They drove us out of our house to join other prisoners in a stockade. After they took us away, my mother begged them to let her go back and get some bedding. So they let her go back and she brought what bedding and a few cooking utensils she could carry and had to leave behind all of our other household possessions.

Rebecca Neugin's family was relatively fortunate. In the process of capture, families were sometimes separated and sufficient food and clothing were often left behind. Over fifty years after removal, John G. Burnett, a soldier who served as an interpreter, reminisced:

Men working in the fields were arrested and driven to stockades. Women were dragged from their homes by soldiers whose language they could not understand. Children were often separated from their parents and driven into the stockades with the sky for a blanket and the earth for a pillow.

Burnett recalled how one family was forced to leave the body of a child who had just died and how a distraught mother collapsed of heart failure as soldiers evicted her and her three children from their homes. After their capture, many Cherokees had to march miles over rugged mountain terrain to the stockades. Captain L. B. Webster wrote his wife about moving eight hundred Cherokees from North Carolina to the central depot in Tennessee: "We were eight days in making the journey (80 miles), and it was pitiful to behold the women & children, who suffered exceedingly—as they were all obliged to walk, with the exception of the sick."

Originally the government planned to deport all the Cherokees in the summer of 1838, but the mortality rate of the three parties that departed that summer led the commanding officer, General Winfield Scott, to agree to delay the major removal until fall. In the interval, the Cherokees remained in the stockades, where conditions were abysmal. Women in particular often became individual victims of their captors. The missionary Daniel Butrick recorded the following episode in his journal:

> The poor Cherokees are not only exposed to temporal evils, but also to every species of moral desolation. The other day a gentleman informed me that he saw six soldiers about two Cherokee women. The women stood by a tree, and the soldiers with a bottle of liquor were endeavoring to entice them to drink, though the women, as yet were resisting them. He made this known to the commanding officer but we presume no notice was taken of it, as it was reported that those soldiers had those women with them the whole night afterwards. A young married woman, a member of the Methodist society, was at the camp with her friends, though her husband was not there at the time. The soldiers, it is said, caught her, dragged her about, and at length, either through fear, or otherwise, induced her to drink; and then seduced her away, so that she is now an outcast even among her own relatives. How many of the poor captive women are thus debauched, through terror and seduction, that eye which never sleeps, alone can determine.

When removal finally got underway in October, the Cherokees were in a debilitated and demoralized state. A white minister who saw them as they prepared to embark noted: "The women did not appear to as good advantage as did the men. All, young and old, wore blankets which almost hid them from view." The Cherokees had received permission to manage their own removal, and they divided the people into thirteen detachments of approximately one thousand each. While some had wagons, most walked. Neugin rode in a wagon with other children and some elderly women, but her older brother, mother, and father "walked all the way." One observer reported that "even aged females, apparently nearly ready to drop in the grave, were traveling with heavy burdens attached to the back." Proper conveyance did not spare well-to-do Cherokees the agony of removal, the same observer noted:

> One lady passed on in her hack in company with her husband, apparently with as much refinement and equipage as any of the mothers of New England; and she was a mother too and her youngest child, about three years old, was sick in her arms, and all she could do was to make it comfortable as circumstances would permit. . . . She could only carry her dying child in her arms a few miles farther, and then she must stop in a stranger-land

and consign her much loved babe to the cold ground, and that without pomp and
ceremony, and pass on with the multitude.

This woman was not alone. Journals of the removal are largely a litany of the burial of
children, some born "untimely."

Many women gave birth alongside the trail; at least sixty-nine newborns arrived in
the West. The Cherokees' military escort was often less than sympathetic. Daniel Butrick
wrote in his journal that troops frequently forced women in labor to continue until they
collapsed and delivered "in the midst of the company of soldiers." One man even stabbed
an expectant mother with a bayonet. Obviously, many pregnant women did not survive
such treatment. The oral tradition of a family from southern Illinois, through which the
Cherokees passed, for example, includes an account of an adopted Cherokee infant whose
mother died in childbirth near the family's pioneer cabin. Although this story may be
apocryphal, the circumstances of Cherokee removal make such traditions believable.

The stress and tension produced by the removal crisis probably accounts for a
postremoval increase in domestic violence, of which women usually were the victims.
Missionaries reported that men, helpless to prevent seizure of their property and assaults
on themselves and their families, vented their frustrations by beating wives and children.
Some women were treated so badly by their husbands that they left them, and this dislocation contributed to the chaos in the Cherokee Nation in the late 1830s.

Removal divided the Cherokee Nation in a fundamental way, and the Civil War
magnified that division. Because most signers of the removal treaty were highly acculturated, many traditionalists resisted more strongly the white man's way of life and distrusted more openly those Cherokees who imitated whites. This split between "conser-
vatives," those who sought to preserve the old ways, and "progressives," those
committed to change, extended to women. We know far more, of course, about "progressive" Cherokee women who left letters and diaries which in some ways are quite
similar to those of upper-class women in the antebellum South. In letters, they recounted
local news such as "they had Elick Cockrel up for steeling horses" and "they have
Charles Reese in chains about burning Harnages house" and discussed economic concerns: "I find I cannot get any corn in this neighborhood, so of course I shall be greatly
pressed in providing provision for my family." Nevertheless, family life was the focus
of most letters: "Major is well and tryes hard to stand alone he will walk soon. I would
write more but the baby is crying."

Occasionally we even catch a glimpse of conservative women who seem to have
retained at least some of their original authority over domestic matters. Red Bird Smith,
who led a revitalization movement at the end of the nineteenth century, had considerable
difficulty with his first mother-in-law. She "influenced" her adopted daughter to marry
Smith through witchcraft and, as head of the household, meddled rather seriously in the
couple's lives. Interestingly, however, the Kee-Too-Wah society which Red Bird Smith
headed had little room for women. Although the society had political objectives, women
enjoyed no greater participation in this "conservative" organization than they did in the
"progressive" republican government of the Cherokee Nation.

Following removal, the emphasis of legislation involving women was on protection rather than participation. In some ways this legislation did offer women
greater opportunities than the law codes of the states. In 1845 the editor of the
Cherokee Advocate expressed pride that "in this respect the Cherokees have been

considerably in advance of many of their white brethren, the rights of their women having been amply secured almost ever since they had written laws." The Nation also established the Cherokee Female Seminary to provide higher education for women, but like the education women received before removal, students studied only those subjects considered to be appropriate for their sex.

Removal, therefore, changed little in terms of the status of Cherokee women. They had lost political power before the crisis of the 1830s, and events which followed relocation merely confirmed new roles and divisions. Cherokee women originally had been subsistence-level farmers and mothers, and the importance of these roles in traditional society had made it possible for them to exercise political power. Women, however, lacked the economic resources and military might on which political power in the Anglo-American system rested. When the Cherokees adopted the Anglo-American concept of power in the eighteenth and nineteenth centuries, men became dominant. But in the 1830s the chickens came home to roost. Men, who had welcomed the Anglo-American basis for power, now found themselves without power. Nevertheless, they did not question the changes they had fostered. Therefore, the tragedy of the trail of tears lies not only in the suffering and death which the Cherokees experienced but also in the failure of many Cherokees to look critically at the political system which they had adopted—a political system dominated by wealthy, highly acculturated men and supported by an ideology that made women (as well as others defined as "weak" or "inferior") subordinate. In the removal crisis of the 1830s, men learned an important lesson about power; it was a lesson women had learned well before the "trail of tears."

Readings For Theda Perdue:

In her larger study, Theda Perdue, *Slavery and the Evolution of Cherokee Society, 1540–1866* (Knoxville: University of Tennessee Press, 1979) deals with aboriginal gender roles in some detail. Another view of the evolving Cherokee society may be found in William G. McLoughlin, *Cherokee Renascence in the New Republic* (Princeton, NJ: Princeton University Press, 1986). Indian gender roles in other parts of the country receive attention in Ramon A. Gutierrez, *When Jesus Came, the Corn Mothers Went Away: Marriage, Sexuality, and Power in New Mexico, 1500–1846* (Stanford, CA: Stanford University Press, 1991), and Lisbeth Haas, *Conquests and Historical Identities in California, 1769–1936* (Berkeley: University of California Press, 1995).

10

BISON ECOLOGY AND BISON DIPLOMACY: THE SOUTHERN PLAINS FROM 1800 TO 1850

DAN FLORES

According to stereotype, the Indians were the first environmentalists in North America, so those who need examples of careful use of resources often point to tribal peoples. Recent scholarship, however, has suggested something rather different. As human beings, Native Americans have altered their environments as often and in as many ways as has any other group of people. Their reverence for nature and their vision of themselves as a part of it have not altered their actions. Hoping to clarify issues related to Indians and nature, researchers in several fields have examined village communities both before and after they became part of the capitalist market system.

This essay demonstrates clearly how the tribes of the Southern Plains adapted to the horse in terms of hunting and agriculture. When still on foot the Plains peoples could only hunt the bison when those animals approached their villages, and they had no way to carry away great quantities of meat if their hunts proved successful. That soon changed. As the analysis in this essay shows, the Plains tribes integrated the horse into their economy so well that their animals had a major negative impact on the grazing lands available to the bison and other wild animals there. It also demonstrates that the increased pressure the mounted hunters put on the southern bison herds started them on their downward path toward near extinction. The author suggests that we need to rethink the impact the Indians had on their local resources.

Dan L. Flores is the A.B. Hammond Professor of History at the University of Montana.

In bright spring light on the Great Plains of two centuries ago, governor Juan Bautista de Anza failed in the last of the three crucial tasks that his superiors had set him as part of their effort to reform New Mexico's Comanche policy. Over half a decade, Anza had followed one success with another. He had brilliantly defeated the formidable Comanche

Source: Dan Flores, "Bison Ecology and Bison Diplomacy: The Southern Plains from 1800 to 1850," *Journal of American History,* 78 (September 1991), 465–85, by permission of the Organization of American Historians, © 1991.

nomnekaht (war leader) Cuerno Verde in 1779, and as a consequence in 1786, he had personally fashioned the long-sought peace between New Mexico and the swelling Comanche population of the Southern Plains. His third task was to persuade the Comanches to settle in permanent villages and to farm.

But the New Mexico governor found the third undertaking impossible. Observers of Plains Indian life for 250 years and committed to encouraging agriculture over hunting, the Spaniards were certain that the culture of the horse Indians was ephemeral, that the bison on which they depended were an exhaustible resource. Thus Anza pleaded with the tribes to give up the chase. The Comanches thought him unconvincing. Recently liberated by horse culture and by the teeming wildlife of the High Plains, their bands found the Arkansas River pueblo the governor built for them unendurable. They returned to the hunt with the evident expectation that their life as buffalo hunters was an endless cycle. And yet Anza proved to be a prophet. Within little more than half a century, the Comanches and other tribes of the Southern Plains were routinely suffering from starvation and complaining of shortages of bison. What had happened?

Environmental historians and ethnohistorians whose interests have been environmental topics have in the two past decades been responsible for many of our most valuable recent insights into the history of native Americans since their contact with Euro-Americans. Thus far, however, modern scholarship has not reevaluated the most visible historic interaction, the set piece if you will, of native American environmental history. On the Great Plains of the American West during the two centuries from 1680 to 1880, almost three-dozen Native American groups adopted horse-propelled, bison-hunting cultures that defined "Indianness" for white Americans and most of the world. It is the end of this process that has most captured the popular imagination: the military campaigns against and the brutal incarceration of the horse Indians, accompanied by the astonishingly rapid elimination of bison, and of an old ecology that dated back ten thousand years, at the hands of commercial hide hunters. That dramatic end, which occurred in less than fifteen years following the end of the Civil War, has by now entered American mythology. Yet our focus on the finale has obscured an examination of earlier phases that might shed new light on the historical and environmental interaction of the horse Indians and bison herds on the Plains.

In the nineteenth-century history of the Central and Southern Plains, there have long been perplexing questions that environmental history seems well suited to answer. Why were the Comanches able to replace the Apaches on the bison-rich Southern Plains? Why did the Kiowas, Cheyennes, and Arapahoes gradually shift southward into the Southern Plains between 1800 and 1825? And why, after fighting each other for two decades, did these Southern Plains peoples effect a rapprochement and alliance in the 1840s? What factors brought on such an escalation of Indian raids into Mexico and Texas in the late 1840s that the subject assumed critical importance in the Treaty of Guadalupe-Hidalgo? If the bison herds were so vast in the years before the commercial hide hunters, why were there so many reports of starving Indians on the Plains by 1850? And finally, given our standard estimates of bison numbers, why is it that the hide hunters are credited with bringing to market only some 10 million hides, including no more than 3.5 million from the Southern Plains, in the 1870s?

Apposite to all of these questions is a central issue: How successful were the horse Indians in creating a dynamic ecological equilibrium between themselves and the vast bison herds that grazed the Plains? That is, had they developed sustainable hunting practices that would maintain the herds and so permit future generations of hunters to follow the same way of life? This is not to pose the "anachronistic question" (the term is Richard White's) of whether Indians were ecologists. But how a society or a group of peoples with a shared culture makes adjustments to live within the carrying capacity of its habitat is not only a valid historical question, it may be one of the most salient questions to ask about any culture. Historians of the Plains have differed about the long-term ecological sustainability of the Indians' use of bison, particularly after the Euro-American fur trade reached the West and the tribes began hunting bison under the influence of the market economy. The standard work, Frank Roe's *The North American Buffalo,* has generally carried the debate with the argument that there is "not a shred of evidence" to indicate that the horse Indians were out of balance with the bison herds. Using the new insights and methods of environmental history, it now appears possible systematically to analyze and revise our understanding of nineteenth-century history on the Great Plains. Such an approach promises to resolve some of the major questions. It can advance our understanding of when bison declined in numbers and of the intertwining roles that Indian policies—migrations, diplomacy, trade, and use of natural resources—and the growing pressures of external stimuli played in that decline. The answers are complex and offer a revision of both Plains history and western Indian ecological history.

Working our way through to them requires some digression into the large historical forces that shaped the Southern Plains over the last hundred centuries. The perspective of the *longue durée* is essential to environmental history. What transpired on the Great Plains from 1800 to 1850 is not comprehensible without taking into account the effect of the Pleistocene extinctions of ten thousand years ago, or the cycle of droughts that determined the carrying capacity for animals on the grasslands. Shallower in time than these forces but just as important to the problem are factors that stemmed from the arrival of Europeans in the New World. Trade was an ancient part of the cultural landscape of America, but the Europeans altered the patterns, the goods, and the intensity of trade. And the introduction of horses and horse culture accomplished a technological revolution for the Great Plains. The horse was the chief catalyst of an ongoing remaking of the tribal map of western America, as Native American groups moved onto the Plains and incessantly shifted their ranges and alliances in response to a world where accelerating change seemed almost the only constant.

At the beginning of the nineteenth century, the dominant groups on the Southern Plains were the two major divisions of the Comanches: the Texas Comanches, primarily Kotsotekas, and the great New Mexico division, spread across the country from the Llano Estacado Escarpment west to the foothills of the Sangre de Cristo Mountains, and composed of Yamparika and Jupe bands that only recently had replaced the Apaches on the High Plains. The Comanches' drive to the south from their original homelands in what is now southwestern Wyoming and northwestern Colorado was a part of the original tribal adjustments to the coming of horse technology to the Great Plains. There is reason to believe that the Eastern Shoshones, from whom the Comanches were derived before achieving a different identity on the Southern Plains, were one of the first intermountain tribes of historic times to push onto the Plains. Perhaps as early as 1500 the proto-Comanches were hunting bison and using dog power to haul their mountain-adapted four-pole tipis east of the Laramie Mountains. Evidently they moved in response to a wetter time on the Central Plains and the larger bison concentrations there.

These early Shoshonean hunters may not have spent more than three or four generations among the thronging Plains bison herds, for by the late seventeenth century they had been pushed back into the mountains and the sagebrush deserts by tribes newly armed with European guns moving westward from the region around the Great Lakes. If so, they were among a complex of tribes southwest of the lakes that over the next two centuries would be displaced by a massive Siouan drive to the west, an imperial expansion for domination of the prize buffalo range of the Northern Plains, and a wedge that sent ripples of tribal displacement across the Plains.

Among the historic tribes, the people who became Comanches thus may have shared with the Apaches and, if linguistic arguments are correct, probably with the Kiowas the longest familiarity with a bison-hunting life-style. Pressed back toward the mountains as Shoshones, they thus turned in a different direction and emerged from the passes through the Front Range as the same people but bearing a new name given them by the Utes: Komantcia. They still lacked guns but now began their intimate association with the one animal, aside from the bison, inextricably linked with Plains life. The Comanches began acquiring horses from the Utes within a decade or so after the Pueblo Revolt of 1680 sent horses and horse culture diffusing in all directions from New Mexico. Thus were born the "hyper-Indians," as William Brandon has called the Plains people.

The Comanches became, along with the Sioux, the most populous and widespread of all the peoples who now began to ride onto the vast sweep of grassland to participate in the hunter's life. They began to take possession of the Southern Plains by the early 1700s. By 1800 they were in full control of all the country east of the Southern Rocky Mountains and south of the Arkansas River clear to the Texas Hill Country. Their new culture, long regarded as an ethnographic anomaly on the Plains because of its western and archaic origins, may not be unique, as older scholars had supposed it to be—at least if we believe the new Comanche revisionists. Irrespective of their degree of tribal unity, however, when they began to move onto the Southern Plains with their new horse herds, their culture was adapting in interesting ways to the wealth of resources now available to them.

To the Comanches, the Southern Plains must have seemed an earthly paradise. The Pleistocene extinctions ten thousand years earlier had left dozens of grazing niches vacant on the American Great Plains. A dwarf species of bison with a higher reproductive capability than any of its ancestors evolved to flood most of those vacant niches with an enormous biomass of one grazer. In an ecological sense, bison were a weed species that had proliferated as a result of a major disturbance. That disturbance still reverberated, making it easy for Spanish horses, for example, to reoccupy their old niche and rapidly spread across the Plains. Those reverberations made the horse Indians thrive on an environmental situation that has had few parallels in world history.

The dimensions of the wild bison resource on the Southern Plains, and the Great Plains in general, have been much overstated in popular literature. For one thing, pollen analysis and archaeological data indicate that for the Southern Plains there were intervals, some spanning centuries, others decades, when bison must have been almost absent. Two major times of absence occurred between 5000 and 2500 B.C. and between A.D. 500 and 1300. The archaeological levels that lack bison bones correspond to pollen data indicating droughts. The severe southwestern drought that ended early in the fourteenth century was replaced by a five hundred-year cycle of wetter and cooler conditions, and a return of bison in large numbers to the Southern Plains from their drought refugia to the east and west. This long-term pattern in the archaeological record seems to have prevailed on a smaller scale within historic times. During the nineteenth century, for example, droughts of more than five years' duration struck the Great Plains four times at roughly twenty-year intervals, in a long-term dendrochronological pattern that seems to show a drying cycle (shorter drought-free intervals) beginning in the 1850s.

More important, our popular perception of bison numbers—based on the estimates of awed nineteenth-century observers—probably sets them too high. There very likely were never 100 million or even 60 million bison on the Plains during the present climate regime because the carrying capacity of the grasslands was not so high. The best technique for determining bison carrying capacity on the Southern Plains is to extrapolate from United States census data for livestock, and the best census for the extrapolation is that of 1910, after the beef industry crashes of the 1880s had reduced animal numbers, but before the breakup of ranches and the Enlarged Homestead Act of 1909 resulted in considerable sections of the Southern Plains being broken out by farmers. Additionally, dendrochronological data seem to show that at the turn of the century rainfall on the Southern Plains was at median, between-droughts levels, rendering the census of 1910 particularly suitable as a base line for carrying capacity and animal populations.

The 1910 agricultural census indicates that in the 201 counties on the Southern Plains (which covered 240,000 square miles), the nineteenth-century carrying capacity during periods of median rainfall was about 7,000,000 cattle-equivalent grazers—specifically for 1910, about 5,150,000 cattle and 1,890,000 horses and mules. The bison population was almost certainly larger, since migratory grazing patterns and coevolution with the native grasses made bison as a wild species about 18 percent more efficient on the Great Plains than domestic cattle. And varying climate conditions during the nineteenth century, as I will demonstrate, noticeably affected grassland carrying capacity. The ecological reality was a dynamic cycle in which carrying capacity could swing considerably from decade to decade. But if the Great Plains bovine carrying capacity of 1910 expresses a median reality, then during prehorse times the Southern Plains might have supported an average of about 8.2 million bison, the entire Great Plains perhaps 28–30 million.

Although 8 million bison on the Southern Plains may not be so many as historians used to believe, to the Comanches the herds probably seemed limitless. Bison availability through horse culture caused a specialization that resulted in the loss of two-thirds of the Comanches' former plant lore and in a consequent loss of status for their women, an intriguing development that seems to have occurred to some extent among all the tribes that moved onto the Plains during the horse period. As full-time bison hunters the Comanches appear to have abandoned all the old Shoshonean mechanisms, such as infanticide and polyandry, that had kept their population in line with available resources. These were replaced with such cultural mechanisms as widespread adoption of captured children and polygyny, adaptations to the Plains that were designed to keep Comanche numbers high and growing. That these changes seem to have been conscious and deliberate argues, perhaps, both Comanche environmental insight and some centralized leadership and planning.

Comanche success at seizing the Southern Plains from the native groups that had held it for several hundred years was likewise the result of a conscious choice: their decision to shape their lives around bison and horses. Unlike the Comanches, many of the

Apache bands had heeded the Spaniards' advice and had begun to build streamside gardening villages that became deathtraps once the Comanches located them. The Apaches' vulnerability, then, ironically stemmed from their willingness to diversify their economy. Given the overwhelming dominance of grasslands as opposed to cultivable river lands on the Plains, the specialized horse and bison culture of the Comanches exploited a greater volume of the thermodynamic energy streaming from sunlight into plants than the economies of any of their competitors—until they encountered Cheyennes and Arapahoes with a similar culture. The horse-mounted Plains Indians, in other words, made very efficient use of the available energy on the Great Plains, something they seem instinctively to have recognized and exulted in. From the frequency with which the Comanches applied some version of the name "wolf" to their leaders, I suspect that they may have recognized their role as human predators and their ecological kinship with the wolf packs that, like them, lived off the bison herds.

The Comanches were not the only people on the Southern Plains during the horse period. The New Mexicans, both Pueblo and Hispanic, continued to hunt on the wide-open Llanos, as did the prairie Caddoans, although the numbers of the latter were dwindling rapidly by 1825. The New Mexican peoples and the Caddoans of the middle Red and Brazos Rivers played major trade roles for hunters on the Southern Plains, and the Comanches in particular. Although the Comanches engaged in the archetypal Plains exchange of bison products for horticultural produce and European trade goods and traded horses and mules with Anglo-American traders from Missouri, Arkansas, and Louisiana, they were not a high-volume trading people until relatively late in their history. Early experiences with American traders and disease led them to distrust trade with Euro-Americans, and only once or twice did they allow short-lived posts to be established in their country. Instead, peace with the prairie Caddoans by the 1730s and with New Mexico in 1786 sent Comanche trade both east and west, but often through Indian middlemen.

In the classic, paradigmatic period between 1800 and 1850, the most interesting Southern Plains development was the cultural interaction between the Comanches and surrounding Plains Indians to the north. The Kiowas were the one of those groups most closely identified with the Comanches.

The Kiowas are and have long been an enigma. Scholars are interested in their origins because Kiowa oral tradition is at odds with the scientific evidence. The Kiowas believe that they started their journey to Rainy Mountain on the Oklahoma Plains from the north. And indeed, in the eighteenth century we find them on the Northern Plains, near the Black Hills, as one of the groups being displaced southwestward by the Siouan drive toward the buffalo range. Linguistically, however, the Kiowas are southern Indians. Their language belongs to the Tanoan group of Pueblo languages in New Mexico, and some scholars believe that the Kiowas of later history are the same people as the Plains Jumanos of early New Mexico history, whose rancherias were associated during the 1600s and early 1700s with the headwaters of the Colorado and Concho Rivers of Texas. How the Kiowas got so far north is not certainly known, but in historical times they were consummate traders, especially of horses, and since the Black Hills region was a major trade citadel they may have begun to frequent the region as traders and teachers of horse lore.

Displaced by the wars for the buffalo ranges in the north, the Kiowas began to drift southward again—or perhaps, since the supply of horses was in the Southwest, simply began to stay longer on the Southern Plains. Between 1790 and 1806, they developed a rapprochement with the Comanches. Thereafter they were so closely associated with the northern Comanches that they were regarded by some as merely a Comanche band, although in many cultural details the two groups were dissimilar. Spanish and American traders and explorers of the 1820s found them camped along the two forks of the Canadian River and on the various headwater streams of the Red River.

The other groups that increasingly began to interact with the Comanches during the 1820s and thereafter had also originated on the Northern Plains. These were the Arapahoes and the Cheyennes, who by 1825 were beginning to establish themselves on the Colorado buffalo plains from the North Platte River all the way down to the Arkansas River.

The Algonkian-speaking Arapahoes and Cheyennes had once been farmers living in earth lodges on the upper Mississippi. By the early 1700s both groups were in present North Dakota, occupying villages along the Red and Sheyenne Rivers, where they first began to acquire horses, possibly from the Kiowas. Fur wars instigated by the Europeans drove them farther southwest and more and more into a Plains, bison-hunting culture, one that the women of these farming tribes probably resisted as long as possible. But by the second decade of the nineteenth century the Teton Sioux wedge had made nomads and hunters of the Arapahoes and Cheyennes.

Their search for prime buffalo grounds and for ever-larger horse herds, critical since both tribes had emerged as middlemen traders between the villagers of the Missouri and the horse reservoir to the south, first led the Cheyennes and Arapahoes west of the Black Hills, into Crow lands, and then increasingly southward along the mountain front. By 1815 the Arapahoes were becoming fixed in the minds of American traders as their own analogue on the Southern Plains; the famous trading expedition of August Pierre Chouteau and Jules De Mun that decade was designed to exploit the horse and robe trade of the Arapahoes on the Arkansas. By the 1820s, when Stephen Long's expedition and the trading party including Jacob Fowler penetrated the Southern Plains, the Arapahoes and Cheyennes were camping with the Kiowas and Comanches on the Arkansas. The Hairy Rope band of the Cheyennes, renowned for their ability to catch wild horses, was then known to be mustanging along the Cimarron River.

Three factors seem to have drawn the Arapahoes and Cheyennes so far south. Unquestionably, one factor was the vast horse herds of the Comanches and Kiowas, an unending supply of horses for the trade, which by 1825 the Colorado tribes were seizing in daring raids. Another was the milder winters south of the Arkansas, which made horse pastoralism much easier. The third factor was the abnormally bountiful game of the early nineteenth-century Southern Plains, evidently the direct result of an extraordinary series of years between 1815 and 1846 when, with the exception of a minor drought in the late 1820s, rainfall south of the Arkansas was considerably above average. So lucrative was the hunting and raiding that in 1813 Charles Bent located the first of his adobe trading posts along the Arkansas, expressly to control the winter robe and summer horse trade of the Arapahoes and Cheyennes. Bent's marketing contacts were in St. Louis. Horses that Bent's traders drove to St. Louis commonly started as stock in the New Mexican Spanish settlements (and sometimes those were California horses stolen by Indians who traded them to the New Mexicans) that were stolen by the Comanches, then stolen again by Cheyenne raiders, and finally traded at Bent's or Ceran St. Vrain's posts, whence they were driven to Westport, Missouri, and sold to outfit American emigrants going to the

West Coast! Unless you saw it from the wrong end, as the New Mexicans (or the horses) seem to have, it was both a profitable and a culturally stimulating economy.

Thus, around 1825, the Comanches and Kiowas found themselves at war with Cheyennes, Arapahoes, and other tribes on the north. Meanwhile, the Colorado tribes opened another front in a naked effort to seize the rich buffalo range of the upper Kansas and Republican rivers from the Pawnees. These wars produced an interesting type of ecological development that appeared repeatedly across most of the continent. At the boundaries where warring tribes met, they left buffer zones occupied by neither side and only lightly hunted. One such buffer zone on the Southern Plains was along the region's northern perimeter, between the Arkansas and North Canadian Rivers. Another was in present-day western Kansas, between the Pawnees and the main range of the Colorado tribes, and a third seems to have stretched from the forks of the Platte to the mountains. The buffer zones were important because game within them was left relatively undisturbed; they allowed the buildup of herds that might later be exploited when tribal boundaries or agreements changed.

The appearance of American traders such as Bent and St. Vrain marked the Southern Plains tribes' growing immersion in a market economy increasingly tied to worldwide trade networks dominated by Euro-Americans. Like all humans, Indians had always altered their environments. But as most modern historians of Plains Indians and the western fur trade have realized, during the nineteenth century not only had the western tribes become technologically capable of pressuring their resources, but year by year they were becoming less "ecosystem people," dependent on the products of their local regions for subsistence, and increasingly tied to biospheric trade networks. Despite some speculation that the Plains tribes were experiencing ecological problems, previous scholars have not ascertained what role market hunting played in this dilemma, what combination of other factors was involved, or what the tribes attempted to do about it.

The crux of the problem in studying Southern Plains Indian ecology and bison is to determine whether the Plains tribes had established a society in ecological equilibrium, one whose population did not exceed the carrying capacity of its habitat and so maintained a healthy, functioning ecology that could be sustained over the long term. Answering that question involves an effort to come to grips with the factors affecting bison populations, the factors affecting Indian populations, and the cultural aspects of Plains Indians' utilization of bison. Each of the three aspects of the question presents puzzles difficult to resolve.

In modern, protected herds on the Plains, bison are a prolific species whose numbers increase by an average of 18 percent a year, assuming a normal sex ratio (51 males to 49 females) with breeding cows amounting to 35 percent of the total. In other words, if the Southern Plains supported 8.2 million bison in years of median rainfall, the herds would have produced about 1.4 million calves a year. To maintain an ecological equilibrium with the grasses, the Plains bison's natural mortality rate also had to approach 18 percent.

Today the several protected bison herds in the western United States have a natural mortality rate, without predation, ranging between 3 and 9 percent. The Wichita Mountains herd, the only large herd left on the Southern Plains, falls midway with a 6 percent mortality rate. Despite a search for it, no inherent naturally regulating mechanism has yet been found in bison populations; thus active culling programs are needed at all the Plains bison refuges. The starvation-induced population crashes that affect ungulates such as deer were seemingly mitigated on the wild, unfenced Plains by the bison's tendency—barring any major impediments—to shift their range great distances to better pasture.

Determining precisely how the remaining annual mortality in the wild herds was affected is not easy, because the wolf/bison relationship on the Plains has never been studied. Judging from dozens of historical documents attesting to wolf predation of bison calves, including accounts by the Indians, wolves apparently played a critical role in Plains bison population dynamics, and not just as culling agents of diseased and old animals.

Human hunters were the other source of mortality. For nine thousand years Native Americans had hunted bison without exterminating them, perhaps building into their gene pool an adjustment to human predation (dwarfed size, earlier sexual maturity, and shorter gestation times, all serving to keep populations up). But there is archaeological evidence that beginning about A.D. 1450, with the advent of "mutualistic" trade between Puebloan communities recently forced by drought to relocate on the Rio Grande and a new wave of Plains hunters (probably the Athapaskan-speaking Apacheans), human pressures on the southern bison herd accelerated, evidently dramatically if the archaeological record in New Mexico is an accurate indication. That pressure would have been a function of both the size of the Indian population and the use of bison in Indian cultures. Because Plains Indians traded bison-derived goods for the produce of the horticultural villages fringing the Plains, bison would be affected by changes in human population peripheral to the Great Plains as well as on them.

One attempt to estimate maximum human population size on the Southern Plains, that of Jerold Levy, fixed the upper limit at about 10,500 people. Levy argued that water would have been a more critical resource than bison in fixing a limit for Indian populations. Levy's population figures are demonstrably too low, and he lacked familiarity with the aquifer-derived drought-resistant sources of water on the Southern Plains. But his argument that water was the more critical limiting resource introduces an important element into the Plains equation.

The cultural utilization of bison by horse Indians has been studied by Bill Brown. Adapting a sophisticated formula worked out first for caribou hunters in the Yukon, Brown has estimated Indian subsistence (caloric requirements plus the number of robes and hides required for domestic use) at about 47 animals per lodge per year. At an average of 8 people per lodge, that works out to almost 6 bison per person over a year's time. Brown's article is not only highly useful in getting us closer to a historic Plains equation than ever before; it is also borne out by at least one historic account. In 1821 the trader Jacob Fowler camped for several weeks with 700 lodges of Southern Plains tribes on the Arkansas River. Fowler was no ecologist; in fact, he could hardly spell. But he was a careful observer, and he wrote that the big camp was using up 100 bison a day. In other words, 700 lodges were using bison at a rate of about 52 per lodge per year, or 6.5 animals per person. These are important figures. Not only do they give us some idea of the mortality percentage that can be assigned to human hunters; by extension they help us fix a quadruped predation percentage as well.

Estimates of the number of Indians on the Southern Plains during historic times are not difficult to find, but they tend to vary widely, and for good reason, as will be seen when we look closely at the historical events of the first half of the nineteenth century. Although observers' population estimates for the Comanches go as high as 30,000, six of the seven population figures for the Comanches estimated between 1786 and 1854 fall into a narrow range between 19,200 and 21,600. Taken together, the number of Kiowas, Cheyennes, Arapahoes, Plains Apaches, Kiowa-Apaches, and Wichitas probably did not exceed 12,000 during that same period. Contemporaries estimated the combined number of Cheyennes and Arapahoes, for example, as 4,400 in 1838, 5,000 in 1843, and 5,200 in 1846. If the historic Southern Plains hunting population reached 30,000, then human hunters would have accounted for only 195,000 bison per year if we use the estimate of 6.5 animals per person.

But another factor must have played a significant role. While quadruped predators concentrated on calves and injured or feeble animals, human hunters had different criteria. Historical documents attest to the horse Indians' preference for and success in killing two- to five-year-old bison cows, which were preferred for their meat and for their thinner, more easily processed hides and the luxurious robes made from their pelts. Studies done on other large American ungulates indicate that removal of breeding females at a level that exceeds 7 percent of the total herd will initiate population decline. With 8.2 million bison on the Southern Plains, the critical upper figure for cow selectivity would have been about 574,000 animals. Reduce the total bison number to 6 million and the yearly calf crop to 1.08 million, probably more realistic median figures for the first half of the nineteenth century, and the critical mortality for breeding cows would still have been 420,000 animals. As mentioned, a horse-mounted, bison-hunting population of 30,000 would have harvested bison at a yearly rate of less than 200,000. Hence I would argue that, theoretically, on the Southern Plains the huge biomass of bison left from the Pleistocene extinctions would have supported the subsistence needs of more than 60,000 Plains hunters.

All of this raises some serious questions when we look at the historical evidence from the first half of the nineteenth century. By the end of that period, despite an effort at population growth by many Plains tribes, the population estimates for most of the Southern Plains tribes were down. And many of the bands seemed to be starving. Thomas Fitzpatrick, the Cheyennes' and Arapahoes' first agent, reported in 1853 that the tribes in his district spent half the year in a state of starvation. The Comanches were reported to be eating their horses in great numbers by 1850, and their raids into Mexico increased all through the 1840s, as if a resource depletion in their home range was driving them to compensate with stolen stock. In the painted robe calendars of the Kiowas, the notation for "few or no bison" appears for four years in a row between 1849 and 1852. Bison were becoming less reliable, and the evolution toward an economy based on raiding and true horse pastoralism was well under way. Clearly, by 1850 something had altered the situation on the Southern Plains.

The "something" was, in fact, a whole host of ecological alterations that historians with a wide range of data at their disposal are only now, more than a century later, beginning to understand.

As early as 1850 the bison herds had been weakened in a number of ways. The effect of the horse on Indian culture has been much studied, but in working out a Southern Plains ecological model, it is important to note that horses also had a direct effect on bison numbers. By the second quarter of the nineteenth century the domesticated horse herds of the Southern Plains tribes must have ranged between .25 and .50 million animals (at an average of 10 to 15 horses per person). In addition, an estimated 2 million wild mustangs overspread the country between south Texas and the Arkansas River. That many animals of a species with an 80 percent dietary overlap with bovines and, perhaps more critically, with similar water requirements, must have had an adverse impact on bison carrying capacity, especially since Indian horse herds concentrated the tribes in the moist canyons and river valleys that bison also used for watering. Judging from the 1910 agricultural census, 2 million or more horses would have reduced the median grassland carrying capacity for the southern bison herd to under 6 million animals.

Another factor that may have started to diminish overall bison numbers was the effect of exotic bovine diseases. Anthrax, introduced into the herds from Louisiana around 1800, tuberculosis, and brucellosis, the latter brought to the Plains by feral and stolen Texas cattle and by stock on the overland trails, probably had considerable impact on the bison herds. All the bison that were saved in the late nineteenth century had high rates of infection with these diseases. Brucellosis plays havoc with reproduction in domestic cattle, causing cows to abort; it may have done so in wild bison, and butchering them probably infected Indian women with the disease.

Earlier I mentioned modern natural mortality figures for bison of 3 percent to 9 percent of herd totals. On the wilderness Plains, fires, floods, drownings, droughts, and strange die-offs may have upped this percentage considerably. But if we hold to the higher figure, then mortality might have taken an average of 50 percent of the annual bison increase of 18 percent. Thirty thousand subsistence hunters would have killed off only 18 percent of the bison's yearly increase (if the herd was 6 million). The long-wondered-at wolf predation was perhaps the most important of all the factors regulating bison populations, with a predation percentage of around 32% of the annual bison increase. (Interestingly, this dovetails closely with the Pawnee estimate that wolves got 3 to 4 of every 10 calves born.) Wolves and other canids are able to adjust their litter sizes to factors like mortality and resource abundance. Thus, mountain men and traders who poisoned wolves for their pelts may not have significantly reduced wolf populations. They may have inadvertently killed thousands of bison, however, for poisoned wolves drooled and vomited strychnine over the grass in their convulsions. Many Indians lost horses that ate such poisoned grass.

The climate cycle, strongly correlated with bison populations in the archaeological data for earlier periods, must have interacted with these other factors to produce a decline in bison numbers between 1840 and 1850. Except for a dry period in the mid- to late 1820s, the first four decades of the nineteenth century had been a time of above-normal rainfall on the Southern Plains. With the carrying capacity for bison and horses high, the country south of the Arkansas sucked tribes to it as into a vortex. But beginning in 1846, rainfall plunged as much as 30 percent below the median for nine of the next ten years. On the Central Plains, six years of that decade were dry. The growth of human populations and settlements in Texas, New Mexico, and the Indian Territory blocked the bison herds from migrating to their traditional drought refugia on the periphery of their range. Thus, a normal climate swing combined with unprecedented external pressures to produce an effect unusual in bison history—a core population, significantly reduced by competition with horses and by drought, that was quite susceptible to human hunting pressure.

Finally, alterations in the historical circumstances of the Southern Plains tribes from 1825 to 1850 had serious repercussions for Plains ecology. Some of those circumstances were indirect and beyond the tribes' ability to influence. Traders along the Santa Fe Trail shot into, chased, and disturbed the southern herds. New Mexican *Ciboleros* (bison hunters) continued to take fifteen to twenty-five thousand bison a year from the Llano Estacado. And the United States government's removal of almost fifty thousand eastern Indians into Oklahoma increased the pressure on the bison herds to a level impossible to estimate. The Southern Plains tribes evidently considered it a threat and refused to abide by the Treaty of Fort Holmes (1835) when they discovered it gave the eastern tribes hunting rights on the prairies.

Insofar as the Southern Plains tribes had an environmental policy, then, it was to protect the bison herds from being hunted by outsiders. The Comanches could not afford to emulate their Shoshonean ancestors and limit their own population. Beset by enemies and disease, they had to try to keep their numbers high, even as their resource base diminished. For the historic Plains tribes, warfare and stock raids addressed ecological needs created by diminishing resources as well as the cultural impulse to enhance men's status, and they must have seemed far more logical solutions than consciously reducing their own populations as the bison herds became less reliable.

For those very reasons, after more than a decade of warfare among the buffalo tribes, in 1840 the Comanches and Kiowas adopted a strategy of seeking peace and an alliance with the Cheyennes, Arapahoes, and Kiowa-Apaches. From the Comanches' point of view, it brought them allies against Texans and eastern Indians who were trespassing on the Plains. The Cheyennes and Arapahoes got what they most wanted: the chance to hunt the grass- and bison-rich Southern Plains, horses and mules for trading, and access to the Spanish settlements via Comanche lands. But the peace meant something else in ecological terms. Now all the tribes could freely exploit the Arkansas Valley bison herds. This new exploitation of a large, prime bison habitat that had been a boundary zone skirted by Indian hunters may have been critical. In the Kiowa Calendar the notation for "many bison" appears in 1841, the year following the peace. The notation appears only once more during the next thirty-five years.

One other advantage the Comanches and Kiowas derived from the peace of 1840 was freedom to trade at Bent's Fort. Although the data to prove it are fragmentary, this conversion of the largest body of Indians on the Southern Plains from subsistence/ecosystem hunters to a people intertwined in the European market system probably added critical stress to a bison herd already being eaten away. How serious the market incentive could be is indicated by John Whitfield, agent at William Bent's second Arkansas River fort in 1855, who wrote that 3,150 Cheyennes were killing 40,000 bison a year. That is about twice the number the Cheyennes would have harvested through subsistence hunting alone. (It also means that on the average every Cheyenne warrior was killing 44 bison a year and every Cheyenne woman was processing robes at the rate of almost one a week.) With the core bison population seriously affected by the drought of the late 1840s, the additional, growing robe trade of the Comanches probably brought the Southern Plains tribes to a critical level in their utilization of bison. Drought, Indian market hunting, and cow selectivity must stand as the critical elements—albeit augmented by minor factors such as white disturbance, new bovine diseases, and increasing grazing competition from horses—that brought on the bison crisis of the midcentury Southern Plains.

That explanation may also illuminate the experience of the Canadian Plains, where bison disappeared without the advent of white hide hunting.

Perhaps that would have happened on the American Plains if the tribes had held or continued to augment their populations. But the Comanches and other tribes fought a losing battle against their own attrition. While new institutions such as male polygamy and adoption of captured children worked to build up the Comanches' numbers, the disease epidemics of the nineteenth century repeatedly decimated them. In the 1820s, the Comanches were rebuilding their population after the smallpox epidemic of 1816 had carried away a fourth of them. But smallpox ran like a brush fire through the Plains villages again in 1837–1838, wiping whole peoples off the continent. And the forty-niners brought cholera, which so devastated the Arkansas Valley Indians that William Bent burned his fort and temporarily left the trade that year. John C. Ewers, in fact, has estimated that the nineteenth-century Comanches lost 75% of their population to disease.

Did the Southern Plains Indians successfully work out a dynamic, ecological equilibrium with the bison herds? I would argue that the answer remains ultimately elusive because the relationship was never allowed to play itself out. The trends, however, suggest that a satisfactory solution was improbable. One factor that worked against the horse tribes was their short tenure. It may be that two centuries provided too brief a time for them to create a workable system around horses, the swelling demand for bison robes generated by the Euro-American market, and the expansion of their own populations to hold their territories. Some of those forces, such as the tribes' need to expand their numbers and the advantages of participating in the robe trade, worked against their need to conserve the bison herds. Too, many of the forces that shaped their world were beyond the power of the Plains tribes to influence. And it is very clear that the ecology of the Southern Plains had become so complicated by the mid-nineteenth century that neither the Indians nor the Euro-Americans of those years could have grasped how it all worked.

Finally and ironically, it seems that the Indian religions, so effective at calling forth awe and reverence for the natural world, may have inhibited the Plains Indians' understanding of bison ecology and their role in it. True, native leaders such as Yellow Wolf, the Cheyenne whom James W. Abert interviewed and sketched at Bent's Fort in 1845–1846, surmised the implications of market hunting. As he watched the bison disappearing from the Arkansas Valley, Yellow Wolf asked the whites to teach the Cheyenne hunters how to farm, never realizing that he was reprising a Plains Indian/Euro-American conversation that had taken place sixty years earlier in that same country. But Yellow Wolf was marching to his own drummer, for it remained a widespread tenet of faith among most Plains Indians through the 1880s that bison were supernatural in origin. A firsthand observer and close student of the nineteenth-century Plains reported,

> Every Plains Indian firmly believed that the buffalo were produced in countless numbers in a country under the ground, that every spring the surplus swarmed like bees from a hive, out of great cave-like openings to this country, which were situated somewhere in the great 'Llano Estacado' or Staked Plain of Texas.

This religious conception of the infinity of nature's abundance was poetic. On one level it was also empirical: Bison overwintered in large numbers in the protected canyons scored into the eastern escarpment of the Llano Estacado, and Indians had no doubt many times witnessed the herds emerging to overspread the high Plains in springtime. But such a conception did not aid the tribes in their efforts to work out an ecological balance amid the complexities of the nineteenth-century Plains.

In a real sense, then, the more familiar events of the 1870s only delivered the *coup de grace* to the free Indian life on the Great Plains. The slaughterhouse effects of European diseases and wars with the encroaching whites caused Indian numbers to dwindle after 1850 (no more than fourteen hundred Comanches were enrolled to receive federal benefits at Fort Sill, in present-day Oklahoma, in the 1880s). This combined with bison resiliency to preserve a good core of animals until the arrival of the white hide hunters, who nonetheless can be documented as taking only about 3.5 million animals from the Southern Plains.

But the great days of the Plains Indians, the primal poetry of humans and horses, bison and grass, sunlight and blue skies, and the sensuous satisfactions of a hunting life on the sweeping grasslands defined a meteoric time indeed. And the meteor was already fading in the sky a quarter century before the Big Fifties began to boom.

Readings for Dan Flores:

As a start for this topic one should look at Richard White and William Cronon "Ecological Change and Indian-White Relations," *Handbook of North American Indians,* 4 (Washington, D.C.: Smithsonian Institution, 1988). Richard White has also analyzed the impact on animals that came from changing economic activities of the Indians after the arrival of the Europeans. See his "Animals and Enterprise," chap. 7 in Clyde Milner, II, Carol A. O'Connor, and Martha Sandweiss, eds., *The Oxford History of the American West* (New York: Oxford University Press, 1994). Two general ecological studies are by Christopher Vecsey and Robert W. Venables, eds., *American Indian Environments: Ecological Issues in Native American History* (Syracuse, NY: Syracuse University Press, 1980), and Frank G. Roe, *The North American Buffalo: A Critical Study of the Species in Its Wild State,* 2nd ed. (Toronto: University of Toronto Press, 1970).

11

INDIAN LAND USE AND ENVIRONMENTAL CHANGE IN ISLAND COUNTY, WASHINGTON: A CASE STUDY

RICHARD WHITE

As noted earlier, scholars of the Native American experience now give increasing attention to environmental themes. Few ethnohistorians now accept the idea that Indians lived in harmony with their natural surroundings—that is, that they used what they found without making any changes in the natural habitat. At the same time, the author demonstrates clearly that tribal people in the Pacific Northwest knew what their home territory offered while they both used local resources and modified their environment through conscious actions. The pioneers who first encountered these Indians had no idea that they did anything more than gather plants growing wild, but White proves that this was not the case. In fact, he claims that local villagers knew their environment thoroughly and used at least fifty separate varieties of plants each year. His discussion focuses on the actions of four Salishian tribes on Whidby and Camano islands in Puget Sound. He shows that through the use of fire and a simple technology, the Indians encouraged the growth of useful plants as they sought to improve their subsistence economy and their food sources. The pioneer whites had no understanding of local Indian diet customs and failed to realize that the tribal people had brought long-term changes in the environments of the two islands. White shows that the pioneers objected to the Indian custom of burning the prairie each year as dangerous and destructive. The discussion points out the different awareness of nature by whites and Indians during the middle of the nineteenth century. It also makes clear the Indians' interactive relationship with the environment before Anglo-Americans entered the region.

Richard White is a professor of history at the University of Washington.

Source: Richard White, "Indian Land Use and Environmental Change: Island County, Washington: A Case Study," *Arizona and the West*, 17 (Winter 1975), pp. 327–338. © *Arizona and the West* 17 (Winter 1975). Reprinted with permission of the publisher.

The first Americans to settle in Island County, Washington Territory, in the late 1850s regarded the region as a virgin wilderness. Heavy coniferous forests and small prairies covered the several islands in Puget Sound which composed the county. On these islands Salish tribes followed age-old practices of fishing, hunting, and gathering, and whites presumed that these people had adapted to the land, enjoying its abundance and suffering its scarcities. The prairies and forests seemed obviously the creation of unrestrained nature. Few observers were aware that the Indians inhabiting the area had actually played an active role in shaping their environment, not indirectly, as any population shapes the ecology of a region merely by occupying it, but consciously and purposefully to fit their own needs. Through the use of fire and a simple technology, the Indians over many generations had encouraged the growth of three dominant plants on the islands—bracken, camas, and nettles—to supplement their regular diet of fish and small game and also had created the conditions that fostered immense forests of Douglas fir. A study of the early Salish experience in Island County demonstrates salient features in the process by which hunting and gathering peoples profoundly altered their natural environment.

At the arrival of white settlers, the Indian population in Island County, an area of approximately 206 square miles, lived wholly on two large islands, Whidby and Camano. In size, Whidby ranks second only to Long Island in the continental United States; Camano is about one fifth the size of Whidby. Small fertile prairies, located largely on the northern part of Whidby Island, comprised about five percent of the county. The remaining terrain was hilly, forested, and infertile.

Four Salish tribes—the Skagit, Kikialos, Snohomish, and later the Clallam—had lived on parts of these islands since about 1000 A.D. Each tribe was a loose aggregation of villages united by language and blood, rather than by a centralized political system. Anthropologists have classified all these tribes as saltwater, or canoe, Indians, who, despite differences in language and kinship, shared basically similar culture traits.

The Salish viewed the land as not only being occupied by humans, plants, and animals, but also by a vast array of spirits associated with specific animals or natural phenomena. This added dimension gave nature an ambience and additional meaning. Plants and animals took on not only economic but also religious significance. Although the settlers dismissed these ideas as superstitions, the Salish possessed an acute knowledge of the natural world. Their understanding of plant life, for instance, was both thorough and refined. They named and classified plants, observing subtle differences in taxonomy and habitat. This knowledge was not solely utilitarian; the Indians observed and studied plants whether they were useful or not.

The Salish quest for salmon—the principal food staple for all Puget Sound Indians—largely determined the location of their villages on the islands. Salmon fishing oriented the tribes toward the rivers, and tribal boundaries in the county were the logical continuations of mainland river systems which lay opposite the islands. As a result, the people of the Snohomish River settled on southern parts of Whidby and Camano islands, while the tribes on the Skagit River built villages on North Whidby. The Kikialos were strictly an island tribe, living on North Camano, but their territory faced the Stillaguamish River and they crossed to the mainland each fall to fish its banks.

At the peak of Salish population (about 1780), the Salish villages contained from 1,500 to 2,500 people, living in more than ninety-three places. Most of the sites were summer camping grounds inhabited seasonally for fishing, hunting, and berry or root gathering; but the Salish occupied at least fifteen permanent villages on the islands. Since the Indians sought safe and protected coves for canoe anchorages and a local supply of fish and shellfish, the selected village locations were principally on northeast Whidby and Camano. Three large Skagit villages on Penn's Cove, on North Whidby, formed the population center of the islands. The Snohomish had three villages on South Whidby, while the Kikialos occupied six permanent sites along the western and northern beaches of Camano. Most of the land on southern Whidby and southern Camano had no permanent population.

The large concentration of nonagricultural people on the islands called for a sensitive adjustment to the environment and a willingness to use every available source of food. This adjustment was reflected in the Salish food cycle of hunting, gathering, and fishing. Although the cycle varied from tribe to tribe, the Salish moved periodically through their territories in Puget Sound following the annual pattern of abundance. From May to October hundreds of mainland Indians joined permanent residents on the islands for root gathering and hunting. For all the Indians in the county, gathering vegetable products comprised a crucial element of their food cycle. At least fifty plants, exclusive of trees, were used by the Skagit alone.

The Salish search for food plants ended in September, when the first salmon of the great fall runs started up the rivers, and the Indians moved off the islands and gathered on the riverbanks to take them. For two months incredible numbers of fish crowded the streams. The large groups of Indians who fished and the immense quantities of fish caught led early settlers to regard salmon as their major food. Salmon were indeed of fundamental importance, but the Salish had other sources of food and were prepared to survive the occasional failure of the salmon to appear.

The Indian food cycle confused most early white observers. At times they saw the Indians as incurably nomadic, wandering across the land in search of food. But this was hard to reconcile with the strong Salish attachment to their permanent villages and their reverence for the graves of their ancestors. The tenacity of this devotion both impressed and bewildered the Americans when they sought to displace them. They found Salish devotion to their villages and lands as formidable as the huge cedar houses in which they lived. Actually the permanent villages and seasonal wandering in search of food formed the poles of the Salish's physical relation to the land. Both were basic.

Even modern anthropologists have tended to view the Salish as moving easily over the land, adapting to natural abundance and leaving no trace, with the settlers inheriting the land much as the first Indians had found it. They described the Indians as living off the "spontaneous product of nature" for generations until they were eventually displaced. Both the settlers and scholars have presumed that the components of the Salish food cycle were gifts of virgin nature. But in the plant communities that existed at the time of early settlement, there was evidence of substantial Salish influence on the environment. Three plants in particular—bracken, camas, and nettles—found in abundance by surveyors and settlers, were closely tied to Salish cultural practices.

Prolonged human occupation of a site usually led to a local enrichment of the soil. Succeeding generations of Indians living at the same village inevitably produced considerable amounts of waste. Shells and bones, plant refuse, ashes from fires, and excrement of humans and animals all gradually rotted and provided the soil with significant

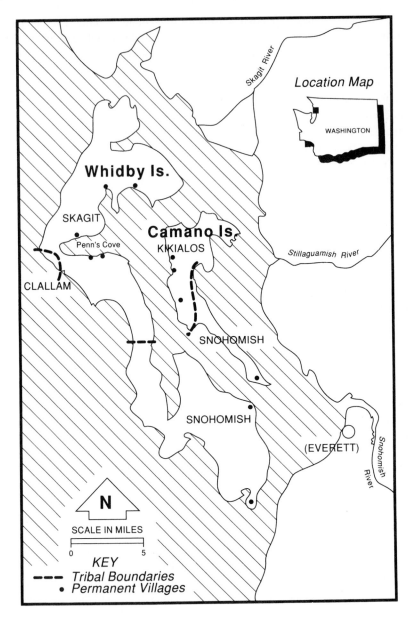

amounts of potash, phosphorous, and nitrogen. These accumulations of waste also provided seedbeds for many of the ancestors of human food crops.

The nettle, for example, preferred rich soils and historically has been associated
with human occupation. The nettle probably spread from the prairies, where it was a native plant, into the vicinity of the Salish villages. As with corn, constant proximity
brought familiarity and eventually the discovery of uses for the plant. The Indians of
Puget Sound made extensive use of the nettle. They extracted a medicine and a dye from

it and peeled, dried, and rolled the bark into a two-ply string for fishing and duck nets. Moreover, as a wild nettle patch generally indicated rich ground, the Indians later used the plant as a guide in starting potato patches. According to their own testimony the Skagit Indians tended the nettles in a manner closely resembling cultivation. They kept the nettle patches free of weeds and burned the plant refuse in the fall after harvesting. The Salish clearly encouraged the nettle over other plant species of the prairies.

The Salish not only burned nettle patches but also regularly burned entire prairies in midsummer or early fall, when the rains had stopped and grass was tall and tinder dry. The first settlers on Whidby found these fires alarming, for they threatened their crops and houses. Because whites refused to tolerate the occasional destruction of their property, the beginning of American settlement saw the cessation of Indian burning on the prairies.

Few settlers gave much thought to the reasons behind these fires. One of the few who did was J. G. Cooper, a botanist with the railroad expedition that reached western Washington in 1854. Cooper recognized that the Salish had definite and sensible reasons for burning and concluded that if they ceased the practice the forest would soon encroach on the open lands. The Indians, he wrote, "burned to preserve their open grounds for game, and for the production of their important root, camas." The introduction of the horse, according to Cooper, had provided a further inducement for firing the grasslands. Fresh pastures sprang up in burned-over country. Cooper's comments on Indian land use were insightful but were largely ignored. Actually they fitted the inland Indians of southern Puget Sound better than they did the saltwater Salish of Whidby.

The Salish of Island County had no reason to burn to increase grazing areas, for they had no horses, nor were they dependent on large game animals for food. Even deer, a relatively minor source of food, were browsers that did not require extensive grasslands for feed. Undoubtedly, Indian burning encouraged game animals by enlarging their feeding areas, but this was not necessarily the rationale for burning. More likely the initial impetus for fires was to increase vegetable production.

The desire to encourage the growth of bracken, a fern which reached heights of seven feet on the prairies, and camas—which Cooper noticed dominating large expanses of open land—were the main reasons for setting fires. Both plants were staples of the Indian diet. The Salish ground dried bracken roots into flour, which they baked for bread. They boiled the fresh camas, eating them like potatoes, or dried and preserved the bulbs. The abundance of these plants on the prairies was not fortuitous. Rather than being major Indian food sources because they dominated the prairies, bracken and camas more likely dominated the prairies because they were major Indian food sources. According to Carl Sauer, the noted geographer, the very existence of people like the Salish depended on "acting intelligently within the range of their experience." Observing the changes that fire brought in its wake and using the altered landscape to their own advantage were "advantageous behavior" that enabled the Salish to survive.

In the Puget Sound region bracken was a pioneer invader of disturbed or burned-over lands. Burning facilitated the plant's spread over the prairies where the dense growth of native grasses often blocked its progress. Once established, the extensive root system of the fern, and the death of its topgrowth in the fall, protected it from fatal damage by fire and gave it an advantage over less resilient rivals. The encouragement of bracken would not have benefited a pastoral people seeking to enlarge their grazing lands. In fact, bracken was a poor feed after its first growth, and pastoral peoples lamented its increase. But the Salish were not herdsmen. They valued the fern as an important source of food and sought to promote its growth.

The camas plant benefited more indirectly from burning. Like bracken, its top growth died off in late summer and fall prairie fires did it little harm. Unlike bracken, however, the mere destruction of competing plants did not contribute to its spread. Direct human or animal intervention was necessary for the plant to widen its range. The Skagit moved camas bulbs into fresh areas, at first perhaps unwittingly, but later with zeal and care. Harvesting enabled the camas to increase, for dropped, split, and discarded bulbs spread the plant to new areas. Gathering the crop with a digging stick became a type of "unplanned tillage." According to Indian and white testimony, cultivation to ensure a better harvest eventually supplemented the digging and transplanting of mature bulbs. Such a technique approached true farming—as did other Salish practices. For example, they also worked in plant refuse around another food plant, the tiger lily. The Indians of the upper Skagit, and probably the Whidby Skagit, practiced a primitive cultivation of both the lily and the wild carrot. When the potato was introduced into Puget Sound, the Salish quickly became adept at the cultivation of that crop without any direct instruction by the settlers.

Indian modification of the vegetational community of the prairies was significant and purposeful. Salish practices involved a rational manipulation of the environment, and this manipulation had profound ecological effects. Burning destroyed conifer seedlings and shrubs that encroached on the prairies, while at the same time it encouraged bracken to become the dominant vegetation of the open lands. Other Salish practices helped spread camas and nettle plants. Unwanted trees or shrubs surviving the fires were pulled out by hand. When the whites arrived, they regarded the prairies as wild. They damned bracken for making plowing difficult, cursed the painful sting of the nettle, and praised camas as pig food. In fulfilling the biblical injunction of sinking plowshares into the earth, they imagined that they were putting the stamp of man upon the land. But the stamp of man was already firmly present.

Salish influence on the landscape extended beyond the limits of the prairies into the surrounding forests. Indians used wood extensively, especially cedar, but also fir, hemlock, and alder. Yet considering the abundance of the forests and the massive size of the towering trees, direct Salish use probably had little impact on forest ecology. The conifers of western Washington were so huge that it took the neighboring Makah Indians two weeks to fell a Sitka spruce by fire and axe. To cut the fir and cedar of Island County would have demanded similar labor. The occasional felling of one of these giants would have made only a minuscule difference in the forest as a whole.

For the Salish the forest yielded other products besides wood. They searched among the trees for berries, fireweed, and game, none of which favored deep forest, but thrived in the clearings and young successional forests that followed fires. The upper-river Indians, fearing the immediate destruction of existing game animals, were wary of fire, but the saltwater peoples of the lowlands apparently burned over berry fields without much hesitation. They particularly sought to promote the growth of fireweed and berries that formed part of the normal successional pattern on such lands. Berries were an important food, while fireweed, along with other materials, was used in the weaving of blankets. The very name *fireweed* given it by the settlers, showed the close connection between this plant and burning.

The first United States surveyors to examine Whidby and Camano islands in the late 1850s made significant comments on the condition of the forests at the time. There had not yet been a decade of settlement, and most of the islands were unoccupied and practically unexplored. The surveyors made two critical observations: (1) they noted that Douglas fir was the dominant forest species of the islands, closely followed by hemlock and Sitka spruce and cedar; and (2) they recorded that large areas in the forests had been burned.

In the hemlock-cedar climax forests in Island County, Douglas fir relied for propagation on the destruction not only of other trees but also of the mature fir itself. Fir not only thrived on catastrophe, it depended on it. Fir seedlings died in the dense shade of mature forests, while hemlock and cedar seedlings survived, spread, and eventually displaced the mature fir as they fell from age and disease. Without interference, the climax forest of the region would have been primarily cedar and hemlock. As Douglas fir of all ages and sizes abounded on the islands, mature forests obviously had been destroyed. This destruction clearly did not result from harvesting, nor was there evidence of extensive kills by disease or insects. The surveyors blamed the destruction on fire.

Normally the fires that had destroyed the virgin forests of Island County could have been ascribed to electrical storms. However, few thunderstorms occurred in western Washington. Thunderstorms swept the mountains on the mainland, but they would have had to be of staggering proportions to reach Puget Sound. Furthermore, such fires could never have reached Island County, simply because Whidby and Camano were islands. Yet fires were so extensive and common on the islands that, of the sixteen townships surveyed in the 1850s, six contained burned-over forests. In five of these the damage was substantial. This burning gave the Douglas fir its advantage and enabled the tree to dominate the forests of the islands.

Extensive forest burning in the county resulted either from prairie fires which accidently spread to the woods or from fires deliberately set to extend berry grounds. With the brisk winds that blew across the islands, a small fire could spread rapidly. As Indian fires were the main source of forest burning in Island County, and probably in the entire Puget Sound region, they played a critical role in determining the species composition of the forests. The result was a large stand of Douglas fir in the lowland forests of Puget Sound and a successional growth of groundsel, fireweed, berries, bracken, and fir, alder, and hemlock seedlings.

In the northern coniferous forests, burning had shaped woodland ecology for centuries. Fire formed a crucial part of the forest environment. It not only liberated mineral nutrients accumulated in the litter, humus, wood, and foliage of the old forest, but it simultaneously prepared seedbeds and triggered the release of some seed supplies. The periodic destruction of old forests kept a significant proportion of each region in young trees and thus reduced the susceptibility of the forest to insects and disease. In a sense, fires were so common and critical that the species composition that would have developed without fire would have been unnatural. The only unusual aspect of the situation on Puget Sound was that such a large percentage of fires were of human origin.

Fire shaped not only the forests but also the animal population that inhabited the woodlands. Both deer and elk were abundant in Island County when settlers first arrived, and according to Miron Heinselman, a forester who had studied forest fires, these animals were "best adapted to recent burns and early succession forests—not climax forests." Thus, by setting fires the Salish provided these animals with their habitat and increased their numbers—as well as the number of their predators, the wolves.

The Salish accomplishment in creating and maintaining their ecosystem was impressive. Because of this the Indian population of 1780 was larger than any human population on the islands before 1910. They populated their islands with spirits and powers, but they did not restrict their manipulation to magic. Their technology was limited, but they used it effectively. Unlike the Indians of the upper rivers, the Salish never suffered seasonal scarcities or periodic famines. Indeed, in terms of camas, berries, bracken, deer, and elk, the islands were a food-exporting region. This had been brought about by Indians learning, through observation and tradition, to alter natural communities to fit their needs, without destroying in the process the ability of these communities to sustain the cultures which had created them. Far from being creatures of their environment, the Indians had shaped their world and made it what it was when the whites arrived.

The stability of the environment the Salish had created in Island County depended on their continued burning, cultivation, and gathering. If they had ceased these activities, the ecology of the area would have been altered. With the coming of the settlers, however, the Salish not only curtailed these practices but began adapting new tools and techniques introduced by white farmers. As a result, the Salish environment changed at a staggering rate in the 1850s. Even as Indians lingered on the prairies and along the coves, pigs and cows destroyed the camas and farmers plowed up the nettles and bracken. The annual fires ceased, and the Indians found themselves powerless to sustain the world that they had created—and that, in turn, had sustained them.

Readings for Richard White:

White considers the same issues in more detail in his *Land Use, Environment, and Social Change: The Shaping of Island County, Washington* (Seattle: University of Washington Press, 1980) and *Roots of Dependency: Subsistence, Environment, and Social Change among the Choctaws, Pawnees, and Navajos* (Lincoln: University of Nebraska Press, 1983. For an eastern example see William Cronon, *Changes in the Land: Indians, Colonists, and the Ecology of New England* (New York: Hill and Wang, 1983). A more recent look at environmental issues is David Rich Lewis, *Neither Wolf nor Dog: American Indians, Environment, and Agrarian Change* (New York: Oxford University Press, 1994).

12

INDIANS IN LOS ANGELES, 1781–1875: ECONOMIC INTEGRATION, SOCIAL DISINTEGRATION

GEORGE HARWOOD PHILLIPS

Usually Native Americans are studied within their social units: bands, villages, or tribes. Not only do most Americans think of Indians in generic terms, but when they think of California tribal people at all, they recall pastoral scenes of Spanish missions in some romantic past. Striving to overcome such ideas, this essay considers the impact that the Spanish, Mexican, and American invasions of California had on the native people there. The author traces Indian experiences with the intruders from aboriginal times through the post–gold rush era. He shows how each of the three imperial powers saw and dealt with the local tribes. The Spanish recruited Indians to labor at the coastal missions, expecting to convert their charges to Christianity while pacifying the region. By the time Mexico gained its independence, most tribal workers labored on farms or ranches or at the missions. In the mid 1830s the government secularized the missions, granting much of the land to ranchers and allowing the Native American workers to remain or leave. Some returned to their tribal homes, but many migrated to the coastal towns and worked as day laborers. Much of the article examines the kinds of jobs open to Native Americans and compares the means used to control their labor first by Mexican and later by American local officials. This discussion explores the impact of white intrusion upon the tribal peoples and explains the process by which some Indians made substantial contributions to the southern California economy.

George Harwood Phillips is retired from the University of Colorado History Department.

As members of sociopolitical units not yet significantly damaged by white contact, Indians had their greatest impact on post-Columbian, North American history. Bands, lineages, villages, chiefdoms, and confederacies rendered decisions and implemented policies

Source: George Harwood Phillips, "Indians in Los Angeles, 1781–1875: Economic Integration, Social Disintegration," *Pacific Historical Review,* 49 (August 1980), pp. 427–451. © 1980 by the Pacific Coast Branch, American Historical Association. Reprinted from the *Pacific Historical Review* by permission of the Branch.

concerning the white intruders that sometimes were of crucial importance in shaping the histories of regions and localities. On occasion, however, Indians actively participated in the historical process as individuals whose traditional corporate existence had been disrupted by white contact. Indians in the Los Angeles region are a case in point.

Seeking work, individual Indians began drifting into the pueblo of Los Angeles almost from the day it was founded. Settlers and Indians thereby established an economic relationship that continued for nearly a century. Unfortunately, historians have overlooked this relationship and have concentrated instead on the social disintegration of the Indian residents. The Indians underwent social disintegration, however, because they became tightly integrated into the pueblo's economic structure. So interconnected were the processes of social disintegration and economic integration that no investigation of Indian urban life would be complete without each receiving equal consideration. This article analyzes the Indian in the history of Los Angeles as both social victim and economic contributor.

At the time of Spanish intrusion into Alta California in 1769 the Indian peoples occupying most of present-day Los Angeles County, half of Orange County, and the islands of Santa Catalina and San Clemente spoke Gabrielino, one of the Cupan languages in the Takic family which is part of the Uto-Aztecan language stock. On the islands and along the densely populated coastal region, the Gabrielino lived in permanent village communities based on kinship ties. For subsistence they relied primarily on hunting, fishing, and collecting wild plants, although they may have engaged in some protoagricultural activity.

In August 1769 Gabrielinos, perhaps from the village of Yangna, located near the Los Angeles River, established friendly contact with the first Spanish expedition passing through their territory. They presented the Spaniards with shell beads and baskets of seeds. The Spanish reciprocated with tobacco and glass beads. That these villagers resided in an incredibly fertile region was not lost on at least one member of the expedition. Fray Juan Crespí remarked: "after crossing the river we entered a large vineyard of wild grapes and an infinity of rosebushes in full bloom. All the soil is black and loamy, and is capable of producing every kind of grain and fruit which may be planted." After the Chumash, their Hokan-speaking neighbors to the north with whom they shared many cultural traits, the Gabrielino became the most intensively colonized people in southern California. Where greater Los Angeles stands today, Spaniards created a mission, pueblo, and three privately owned ranchos in just thirteen years.

In September 1771 Mission San Gabriel Arcángel was founded, the fourth Spanish mission to be established in Alta California. It was moved to its present location, near the Indian village of Sibangna, in 1774. By the end of the year 154 neophytes (the term used to designate the Indian converts) resided at the mission. Ten years later 739 neophytes were associated with the mission, although many lived on inland mission ranchos. Politically and culturally San Gabriel was much the same as the other missions, but economically it differed considerably. More than the others, it emphasized viticulture, and its large vineyard was recognized as the *viña madre* of Spanish California. Many of its neophytes acquired the skills of planting, tending, and harvesting grapes and manufacturing wine and distilled spirits. They also became masons, carpenters, plasterers, soapmakers, tanners, shoemakers, blacksmiths, millers, bakers, cooks, brickmakers, cartmakers, weavers, spinners, saddlers, shepherds, and vaqueros. In short, the neophytes of San Gabriel as well as those of the other southern missions—San Fernando, San Juan Capistrano, San Luis Rey, and San Diego—became *the* skilled labor force of southern California.

In September 1781, ten years to the month after the establishment of Mission San Gabriel, a party of forty-four men, women, and children founded the pueblo of Los Angeles near the village of Yangna and only three leagues from the mission. Racially and ethnically the colonists were heterogeneous; only two adults were true Spaniards, the others being of Indian, African, and mixed ancestry. But to distinguish themselves from the California Indian population, they adopted the label *gente de razón,* or people of reason. Included were a few farmers, a hoemaker, a cowherd, a mason, and a tailor. By 1790 the population of the pueblo totalled 141 persons.

Privately owned ranchos, the first to be established in Alta California, were also created in Gabrielino territory. In 1784 the governor of the province granted soldiers Juan José Domínquez, José María Verdugo, and Manuel Pérez Nieto permission to raise livestock on vast tracts of land, provided their claims did not encroach upon the holdings allotted to the pueblo and the mission. Each grantee was required to construct a stone house, stock his rancho with two thousand head of cattle, and employ as many vaqueros as needed to manage the animals.

Based on crop growing and stock raising, the mission, pueblo, and ranchos were designed to be economically self-sufficient. The mission relied mainly on neophyte labor, but initially the pueblo and the ranchos recruited most of their workers from the gentiles (a term applied by the gente de razón to the unconverted, politically independent Indians). The gentiles, however, consented to work only when it did not interfere with their traditional subsistence activities. In 1784 Lieutenant Francisco Ortega noted the dependence of the pueblo on Indian labor and the independence of the Indian laborers: "I feel that only with the aid of the gentiles have . . . [the settlers] been able to plant the . . . crops of wheat and corn but as . . . [the Indians] are at present harvesting their abundant wild seeds, they justly refuse with this good reason to lend a hand in digging and weeding."

Apparently concerned about the familiarity established between settlers and gentiles, the governor attempted to regulate Indian-white relations in the pueblo. In 1787 he issued instructions to the corporal of the guard which outlined how the Indians were to be treated. Never were they to be allowed inside the settlers' houses, certainly not to sleep or even to grind corn. Indians from distant villages were not to settle permanently in the pueblo, while those who came for only a few days' work were to reside near the guardhouse, where they could be easily observed. Large groups were not to be allowed in the town for their own amusement. Tact and diplomacy were to be used to encourage the Indians already residing near the pueblo to move from the immediate area. A settler seeking to recruit Indian workers from outside the pueblo had to obtain permission from the authorities, and a person who traveled alone to a village without authorization was liable to a week's punishment in the stocks. The directive forbade forced labor and false promises and demanded that Indian complaints be heard. An individual caught mistreating an Indian was to be punished in the presence of the victim. If Indians were apprehended in the act of stealing or stock killing, they were to be told the reason for the punishment and then lashed fifteen or twenty times in the presence of their leaders. Most likely these instructions were often ignored, but they do indicate that the pueblo, a tiny foreign enclave in a vast Indian territory, was both suspicious of and dependent upon its Indian neighbors.

By the beginning of the nineteenth century a sizable body of Indians, most of them from beyond the Los Angeles–San Gabriel region, had settled, at least temporarily, near the town. The corporal of the guard, Francisco Xavier Alvarado, reported in 1803 that 150 of the 200 gentiles were from outside the immediate area. Six years later he noted that the resident Indians spent much of their time gambling and drinking and a few had been put in the stocks as punishment. About this time some of the gentiles probably contracted the same venereal disease that had recently infected a large number of the neophytes at the nearby mission.

When the gentiles were not available or when skilled labor was demanded, the pueblo employed neophytes from the southern missions. In 1810, for example, a hundred Indians from San Juan Capistrano assisted the settlers in raising hemp and flax. And in 1819 neophytes from San Luis Rey constructed a church, receiving one *real* (12½¢) a day plus board and lodging for their efforts. But until the mid 1830s the pueblo and the ranchos depended mainly on gentile labor.

This dependency became a major concern of the Spanish missionaries, and from their accounts emerges a picture of Indian industriousness and settler indolence. The padres were convinced that the employment of gentiles sapped the initiative of the gente de razón and prolonged traditional Indian religious practices. In 1795 Father Vincente de Santa María wrote: "The whole of pagandom . . . is fond of the Pueblo of Los Angeles, of the rancho of Mariano Verdugo and the rancho of Reyes, and of the Zanja. Here we see nothing but pagans passing, clad in shoes, with sombreros and blankets, and serving as muleteers to the settlers and rancheros, so that if it were not for the gentiles there would be neither pueblo nor rancho. . . . Finally these pagan Indians care neither for the Mission nor for the missionaries." The following year Father José Señan expressed a similar view:

> The main fault . . . lies in the indifference of the colonists and their disinclination toward hard work; they prefer to hold in hand a deck of cards rather than a hoe or plow. What little progress is being made must be credited to the population of neighboring gentile rancherías and not to the settler. The Indians cultivate the fields, do the planting, and harvest the crops. . . . Still more painful is the effect of all this upon the natives who, being in contact with the colonists, or *gente de razón,* should have been the first to receive Holy Baptism. But because of the bad example set them, and perhaps for their own private reasons, these natives still abide in the shadows of paganism.

A report on the condition of the Indians at San Gabriel, issued in 1814 by the mission's padres, echoed the same concern:

> In the town and on the ranchos of the people of the other classes both men and women who are pagans assist in the work of the fields. Also they are employed as cooks, water carriers and in other domestic occupations. This is one of the most potent causes why the people who are called *gente de razón* are given so much to idleness. Since the pagan Indians are paid for their labor by half or a third of the crops, they remain content in the service of their masters during the season of planting and harvesting. The latter, with few exceptions, never put their hands to the plow or sickle. As a result of this another drawback arises, namely the [Indian] adults delay having themselves baptised. In the service of their masters, they live according to their pagan notions and practices.

By the time of Mexico's independence in 1821 Los Angeles had become a thriving agricultural community, a development noted by foreign visitors. A. Duhaut-Cilly passed through in the late 1820s and "counted eighty-two houses comprising the pueblo, which I inferred it might have one thousand inhabitants, including in this number two-hundred Indians, servants or laborers. . . . The principal produce consists of maize and grapes. The vine succeeds very well." About the same time, Alfred Robinson arrived. "The population of this town," he wrote in *Life in California,* "is about fifteen hundred; and has an alcalde, two regidores, and a syndico who compose its *'Ayuntamiento'* or Town Council. In the vicinity are many vineyards and cornfields, and some fine gardens, crossed by beautiful streams of water. The lands[,] being level and fertile, are capable of great agricultural improvement." To irrigate the vineyards, gardens, and orchards an efficient water system was developed. It consisted of a *zanja madre,* or main ditch, which channelled the water from the Los Angeles River to the town and several branch zanjas, eventually numbering eight, which carried the water to the growers' plots.

The pueblo's first vineyard was planted about 1803, probably with cuttings from Mission San Gabriel. The grape was of the "mission" variety, best suited for the table, but also made into a brandy called *aguardiente* and a wine of poor quality. Louis Vignes, originally from Bordeaux, is generally credited with establishing California's commercial wine industry. He settled in the pueblo in 1831, imported cuttings from France, and soon had a large vineyard under cultivation.

As the pueblo's grape and other agricultural industries expanded, the demand for cheap labor increased sharply. Indians supplied this need. The census of 1830 put the number of Indians in the pueblo at 198 as compared to 764 gente de razón. The census taker divided the Indians into two classes: Domesticated Indians (ex-neophytes who had once been attached to the missions) and Domesticated Heathens (gentiles who had never been converted or missionized). At this time the gentiles outnumbered the ex-neophytes 127 to 71 in the pueblo and 157 to 104 in the entire district. According to the census taker, amicable relations prevailed between the gentiles and the gente de razón. "The heathens of the neighborhood," he noted, "who come here and work with the whites, are treated well and live a civilized and quiet life."

Within a few years, however, Indian-white relations in the town changed significantly. In August 1833 the Mexican government enacted a law secularizing the missions of Alta and Baja California. Originally designed to convert the missions into Indian pueblos and distribute land to the neophytes, in effect the law opened up thousands of square leagues to private white ownership and thus established the rancho the dominant economic and social institution of Mexican California.

Even with the promise of land, most neophytes exhibited scant interest in remaining at or near the missions. They drifted into the interior, sought work on the ranchos, or wandered into the towns. Although most of the neophytes from San Gabriel fled to the north, those from the southern missions of San Diego, San Luis Rey, and San Juan Capistrano overran the Los Angeles area. The census of 1836 identified 533 Indians in the district as compared to 1,675 gente de razón. Residing in the town proper were 223 ex-neophytes and 32 gentiles. Eight years later another census recorded 650 Indians in the town, over 400 coming from the southern missions. Thus, in the decade after secularization began, ex-neophytes replaced the gentiles as the town's Indian majority and the total number of Indian residents tripled.

Because the town's economic structure could not absorb such a dramatic increase in the work force, a large number of Indians remained perpetually unemployed. The social and political ramifications of this economic situation were extensive. Incidents of Indian drunkenness increased and alarmed the Mexican authorities. The problem was linked to the development of a retail liquor business that by the mid 1830s had become an important part of the local economy. But rather than regulate the business in order to curtail Indian consumption, the ayuntamiento increased its authority over the Indian consumers. In January 1836 it authorized the *regidores* (councilmen) to arrest all drunken Indians and assign them to work on the zanja madre which needed improvement. Although hardly an act of great repression, the authorization initiated a system of labor recruitment that steadily integrated Indians by force into the pueblo's economic structure.

Over the years, Indians established several settlements in and adjacent to the pueblo. The smallest consisted of Pipimares, Gabrielino-speakers most likely from Santa Catalina Island. These survivors of a once thriving island population had been removed to the mainland sometime in the 1820s. Those who eventually settled in the pueblo clustered together in a few huts and tenaciously maintained their distinct identity. The majority of the Indians, however, resided on a tract of city property that the ayuntamiento granted them in 1836.

Three Indian *alcaldes* nominally governed the main settlement. While possessing limited influence with the white authorities, these officials sometimes pressed for Indian rights. On April 27, 1838, for instance, Alcaldes Gabriel, Juan José, and Gandiel petitioned the ayuntamiento to force a white neighbor, Juan Domingo, to vacate land that belonged to the Indians. The Mexican authorities ruled in favor of the Indians, fined Domingo $12, and ordered him off the property. The Indian residents, however, achieved few such legal victories, and it was not long before their rights were severely curtailed.

In January 1844 the ayuntamiento passed a resolution stating that all persons without occupation or some manner of making a living were liable to a fine or incarceration. Upon discharging servants or day laborers, employers were to issue each a document indicating the circumstances of their release and whether they were at liberty to work for someone else. No servant or worker could be hired without this document, and those seeking employment for the first time had to secure a certificate from the authorities. Persons failing to present their documents were to be arrested and tried immediately and, if found guilty, jailed as prisoners of the city.

The resolution emerged in response to a sharp rise in Indian crime and violence, although the hostilities were primarily intra-Indian and confined to the main Indian settlement. Most of those arrested were charged with being drunk and disorderly and usually received a sentence of fifteen days of hard labor on public works projects. On occasion, however, Indian prisoners worked out their sentences in the custody of private citizens who paid their fines and who were responsible for their whereabouts and behavior.

In May and June 1845 the Indian residents became so disorderly that two petitions presented to the ayuntamiento sought their removal from the town. The commission that was formed to study the problem recommended removal, and late in the year the Indians were forced to move across the river, where they constructed a new settlement called Pueblito. The following year two more petitions called for the removal of the Pipimares. The first was rejected on the grounds that these Indians had resided in the town for years and that no complaint had been issued against them. The second petition, however, led to the formation of a commission which reported that the few Pipimares who remained should be domiciled on the premises of their employers or relocated in the main Indian settlement. The commission's recommendations were approved and the Pipimares were dispersed.

The new settlement of Pueblito became as crime ridden as the old. In February 1846 twenty-six citizens petitioned directly to the Governor of California: "When the 'Indian Rancheria' was removed to the 'Pueblito' we thought that the isolation of these aborigines would prevent the committing of excess and thefts . . . but we are sorry to say it has proved to the contrary. Taking advantage of their isolation they steal all neighboring fences and on Saturdays celebrate and become intoxicated to an unbearable degree." The petitioners were also concerned about the spread of venereal disease among the Indians, blaming it on the "vice" of polygamy. They feared that the Indian population would soon disappear if corrective measures were not taken. The Indians, they recommended, should either be placed in an area where they could be strictly policed or provided with living quarters by their employers.

Late the following year Rafael Gallardo submitted a petition to the common council (the city government under American rule) that sought to remove the Indians from Pueblito. On November 8, 1847 the council passed an ordinance authorizing the destruction of the settlement. This required housing servants and workers on their employers' premises, relocating self-sufficient Indians outside the city limits in widely separated settlements and assigning vagrants of either sex to public works projects or confining them in jail. Twenty-four dollars were raised to assist the Indians in moving, and by the end of the month Pueblito had been razed.

American rule introduced new and serious problems to the resident Indians. As unruly Yankees, Californios, and immigrants from Mexico (especially Sonora) and Europe drifted into the pueblo, Los Angeles became one of the most volatile and lawless towns in the Far West. "Gambling, drinking, and whoring are the only occupations," wrote an American military officer in 1849," and they seem to be followed with great industry, particularly the first and second. Monte banks, cock fights, and liquor shops are to be seen in all directions." In *Reminiscences of a Ranger,* Horace Bell recalled "that in the years of 1851, '52 and '53, there were more desperadoes in Los Angeles than in any place on the Pacific coast, San Francisco with its great population not excepted."

Given the general disorder that characterized Los Angeles in the early 1850s, it is hardly surprising that the semblance of social stability the Indians had maintained under Mexican domination quickly gave way to internal dissension and conflicts. The worst incident of intra-Indian violence occurred in 1851 during a traditional gambling game called *peon.* A fight erupted between local Indians and Cahuillas visiting from the interior. "We found thirteen dead in the vicinity of the fight," recalled Joseph Lancaster Brent. "These all had their heads mashed beyond recognition, which is the sign manual of Indian murder; but these Indians did not scalp. Dead and wounded Indians were discovered everywhere, and it was a moderate estimate that fifty lost their lives." In May 1851 the common council prohibited the playing of peon within the city limits. The games continued, however, often resulting in Indian casualties and arrests.

Throughout the 1850s seldom a week went by without the local newspapers reporting incidents of Indian violence and crime. Bodies of dead—usually murdered and mutilated—Indians were a common sight in the streets. Nearly all the homicides went unsolved, the coroner usually rendering a verdict of "death by violence from persons unknown." Arrested for theft, forgery, rape, assault, and sometimes murder, Indians were whipped, imprisoned, and executed for their misdeeds. Perhaps the most revealing statement on intra-Indian violence—indeed, on town violence in general—came from the *Los Angeles Star* on September 13, 1856. Mentioning no specific cases, it reported with icy indifference and caustic cynicism that "Indians continue to kill each other. One or two instances of stabbings have come under our notice this week. We cannot learn that any white person had developed his manhood within the last seven days."

By the mid 1850s the Indian residents were obviously undergoing social disintegration, a process that drew comments from travelers and local citizens. An American visitor remarked in 1852 that he "saw more Indians about this place than in any part of California I had yet visited. They were chiefly 'Mission Indians' . . . [and] are a miserable squalid-looking set, squatting or lying about the corners of the streets, without occupation. . . . No care seems to be taken of them by the Americans." In the same year, Benjamin Wilson reported on the condition of the Indians of southern California, stating that those in the pueblo had "become sadly deteriorated, within the last two years." In 1855 a local physician estimated that nine tenths of the town's Indians were infected with syphilis.

Despite the social disorder, Los Angeles continued to develop economically. "The pueblo of Los Angeles is extremely rich . . . ," reported Eugène Duflot de Mofras in 1842. "Vineyards yield 600 barrels of wine, and an equal amount of brandy. . . . El pueblo has in addition sixty *huertas,* or gardens, planted out to vines that cover an area roughly estimated at 100 hectares." A few years later Edwin Bryant noted: "The yield of the vineyards is very abundant and a large quantity of wines of good quality and flavor, and *aguardiente,* are manufactured here. Some vineyards, I understand, contain as many as twenty-thousand vines."

In late 1852 the *Star* estimated that there were 400,000 vines within the city limits and that each vine would conservatively yield five pounds of grapes. On the vine, grapes brought between two to six cents per pound in the town and its environs but averaged twenty cents a pound in San Francisco. In 1859 approximately 300,000 pounds of grapes and 150,000 gallons of wine—valued at $36,641 and $113,180, respectively—were exported. Three years later 6,340 tons of grapes were harvested, resulting in 352,223 gallons of wine and 29,789 gallons of brandy. And by 1875 the production of wine had risen dramatically to 1,328,900 gallons.

Indian residents did not share in the agricultural wealth of Los Angeles County. The federal census of 1850 identified only 334 Indians as taxpayers, and only three in the county and none in the town had enough personal wealth to be listed in a column labeled "Value of Real Estate Owned." Those listed were Urbano Chari, a farmer worth $500; Roman, a farmer worth $1,000; and Samuel, a laborer worth $250. Yet according to the state census of 1852 the county's Indian population of 3,693 approximated that of the whites at 4,093.

At this time about four hundred Indians were employed in the pueblo, many as domestic servants. The Benjamin Wilson report of 1852 asserted that the Indians, "with all their faults, appear to be a necessary part of the domestic economy. They are almost the only house or farm servants we have. The San Luiseño is most sprightly, skillful, and handy; the Cahuilla plodding, but strong, and very useful with instruction and watching." The town servant earned a maximum of a dollar per day, but most received less. For attending to most of the household duties, an Indian and his wife received fifty cents a day from their Anglo-American employer. Domestics, moreover, could be discarded with blatant callousness. Upon discovering that his young servant was terminally ill, a Spanish-speaking citizen, apparently to avoid burial expenses, hauled her out of town to die beside the road. Competition was fierce among the Indians for the limited number of domestic jobs, so employers had no difficulty in finding replacements. In May 1860, for example, an Indian informed a Mr. Laventhal that his servant had been killed the previous night and that he had come to take his place.

Most of the labor performed by the Indians related to the town's most important industry. Indians maintained the vineyards and repaired the irrigation ditches throughout the year, but during the fall harvest their services were of special importance. Harvesting just one large vineyard called for a large body of organized workers. William Wolfskill, for example, employed about forty laborers, two thirds of whom picked the grapes and hauled them to a central location. Indians also provided valuable, if extremely tedious, labor in the processing of the grapes. "There were no wine presses," recalled an Anglo-American resident, "and the grapes were placed in huge shallow vats placed near the 'sanja' or water ditch. The Indians were made to bathe their feet in the sanja and then step into the vats where they tread rhythmically up and down on the grapes to press out the juice. Quite a number of Indians were in the vats at one time." Harris Newmark wrote in *Sixty Years in Southern California* that the Indians, "Stripped to the skin, and wearing only loin-cloths, . . . tramped with ceaseless tread from morn till night, pressing from the luscious fruit of the vineyard the juice so soon to ferment into wine."

During the 1850s and 1860s the Indian residents increasingly were integrated by force into the pueblo's economic structure. The impetus behind this development came from both state and local legislation. At its first session in late 1849 and early 1850 the California legislature authorized the mayor or recorder of an incorporated town or city to arrest, on the complaint of any citizen, Indians caught begging, loitering, or "leading an immoral or profligate course of life." Those arrested could then be hired out to the highest bidder for a term not to exceed four months. Imitating the legislature, the Los Angeles common council issued the following ordinance in August 1850: "When the city has no work in which to employ the chain gang, the Recorder shall, by means of notices conspicuously posted, notify the public that such a number of prisoners will be auctioned off to the highest bidder for private service."

Nearly every Monday morning for some twenty years local ranchers and growers assembled at the mayor's office to bid on the Indian prisoners. That the practice became callously routine is demonstrated in a letter written in 1852. The administrator of Rancho los Alamitos called upon his employer to "deputize someone to attend the auction that usually takes place at the prison on Mondays, and buy me five or six Indians." In his characteristically flamboyant yet often poignant way, Horace Bell described the system in which the Indians were caught.

The cultivators of the vineyards commenced paying the Indian peons with *aguardiente,* a veritable fire-water and no mistake. The consequence was that on being paid off on Saturday evening, they would meet in great gatherings called peons, and pass the night in gambling, drunkenness, and debauchery. On Sunday the streets would be crowded from morn till night with Indians, males and females of all ages, from the girl of ten or twelve, to the old man and woman of seventy or eighty. . . .

About sundown the pompous marshal, with his Indian special deputies, who had been kept in jail all day to keep them sober, would drive and drag the herd to a big corral in the rear of Downey Block, where they would sleep away their intoxication, and in the morning they would be exposed for sale, as slaves for the week. Los Angeles had its slave mart, as well as New Orleans and Constantinople—only the slave at Los Angeles was sold fifty-two times a year as long as he lived, which did not generally exceed one, two, or three years, under the new dispensation. They would be sold for a week, and bought up by the vineyard men and others at prices ranging from one to three dollars, one-third of which was to be paid to the peon at the end of the week, which debt, due for well performed labor, would invariably be paid in *aguardiente,* and the Indian would be made happy until the following Monday morning, having passed through another Saturday night and Sunday's saturnalia of debauchery and bestiality. Those thousands of honest, useful people were absolutely destroyed in this way.

Many Indian prisoners, however, paid their fines and thus were spared the indignity of the auction. In fact, the town government met part of its operating expenses with the revenue collected from Indians. On October 2, 1850 the common council authorized the recorder to pay the Indian alcaldes one real (12 ½) out of every fine collected from an Indian they had brought to trial. Evidently they did their work well, for on November 27 of the same year the council appointed $15.75 for the alcaldes. At the rate of eight Indians to the dollar, it seems that these officials had rounded up well over 100 souls, of whom 126 had paid their fines. The alcaldes so abused their authority that in September 1852 the council encouraged the mayor to curtail their activity.

The practice of arresting and fining drunken Indians brought a strong condemnation from the *Los Angeles Star* on December 3, 1853.

It has long been the practice with the Indians of this city, to get drunk on Saturday night. Their ambition seems to be to earn sufficient money, through the week, to treat themselves handsomely at the close of it. In this they only follow white examples, and like white men, they are often noisy about the streets.—It has also been the practice with the City Marshal, and his assistants, to spend the Sabbath in arresting and imprisoning Indians, supposed to be drunk, until Monday morning, when they are taken before the Mayor and discharged on paying a bill of two dollars and a half each, one dollar of which is the fee of the Marshal. Sometimes of a Monday morning we have seen the Marshal marching in a procession with twenty or twenty-five of these poor people, and truly, it is a brave sight.—Now, we have no heart to do the Marshal slightest prejudice, but this leading off Indians and locking them up over night, for the purpose of taking away one of their paltry dollars, seems to us a questionable act.

Apparently the criticism went unheeded, for seven years later the *Star* was still issuing sarcastic broadsides: "On last Sunday, our vigilant City Marshal and his assistants brought *forty one* Indians to the stationhouse, generally on charges of drunkenness. We do not know whether the officers are becoming more vigilant, or the aborigines more dissipated."

The Indians purchased aguardiente at the numerous local taverns. According to the Wilson report, "In some streets of this little city, almost every other house is a grog-shop for Indians." In mid May 1851 Mayor Benjamin Wilson called for a city ordinance that would prohibit the selling of liquor to Indians, and later in the month the common council amended the existing police ordinance to achieve this end. Those convicted were to be fined not less than $20 or imprisoned for five days or both. But the ordinance was blatantly ignored, and on November 16, 1854 the *Southern Californian* demanded that the council take the necessary action to correct the situation and identified several grog-shop owners—Alexander Delique, Pedro María, Ferrio Abilia, and J. B. Guernod—as the worst offenders. So profitable was this business, however, that the tavern owners could sustain the fines levied against them. In 1855 Vicente Guerrero paid a fine of $30 but kept his business active. A week later he paid another fine—this one for $200!

Although a few of the white citizens of Los Angeles expressed sincere concern about the social disintegration of the local Indians and sought to ameliorate what was considered to be the cause of their decline, no one urged elimination of the labor system. This point was made by California's Superintendent of Indian Affairs who visited the town in 1855. "If it were practicable or desirable in their demoralized condition, to remove them to the Reservation," he wrote to his superior in Washington, D.C., "it could not be accomplished, because it would be opposed by the citizens, for the reasons that in the vineyards, especially during the grape season, their labor is made useful and is obtained at a cheap rate."

Because the pueblo and its environs had a surplus of cheap Indian labor, white workers found the region closed to their services and skills. The Wilson report claimed that in 1852 no white man would work for the wages received by the Indians. In 1860, according to Harris Newmark, "Small as was the population of Los Angeles County about this time, there was nevertheless for a while an exodus to Texas, due chiefly to the difficulty experienced by white immigrants in competing with Indian ranch and vineyard labor." Less objectively, the *Semi-Weekly News* on February 11, 1869 asserted that the Indian, "being brought into competition with that class of labor that would be most beneficial to the country, checks immigration, and retards the prosperity of the country." Ignoring their contributions to the development of the pueblo, the editorial complained that the Indians "build no houses, own no lands, pay no taxes and encourage no branch of industry. . . . They have filled our jails, have contributed largely to the filling of our state prison, and are fast filling our graveyards, where they must either be buried at public expense or permitted to rot in the streets and highways."

Indeed, Indians were filling up the graveyards, for by this time the town's Indian population was in rapid decline. Between 1850 and 1860 the number of Indians recorded in Los Angeles County dropped from 3,693 to 2,014. By 1870 the figure had plummeted to 219. Some may have blended in with the Spanish-speaking population and thus were not counted as Indians in the census reports. Presumably others left the town for the ranchos or the interior. But intra-Indian violence and contagious diseases account for much of the population reduction.

Many perished during the smallpox epidemic of late 1862 and early 1863. The disease, of course, respected no race or class, but social and economic factors largely determined its demographic impact. An American resident concluded that the Indians "succumbed *en mass*" because their constitutions had been undermined by years of dissipation. According to Harris Newmark, "The dread disease worked its ravages especially among the Mexicans and Indians, as many as a dozen of them dying in a single day; and these sufferers and their associates being under no quarantine, and even bathing *ad libitum* in the *zanjas,* the pest spread alarmingly." The *Star* reported in late January 1863 that two hundred cases had been identified and that two hundred persons had already died. Accurate death statistics are lacking, but since immunization was not compulsory and was initially resisted by the Indians, their toll must have been devastatingly high.

Irrespective of their declining numbers, Indians continued to be jailed and auctioned off to private individuals throughout the 1860s. J. Ross Browne attested in 1864 that Indians were "paid in native brandy every Saturday night, put in jail the next morning for getting drunk, and bailed out on Monday to work out the fine imposed upon them by the local authorities. This system still prevails in Los Angeles, where I have often seen a dozen of these miserable wretches carried to jail roaring drunk of a Sunday morning." And in early 1869 the *Semi-Weekly News* reported that farmers continued to assemble at the mayor's office on Monday mornings to obtain the services of the Indian prisoners. By the mid 1870s, however, the town's Indian labor force had practically disappeared. A newspaper article dated November 3, 1875 stated that a band of Luiseños from San Diego County would soon arrive to participate in the grape harvest. Los Angeles, it seems, was now importing its Indian labor.

From 1781 to the 1870s the white residents of Los Angeles relied almost exclusively on Indian labor, domestic and agricultural. Initially, local Gabrielinos, the so-called gentiles, constituted the town's work force, and given their political independence, they were not without some economic leverage. They labored for the gente de razón only when it did not interfere with their traditional subsistence activities. So long as the gentiles provided most of the labor, Indian-white relations remained firmly based on a practical exchange of service for goods. But once the politically powerless ex-neophytes replaced the gentiles, relations between Indians and whites quickly deteriorated into economic exploitation. The quality of Indian-white relations, therefore, was determined as much by which Indian group (gentile or ex-neophyte) constituted the labor force at a given time as by which white group (Spanish, Mexican, or American) was in political control.

The shift from gentile to ex-neophyte labor came with the secularization of the missions. Ex-neophytes overran the Los Angeles area, providing the pueblo with many more workers than it could absorb. The domestic servants who found steady employment did not fare too badly, but the agricultural laborers, whose work was usually seasonal, often suffered unemployment for long periods of time. The social consequences of this economic situation were despondency, drunkenness, and violence. As disorderly Indians became a major concern of the Mexican and then the American city administrations, stringent laws were enacted to correct the problem.

Beginning in 1836, when the ayuntamiento authorized the regidor to arrest drunken Indians and assign them to public works projects, a labor recruitment system developed that increasingly integrated Indians by force into the town's economic structure. After 1850, when the common council authorized the recorder to auction off jailed Indians to private individuals, the system ensured that the demand for labor was always met with a plentiful supply.

Although it is impossible to discern the percentage of Indian workers recruited by force during the 1850s and 1860s, any rise in the Indian crime rate would have resulted in an increase in the number of Indians arrested and put up for auction. And a rise in the number of Indians recruited by force would have reduced the number of those freely employed. Furthermore, since forced labor was cheaper than free, it was in the best, albeit short-term, interests of the growers to see that there were always Indians available for auction. By paying their workers, at least in part, in aguardiente, they virtually ensured that some Indians would be arrested for drunkenness and immediately forced back on the job market. Serving the same end were the grog shop owners who persisted in illegally selling to the Indians the brandy they acquired from the growers.

This kind of economic system could not be maintained over the long run, however, because labor recruitment depended in large part on the perpetuation of Indian social instability. In effect, the system bred its own destruction, for the process of economic integration generated a process of social disintegration, which in turn led to drastic population reduction. The resident Indians, it seems, were caught not so much in a vicious circle as in a downward spiral from which few escaped or survived. But they were more than just social victims; they were economic contributors as well. In their descent to disappearance, they engaged in activity, both productive and destructive, that contributed significantly to the social and economic history of the pueblo's first century.

Readings for George Phillips:

California Indians have received increasing attention and Phillips is one of those who has focused on their histories. He has several books on this topic including *Chiefs and Challengers: Indian Resistance and Cooperation in Southern California* (Berkeley: University of California Press, 1975) and The Enduring Struggle: Indians in California History (San Francisco, CA: Boyd & Fraser, 1981). James J. Rawls, *Indians of California: The Changing Image* (Norman: University of Oklahoma Press, 1984) and Albert T. Hurtado, *Indian Survival on the California Frontier* (New Haven, CT: Yale University Press, 1988) provide other parts of the story. For a comparative view on the impact of alcohol on other Indians see Peter Mancall, *Deadly Medicine: Indians and Alcohol in Early America* (Ithaca, NY: Cornell University Press, 1995).

13

THE NAVAJO AT THE BOSQUE REDONDO: COOPERATION, RESISTANCE, AND INITIATIVE, 1864–1868

KATHERINE MARIE BIRMINGHAM OSBURN

Throughout the nineteenth century American planners sought to move Indians into the majority culture and society. Usually such programs depended on experience and knowledge gained at school, in church, or on the farm. The officials delegated to help "civilize" tribal people assumed that the examples these institutions provided would help them achieve their goal of changing Indians quickly. Occasionally the elements combined successfully and a few Native Americans actually adopted much of the majority culture, but that proved uncertain and most Native Americans rejected the whites' overtures whenever they had a chance. This selection discusses the experiences of the Navajos after their 1863–64 defeat by federal troops in northern New Mexico. Having defeated the tribe, General James H. Carleton decided to force acculturation upon his captives. He moved the Indians into the southeastern corner of New Mexico, where the army herded them onto a forsaken area known as the Bosque Redondo. There the general ordered his subordinates to establish a reservation and to begin the process of forced acculturation. The author considers the variety of Native American responses and initiatives begun while having to farm in a sterile region, send their children to school, and see their culture gradually destroyed. Much of the article relates Indian efforts to avoid cooperating with the soldiers, to sabotage its program, and to retain their tribal religion, economy, and identity. In 1868 the tribe signed a treaty with the United States that allowed the Indians to return to their traditional homeland, where they remain today.

Katherine Marie Birmingham Osburn is an assistant professor of history at Tennessee Technological University.

Source: Katherine Marie Birmingham Osburn, "The Navajo at the Bosque Redondo: Cooperation, Resistance, and Initiative," *New Mexico Historical Review*, 60 (October 1985), pp. 399–413. Reprinted with permission of the editor.

Despite the traumatic experience of military defeat and incarceration in a strange and hostile environment, the Navajo at the Bosque Redondo, 1864–68, did not respond passively to the reservation experience. Rather, they devised active adaptive strategies using a pattern of cooperation, resistance, and initiative. While Navajo religion furnished the Indians with a means of devising their own responses to many problems they faced, it also acted as a basis for solidarity in an experience potentially devastating to the Navajo's cultural survival. Since Indian behavior worked against the military's purposes and functioning at the Bosque Redondo, Indians were a variable in the reservation's demise, actively participating in its failure—not merely observing its collapse. Thus, while administrative and military aspects of the Bosque are important, the Navajo's behavior warrants equal consideration.

As a result of the Kit Carson campaign of 1863–64, Brig. Gen. James H. Carleton, commander of the military department of New Mexico, moved the Navajo to a plot in southeastern New Mexico known as Bosque Redondo. There he had established a military post, Fort Sumner, and a reservation, where he planned to transform the Mescalero Apache and the Navajo into peaceful, Christian Americans. The Navajo who arrived at the Bosque Redondo were starving and impoverished, and over the next four years their miserable condition did not improve greatly. Shortages of food and fuel were continual, and the alkaline water caused dysentery. Other illnesses at the reservation included malaria, pneumonia, rheumatic fever, measles, and venereal disease. The Indians reported that sometimes military personnel beat them and that Navajo women were raped. Further, the Navajo were raided by other Indian tribes.

Despite this evidence, Carleton interpreted the Navajo's degraded condition as an indication that they were now passive and dependent. "It is a mockery," he wrote, "to hold councils with a people who . . . have only to await our decisions. [We should] care for them as children until they can care for themselves." In his view the Navajo were his to transform. The Indians initially proved cooperative. As a condition of their surrender the Indians agreed, as former Indian Superintendent James L. Collins noted in 1864, "to abandon their nomadic, marauding way of life, to settle on a reservation away from their cherished mountain homes, and to devote themselves to the pursuit of industry as their means of support."

Observers at the Bosque Redondo generally commented on how industriously the Indians worked. In 1865 the Indians testified before the Doolittle Commission, a Senate investigative committee, that they were more than willing to farm despite the problems involved. In addition, Michael Steck, superintendent of Indian Affairs in 1864, commented that "the tribe has for three centuries been engaged in planting and they are also far in advance of all other wild tribes in various fabricks such as blankets, baskets, ropes, saddles and bridle bits." Thus it appeared to individuals who visited the reservation in the early years that the experiment had tremendous potential and that the Indians were hard-working and cooperative.

Indian cooperation was, however, more complex than it first appeared. Although the Navajo recognized that farming was a necessity—because the rations provided by the United States government were inadequate—the Indians had more choice in this area than is initially apparent. In 1868, for instance, they staunchly refused to plant any crops, explaining, "We have done all that we could possibly do, but we found it to be labor in vain and have therefore quit it; for this reason we have not planted or tried to do anything this year." Thus cooperation, though mandated by hunger, was also a choice, for the Indians did refuse to farm. In this act they demonstrated their ability to decide for or against cooperation, regardless of the circumstances.

Similarly, the Navajo considered the benefits of the education programs at the Bosque and chose to accept training in carpentry, leatherworking, and blacksmithing. Delgadito, the Navajo headman, realized his people's need to repair their newly acquired farm implements and also concluded that they would now have to learn how to make a living. The Navajo also perceived that the trades provided them with such an opportunity. Accommodation in this realm, then, was a strategy born of immediate needs and of an understanding of the new economic realities facing the Indians.

While the Navajo appreciated instruction in the trades, they were much more reticent about the benefits of other types of education. For example, although General Carleton established a school at the Bosque Redondo in 1865, the Indians rarely utilized it. Apparently they were more interested in receiving the ration coupons that the school distributed than in procuring an education for their children. As post surgeon Dr. George Gwynther noted:

> I do not think that the juvenile savages shared either love of or aptitude for the alphabet, nor rightly appreciated the treasure to which it was the key; inasmuch as they often stipulated for additional bread rations as a condition of longer attendance at school.

The Navajo's resistance to the reservation school was a serious blow to Carleton's plans for acculturation. Yet the Indians claimed they were not opposed to education; they were simply more absorbed with the immediate concerns of daily survival and considered the benefits of education to be peripheral to more urgent matters, such as obtaining enough food to fend off starvation. Their attempt to procure money and extra ration coupons for sending their children to school demonstrates the Indians' shrewd survival strategy.

The Navajo gave top priority to procuring more food. They often tried pleading for larger rations. While officers struggled to find a solution, sometimes increasing the size of the ration, other times shifting its frequency, the Indians acted to meet their needs by their own methods. They stole any available food and also produced some three thousand extra ration coupons. By forging metal coupons, the Navajos were utilizing an old skill to meet a new need. In addition, since the number of forged tickets increased from January to May of 1865, the number of Indians who benefited from this practice probably increased. Apparently, however, this strategy profited some Indians at the expense of others.

Another method of obtaining extra food was prostitution, which was not a standard practice under less stressful conditions. Navajo women were generally considered to be modest and decent before and after the Bosque Redondo years. Indeed, the Navajo moral code discouraged promiscuity, and Navajo religion had a ritual designed for "the removal of prostitution or mania," called The Prostitution Way. While the Navajo recognized the degradation of prostitution at Fort Sumner, they also indicated that the women were compelled to set aside their moral prescriptions because of poverty and hunger.

Although some Navajo disregarded the moral injunctions of their culture against prostitution, the taboos governing residence were generally upheld. Carleton had originally planned to house the Navajo in neatly ordered barracks similar to the type of housing found in Pueblo villages. The Navajo, however, found this scheme unacceptable because their traditional housing was widely dispersed. Furthermore, they rejected the notion of permanent homes because of their beliefs about departed souls. "The custom of our tribe," the chiefs claimed, "is never to enter a house where a person has died, but abandon it." Consequently, they settled "in scattered and extended camps, unorganized by bands or otherwise."

The Navajo's refusal to adhere to Carleton's plans for their housing represents another assertion of their autonomy. Instead of conforming to the military's plans, the Navajo forced the military to restructure their administration procedures. As Nelson H. Davis complained, the dispersed Indians were difficult to control and his troops were severely taxed in their efforts to round up Indians for work. Thus the defiance of the Indians allowed them to continue their traditional settlement patterns in spite of their captivity and to exert some control over the decisions that affected their lives.

For similar reasons the Navajo refused medical treatment at the post hospital. The Indians explained that they shunned the hospital because "all that have reported there have died." Because of this belief, Dr. Gwynther insisted on removing from the hospital all patients who were near death. Thus the Indians' behavior helped to dictate hospital policy.

Resistance to the hospital can also be traced to the Navajo's preference for their native medicine men. Dr. Gwynther complained that "the relations of the sick person have [occasionally] carried the patient off clandestinely, to get such benefits as may accrue from the practice of their native medicine-men." The Indians admitted that the medicine men were often ineffectual in combatting diseases on the reservation, but explained that they lacked the plants necessary for native cures.

Army doctors viewed illness as a natural occurrence treatable with scientific methods, but the Navajo had a different interpretation. In the Navajo world view, illness is an example of disharmony in the cosmic order that the performance of a religious ceremony can correct. During the ceremony, the Navajo invoke their Holy People to rectify the disturbance of order. If the ritual is correctly carried out, the deities are obligated to grant the mortal's requests, for a principle of reciprocity governs the exchange. In this regard, Navajo oral tradition emphasizes the importance of healing ritual at the Bosque. Charlie Mitchell, a Navajo who had been a child at the reservation, explained that ceremonies were performed to prevent the Navajo from dying in captivity.

In seeking solutions to disease, the Navajo rejected Anglo cures but embraced some from other Indians. They borrowed, for instance, the Chiricahua Windway from the Apache at the fort. This ritual cures a variety of sicknesses: those caused by the winds—being knocked over by wind, cooking with a tree felled by wind, or sleeping in a place hollowed out by winds; those caused by snakes—eating food touched by a snake, injury to a snake, or snake bites; those from a cactus—because of cooking with tree cactus; or those by flooding. Another Navajo explanation for sickness at the Bosque Redondo was witchcraft. To help combat illness resulting from witchcraft, the Navajo also adopted the Apache's Suckingway ritual technique for curing a witchcraft victim: sucking out the witch's darts.

To bring about other cures, the Navajo also performed many of their own ceremonies. For instance, the Squaw Dance, a ritual of the Navajo Evilway, which purifies an individual from disease-inducing contacts with foreigners, was used at the Bosque. According to this ceremony some sicknesses are the result of the ghosts of aliens, either those whom a Navajo warrior has killed or those who died from other causes and with whom the Navajo may have had contact, sexual or otherwise. Touching the corpse or stepping on the grave of an "outsider" may also cause alien ghosts to torment a Navajo with sickness. Because the Navajo were in close contact with Apache and Anglos who died, they no doubt felt that at least some of their sicknesses necessitated the performance of the Squaw Dance.

Other reasons for enacting the Squaw Dance were probably connected with Navajo raids from the Bosque reservation. Since Navajo warriors were killing enemies during this time, they required a Squaw Dance to prevent or cure a retaliating illness. In March of 1866, as an example, seven Navajo went on a foray against the Utes who had killed one of their children. The Navajo pursued their enemies for approximately twelve days and then attacked them, killing five and capturing a ten-year-old Ute boy, twenty-four horses, and saddles and guns. Another account of a Navajo campaign from Fort Sumner does not end so happily. While on a raid in the Comanche country, the Navajo lost four of their war party. The raid had been doomed, the raiders concluded, when a coyote appeared one night in the warriors' camp. In October 1867 a contingent of Navajo retaliated against the Comanches for a raid on 9 September. The Navajo had pursued their attackers and killed twelve.

In addition to retaliatory raids, the Indians also committed offensive raids aimed at obtaining more stock. In this regard, settlers in eastern New Mexico claimed that Navajo from Fort Sumner attacked their homes and stole their livestock. Yet while some Navajo did engage in such activities, it is important to note that a large number of the complaints were probably exaggerated and that the Navajo were often blamed for depredations that other Indians committed. Regardless of blame, warfare conducted at the Bosque Redondo required ceremony to counteract the disturbance it wrought in the natural order.

The Navajo also performed the Fire Dance, a ritual of the nine-night Mountainway or Nightway ceremonies that restore harmony. The Fire Dance combines in a single ceremony the abbreviated forms of many ceremonials. Dancers representing a variety of other Holyway ceremonies, such as Beautyway, Windway, or Waterway, perform a portion of their chant. The patient receives the specific benefits of each without undergoing the entire ceremony. Thus the Fire Dance saves time and expense and would serve the Navajos by adapting their more elaborate ceremonies to the limited resources of the reservation.

The Fire Dance was also possibly connected with the food problems at the Bosque. Certainly corn-growing rites and the ritualistic treatment of food employed in the dance were relevant to experiences of the Navajo on the reservation. According to their eschatology an individual who has eaten another person's food without ritualistic preparation may be in danger of being transformed into that person. Therefore the Navajo may have performed Fire Dances as protection from being "transformed" by the white person's food. The recitation of rituals concerned with agriculture suggests that although the Navajos utilized the American's technology, they were convinced that their success in farming was contingent upon their controlling the forces of nature that were responsible for the harvest.

While the Navajo employed a variety of responses in order to survive at the Bosque, their ultimate goal was to return to their homeland. From April to August 1865 approximately 1,300 Navajo left the reservation, hoping to return to their old country, where roughly 1,000 to 2,000 Navajo remained, having escaped the roundup. General Carleton dealt sternly with the runaway problem, telling his newly appointed post commander Maj. William McCleave that he would kill every Indian found off the reservation without a passport. Despite this threat Indians continued to leave the reservation over the next several years. In 1868, for example, 250 to 300 more Navajo escaped.

The majority of Navajo, however, remained at the Bosque Redondo and attempted to obtain their liberty through pleading and ceremony. As early as 1865 the Indians begged for their release, warning that if they were forced to remain upon the reservation they would "all die very soon." They explained that they had been instructed by their Holy People to remain within the boundaries of three rivers, the Rio Grande, the Rio San Juan, and the Rio Colorado, and that their violation of this restriction was responsible for their current suffering. They extolled the productivity of their old country, where they had enough food and firewood and were safe from their enemies.

According to Navajo oral tradition it was not pleading alone that secured the Navajo's release, but also the performance of the Coyote Way ritual. Although some informants claimed that the ritual was divinatory, indicating that the government was now ready to free the Navajo, other Navajo attributed their freedom to this ceremony. The years of pleading had been unsuccessful, they claimed, until the performance of the Coyote ritual, "during which our leader was blessed with Coyote power." Because of this ceremony, the next request to leave was approved.

Moreover, the Navajo called on their religious ritual to aid them in interaction with the reservation personnel. Recognizing that Anglos controlled the reservation, the Navajo attempted, at the same time, to circumvent government officials and to procure release by petitioning their Holy People. To this day some Navajo believe that, ultimately, their Holy People, not the United States government, returned them to their current reservation. Whatever the cause of release on 1 July 1868, the Navajo signed a treaty with the U.S. government allowing them to return to their traditional homeland.

An examination of the Navajo's behavior at the Bosque Redondo reveals that the Indians worked toward two primary goals, survival and release, by using a pattern of cooperation, resistance, and initiative. Cooperation meant farming and learning the trades, while resistance was manifested in refusing formal education, barracks housing, and Anglo medical treatment. In addition, prostitution, forgery, raiding, fleeing, and ceremony represented Indian initiative. These varied activities indicate that the Navajo had no single survival strategy. In fact, solutions that individuals employed sometimes clashed with the interests of the tribe as a whole. For example, when Navajo leaders promised to curtail raiding, while other Navajo raided, the Indians were factionalized, increasing the potential for cultural disintegration.

Navajo religion, however, was an important element in avoiding this fate. Oral histories recount how special the ceremonies were to the Indians during captivity and indicate their belief that their Holy People sustained the tribe at the Bosque. In addition to providing comfort, religion was also a source of social cohesion. Navajo ceremonies require large gatherings of people, some of whom are involved with the ceremony while others come to meet friends and family. The largest number of spectators gather during the final day and night of a sing, and the patient's kinsmen are expected to feed them. Consequently there is social pressure on all nearby relatives to contribute time and labor to help defray the costs of a ritual. Thus kinsmen and neighbors are bound together by reciprocal obligations governing the ceremony.

Ceremony also functions ideally as a means of reducing intergroup tensions by redistributing wealth. The singer is expected to give a large portion of his fee to friends and relatives. Navajos who stint on ceremonies risk accusations of witchcraft, and prosperous Navajos must sponsor elaborate ceremonies to avoid similar suspicions. In a situation such as that at the Bosque Redondo, where resources were limited and tensions great, ceremony would have provided a means of reducing the stress the uneven distribution of resources generated. Religion, then, was the key to the Navajo's survival as a cultural unit during their stay near Fort Sumner.

The Bosque Redondo experiment failed for a number of reasons, most of which historians have discussed. The reservation was not economically feasible because of environmental and administrative problems, yet the failure of the Bosque Redondo cannot be understood without discussing Navajo activities. Clearly their behavior taxed the labors of the military in administering them—because of their dispersed settlement pattern—and in containing them—because they left the post without the proper papers. Their refusal to accept the Bosque Redondo, seen in their nearly constant begging to go home, also contributed to the realization that Carleton's plan was not workable. The Navajo at the Bosque Redondo were not passive observers of the reservation's rise and fall, but were instead active participants in the successes and failures of the experiment.

Readings for Katherine Marie Birmingham Osburn:

The most complete discussion of the Navajos' "Long Walk" is Gerald Thompson, *The Army and the Navajo: The Bosque Redondo Reservation Experiment 1863–1868* (Tucson: University of Arizona Press, 1976). For the general context of Navajo relations with Europeans and Americans see Edward Spicer, *Cycles of Conquest: The Impact of Spain, Mexico, and the United States on the Indians of the Southwest, 1553–1960* (Tucson: University of Arizona Press, 1962). Norman Bender Examines the Navajos' experiences after their return from the Bosque Redondo in *'New Hope for the Indians': The Grant Peace Policy and the Navajos in the 1870s* (Albuquerque: Historical Society of New Mexico/University of New Mexico Press, 1989). See also Peter Iverson, *The Navajo Nation* (Westport, CT: Greenwood Press, 1981).

14

THE CONSEQUENCES OF RESERVATION LIFE: NATIVE CALIFORNIANS ON THE ROUND VALLEY RESERVATION, 1871–1884

TODD BENSON

California is a large state and this essay presents a story of Indian experience that differed substantially from what happened in Los Angeles. Certainly the influx of Anglo-Americans into the region brought near disaster for many native people. Much of the discussion of late nineteenth-century reservation activities depicts the tribal people as the targets of aggressive American efforts to destroy their culture. This suggests that government officials working through the farm, school, and church on each reservation demanded cultural, psychological, and economic submission by the Indians. While that certainly took place, such a view of events characterizes the tribal people solely as victims. That they were, but, as Benson shows, their story was more complicated.

The New Social Historians have discussed the idea of agency or of initiative as an important way to understand minority actions in American society, and that approach certainly fits the circumstances of the northern California people who were placed on the Round Valley Reservation. They were expected to follow orders and gradually to become like other Americans. The author suggests that, while some of this happened, there is more to the story. Rather than acquiesce, these Indians had goals of their own. The essay examines these by looking at the internal cultural workings of the reservation population, and shows the methods they used to resist, block, or avoid doing what the agents expected them to do. In doing so it makes clear the continuing need for students of ethnic issues to study the actions of all the groups present in the story.

Todd Benson is the Director of Freshman and Sophomore Programs at Stanford University and a lecturer in the history department there.

Source: Todd Benson, "The Consequences of Reservation Life: Native Californians on the Round Valley Reservation, 1871–1884," *Pacific Historical Review.* 60:2 (May 1991), pp.221-44. © 1991 The Regents of the University of California.

During the past decade, the theme of resistance has dominated American Indian historiography. Scholars have begun portraying indigenous people as historical actors in their own right, rather than depicting them, as did most previous historians, as the passive victims of advancing white civilization. Recent works have thus emphasized initiative, survival, and cultural resilience as central to the American Indian experience.

Still, historians of the early reservation period have resisted this approach, arguing that removal to reservations represents a watershed experience for American Indians which held devastating consequences for both Indian culture and Indian psychology. Francis Paul Prucha, for example, writes that life on reservations was, for "most" tribal members, "shattering" and "demoralizing." Robert Utley similarly argues that "the reservation program tore down the traditional culture" and left Indians "beset by more or less cultural disintegration and by feelings of helplessness and hopelessness."

It might be argued that if reservation life had a destructive impact on American Indian cultures anywhere, it did so in California, since tribes there experienced unparalleled devastation as a result of contact with whites. Following the discovery of gold in 1848, Euro-American settlers, hungry for wealth, poured into the state by the thousands, bringing with them germs, guns, and, most important, a racist disregard for the value of Indian lives. By 1860, the combined effect of exposure to both white diseases and violence had reduced the Native Californian population from 100,000 to 35,000. Ten years later, the population had dwindled to 30,000, and over half of the survivors, as a result of either forced or voluntary removal, lived on reservations.

It is, perhaps, not surprising, given the magnitude of this demographic disaster, that the "watershed" thesis remains virtually unchallenged by historians of Indians in California. George Harwood Phillips, for example, has attacked the notion of Indian passivity during the earlier mission period, but bases his argument, ironically, on a "perception of Indian passivity by Anglo-Americans who observed Indians after they had been colonized and demoralized" during the late-nineteenth century. Although Phillips only implicitly blames reservation life as the cause of this alleged demoralization, other historians have argued directly that reservations had a devastating effect on Indian behavior and culture. In his *Indian Survival on the California Frontier*, Albert Hurtado seeks to emphasize the theme of Indian initiative, but ultimately concludes that the labor system employed on California reservations helped to make the native family "a casualty on the California borderland frontier." Edward Castillo agrees, arguing that removal to reservations "was bound to result in serious social upheaval—the disintegration of both family and community life," to which Robert Chandler adds that white domination in most cases "doomed" the California Indians to become "emotional and physical cripples."

This paper challenges such views on the basis of the experiences of the surviving tribal members on one California reservation, the Round Valley agency in Mendocino County, between 1871 and 1884, the period immediately following the worst of the violence directed against northern California's Indians. Round Valley represents an appropriate test case because it served during these years as home to Indian agents of the Methodist church, among the most assimilationist-minded of Protestant denominations, and one which waged an unusually ardent campaign to eradicate Indian cultures. Round Valley was also the residence of the remnants of several tribes—the Yuki, Konkow, Nomlaki, Wailaki, Achumawi, Whilkut, and Pomo—which had suffered devastating losses, extending in the case of the Yuki and Wailaki to over ninety percent of precontact population. The magnitude of this demographic catastrophe, coupled with the intensity of the assimilationist pressures on these tribes, suggests that if cultural disintegration occurred anywhere, it did so at Round Valley. The evidence reveals, however, that Round Valley tribal members not only stoutly resisted white domination, but also pursued their own goal of self-sufficiency.

Two Views of the Reservation

The U.S. government established the Round Valley reservation, together with several others in California, in the 1850s as a solution to what it deemed the state's Indian "problem." According to most whites, California tribes represented a danger to property, safety, and the unhindered development of "white civilization." Removal of native peoples to reservations would, they believed, erase this danger while also protecting tribal members from the threat of violence and their own supposed ignorance. Indians who failed to learn the ways of white society would be condemned to lives of poverty and suffering, if not to extinction. Reformers saw reservations as schools where individual Indians would learn these ways, thus guaranteeing their survival. California reformers envisioned that Indians would receive this education in part by working on reservation farms, where they would not only learn the work ethic and a sedentary agricultural lifestyle, but also produce profits that would be used to make the reservations self-sustaining.

The plan failed abysmally. Tribal members removed to California reservations in the 1850s and 1860s faced conditions little different from those they had experienced outside reservation boundaries. At Round Valley, settlers coveting land or avenging alleged Indian depredations ignored borders and continued to attack tribal members even after they had come under the agency's protection. Chronic shortages of food and supplies forced Indians to subsist by hunting and gathering their own food, or by performing wage labor off the reservation. As on other reservations, many migrated to the reservation only during periods when jobs, food, and supplies were available there.

Corrupt agency administrators aggravated the situation by stealing the reservation's supplies and diverting its resources for their own use. Such profiteering plagued the administration of reservations nationwide, leading President Ulysses S. Grant in 1869 to promulgate a new approach to federal Indian policy. Grant's plan, his so-called Peace Policy, transferred control over the selection of Indian agents from the federal government to the churches. Grant envisioned that these religious organizations would choose as agents individuals known for their integrity and religious beliefs rather than for their political connections. Honest, Christian agents committed to the task of reform, rather than to expanding their personal fortunes, would save the government money and prove more effective than their predecessors at assimilating tribal members. The President granted the power to select Indian agents in California to the Methodist church, whose leaders ultimately chose three agents to serve at Round Valley: Hugh Gibson from 1871 to 1872, James Burchard from 1872 to 1877, and Henry Sheldon from 1877 to 1884. These agents zealously followed the goals of Grant's policy, waging a continuous battle to convert Round Valley's tribal members to the ways of white society.

The agents focused their assimilationist campaign around two objectives. The first was instruction in the Christian religion. The agents proselytized tribal members tirelessly, an activity which, in the case of agent Burchard, appeared to meet with success in 1874. In February of that year nearly five hundred Indians converted to Christianity. By April, Burchard reported that, as a result of the conversions, he had not "known of a quarrel or fight" on the reservation, and that not a single Indian had "had to be punished for disobedience or other faults." This was, he concluded, "the best fruit of the Peace Policy of President U. S. Grant." By the following September, Burchard had admitted almost a thousand Indians to membership in the Methodist church. The effect of the conversions, in his mind, was spectacular. "The Indians," he wrote, had, for the first time, become "quiet, peaceable, orderly, and easily managed." Acceptance of Christianity appeared not only to render tribal members more docile, but also, according to Burchard, to improve their moral and sexual behavior, which he had viewed as suspect. The agent exulted over what he saw as the effects of the mass conversions. "All dancing, swearing, drinking, Gambling, Sabbath Breaking, and all the Pagan practices and habits have been abandoned," he wrote in September 1874. Increasing numbers of Indians, he added a year later, had accepted Christian principles of marital fidelity and taken Christian vows of marriage.

Like other reformers, the Round Valley agents coupled their missionary efforts with instruction in the more secular subject of "civilization," by which they meant the everyday norms of middle-class European-Americans. This required, first, that they abandon their "dissolute" hunting-and-gathering means of subsistence and learn techniques of sedentary agriculture. It further required that tribal members learn to live in the proper kind of dwelling. The agents constructed over a hundred frame houses with which to replace the traditional native wickiups, which they saw as unhealthy. Many contained bed frames, included so as to allow the Indians to sleep off the ground, a practice the agents believed necessary to prevent the spread of disease. Also included in the assimilationist curriculum was instruction in the theory and practice of American democracy. Burchard held a gala celebration on the nation's 4th of July centennial, complete with fireworks and the reading of the Declaration of Independence. In addition, he attempted to dismantle the Indians' hereditary system of chieftainship and institute an open-ballot system whereby tribal elders democratically elected their leaders. At one point he tried to establish an Indian House of Representatives and Senate as tribal legislative bodies. Democracy had its limits, however: the agent installed himself as President of the new reservation republic.

That Burchard would attempt to teach tribal members lessons in democratic theory—however imperfect—suggests the comprehensiveness of the agents' vision. Round Valley, in their minds, represented a social laboratory where Indians would learn to think and act completely as whites. The Indians themselves saw things differently. To them, the reservation represented an immediate source of supplies and, because of its land resources, a potential hope for economic independence. While achieving these goals might require them to adopt white concepts of land ownership or white methods of agriculture, it did not, contrary to the beliefs of the agents, require that they yield to the agents' demands.

In the short term, tribal members saw the reservation as only a seasonal source of sustenance. The onset of Methodist administration did not end the chronic shortages of food and supplies which had previously plagued the agency, forcing the Indians to continue the seasonal pattern of migration on and off the reservation that they had practiced before the Methodists came to power. Many, during such shortages, moved off the reservation to perform seasonal wage labor for surrounding settlers, the men working in the fields and the women "doing the washing and ironing." Income from such labor, agent Sheldon reported in 1879, was a necessity: the Indians depended on it "to obtain the means of living and clothing." This periodic lack of supplies undoubtedly explains the variations in Round Valley's annual population, which ranged from a high of 1,700 in 1872 to a low of 534 in 1880, as well as the yearly migrations made by Konkow tribal members between the reservation and their homes in Butte County.

The most severe supply shortage occurred in the winter of 1877–1878, when outside jobs could not be had. According to agent Sheldon, cold weather in November and December, when coupled with a lack of clothing and blankets, brought "much suffering" to the Indians. By the first week in January, many men had no shirts or worked "nearly barefooted," while women were prostituting themselves for clothes. "Many are nearly naked," reported Sheldon eleven days later, "and the seeds of death are being scattered widely." The agent had no doubt about the eventual effect of the clothing shortage. Many tribal members, he predicted in February, would leave Round Valley "if the supplies asked for cannot be obtained." His forecast came true the following summer, when many members of the Potter Valley band of Pomo fled the reservation. They were, said Sheldon, "dissatisfied because I had not the clothes to issue to their men and women." More would have fled, he thought, had he not pursued and captured those who first ran away.

That Indians remained on the reservation at all during the harsh winter suggests that the alternatives available to them were limited; that some later fled suggests that those alternatives, although limited, did exist, and that tribal members expected the reservation to provide at least a bare minimum of food and goods. Indian actions at Round Valley's annual census reflected this view of the reservation. Tribal members allowed themselves to be counted as wards of the reservation only if they drew issues of reservation supplies. In 1875, agent Burchard experienced difficulties because he did not issue the reservation's annual supply of goods until after the census was finished. Because Indians had "an aversion" to being counted until after they had received their supplies, he acknowledged, it became "impossible to get all present."

While tribal members' short-term view of the reservation was as a seasonal source of food and clothing, their long-term view of it was as a possible means to independence. Indians whose land had been violently appropriated by white settlers hoped that they could use reservation lands to become self-supporting. "We want land, plow, garden, and work," said James Sherwood, chief of the Little Lake band of Pomo, in 1878. Henry Clay, chief of the Achumawi on the reservation, agreed. "We want our own farms and so help ourselves," he said. "We want home, be somebody," added Peter Hudson, chief of the Huchnom, a tribe closely related to the Yuki. "Don't want be beggars, we don't want to beg. We want get land, we know we can support ourselves . . . [and] we want to do something for ourselves."

Many Indians had been promised land as an incentive to migrate to the reservation. Sustaining these pledges was the passage of a congressional bill in 1873 which extended the reservation's boundaries so that over a hundred thousand acres were available for the Indians' use. The bill also allocated money to compensate nearby settlers for the loss of property located within the new boundaries. But the settlers rejected these payments as insufficient, and over the next two decades, they issued a series of legal challenges to block implementation of the legislation.

Tribal members, in the meantime, grew increasingly frustrated over the government's failure to deliver the lands which they had been promised. "A large proportion" of
Indians, Sheldon wrote in 1878, were "discontented" because of the government's apparent inactivity. "The Indians are getting tired of waiting," he added four years later, especially when "they see the horses, cattle, and sheep of the settlers occupying the very lands
long ago promised to them." Earlier that year, Sheldon had stopped using promises of land
as an enticement to encourage Indians to migrate to the reservation. By 1883, there was
"widespread dissatisfaction" with the government's failure to resolve the settler's claims.

By then, as well, many on the reservation had tired of waiting and acted on their
own to obtain land. Some tribal members volunteered their labor to local ranchers in exchange for offers of small plots, while others sought to buy land. A chief of the Potter
Valley band of Pomo, whom Sheldon called Captain Jack, led a group of Indians, who
had apparently decided to remain at Round Valley when others of their band had fled
five months earlier, off the reservation in October 1878. With money earned picking
hops, they purchased a plot, paying a poll tax to register themselves as its legal owners.
Sheldon did not approve of the Indians' action and set out the following month to re-
capture them. The band refused to return, however, citing the advice of a white lawyer
they had hired who instructed them "not to stir a step." Their plan, reported Sheldon,
"was should I take any of them, a writ of 'Habeas Corpus' would be issued, and they
would be brought before the County Judge, and I was to be arrested for kidnapping."

The actions of Captain Jack's band demonstrate that the realities of life in a white-
dominated world could sometimes force tribal members to modify their traditional
ways. By purchasing land, after all, they appeared to have adopted the Euro-American
concept of landownership, thus violating the traditional California Indian belief that the
earth, as an object of worship, could not be bartered. The expressed desire of tribes at
Round Valley to cultivate their own land represented a similar adaptation, since sedentary agriculture, far from an indigenous form of subsistence, signified the livelihood
which the Indian agents strove to teach tribal members. Contrary to the arguments of the
anthropologist Virginia P. Miller, however, who finds in these adaptations evidence of
the complete "acculturation" of Indians at Round Valley, acceptance of white notions of
property or of how best to subsist did not mean acceptance of white civilization, a point
which Sheldon's pursuit of the fleeing band of Pomo suggests he realized. Tribal members saw the Round Valley reservation as a possible source of short-term sustenance and,
in the long term, of independence. When the reservation failed to fulfill those expectations, the Indians simply pursued them elsewhere. Sheldon and his fellow agents, however, saw the reservation as indispensable. In their minds, the Indians could not learn the
lessons of civilization outside Round Valley's boundaries.

Conflict and Resistance

Different ideas about the reservation's purpose fostered unremitting conflict at Round
Valley. Agents and Indians confronted each other as adversaries, each group struggling
to achieve its own goals while preventing its opponent from doing likewise. The contest
was, in one sense, ironic, since both parties shared a common enemy. Surrounding settlers, who wanted the reservation lands for themselves, saw both agents and Indians as
obstacles in their path, and targeted both for intimidation.

The Indians, not surprisingly, bore the brunt of this aggression. They sustained frequent losses to their food supplies when settlers drove their hogs and cattle through the reservation fields and into the Indians' gardens. Although not as prevalent as they had been prior to 1865, instances of physical threats and violence also occurred. Surrounding settlers used the threat of violence to drive Indians from their camps, fired upon them while they were gathering acorns just outside the reservation, raped them, and sometimes even murdered them. Nor were the agents immune from threats of violence. To furnish the legal authorities with the names of the armed whites who trespassed onto the reservation to buy sex from Indian women, wrote Burchard in 1874, "would put the agent's life in great jeopardy." Four years later Sheldon had a man arrested and charged in the attempted rape of an Indian schoolgirl. The case was dismissed, but as Sheldon left the courtroom, the father and brother of the man he had accused attacked him with a club and repeatedly pistol-whipped him.

The settlers' attempts to intimidate the agents embodied a certain logic, since the agents, like the Indians, shared the goal of obtaining more land for the reservation, and thus represented a direct threat to the settlers' interests. Indeed, the agents thought it would be impossible for them successfully to civilize tribal members without receipt of the additional lands which had been promised. Sheldon grew frustrated at the continual demands placed on him to demonstrate his success at assimilating the Indians. Complete assimilation, he told the Commissioner of Indian Affairs, could not occur until the reservation received the lands it had been promised. "Please remember," he said, "that it is impossible to make brick, without clay. . . ."

A shared interest in acquiring land did not, of course, reflect a shared faith in the virtues of assimilation, producing, rather than even the most superficial of alliances, continual confrontations between agents and Indians. The agents' authority gave them a clear advantage in this contest. To ensure that Indians performed the work which was required of them, for example, they tied receipt of reservation rations to the performance of agricultural labor, such as planting, harvesting, or tending stock. A bill passed by Congress in 1875 codified this requirement by outlawing the distribution of rations on federal reservations to able-bodied men who did not work.

After 1873, the agents also held the power to restrict tribal members' movements. In that year, the Secretary of the Interior issued an order which granted the agents, and their colleagues nationwide, the authority to restrict Indian migrations off the reservations. "Under no pretext," read the order, were tribal members to leave "without a special permit in writing from the Agent." Such permits would not be granted, "except it shall be made to appear to his satisfaction that the issuance of same will inure to the benefit of the applicant."

At Round Valley, agent Burchard did not wait for official word before he began seeking to control Indian migrations. In 1872 he twice used soldiers stationed at nearby Camp Wright to capture Indians who had fled the reservation. After the military post was disbanded four years later, agent Sheldon used reservation employees to capture fleeing Indians. Since the agents also controlled the administration of justice on the reservation, Indians whom they deemed to have misbehaved, whether because of either unauthorized migrations or other transgressions, might find themselves indefinitely confined to the guardhouse, or worse. Sheldon punished one fifteen-year-old boy, who had continued to visit his girlfriends even after the agent, "for their protection," had placed them in surrounding white homes, with four weeks of daytime labor while shackled to a ball and chain, and six weeks of night-time confinement. And until 1875, Burchard whipped tribal members whom he found to have seriously misbehaved.

The agents' authority did not inhibit Indian resistance, however. Sheldon, for example, found that confinement in the guardhouse did not deter flights from the reservation, since tribal members viewed incarceration as a luxury. "They get fed," he wrote, "and don't have to work." Once Indians did flee, it was not always possible to capture them. In June 1878, Sheldon succeeded in capturing "only a few" of a "large number" of tribal members who had left the reservation.

Just as the agents' disciplinary powers proved ineffective in deterring Indian migrations, so too their control of the distribution of reservation rations proved inadequate for managing labor. Tribal members could use the threat of withheld labor to force the agent to pay them cash. In 1879, Sheldon began supplementing Indian farm workers' rations with cash payments as an incentive to keep them on the reservation. "They can get higher wages and money," he wrote, "working out side [*sic*]." By 1884, he found it necessary to raise wages in order to attract enough laborers to harvest the reservation hop crop. "Last year," he reported, "we only paid 1 1/4 cts per lb but others paid 2 cts and we may have to." Skilled Indian workers, such as blacksmith's and carpenter's apprentices, also used the tight local labor market to win higher pay. Wages for outside labor, Sheldon wrote in 1881, were high enough that an Indian apprentice "would laugh at me to offer him less than $10 per month, and some I can hardly induce to stay at $15—and without them we could not do our work."

Indians not only could wring higher wages out of the agent, but also could deceive him into misinterpreting their actions. Tribal members did not acculturate as rapidly as the agents believed, most notably in the case of the conversions to Christianity, described earlier in this paper, which occurred during the mid-1870s. Contrary to what agent Burchard had thought, the Indians converted not because they accepted the wisdom of what he taught them, but because conversion furthered their own goals. This became evident as early as 1878, when agent Sheldon reported that most of the earlier religious converts had abandoned their beliefs. He did not explain the cause of the recidivism to his superiors until five years later, however, probably because he did not want to undermine his efforts to expand the reservation's size. The conversions, he recalled, had occurred at a time when the prospects for more land looked excellent. Congress had recently extended the reservation's boundaries, and the Indians "were promised by Commissioners, Inspectors, and Agent, that if they were 'good' Government would soon give each of them a piece of land." Methodist preachers on the reservation simultaneously were urging the Indians "to become good" in revival meetings. "In their minds," according to Sheldon, "becoming good, became connected with getting lands, and as all wanted lands they *became good*, i.e. joined the Church." As the prospects for land faded, so too did the Indians' enthusiasm for Christianity. "Is all good Christians," said an unidentified Indian living on the reservation, "long as sugar barrel not empty, but timeby sugar all gone, mos' all slide back."

Unless it served their interest, as in the case of the conversions, Indian acceptance of "civilization" rarely occurred. Native cultures proved remarkably resistant both to the powers of the agents and to the hardships of reservation life. Contrary to the arguments of Edward Castillo and Albert Hurtado, the Indian family at Round Valley remained strong. Sheldon noted that some tribal members would have been able to live quite well off the reservation, "if they only had themselves to support." They did not choose to do so, however: "They all," said the agent, "have relations, and friends, that they will not desert, unless compelled by the direst necessity, and then only for a short time."

The strength of family bonds created severe administrative problems for the agents. Burchard found that he could not enforce restrictions on Indian movement as long as some tribal members remained at large: reservation Indians "want to go, and see their relations who are living in some other county, they have heard some of them are sick, they *must* go." He also found it necessary to distribute the free rations given to sick Indians only in minuscule quantities: "two or three ounces of tea, four or five ounces of sugar, one fourth of a pound of meat, a teacup full of rice, or the same amount in syrup." "If larger quantities were issued," he explained, "they would divide with their poor relations or friends."

The strength of family bonds also undoubtedly contributed to the persistence of Indian culture on the reservation. Gambling games, for example, remained an important social event for tribal members, as they had been in the years before white immigration. Families and relatives living off the reservation travelled great distances to attend these games, which occurred over several consecutive days. Sheldon tried to stop the practice soon after assuming office, directing "all employees to break it up any and all times when found." The Indians, however, simply "went off into the brush," or to the nearby town of Covelo, and continued playing.

Tribal members also persisted in traditional medical practices, rather than relying on the reservation physician. The Indians had a "frequent preference for native doctors," said Gibson, and native healers continued to draw complaints from agents until as late as 1880. Sweathouses, in addition, remained important social institutions on the reservation, as they had been during precontact times. Indian men held contests to see who could withstand the smoke from a fire in the center of the sweathouse and dance the longest. In 1873, agent Burchard closed down the sweathouses on the reservation. Sweating ceremonies continued at night, however, primarily at two sweathouses operated by Indians who lived and worked on the property of local ranchers. Some of the Yuki Indians, complained Burchard in January 1875, "go to these sweat-houses on week evenings and spend the entire night (and often for several nights in succession) in sweating, gambling, dancing &c., thereby totally unfitting them for work when they return, being very sleepy . . . for days afterward." Two months later he requested permission to destroy the two offending sweathouses. Sweating ceremonies continued, however, drawing complaints from agents until at least 1881.

Indians challenged the agents' authority not only by maintaining their traditional ways, but also by abusing reservation property. They obtained household goods, for example, by stealing them from the agency cookhouses, and grain by clandestinely raiding the reservation granaries. And since a broken tool had to be repaired before it could be used again, the Indians at Round Valley became adept at interrupting their work routines by breaking reservation equipment. "It is surprising how skillful they are at breaking tools and machinery," agent Sheldon reported. The reservation harness-maker spent many hours fixing harnesses broken by the Indians. "A great amount of repairing is needed," Sheldon said, "as the Indian drivers are so careless. . . ." In his view, Indian workers needed to be constantly watched, for if they were left unsupervised, "property would be destroyed."

Indian resistance on one occasion brought economic rewards in addition to a reduced workload. In 1881, Sheldon decided simultaneously to teach tribal members animal husbandry and to accomplish the milking of the cattle herd by entrusting each Indian family with the care of a cow and her calf. The attempt failed. Tribal members responded by "leav[ing] the calf in the corral without food several days, or turn[ing] out cow and calf." The agent ended up having to pay Indian boys to do the milking.

The Indians reserved their most determined resistance not for increases in their work load, but for the agents' school programs. Efforts to educate Indian children began in 1871, when Gibson's wife opened a day school. A second school opened in 1873, but later closed its doors, due to cutbacks in funding. The purpose of these day schools extended beyond elementary instruction in reading and writing to encompass the agents' entire assimilationist vision. They, like Indian reformers across the country, believed that the best hope for civilizing Indians was through their children. Children were more tractable, more receptive to the teachings of the reformers than were their elders, who had to be dispossessed of customs ingrained over a lifetime. The place to educate Indian children about civilized life was in the schools.

Learning to become civilized, of course, meant learning to become Christians, and Bible readings thus formed an essential part of lessons at the Round Valley day schools. Civilization also meant learning to work. Indian boys, supervised by reservation employees, learned agricultural techniques in Round Valley's fields, while girls stayed inside the school to study domestic arts, such as cooking, sewing, and housework. Agent Sheldon found this regimen insufficient, however. True educational progress, in his view, would not occur so long as children returned from school each day to be with their families. "The associations of the [Indian] camps," he wrote in 1877, "is [*sic*] anything but healthy for their mental, or moral being." He repeated himself two years later: "We greatly need a boarding school so that we can take the children from the corrupting influences of the camps."

Sheldon got his wish when a boarding school opened on the reservation in 1881. He immediately forbade its students from having contact with outside friends. "I deemed it absolutely necessary," he recalled two years later, "to keep them as isolated as possible." Such stringent measures did not prevent the school from experiencing difficulties, however. Funding limits set by the Commissioner of Indian Affairs did not allow Sheldon to hire a sufficient number of staff, forcing him to limit the school's operations.

Moreover, the Indian students refused to acquiesce in Sheldon's efforts to "civilize" them. Flights from the school occurred regularly, even if they were not always successful. Sheldon had particular trouble controlling the older students. "I find it difficult to retain the larger boys in school regularly," he noted in June 1882, "as they can earn from 75 cents to $2 per day shearing sheep and harvesting, and to have them out and in is demoralizing in its effects on the others." By the following November, none of the older boys remained at the school. Their absence sparked dissatisfaction among the eight older girls, five of whom asked the agent for permission to leave. Sheldon strongly opposed their request: the loss of the girls, he wrote, "would be disastrous," because they performed most of the labor that kept the school operating. Yet resistance to his authority had reached a point where the agent required reinforcements: he did not reject their request out of hand, but promised to forward it to the Commissioner of Indian Affairs for his consideration. "I think that a word from *you*," he wrote the commissioner, "would show that I am not alone in my earnest purpose to benefit them." The Commissioner obliged shortly thereafter, and the girls agreed to remain in the school.

Resistance to Sheldon's authority continued, however, finally exploding in July 1883. On the night of the twenty-first, the school dining hall and kitchen burned to the ground. Two days later, the main school building also burned. Sheldon suspected arson, and in August he arrested five boys, ranging in age from twelve to sixteen, after they confessed to starting the fires. To partially fill the holes which the blazes had left, he quickly opened a new day school on the reservation, hiring one of the boarding school teachers and a nurse to teach Indian girls to sew. He also entrusted the two employees with the twenty-four-hour care of some Indian girls whom he "felt should be kept from the camps at present." The damage, however, had already been done.

An Indian Victory

Regardless of the determination with which the Indians resisted the agents' attacks on their culture, the agents themselves remained steadfastly convinced of the virtuousness of their mission. Burchard, for example, knew exactly whom to credit when the Indians began to convert to Christianity. "To God be all the praise for this wonderful change in their character and life," he wrote. Sheldon in 1879 had declared his intent to do only that which was right. *"I will not,"* he wrote, *"do anything else knowingly."*

Even as crushing a failure as the burning of the boarding school did not lead Sheldon to doubt his own sense of self-righteousness or inspire him to engage in self-criticism. He simply did not—or could not—consider the possibility that the arson represented a reaction to his own strictness. But if he could not blame himself, neither could he blame the Indians: to do so would have been to admit that he had failed to civilize them. Responsibility for the two blazes, in Sheldon's mind, rested not with the Indian students who had actually started them, but with whites, both inside and outside the school, who had resisted the agent's authority.

Sheldon's zealousness had, in fact, inspired opposition from some of the school's white employees. The agent had repeatedly enjoined teachers to enforce absolute segregation by sex among the Indian pupils, a practice he deemed necessary to prevent any illicit sexual contact. One of the instructors, a Mr. Reasoner, found the agent's restrictions too severe. Sheldon was furious to learn that Reasoner had allowed boys and girls to play together when the agent and his wife—who also served as a teacher at the school—were absent. He was even more outraged to find that the school's missionary had twice taken a vote among the schoolchildren to determine whether they thought Mrs. Sheldon, who was, like her husband, a strict disciplinarian, should be relieved of her duties. According to Sheldon, the missionary had told the children that the agent should allow them to meet in Sunday school with their outside friends, and had even tried to arrange marriages for two Indian girls—ages fourteen and sixteen—whom Sheldon had forbidden to wed.

That even the missionary would balk at implementing Sheldon's demands suggests the strictness with which the agent wielded his authority. Yet in spite of such opposition, the truth remained that Indians, and not white employees, had lit the fires which burned the agency buildings. Sheldon persisted, however, in blaming reservation workers for creating a climate in which the arson could occur. A group of employees who feared that he would fire them, Sheldon reported, had opposed him and had "worked upon" the teachers and "prejudiced" the missionary until they too became set against him. The missionary, in turn, had kindled "a spirit of discontent, and insubordination, which culminated in the burning of both . . . buildings." Sharing the blame with the school's employees were the surrounding settlers. The burning of the school, the agent wrote, represented "the outcropping of a spirit of hostility that has been more or less expressed since I began to prepare the buildings for that purpose." Certain settlers were "disappointed that the Agent has staid [*sic*] so long. He knows too much to suit them." Indeed, the arson, far from illustrating failure, testified to the agent's success. *"The truth is,"* wrote Sheldon three months after identifying the arsonists, "that I have done too much for the Indians to suit the people of this valley."

In the summer of 1884, U.S. Indian Inspector Paris Folsom spent six weeks investigating conditions at the Round Valley Reservation and then summarized his findings in a report which was sent to the Bureau of Indian Affairs. Folsom did not discuss the burning of the school, but he found Sheldon to be neither as successful nor as blameless for the problems of the reservation as the agent had thought. "Nothing whatever," said Folsom, indicated "a healthy condition of affairs at this agency." The agent was guilty of "inexcusable weakness, and gross carelessness in the management of the details of the agency." Folsom asked for, and received, Sheldon's resignation. The administration of the Methodists at Round Valley was over.

In a small, but significant, way, the Indians had defeated the agents. Even after enduring the deprivations, epidemics, and near-genocidal violence which had preceded their removal to Round Valley, they had, far from collapsing culturally or psychologically, resisted the agents' assimilationist attacks. Moreover, they had continued to pursue their own goal of independence, at one point even faking a conversion to Christianity which was intended to win more land. Sheldon had to resign because he failed to address, or to accept, the realities of Indian resistance.

Proponents of the watershed thesis have committed the same mistake. The realities of life in a white-dominated world, to be sure, did require adaptations, as in the case of the Indians' desire to cultivate reservation lands. But adaptation did not mean demoralization or assimilation. Tribal members sought to become farmers, not because they had internalized the agents' assimilationist ideology, but because agriculture represented their best hope for becoming self-sufficient. Rather than a place where they would become *like* whites, Round Valley tribes envisioned the reservation as the place where they could become independent *from* whites.

While the appropriation of assimilationist ideas for their own purposes was not something unique to these Indians, as Frederick Hoxie has demonstrated in the case of the Cheyenne River Sioux, what was unusual was the slimness of the margin by which they had escaped genocide. That even tribal members who had endured such unimaginable violence could pursue their goal of self-sufficiency while successfully resisting the agents' efforts suggests that the idea of the reservation as a turning point in American Indian history needs revision. Indeed, if the experience of tribal members at Round Valley is representative, the shape of Indian history after the beginning of the reservation period does not fundamentally differ from that of the period which preceded it. Reservations signalled not a pivotal shift from an Indian past of initiative to a future of passivity, but only a change in setting. The circumstances of the struggle may have changed, but the struggle itself did not.

Readings for Todd Benson:

Albert T. Hurtado, *Indian Survival on the California Frontier* (New Haven, CT: Yale University Press, 1988) considers similar issues. Malcolm Margolin, *The Ohlone Way: Indian Life in the San Francisco Bay Area* (Berkeley, CA: Heyday Books, 1978) examines the pre-mission Indians of northern California.

George H. Phillips, *Chiefs and Challengers: Indian Resistance and Cooperation in Southern California* (Berkeley: University of California Press, 1975) looks at another part of that state. In a series of essays demographer Sherburne F. Cook provides ideas about the biological and cultural impacts whites made on California native groups in *The Conflict Between the California Indian and White Civilization* (Berkeley: University of California Press, 1976).

15

THE LAKOTA GHOST DANCE: AN ETHNOHISTORICAL ACCOUNT

RAYMOND J. DEMALLIE, JR.

Of all of the Indian religious and revitalization movements in the nineteenth century, the Ghost Dance of the late 1880s and 1890s is the best known. Following the open-ended teachings of the Nevada Paiute Wovoka (Jack Wilson), many tribes on the northern plains adopted the Ghost Dance at a time of immense cultural stress. They had been forced onto dreary reservations, lost many of their horses and firearms, watched the bison disappear, and faced the prospect of having to become dirt farmers. The long-standing interpretation of these events suggests that in response to these pressures the northern plains tribes turned to the Ghost Dance hoping somehow to escape from their wretched conditions. Thus the Lakota version of these ceremonies has been depicted as a response to social and economic circumstances, as an effort to retreat into some mystical past or as a perverted effort to recast peaceful teachings into a militant call for renewed warfare.

Surely some of the participants may have hoped to bring about better times, but as earlier discussions of tribal revitalization movements suggest, that is too simplistic. In this essay the author suggests that an analysis of symbols and of the Indians' view that they were a part of nature are needed to understand what Lakota Ghost Dancers believed and where these ideas fit into their existing religious beliefs. He shows how many historical treatments of the movement have erred because they ignored these elements of Indian life and belief, and then presents a multi-layered explanation of what these spiritual ideas meant in the context of historical Lakota culture.

Raymond J. DeMallie, Jr., is a professor of anthropology at Indiana University.

The Lakota Ghost dance (*wanagi wacipi*) has been the subject of extensive study, first by newspapermen, who made it a true media event, and later by anthropologists and historians. The chronology of the contextual events in Lakota history—the 1888 and 1889 land cession commissions and their subsequent delegations to Washington, the

Source: Raymond J. DeMallie, Jr., "The Lakota Ghost Dance: An Ethnohistorical Account," *Pacific Historical Review,* 51:4 (November 1982), pp. 385–405. © 1982 The Regents of the University of California.

beef ration cuts at the agencies, the spread of the ghost dance ritual among the Lakotas in 1890, the death of Sitting Bull, the calling in of U.S. troops, the flight of Lakota camps to the badlands, the blundering massacre at Wounded Knee, and the eventual restoration of peace under U.S. army control of the Sioux agencies—is voluminously detailed in the printed literature.

The historiography of the Lakota ghost dance period begins with two contemporary works drawn primarily from newspaper sources, James P. Boyd's *Recent Indian Wars* (1891) and W. Fletcher Johnson's *Life of Sitting Bull and History of the Indian War of 1890–91* (1891). Despite the sensationalist tone, both volumes compiled a substantial body of important historical material. James Mooney, in his anthropological classic, *The Ghost-Dance Religion and the Sioux Outbreak of 1890* (1896), included a balanced historical discussion based on unpublished government records, newspaper accounts, and interviews with Indians. Mooney stressed the revivalistic aspects of the ghost dance and the hope it offered for regeneration of Indian culture. Subsequently there have been numerous historical studies of the Lakota ghost dance, most of which are partisan, focusing either on the Indian or military point of view. George E. Hyde's *A Sioux Chronicle* (1956) attempted to reconcile both perspectives and present the ghost dance in its political and economic context. The definitive modern historical study is Robert M. Utley's *The Last Days of the Sioux Nation* (1963), the best presentation of the military perspective.

The so-called "Sioux Outbreak" with the associated troop maneuvers and the resultant Wounded Knee massacre were, from the moment they began, linked with the ghost dance. This new religion had come into Sioux country from the West, originating with Jack Wilson (Wovoka), a Paiute prophet living in Nevada. Lakota acceptance of the ritual has been interpreted as a response to the stress caused by military defeat, the disappearance of the buffalo, and confinement on a reservation. The ghost dance religion itself has been seen as an epiphenomenon of social and political unrest. As the redoubtable Dr. Valentine T. McGillycuddy, the former dictatorial agent of Pine Ridge, diagnosed the situation in January 1891: "As for the ghost dance, too much attention has been paid to it. It was only the symptom or surface indication of deep-rooted, long-existing difficulty. . . ."

Such an analysis has become standard in the writings of both historians and anthropologists. Mooney wrote that among the Sioux, "already restless under both old and new grievances, and more lately brought to the edge of starvation by a reduction of rations, the doctrine speedily assumed a hostile meaning." Similarly, Robert H. Lowie asserted in *Indians of the Plains* (1954), a standard text: "Goaded into fury by their grievances, the disciples of Wovoka in the Plains substituted for his policy of amity a holy war in which the Whites were to be exterminated." However, this consensual interpretation of the ghost dance has not gone unchallenged. For example, in an anthropological overview, Omer C. Stewart explicitly rejected the characterization of the ghost dance as a violent, warlike movement. Nonetheless, this is a minority viewpoint in the literature.

Reevaluation of the ghost dance starts with an examination of the consensual interpretation exemplified in Robert M. Utley's work. He wrote:

> Wovoka preached a peaceful doctrine, blending elements of Christianity with the old native religion. . . . The Ghost Dance gripped most of the western tribes without losing this peaceful focus. Among the Teton Sioux, however, it took on militant overtones. . . . In their bitterness and despair, the Sioux let the Ghost Dance apostles, Short Bull and

Kicking Bear, persuade them that the millennium prophesied by Wovoka might be facilitated by destroying the white people. Wearing "ghost shirts" that the priests assured them would turn the white man's bullets, the Sioux threw themselves wholeheartedly into a badly perverted version of the Ghost Dance.

Before this analysis can be evaluated, a number of fundamental assumptions underlying it must be made more explicit. First, the statement that Wovoka's doctrine blended Christianity with "the native religion" implies that there was some fundamental similarity between the native religions of the Paiutes and the Lakotas. This assumption underestimates the significance of the vast cultural differences between these two tribes.

Second, the analysis asserts that the Lakotas perverted a doctrine of peace into one of war. This assertion incorrectly implies that the Lakota ghost dance religion was characterized by a unified body of doctrinal teaching. Lakota accounts of visits to the prophet clearly show that his teachings were not formulated into a creed; each man went away from meeting Wovoka with a personal interpretation of the ghost dance religion. For the Lakotas, this behavior was very much in accord with traditional religious practices, which defined loci of power (*wakan*) in the universe and devised rituals to tap this power, but which left each individual free to contribute to the understanding of the totality of the power (*Wakan Tanka*) through his own individual experiences. Within the context of a nondoctrinal religion, there can be no heretics, only believers and nonbelievers.

Third, the analysis asserts that the leaders of the ghost dance misled their followers for political reasons, even to the point of making false claims that their sacred shirts would ward off bullets. This assertion assumes *a priori* that to its leaders the ghost dance was a political movement merely masquerading as religion.

Fourth, the claims that the ghost dance "gripped" the tribes and that "the Sioux threw themselves wholeheartedly into" the ritual suggests irrational fanaticism. But the historical record makes it clear that the period of Lakota participation in the ghost dance was basically confined to the fall and early winter of 1890 and that the majority of the Lakota people in the ghost dance camps had only gone to them because they feared that an attack from the U.S. army was imminent. This factor explains why these camps fled to the safety of the badlands.

The standard historical interpretation of the Lakota ghost dance takes too narrow a perspective. It treats the ghost dance as an isolated phenomenon, as though it were divorced from the rest of Lakota culture. It also refuses to accept the basic religious nature of the movement. The so-called ghost dance outbreak has broader implications and interconnections than historical studies have indicated. To dismiss the ghost dance as only a reaction to land loss and hunger does not do it justice; to dismiss it as merely a desperate attempt to revitalize a dead or dying culture is equally unsatisfactory. Even though it was borrowed from outside sources, the ghost dance needs to be seen as part of the integral, ongoing whole of Lakota culture and its suppression as part of the historical process of religious persecution led by Indian agents and missionaries against the Lakotas living on the Great Sioux Reservation.

The primary reasons why previous historical analyses of the Lakota ghost dance have been inadequate lie in our reluctance to consider seriously the symbolic content of Indian cultures—in this instance, to allow the Lakotas their own legitimate perspective. Instead, empathetic writers have characterized the Lakotas as though they were either uncomprehending children or were motivated by precisely the same political and economic drives as white men. Both attitudes are as demeaning as they are misleading, and they fail to treat Indian culture with the same serious consideration afforded other cultures.

Writing history that deals with the meanings and conflicts of peoples with different cultural systems is a complex task. In recent years historians of the American Indian have turned to ethnohistory to provide methods for understanding the complexities of interactions between participants coming from totally different cultures. In a discussion of the new perspectives available from political, ecological, economic, and psychological anthropology, Calvin Martin has demonstrated the utility and contributions of each to the writing of ethnohistory. Within the discipline of anthropology, however, there is a more general theoretical perspective that may profitably be applied to ethnohistorical study—namely, symbolic anthropology. This method attempts to isolate differing significant symbols—units of meaning—that define perspectives on reality within different cultural systems. In the context of ethnohistory, it attempts to compare epistemological and philosophical bases for action from the perspective of the different cultures involved. Its focus is on ideas systematically reconstructed for each cultural system. It does not reduce history to ideological conflicts, but uses ideology to understand the motivation that underlies behavior.

It must not be assumed that the intention of a symbolic approach to ethnohistory is to penetrate the minds of individuals in the past. Psychological approaches to history are necessarily highly speculative, and any claim to intersubjectivity is no more possible with individuals in the past than with those of the present. Rather, the symbolic approach attempts to delineate collective understandings from each of the cultural perspectives involved, and thus to describe the cognitive worlds of the participants in the events under study. Using this as background, the ethnohistorian has a basis for ascribing motives and meanings to past actions. Robert Berkhofer expressed it well when he wrote: "Historical study, then, in my view, is the combination of the actors' and observers' levels of analysis into a unified representation of past reality."

In attempting to reconcile and combine both Lakota and white perspectives on the ghost dance, it is essential to compare causal notions of change as understood by the two cultures. During the late nineteenth century the basic issues on the Great Sioux Reservation were what kinds of change would occur in Indian culture and social life and who would direct this change. Whites assumed that Indian culture was stagnant and that the Indians could be transformed for the better only by the imposition of Western civilization. Indians, on the other hand, sought to control the process of change themselves.

For the Lakota people, the nineteenth century had been a period of continual changes: further explorations on the Plains, the complete integration of the horse into their culture, the flourishing of the sun dance as the focal point of ritual activity, the slow takeover of their country by the whites, the disappearance of the buffalo, and finally the adjustment to reservation life. A discussion of the Lakota view of the relationship between mankind and the natural world, particularly the buffalo, can help us begin to understand these changes from the Lakotas' perspective.

During the 1860s, when commissioners traveled up the Missouri River to sign treaties with the Indians, they found the attitude of the Lakotas toward the buffalo to be particularly unrealistic. To the commissioners it was evident that the buffalo were being exterminated and would soon be gone from the region. To the Indians this decline did not appear to be an irreversible process. For example, the chiefs told the commissioners that they hoped the whites would take away the roads and steamboats and "return us all the buffalo as it used to be." Baffled at this illogic, the commissioners reported that the Indians "are only too much inclined to regard us possessed of supernatural powers." This complete failure to communicate stemmed from the commissioners' assumption that the facts of the natural world must have appeared the same to the Indians as they did to the whites. Yet the Indians themselves recorded testimony which showed dramatically that the Lakotas thought of the land, the animals, and the people as a single system, no part of which could change without affecting the others. Thus when the commissioners asked if the Indians would consent to live on the Missouri River, they were told: "When the buffalo come close to the river, we come close to it. When the buffaloes go off, we go off after them." The Indians, the animals, and the land were one; while the people lived, talk of buffalo extinction was without meaning. Much later, Black Elk expressed the same attitude when he commented to poet John G. Neihardt: "Perhaps when the wild animals are gone, the Indians will be gone too."

To understand this interrelatedness of man, land, and animals—particularly the buffalo—it is necessary to understand the Lakota view of their origins. During the early twentieth century, the old holy men at Pine Ridge instructed Dr. James R. Walker, the agency physician, in the fundamentals of their religion. A cornerstone of their belief was that both mankind and the buffalo had originated within the earth before they emerged on the surface. When the buffalo became scarce, it was believed that they went back inside the earth because they had been offended, either by Indians or whites. At any given time, this explanation accounted for the scarcity of buffalo. Later, Black Elk told Neihardt about a holy man named Drinks Water who had foretold during the mid-nineteenth century that "the four-leggeds were going back into the earth." But this explanation also allowed for the return of the buffalo. The ghost dance Messiah's promise of a new earth, well stocked with buffalo, was completely consistent with the old Lakota system of cause and effect by which they comprehended the ecology. If the buffalo had been driven back into the earth by the white man, they could be released again by the Messiah.

The Lakotas' causal model of change was vastly different from the white man's. The Lakota world was a constant, with relationships among its parts varying according to external pressures. As the nineteenth century wore on, these pressures came more and more from the whites. But these pressures were not conceived of by the Lakotas as cumulative or developmental. All that *was* existed in its potentiality before the whites intruded; if they would leave, the world could be again as it had been. From the 1850s through the 1870s the Lakotas tried to get rid of the whites by war; in 1890 they tried ritual dancing and prayer. The white view, of course, was diametrically opposed. This was the age of the developmental social philosophers preaching the doctrine of individual competition for the evolution of humanity. The history of mankind was religiously believed to be progressive; changes were accepted as good and cumulative, leading from earlier stages of savagery and barbarism (in which the Indians still lived) to civilization, which was believed to be becoming progressively better, not only technologically, but morally as well.

It is within this general context of cross-cultural misunderstanding that a symbolic approach can contribute to an analysis of the Lakota ghost dance and subsequent military action. The dance itself, the actual ritual, became the focus of misunderstanding between Indians and whites. Most importantly, dance was a highly charged symbol. For the Lakotas the dance was a symbol of religion, a ritual means to spiritual and physical betterment. Even Lakota nonbelievers accepted the religious motivation of the ghost dance. For the whites, on the other hand, Indians dancing symbolized impending war. Similarly, Indian and white conceptions of ghosts were different. For the Lakotas, the ghost dance promised a reunion with the souls of their dead relations. For the whites it suggested that the Indians were expecting to die, caught up in a frenzy of reckless fatalism.

This clash over the meaning of the ghost dance is fully documented in the literature. For example, in 1890, according to James Boyd's *Recent Indian Wars:*

> The Indians mingled tales of their hard treatment with their religious songs, and their religious dances assumed more and more the form of war dances. . . . The spirit of fatalism spread and they courted death at the hands of white men, believing that it would be a speedy transport to a happier sphere.

However, Boyd's sources—both Indian and white—do not provide factual support for his interpretation. Nonetheless, this seems to have been the general opinion held by whites living on the frontiers of the Great Sioux Reservation. Boyd wrote:

> Older residents, and those acquainted with Indian warfare, knew well that an outbreak was always preceded by a series of dances. While these men were quite familiar with Indian nature, they failed to discern between a religious ceremony and a war dance.

Boyd reviewed the progress the Sioux had made in Christianity, home building, farming, and ranching, and he raised the question of why they would wish to precipitate war. One possible answer came from Red Cloud, who said in an interview:

> We felt that we were mocked in our misery. . . . There was no hope on earth, and God seemed to have forgotten us. Someone had again been talking of the Son of God, and said He had come. The people did not know; they did not care. They snatched at the hope. They screamed like crazy men to Him for mercy. They caught at the promises they heard He had made.

Towards the end of the book, Boyd revealed his personal interpretation of the cause of the trouble: "The Indians are practically a doomed race, and none realize it better than themselves."

Doubtlessly, some individual Lakotas shared this sense of despair. There were no buffalo; the government systematically broke its promises to support the Sioux until they could provide for themselves; and the Indians were starving. The ghost dance, arising at this opportune time, held out hope for the Lakotas. But if the Lakotas truly had believed themselves to be a doomed people, they would have paid no attention to the ghost dance. The religion was powerful because it nurtured cultural roots that were very much alive— temporarily dormant, perhaps, but not dying.

Is it reasonable to dismiss the Lakota ghost dance as insignificant, the mere "symptom" of other troubles, to use McGillycuddy's medical metaphor? This depiction does not explain the popularity of the ghost dance as a religious movement among other tribes. Perhaps it could be used to explain the warlike twist that the ghost dance took among the Lakotas. But when the record is evaluated objectively, it seems clear that the Lakota ghost dance did not have warlike intentions. Hostility was provoked only when Indian agents demanded that the dance be stopped, and violence came only after extreme provocation—the assassination of Sitting Bull by the Standing Rock Indian Police and the calling in of the army. For all intents and purposes, Sitting Bull's death was unrelated to the ghost dance. Agent McLaughlin had been clamoring for the old chief's arrest and removal from the reservation for some time, ever since Sitting Bull had refused to take up farming and be a model "progressive" Indian, to use McLaughlin's own term.

Lakota ghost dancers were enjoined to put away whatever they could of the white man's manufacture, especially metal objects. George Sword, captain of the Pine Ridge Indian Police, noted that some of the ghost dancers did have guns. When the agent demanded that the dance at No Water's camp cease, he was threatened with guns and retreated to the agency. Apparently, the purpose of the weapons was to ward off outside interference with the ritual. However, Boyd quoted a ghost dancer named Weasel: "We did not carry our guns nor any weapon, but trusted to the Great Spirit to destroy the soldiers." This statement was made after troops had arrived at Pine Ridge. Weasel related: "The priests called upon the young men at this juncture not to become angry but to continue the dance, but have horses ready so that all could flee were the military to charge the village." However, even this precaution was not considered necessary by fervent believers. Short Bull, one of the ghost dance leaders, assured his people that they would be safe from the white soldiers:

> If the soldiers surround you four deep, three of you, on whom I have put holy shirts, will sing a song, which I have taught you, around them, when some of them will drop dead. Then the rest will start to run, but their horses will sink into the earth. The riders will jump from their horses, but they will sink into the earth also. Then you can do as you desire with them. Now you must know this, that all the soldiers and that race will be dead.

Historical sources provide more information about the ghost dance from Short Bull than from any other of the leaders. Talking to Walker, he outlined his understanding of the prophet's teachings: "It was told that a woman gave birth to a child and this was known in heaven." Short Bull went to meet him. "This man professed to be a great man, next to God." The prophet told Short Bull and the other Lakotas "that he wished to be their intermediator. He said 'Do nothing wrong.'" On another occasion Short Bull said:

> Who would have thought that dancing could have made such trouble? We had no wish to make trouble, nor did we cause it of ourselves. . . . We had no thought of fighting. . . . We went unarmed to the dance. How could we have held weapons? For thus we danced, in a circle, hand in hand, each man's fingers linked in those of his neighbor. . . . The message that I brought was peace.

The messianic and strongly Christian nature of the ghost dance is very clear in Short Bull's teachings:

> The Father had commanded all the world to dance, and we gave the dance to the people as we had been bidden. When they danced they fell dead and went to the spirit-camp and saw those who had died, those whom they had loved . . . .
>
> In this world the Great Father has given to the white man everything and to the Indian nothing. But it will not always be thus. In another world the Indian shall be as the white man and the white man as the Indian. To the Indian will be given wisdom and power, and the white man shall be helpless and unknowing with only the bow and arrow. For ere long this world will be consumed in flame and pass away. Then, in the life after this, to the Indian shall all be given.

Through the teachings of the ghost dance, and statements about it by Lakotas recorded from 1889 until about 1910, it is possible to proliferate evidence to demonstrate the peaceful intentions of the leaders of the ghost dance. The historical record does not support the accusation that the Sioux "perverted" the ghost dance doctrine of peace to one of war.

Simple refutation of the consensual historical interpretation does little to advance an understanding of the ghost dance. Since it had a short life among the Lakotas, at least as far as active performance of the ritual, perhaps it might be dismissed as an isolated reaction to social stress, a revitalization movement that failed. After all, Mooney estimated that only half of the Sioux were affected by the ghost dance and his sources suggest that of these, only a small number were real believers in the religion. But this conclusion ignores the extreme importance that the Lakotas of 1890 placed on the dance, as well as the extent to which its suppression has served in later years as a symbol of white oppression. When Mooney visited Pine Ridge in 1891 as part of his comparative study of the ghost dance, he found the Lakotas uncooperative. He wrote: "To my questions the answer almost invariably was, 'The dance was our religion, but the government sent soldiers to kill us on account of it. We will not talk more about it.' "

The study of Lakota history from 1880 to 1890 suggests that it is a mistake to treat the ghost dance as an isolated phenomenon. Its prohibition was only another step in the systematic suppression of native religious practices that formed an integral part of the U.S. government's program of Indian civilization. Missionary observers felt that the ghost dance was only one more eruption of the "heathenism" that necessarily underlay the Indian pysche, a heathenism to be conquered and dispatched when Indians, as individuals, raised themselves from barbarism to civilization. The evolutionary social theory of the times held sway in the rhetoric of Indian policy. *The Word Carrier,* a Protestant missionary newspaper published at the Santee Agency in Nebraska, argued in 1890 (before Wounded Knee) that it was the government's responsibility to end the ghost dancing because of its political potential. The argument was an insidious one, expressed as follows:

> Their war dances have been suppressed simply as a political measure. The sun dance was forbidden in the name of humanity, as cruel and degrading. The Omaha dances should be summarily suppressed in the name of morality. But all of these alike, as well as all other of their heathen dances, should be prevented as far and as fast as possible until utterly eradicated, because they are potentially dangerous. We ought not to touch them as religious ceremonials, but, as breeders of riot and rebellion, we must.

The callousness of missionary zeal for the suppression of heathenism is nowhere more dramatically revealed than in *The Word Carrier*'s editorial on the Wounded Knee massacre printed in the January 1891 issue:

> The slaughter of a whole tribe of Indians at Wounded Knee was an affair which looks worse the more it is investigated. But aside from the question of culpability there is a providential aspect which demands notice. Taking it in its bearings on the whole condition of things among the rebellious Titon [*sic*] Sioux it was a blessing. It was needful that these people should feel in some sharp terrible way the just consequences of their actions, and be held in wholesome fear from further folly.

Commentary is perhaps unnecessary, but we can suggest that the fanaticism of Christian missionaries was no less than that of the ghost dancers themselves. Stanley Vestal, in his biography of Sitting Bull, takes the Christian aspects of the ghost dance at face value and seizes the opportunity to comment on the missionaries:

> The Ghost dance was entirely Christian—except for the difference in rituals. However, it taught nonresistance and brotherly love in ways that had far more significance for Indians than any the missionaries could offer. No wonder the missionaries became alarmed; they were no longer sure of their converts.

However, the dominant interpretation of the ghost dance, contemporarily and historically, places little significance on Christian parallels.

Some contemporary observers felt that the ghost dance showed striking resemblances to the sun dance, a suggestion that seems at first unfounded, but which gains credibility by reading descriptions of the ritual. Mary Collins, a missionary, witnessed the ghost dance in Sitting Bull's camp and recorded the following description:

> I watched all the performance, and I came to the conclusion that the "ghost dance" is nothing more than the sun dance revived. They all looked at the sun as they danced. They stopped going round now and then, and all faced the sun, with uplifted faces and outstretched arms, standing in straight lines and moaning a most horrible sound. Then they raised themselves on the toes, and then lowered themselves, raising and lowering their bodies in this way, and groaning dismally, then joined hands with heads strained backwards, watching the sun and praying to it until, with dizziness and weariness, one after another fell down, some of them wallowing and rolling on the ground and frothing at the mouth, others throwing their arms and running around and whooping like mad men, and all the time, as much as possible, still gazing sunward. They have not yet cut themselves, as in the old sun dance, but yesterday I heard this talk: Some said, "If one cuts himself, he is more 'wakan,' and can see and talk with the Messiah."

These similarities to the sun dance—gazing sunward and the dance step of the sun dance—are suggestive. Also, Mooney notes that of all the tribes who adopted the ghost dance, the Sioux were one of the few to dance around a sacred tree (or pole), the structural form of the old sun dance. This element may be superficial, serving only to indicate that when people borrow new ideas, they adapt them to older cultural forms as closely as possible. However, it reinforces the Lakotas' sense of religious loss and their deep felt need to establish continuity with their past. It seems that the new religion, believed to come from a reincarnated Christ wearied of the faithlessness of the whites and ready to aid his Indian children, was incorporated in a ritual form that merged the circle dance of the Paiutes (in which men and women danced together in a circle, holding hands—an innovation for the Lakotas) with the sacred dance circle and center pole of the traditional Lakota sun dance.

A speech by Short Bull to his people on October 31, 1890, points out the importance of the tree or center pole as defining the sacred space for the ghost dance ritual: "Now, there will be a tree sprout up, and there all the members of our religion and the tribe must gather together. That will be the place where we will see our dead relations." Short Bull's ghost dance preachings incorporated traditional Lakota symbolism of the four directions to suggest the unifying effects of the ghost dance on all Indian tribes. "Our father in heaven has placed a mark at each point of the four winds," indicating a great circle around the central tree. To the west was a pipe, representing the Lakotas; to the north, an arrow, representing the Cheyennes; to the east, hail, representing the Arapahoes; and to the south, a pipe and feather, representing the Crows. "My father has shown me these things, therefore we must continue this dance." He promised that the ghost dance shirts would protect them from the soldiers. "Now, we must gather at Pass Creek where the tree is sprouting. There we will go among our dead relations." Many years later one Lakota who had participated in the ghost dance as a boy commented: "That part about the dead returning was what appealed to me."

In practice, the millenialism of the ghost dance was merged with the symbols of the old religion. The tree, which had symbolized the body of an enemy in the old sun dance, became in the ghost dance symbolic of the Indian people themselves; this tree was dormant, but it was about to sprout and bloom. The tree symbol is best known from Black Elk, who found the outward symbols of the ghost dance so strikingly similar to his own vision during childhood that he was immediately caught up in the new religion. He felt it as a personal call, a reminder that he had not yet begun the work assigned him by his vision. "I was to be intercessor for my people and yet I was not doing my duty. Perhaps it was the Messiah that had appointed me and he might have sent this to remind me to get to work again to bring my people back into the hoop and the old religion."

It seems clear in Black Elk's case that the ghost dance, while seen as a new ritual, inaugurated by a new prophet—perhaps Christ himself—was in no way felt to be a sharp break with the old religion. It was rather a means to bring the old religion to fulfillment. There is no denial that this new hope for religious fulfillment was born of frustration and unhappiness bordering on despair. The ghost dance was to bring about the transformation to a new life on a rejuvenated earth filled with all the Lakota people who had ever lived before—living again in the old ways, hunting buffalo unfettered by the demands of whites, and freed from the cares of the old earth. Years later, one ghost dancer recalled the wonderful promise of the ghost dance visions:

> Waking to the drab and wretched present after such a glowing vision, it was little wonder that they wailed as if their poor hearts would break in two with disillusionment. The people went on and on and could not stop, day or night, hoping perhaps to get a vision of their dead, or at least to hear of the visions of others. They preferred that to rest or food or sleep. And I suppose the authorities did think they were crazy—but they weren't. They were only terribly unhappy.

In order to put the ghost dance in its proper perspective in Lakota religious history, it is imperative to review the process of religious persecution that marked the Lakota experience during the 1880s. At Pine Ridge, from the beginning of the decade, Agent McGillycuddy preached against the evils of the sun dance. Finally, in his annual report for 1884, he wrote that "for the first time in the history of the Ogalalla Sioux and Northern Cheyennes" the sun dance was not held. Though McGillycuddy did not fully understand the reasons why, the prohibition of the sun dance was indeed a drastic blow. As a public festival it brought together Lakotas from all the agencies into old-time encampments, with opportunities for courting and fun. In addition to the actual ritual of the ceremony, the sun dance provided the time and place for many additional rituals, including the acting out of visions, dances by groups of people with shared vision experiences, demonstrations of the powers of medicine men (healers), the piercing of babies' ears (essential for identity as a Lakota), and lavish giveaways. Camped around the sacred circle with the sacred tree at its center, the occasion of the sun dance was a real affirmation of Lakota identity and power, in both physical and spiritual senses. In the words of Little Wound, American Horse, and Lone Star, as they explained their traditional religion to Dr. James R. Walker in 1896: "The Sun Dance is the greatest ceremony that the Oglalas do. It is a sacred ceremony in which all the people have a part. . . . The ceremony of the Sun Dance may embrace all the ceremonies of any kind that are relative to the Gods."

In 1888, as the Oglala winter counts—native pictographic calendars—record, a further government prohibition was enforced on the Lakotas: "Bundles were forbidden." It had been the custom when a beloved person died to cut a lock of his or her hair and save it in a ritual bundle for a year, thus causing the spirit (*wanaǧi*) to remain with the people. At the end of the period, the spirit was released, and a great giveaway was held; throughout the year goods were amassed to give away in honor of the departed one. In some cases, as upon the death of a first-born son, the parents gave away everything they owned, although, according to tribal customs of sharing, they would in return be given the necessities of life and thus reestablished in a new home to help put the past out of their minds. Agent H. D. Gallagher at Pine Ridge decided in 1888 that although this custom had been allowed unchecked by his predecessors, he would put an immediate stop to it. Yet, he wrote in his annual report, "I found myself opposed by every Indian upon the reservation." To the Lakotas it was a final horror: not even in death was there escape from the white man's restrictions. The giveaway after death was prohibited and became an offense punishable by arrest. Ten years later, in 1898, Short Bull, in his capacity as religious leader, sent a plea to the agent begging for understanding:

> The white people made war on the Lakotas to keep them from practicing their religion. Now the white people wish to make us cause the spirits of our dead to be ashamed. They wish us to be a stingy people and send our spirits to the spirit world as if they had been conquered and robbed by the enemy. They wish us to send our spirits on the spirit trail with nothing so that when they come to the spirit world, they will be like beggars. . . . Tell this to the agent and maybe he will not cause us to make our spirits ashamed.

Such requests fell on deaf ears. From the agents' point of view, every vestige of heathen religion had to be eliminated before civilization could take firm root. The powers of the agents were dictatorial in the matter.

Following the prohibition of public rituals surrounding the sun dance, as well as the rituals of death and mourning, came the prohibition in 1890 against the new ritual of the ghost dance. Then came the murder of Sitting Bull and the massacre at Wounded Knee. It was a period of grave crisis for the Lakota people, physically and emotionally. Their religion had been effective before the whites came, but now the *Wakan Tanka* seemed no longer to hear their prayers. Under the restraints of reservation life, traditional customs relating to war and hunting were abandoned. For spiritual renewal there were only two places to turn: secret rituals of the purification lodge, vision quest, *yuwipi,* and attenuated versions of the sun dance, or alternatively to the various Christian churches which were clamoring for converts.

But the years immediately following the ghost dance were bad ones for missionaries to make new converts. According to Agent Charles G. Penney, in his annual report for 1891, there were yet "a considerable number of very conservative Indians, medicine men and others, who still insist upon a revival of the Messiah craze and the ghost dancing." The following year the missionary John P. Williamson, a perceptive observer, reported from Pine Ridge that "the effect of the ghost dances in the former years was very deleterious to Christianity, and is still felt among the Ogalallas. The excitement of a false religion has left a dead, indifferent feeling about religion."

The Lakota religious leaders at Pine Ridge who shared their thoughts with Dr. Walker at the beginning of the twentieth century were disappointed, but not defeated. Little Wound, after revealing the sacred secrets of the *Hunka* ceremony, said to Walker:

> My friend, I have told you the secrets of the *Hunkayapi*. I fear that I have done wrong. But the spirits of old times do not come to me anymore. Another spirit has come, the Great Spirit of the white man. I do not know him. I do not know how to call him to help me. I have done him no harm, and he should do me no harm. The old life is gone, and I cannot be young again.

Afraid of Bear commented: "The spirits do not come and help us now. The white men have driven them away." Ringing Shield stated: "Now the spirits will not come. This is because the white men have offended the spirits."

One of the most eloquent testimonies comes from a speech by Red Cloud, recorded by Walker, in which he outlined his understanding of the Lakota *Wakan Tanka*. Then he added:

> When the Lakotas believed these things they lived happy and they died satisfied. What more than this can that which the white man offers us give? . . . *Taku Skanskan* [Lakotas' most powerful god] is familiar with my spirit (*nagi*) and when I die I will go with him. Then I will be with my forefathers. If this is not in the heaven of the white man, I shall be satisfied. *Wi* [Sun] is my father. The *Wakan Tanka* of the white man has overcome him. But I shall remain true to him.

Outwardly, the white man's victory over Lakota religion was nearly complete. Inwardly, even among those who—like Red Cloud—accepted Christianity for what it was worth, the recognition of the existence of *wakan* in the life forms of the universe provided foci of belief and hope.

Any meaningful understanding of the Lakota ghost dance period must begin with an analysis of the foundations for cultural conflict. Lakotas and white men operated under radically different epistemologies; what seemed illogical to one was sensible to the other and vice versa. Objects in the natural world symbolized totally different realms of meaning in the two cultures. This difference has important implications for the writing of history. For example, Utley suggests that "when the hostile Sioux came to the reservation, they doubtless understood that the life of the future would differ from that of the past." But we can raise a reasonable doubt that this statement truly characterized the Lakota point of view. When Utley writes: "That the vanishing herds symbolized their own vanishing ways of life cannot have escaped the Sioux," we must deny the assertion. This is the unbeliever's attitude, totally dependent on acceptance of western philosophy. Similarly, it is necessary to take issue with Utley's claim that "after Wounded Knee . . . the reality of the conquest descended upon the entire Nation with such overwhelming force that it shattered all illusions." This is political rhetoric to justify the defeat of the Indians, not reasoned historical assessment.

The vast differences between the rhetoric of whites and Indians gives special significance to the ghost dance as the last step in a decade-long series of events aimed at crushing every outward expression of Lakota spirituality. From the believer's standpoint, the social and political problems—the so-called outbreak and the Wounded Knee massacre—were but epiphenomena of religious crisis. The ghost dance was inextricably bound to the whole of Lakota culture and to ongoing historical processes in Lakota society. Although it was introduced from the outside, it was rapidly assimilated to the Lakota system of values and ideas, especially because it promised resolution to the grave problems that beset the people. To recognize it as a religious movement in its own right does not deny its interconnection with all other aspects of Lakota life or negate its intended practical consequence to free the Lakotas from white domination. However, such recognition does retain the Lakotas' own focus on the ghost dance as a fundamentally religious movement which was to bring about radical transformation completely through religious means. Virtually all historical data point to the non-violent intentions of the ghost dance religion and the commitment of the believers to achieving their ends non-violently. It was the explicit command of the Messiah. In a cultural sense, this understanding of the ghost dance was shared by all Lakotas, believers and nonbelievers alike.

The importance of the ghost dance is not to be measured in the simple number of participants or in the unhappiness or despair that it reflected, but rather as part of the religious history of the Lakota people. For a time it held out such hope to the Lakotas that its ultimate failure, symbolized by the tragic deaths of the believers at Wounded Knee, generated a renewed religious crisis that forced a final realization that the old ways, with the hunting of the buffalo, were actually gone forever. Out of this religious collapse, new beliefs, new philosophies, eventually developed that would entail a major intellectual reworking of the epistemological foundations of Lakota culture.

Among the writers on the Lakota ghost dance, only John G. Neihardt accepted it as a legitimate religious movement and saw it as an attempt by the holy men of the Lakotas to use sacred means to better the condition of their people. A symbolic approach forces examination of the religious aspects of the ghost dance, not only because it *was* primarily religious from the Lakotas' perspective, but also because at least some contemporary white observers—the missionaries—understood that the ritual's true power lay in its religious nature. To the white men the ghost dance was seen as the last gasp of heathenism; to the Indians it offered renewed access to spiritual power.

The ghost dance ritual itself was a powerful symbol, but one on whose meanings the whites and Lakotas were incapable of communicating. They shared no common understandings. That the ghost dance could be a valid religion was incomprehensible to the whites, just as the whites' evolutionary perspective on Lakota destiny—that the barbaric must develop into the civilized—was incomprehensible to the Lakotas. Religion, dancing, ghosts, the processes of social change, and animal ecology were all important symbols to both whites and Indians but the meanings of these symbols in the two cultures were diametrically opposed. By focusing on these symbols it is possible for the ethnohistorian to reconstruct the meanings of events from the perspective of the participants and to arrive at an analysis that has both relevance and insight, and which contributes to an understanding of the historical realities of the Lakota ghost dance.

Readings for Raymond J. DeMallie, Jr.:

Placing the Ghost Dance among Indian revitalization movements, but yet a part of traditional Lakota religious practice gives it ties to many other groups and regions. Raymond J. DeMallie, Jr. and Douglas R. Parks, *Sioux Religion: Tradition and Innovation* (Norman: University of Oklahoma Press, 1987) is a good place to start. Russell Thornton, *We Shall Live Again: the 1870 and 1890 Ghost Dance Movement as a Demographic Revitalization* (New York: Cambridge University Press, 1986) deals with some of the same issues. Robert M. Utley, *The Lance and the Shield: The Life and Times of Sitting Bull* (New York: Henry Holt, 1993) gives a sympathetic account. For an analysis of another Indian religious movement of the nineteenth century see Robert H. Ruby and John A. Brown, *Dreamer Prophets of the Columbia Plateau: Smohalla and Skolaskin* (Norman: University of Oklahoma Press, 1989).

16

THE ALLOTMENT PERIOD ON THE NEZ PERCE RESERVATION: ENCROACHMENTS, OBSTACLES, AND REACTIONS

ELIZABETH JAMES-STERN

In 1887 the General Allotment Act went into effect. Also known as the Dawes Act or the Severalty Act, this legislation was the logical result of nineteenth-century efforts to incorporate Indians into the general society. That objective brought little benefit and often considerable misery to the tribal people. For generations pro-Indian groups and individuals had promoted the idea that assimilation offered the only chance to save these people from complete destruction. By the late nineteenth century the idea that Indians represented a dying race had wide public acceptance in American society, so efforts to help them received considerable public support.

Throughout American history the so-called friends of the Indian had depended on the church, the school, and the farm as the basic instruments needed to transform the tribal societies, and the allotment program built on that base. It called for assigning each reservation family a plot of land so that they could become farmers. This essay examines how allotment was implemented on the Nez Perce Reservation in Idaho. It analyzes the personnel involved in getting individuals onto farms, the actions of local white farmers, ranchers, and town builders as well as the Indian responses and initiatives regarding the reform efforts. The author provides a clear case study of how allotment functioned, of who gained and who lost through its operation and how the Indians shaped their lives because of it.

Elizabeth James-Stern is a doctoral student in history at Arizona State University.

The last years of the nineteenth century marked the beginning of a new era of Indian policy in the United States. Led by political and social reformers, the new philosophy

Source: Elizabeth James-Stern, "The Allotment Period on the Nez Perce Reservation: Encroachments, Obstacles, and Reactions," *Idaho Yesterdays* 37:1 Spring 1993 pp. 11–23. © 1993 Idaho State Historical Society.

sanctioned assimilation of Native Americans into the mainstream of Anglo-American society and culture. The General Allotment Act, passed by Congress in 1887, represented the crowning achievement for this group of reformers. Also known as the Dawes Act or Severalty Act, it provided for the allotment of 160 acres of reservation lands to heads of households, and 80 acres per person to orphans and unmarried adults, who were enrolled members of Indian tribes. Remaining reservation lands would then be made available for Anglo agricultural settlement in tracts of not more than 160 acres.

A clear rationale lay behind the Dawes Act, which was to serve as a primary vehicle for assimilation. Proponents intended to transform Native Americans into Anglo-American farmers, changing not only their livelihood but their values and culture as well. Opening unallotted reservation lands to white settlement could, they believed, encourage the Indians toward that end as their new neighbors provided example and advice.

Like so many other plans to improve the lot of people, the provisions and intentions of the Severalty Act appeared at the time of its enactment to be both logical and possible. Instead, the act worsened reservation conditions as many Native Americans began to feel cheated or discouraged. Many non-Indian people took advantage of opportunities created by changes in the Indian estate. Foremost among this group stood farmers and ranchers who generally cared little for the fate of Native Americans but coveted reservation lands.

Anthropologist Alice Fletcher contributed an active role in the drafting of and lobbying for passage of the Dawes Act. She believed that assimilation was the only hope for Native American survival and allotment was the best means of assimilation. Fletcher had previously spent some time with Native Americans and had allotted land on the Omaha and Winnebago reservations. With the change in federal policy, she held high hopes for the future of Native Americans. In 1889, she accepted a position as special agent in charge of allotment on the Nez Perce reservation in Idaho. When Fletcher arrived on May 28, she found a reservation surrounded by eager settlers, trespassers, and squatters.

Before and after the passage of the General Allotment Act, local newspapers avidly reported to residents in the nearby town of Lewiston the progress of the proposed policy and its implementation. Five years prior to the passage of the Dawes Act, the *Nez Perce News* had published an editorial recommending the use of the Nez Perce Reservation as an experiment in severalty and settlement—an arrangement that supposedly would benefit everyone concerned. When the government changed Indian policy as the paper urged, the Nez Perce could serve as a prototype of success in farming, education, and self-sufficiency. The editor's suggestion never materialized, but the coverage demonstrates Lewiston's early interest in the administration of reservation land.

Two days after Alice Fletcher's arrival in Idaho, the *Lewiston Teller* boldly announced: "Nez Perce Reservation to be Allotted at Once." The reports proclaimed the success of allotment on other reservations and praised Fletcher for her efficiency and reliability. The *Teller* predicted that the allotment process would be completed within fifteen months and expressed hope that Fletcher's efforts with the Nez Perce would result in the satisfaction of all concerned. No one could foresee the time and effort Alice Fletcher eventually expended in four tedious years of surveying land and tracing family relationships.

The *Lewiston Teller* most noticeably, but other newspapers such as the *Nez Perce News,* followed Fletcher's progress with care and reported every detail to the public. In November of 1891, another *Teller* headline proclaimed: "Nez Perce Reserve: It is Virtually Thrown open to Settlement and Cultivation." The newspaper reported that leasing could allow Anglos to farm land legally on the reservation and that thousands of acres would likely be available. In its continual advertising for more settlers, the paper also described Northwest Indian land as not only cheap but "far more desirable than the lands recently opened to settlement near Oklahoma." Concentrating on the amount of unallotted land, the newspaper illustrated the prevailing local attitude that Native Americans made no good use of the reservation: "the day is not far distant when actual settlers will be cultivating and rendering productive these broad acres so long locked up in the unused public domain." The *Teller* plainly reflected a significant amount of public interest in acquiring Nez Perce lands.

Another example of local attention took the form of an angry editorial written during or immediately after the negotiations for the sale of surplus lands. At first, enough Nez Perce objected to the cession of any land to block passage of an official agreement. The author referred to these Nez Perce leaders as "contemptable [sic] dogs" because they prevented the opening of the reservations to Anglo settlement. He claimed that "thousands of ready hands are now waiting for the privilege" of working Nez Perce lands. To gain the number of Nez Perce signatures needed, the editor advocated mass meetings that would force compliance. He then suggested that "a little rope" might be necessary to achieve their goal. If the editorial's tone indicated public sentiment, then settlers cared little for the concerns and desires of the Nez Perce. They believed that they had every legal and moral entitlement to reservation land.

Not satisfied to wait for the completed allotment process, local ranchers approached Alice Fletcher before she even entered the reservation. They demanded respect for their "rights" on the reservation. Fletcher's companion, Jane Gay, interpreted the situation as exactly what it represented, noting the cattlemen's ignorance of the intent of allotment. She wrote that they believed severalty "a skilful contrivance to dispossess the aborigines and facilitate the opening up of their lands to squatter sovereignty." Fletcher defended the Nez Perce and her own integrity, patiently explaining to the cattlemen that her duty consisted of placing the Indians on the best lands. The Allotment Act was intended to benefit Native Americans, making them "self supporting and valuable citizens." Fletcher sometimes allowed people such as the cattlemen to believe that she possessed naive faculties. In this case she also did not discourage their assumption that because she was female, she therefore was apolitical and morally pure. Gay, who observed the whole proceeding, wrote that the men seemed baffled not only by Fletcher's words, but even more by the fact that a woman had spoken them. As they left, Gay overheard one grumble that a man would have been more easily intimidated.

While Fletcher did not let them intimidate her, the ranchers were equally determined to have their way. Other cattlemen approached her with the same intention and received the same polite response. The General Allotment Act authorized grazing lands to double the acreage of an allotment, and several people attempted to persuade Fletcher to give the Nez Perce less land by declaring it agricultural. If she did so, she increased the amount of land left over and therefore allowed more room for settlement. However, Alice Fletcher did not earn her exceptional position or fame through gullibility or ignorance.

She knew only too well that thousands of non-Indian-owned cattle already grazed illegally on the reservation and prospective settlers surrounded the reservation in anticipation of its opening. Some had built houses inside the boundary, while other impatient squatters had already moved in to stake their claims.

Illegal entry on reservation lands was not new. Many cattle ranchers had simply ignored reservation boundaries and grazed their cattle on Nez Perce land throughout the later part of the nineteenth century. Agent George Norris first reported violations in his 1888 report. The year before, he had observed the reservation's excellent conditions for stock raising. He mentioned nothing of trespassing cattle, but he had held the office of agent for no more than a few weeks when he prepared the first report. By the time of his second report, the situation had become Norris' first order of business. Herds grazed freely on the reservation, and the settlers justified their use of the land by claiming the Nez Perce used none of it—and no fences existed to indicate that they did. The small reservation police force of five men could do little to remedy the situation. They patrolled 150 miles of boundary while remaining responsible for their other regular duties. They could drive trespassing stock off the reservation, but more often than not the same animals found their way back onto Nez Perce land. The crux of the matter, Norris noted, lay in the fact that local ranchers and farmers simply ignored the rights of the Nez Perce and the treaty obligations of the government to them.

   Agent Warren Robbins also reported the presence of illegal stock in 1890. He conceded that they provided a "source of constant annoyance" but claimed "there are no great herds," only a few scattered about the reservation. A year previously, Jane Gay had dryly remarked: "We are told that there are approximately ten thousand head now eating the grass of the Indians . . . ." Robbins' next report expressed more concern over the matter. He complained that keeping trespassing cattle off the reservation constituted an impossible task. In 1890, Nez Perce-owned cattle totaled approximately 7,000 head. Few Nez Perce owned 100 or more head; the majority of stockmen raised small numbers of cattle. Statistics varied throughout the years, but at least as many Anglo-owned cattle grazed on the reservation as did Nez Perce-owned livestock.

   Semiannual investigations by the Board of Indian Commissioners presented a more precise view of trespassing cattle. The earliest report of boundary violations came in 1884, from inspector W. A. Newell. He relayed complaints from the Nez Perce that not only did cattle invade their land., they lost approximately 500 head themselves when their own cattle wandered off the reservation and were branded by Anglo ranchers. Other complaints reached the Secretary of the Interior in 1887, and finally in 1889 inspector T. D. Marcum conducted an inquiry into the matter. Two men stood in the center of the controversy: Indian agent Charles Monteith and W. A. Caldwell. Other names surfaced in the testimony, but these two appeared repeatedly.

   Caldwell had lived on the reservation since 1865, operating a mail station and raising stock. Other agency employees, such as blacksmith Thomas Barton, admitted to running cattle illegally on Nez Perce land with or without various agents' knowledge but claimed they were never ordered to stop. Several witnesses named Caldwell specifically as the most flagrant offender. Charles Fairfield, a reservation farmer, charged Monteith with having a financial interest in Caldwell's cattle business. Monteith and Caldwell denied the allegation, and it was never proven. Fairfield estimated Caldwell's herd at 500 to 600 cattle, but Caldwell claimed to have averaged only 100 head annually for the twenty years he resided on the reservation. Other witnesses supported Fairfield's statements.

Agency miller and sawyer W. W. Johnson testified that Nez Perce herds died of starvation because of the great amount of trespassing cattle. James Reuben, a respected tribal leader, spoke of Nez Perce-owned cattle bearing Caldwell's brand. Several other witnesses came forward to testify, including John P. Vollmer, president of the First National Bank of Lewiston. He reported that many Nez Perce objected to Monteith's second appointment as agent in 1889 and asked him to intercede on their behalf. While he declined to do so, Vollmer did tell Marcum that he believed local cattlemen supported Monteith's appointment because they felt he would allow them to graze their herds on the reservation "without hindrance."

No one presented proof supporting the allegations against Monteith, who seemed not to believe that a problem existed. He never addressed the issue of trespassing stock in any of his annual reports and only discussed it with representatives of the Indian Department when asked directly. He asserted that Nez Perce cattle grazed outside the reservation as well as inside and that he was too busy to deal with the issue, and he suggested that either the Indian Department charge a fee and permit the cattle on the reservation or the agency simply purchase trespassing cattle for a school herd. Monteith also claimed to have ordered Caldwell and others off the reservation, but no witness or statement confirmed that assertion. Obviously, Monteith's concerns differed significantly from those of the Nez Perce. Even if he did not personally profit through Caldwell's business, he failed to acknowledge how important the Nez Perce considered the issue of trespassing stock. Monteith often disagreed with Nez Perce about various reservation issues, and the tribe was concerned enough about his reappointment as agent in 1889 to dispatch James Reuben to Washington, D.C., to protest the department's decision.

The Nez Perce problem was not unique. Stock owners commonly encroached on Indian reservations throughout the Northwest during the latter part of the nineteenth century, when cattle ranching reached its peak in the region. The Klamath, Warm Springs, Malheur, Umatilla, Yakima, and Nez Perce reservations all suffered to some degree from illegal cattle grazing. A government order forced many stockmen off the Nez Perce reservation in 1890. The injunction was apparently not an agency ruling but may have resulted from Marcum's investigation in 1889. Whatever its source, many stock owners complied with the order. However, agent Robbins reported incidents again in 1891 and federal inspectors discovered additional violations in 1893.

Both lax Indian policy on the part of the federal government and the ruthlessness of stock owners share blame for excessive cattle trespassing. In the Nez Perce case, the cursory interest of agent Monteith also contributed to the problem. While people such as Alice Fletcher and several missionaries worked diligently to promote what they considered the Nez Perce's best interests, others such as Caldwell took advantage of every circumstance available. They profited at the expense of the Nez Perce and disregarded the effects their actions had on the Indians.

The opening of the reservation to settlement may itself have helped to end the problem. After 1890, agriculture, sheep breeding, and general overgrazing caused a rapid decline in the land available to run cattle. While other factors also affected the livestock industry's decline, allotment and settlement irreversibly divided up the reservation. Running large numbers of cattle eventually became more and more difficult for both Nez Perce and Anglos as the open range of the reservation gave way to agriculture. In 1905, Nez Perce agent F. G. Mattoon reported that the Nez Perce themselves collectively owned 3,000 head of cattle—an estimate less than half the 1890 figure.

The controversy over trespassing cattle peaked just before the opening of the reservation. With the implementation of the Allotment Act, other issues developed. The influx of settlers was perhaps the most obvious change. Many local whites settled on Nez Perce lands in 1895 and still others traveled specifically to Idaho to homestead on the reservation. Father Alexander Diomedi, long a missionary in the Northwest and a former priest in Lewiston, wrote a letter to a midwestern German settlement encouraging its residents to settle on the Idaho reservation. The recipients appointed a delegation to investigate the possibilities and its members reported favorably. Several families from the settlement thus moved to Idaho and purchased Nez Perce land. Still others discovered a new opportunity in the opening of Native American reservations after the depression of 1893, as surplus Native American lands provided a new start for many farmers who had lost everything they owned. Certainly a variety of settlers attempted farming on the reservation, all with their own stories. Their success with the opening of surplus land overshadowed any objection the Nez Perce might have had. After all (from the viewpoint of settlers), the government had passed a law and the Indians had agreed to sell their unallotted land.

A promoter for the Lewiston area justified allotment in the name of progress and development. A pamphlet entitled "Highlights in Lewiston History," published early in the twentieth century, included the 1895 opening. Lewiston, its author said, benefitted from allotment because the reservation had previously "blocked entrance . . . to the whole inland country. . . ." The booklet continued by describing the aftermath of the opening as "red letter days for Lewiston" because of the influx of Anglo settlers, available land, and the money spent by both the new arrivals and the Nez Perce from their payments.

Surely the Nez Perce perceived the loss of their land as something less than a landmark event. A tribal history published in 1972 compared the opening of the Nez Perce reservation to the Oklahoma land rush of 1893. Indeed, the Meriam Report of 1928, which surveyed conditions on reservations across the country, revealed that by then the reservation as defined by the terms of the 1863 treaty contained only 1,300 Nez Perce residents—compared to 20,000 Anglos. Allotment terminated any concept of a physical area of land that might be considered "Nez Perce country," despite contrary views of map makers, agents, and lawyers. The Indians became "strangers on their own land."

The town of Orofino provided an example of the determination of Anglo settlers to establish their own communities. C. C. Fuller filed the original homestead claim on the site and took up residence on November 19, 1895, just one day after the official opening of the reservation. He first operated a trading post, while others established various businesses and enterprises. Determined to organize their new community, Fuller and others fought to acquire Nez Perce land titles, but the process was slow although few Nez Perce had the means to fight for their land in court, even if they desired to keep their allotment. Through settlers' perseverance and numerous litigations, Orofino finally became a town by the turn of the century.

As on many Native American reservations after allotment, few Nez Perce became Anglicized farmers as reformers and the federal government had intended. The twenty-five-year term of trust patents failed to provide a successful conversion period for two reasons: leasing and heirship problems. Many Nez Perce agreed to leases in which Anglo farmers worked the land and the owners lived off the rental money.

Even if a Nez Perce farmed his or her own land, a death reduced any heirs' land base by at least half and usually more. The Nez Perce reservation gradually became more and more owned or operated by Anglos. As early as five months before the official opening of the reservation in 1895, inspector P. M. McCormick found "the greater portion" of Nez Perce renting their farms. Leasing became so prevalent nationwide that in 1906, the Burke Act eased federal restrictions on the practice. In June of the same year, Congress approved a special act specifically to allow Nez Perce the privilege of leasing.

Every annual report from the Nez Perce agency between 1895 and 1905 reported on leasing. In 1895, agent S. G. Fisher estimated that Anglo leasers had worked nine-tenths of the 10,000 acres in cultivation. The number increased annually, and by 1900 agent C. T. Stranahan admitted that most of the Nez Perce had become discouraged with farming. Two years later he asserted that the demand for leasing continued "unabated." In 1904, F. G. Mattoon, school superintendent in charge of the agency, acknowledged that the practice of leasing was subject to abuse. Leasing did not benefit the Nez Perce; in fact, it had the opposite effect. It made them dependent on lease income, a situation Mattoon compared to the old annuity and ration system. Indeed, the practice of leasing allotments undermined the very intentions of the Severalty Act. Native Americans no longer had to attempt to farm or develop their land. Nor did they have significant reasons to accept Anglo culture or society. They could live as they wanted, supported by the money from lease incomes.

Stranahan also complained of many Nez Perce negotiating their own leases. All contracts needed the approval of the agent as a representative of the Interior Department. Without his consent on the leases, Stranahan feared, agreements would cheat the Nez Perce. However, the agent refused to issue permits to some Nez Perce. If they did not want to farm, they then simply rented out the land with or without the agent's permission. Stranahan also pointed out the widespread disillusionment with farming but apparently did not connect the two situations.

Fractionated heirship contributed to the opposition of many Nez Perce to farming. A significant and widespread problem on most allotted reservations even to the present day, fractionated heirship results from nothing more than the death of an allottee. The heirs divide the land between themselves, the amount depending on that person's relationship to the deceased. As each of these heirs dies, the plot of land is further divided among next-generation heirs—and so on, until the acreage becomes incomprehensibly small fractions of a single allotment. As that occurs, each person takes less interest in the inheritance: the share of profit is simply too small to worry about. Often, heirs agree to lease or sell the allotment and divide the income. The problem of fractionated heirship developed almost from the start of allotment and obviously became more complicated with time.

Even with the best of all other conditions, one understands why the Nez Perce quickly became discouraged. As early as 1899, C. T. Stranahan noted the "quite perplexing" problem of distributing heirship allotments. He recommended that the government put forth a special effort to alleviate the already developing entanglements. His admonition went unnoticed and the problem became increasingly difficult to rectify. One particular allotment on the Nez Perce reservation eventually gained over sixty heirs with interests ranging from 10,800/103,680 to 90/103,680—a situation not particularly unusual for the Nez Perce or any other allotted reservation.

Even among those willing to attempt farming, such fractionated heirship discouraged their descendants. But ethnohistorical reasons also impeded the success of allotment in Idaho. Traditional Indian kinship patterns differed significantly from the Anglo-American ideals set forth by the Dawes Act. Prior to allotment, Nez Perce lived in extended family groups, but severalty required people to live with immediate family only and in isolated farmhouses. Traditional families consisted of several nuclear families, with no particular identifiable head of household. Continuing aboriginal family structures deterred the Nez Perce from segregating themselves on individual farms.

Writing in 1923, Oscar Lipps, superintendent of the Nez Perce Reservation, acknowledged problems stemming from allotment—particularly heirship and the disproportionate Anglo population. He noted that by then the Nez Perce held 100,000 acres of allotted and tribal lands, but Anglo settlers owned 650,000 acres. Almost every Nez Perce under the age of 27 owned land only through heirship, and often a dozen or more heirs received a tract of 80 acres to divide up among them. The only practicable solution, Lipps argued, consisted of selling the land and distributing the profit. Under existing conditions, the heirs could not even begin their own farms if they wanted to because all the productive land was gone.

The Nez Perce spent centuries adapting to new institutions and ideas, most evidently after white contact. Allotment presented special difficulties, however. Certainly few would have unconditionally accepted the Dawes Act, given a choice; but Native Americans were not given such a choice to accept or reject allotment, which in theory required them to throw away their entire culture and start anew. The government forced the Dawes Act on Native Americans. No question was raised about its ultimate goals, and no one offered the tribes an option. Ironically, on the Nez Perce reservation the height of Native American agricultural activity occurred before 1890. Nez Perce farming actually declined after allotment.

By 1911, many Nez Perce had lost land or money or both either directly or indirectly through severalty. The agency had cancelled over one hundred allotments and many more had been sold, leased, or erroneously awarded to the wrong heirs. The Nez Perce agent controlled the management, contracts, and legal decisions of many allotments. All lease payments went through his office, as did probate questions. At the direction of the Indian Office, the agent collected money and allowed each individual to withdraw only twenty-five dollars per month on his or her account. To further complicate matters, in 1909 the Commissioner of Indian Affairs prohibited merchants from issuing credit to Native Americans. Anyone who did so risked his license.

The Nez Perce considered that directive libelous in its suggestion of their untrustworthiness, and economically disastrous as well. They needed either credit or their full amounts of money. Twenty-five dollars a month scarcely allowed families to meet their needs, and it hindered them from making any major improvements on their land. The Nez Perce also had cause for complaint regarding treaty violations, unauthorized construction of roads and railroads through the reservation, and indiscriminate heirship rulings.

The Nez Perce asserted their rights as state and federal citizens. They sought access to the courts and other means of arbitration. Led by Starr J. Maxwell, Nez Perce tribal attorney, the Nez Perce presented their grievances to Congress. They introduced, via Idaho's senator William Borah, a document containing 131 exhibits, most of which were personal affidavits. The majority of witnesses specified the agent's control of their personal finances as a cause of hardship. Others reported their allotments diminished by roads and railroads built without permission or compensation. Still others objected to state hunting and fishing laws. Treaties had guaranteed fishing and hunting rights to the Nez Perce, but several tribal members had been arrested for violating game laws.

Many Nez Perce also complained about losing their first per-capita payments in 1895. Tom Williams' story echoed that of others. The agent induced him to deposit his money in the First National Bank at Moscow, Idaho. Shortly afterward, the bank failed. Charley Wat-to-lina, who also lost his deposits, estimated that the First National had accepted $200,000 to $300,000 from Nez Perce. Few, if any, received their money back.

The affidavits also documented some of the unfair heirship decisions. This problem affected many women, such as Mary Types, whose husbands had been previously married. When Types died, the superintendent awarded half of his allotment to their daughter and the other half to his first wife. Mary Types received nothing and wanted the case reviewed. He-yum-ka-yon-mi also requested an investigation into her claims. When her husband died, the agent awarded his allotment to his parents and she received nothing. In still another case, You-hoy-ta-mut-Kickt asked to recover her daughter's allotment. The agent had cancelled it because another woman by the same name as the daughter also owned an allotment. You-hoy-ta-mut-Kickt's daughter had died, but the other woman was still living.

In almost all the affidavits, the Nez Perce appear to have had legitimate concerns and objections. Severalty and the opening of the reservation created numerous difficulties. Even if federal policy failed to recognize the reality of allotment's impact until the 1930's, Native Americans did not. The Nez Perce memorial represented an effort to resolve their grievances within the legal framework of the government. The affidavits were not simply a list of complaints; individually they conveyed real problems, and collectively they showed a determination to be heard by Congress and the Indian Department.

Despite such problems, Superintendent Lipps believed wholly in the efficacy of the Dawes Act. Yet he realized how and why it created problems. He cited a new government study of Native American conditions, presumably the Meriam investigation, that offered a framework for ameliorating any negative situations for Native Americans. In his view, the Nez Perce lived better after allotment than they had in the eighteenth century. Before Lewis and Clark met the Nez Perce, in Lipps's view they were poverty stricken, leading a day-to-day existence in a futile search for food. At least after allotment, he suggested, few "blanket Indians" remained and most wore short hair. Lipps's faulty logic, ethnocentric interpretation, and vision of progress lack validity today, but he did recognize that allotment created drastic changes for Native Americans. While assimilation represented a primary goal of the legislation, short hair and Anglo clothing did little to help Native Americans become successful farmers. Lipps and many of his colleagues believed that these were signs of success for the Dawes Act and other measures aimed at assimilation. A contrasting Nez Perce view is that the Severalty Act attempted to prevent Native Americans "from being Indian."

In addition to agriculture, education was also an important aspect of the assimilation campaign. "Industrial training" prepared young Native Americans to take over their parents' allotments. Lapwai boasted its own government school, later moved to nearby Fort Lapwai. Its capacity held steady at about sixty pupils in industrial and academic training. The Catholic mission school at Slickpoo operated classes well into the twentieth century. Several Nez Perce also attended Carlisle in Pennsylvania and Chemewa in Oregon.

Lapwai Rural High School Number One became in 1909 the first white-Indian integrated school in the country. Mrs. John N. Alley, wife of the agency physician, initiated the plan. With the support of Presbyterian missionaries Kate McBeth and Mary Crawford, Alley served on the local board of education beginning in 1903. One of her first projects involved the construction of a new school building for Anglo children. Soon after its completion, she and others began planning a separate high school. They advocated an integrated school and held meetings with government officials and Nez Perce spokesmen. A local election in 1909 approved the plan, which included the use of already existing government school buildings and federal subsidies to the school system for Nez Perce students. By December of that year, approximately 300 students attended Lapwai Rural High School, 40 percent of whom were Nez Perce.

While education formed a major part of the assimilation campaign, as with severalty, reality differed significantly from the hopes and ideas of reformers. One of the major problems in Native American education during the allotment era was the lack of concern about it among land-seeking westerners who cared little for the fate or welfare of Native Americans. Their primary interest lay in freeing reservation land. These individuals considered any time, thought, or money spent on the matter wasted. On the Nez Perce reservation, school integration fell victim to his attitude; there was little concern on the part of non-Indian residents for equal opportunity in the district. Integrating the high school allowed government-salaried teachers to work there, but with minimal contributions from the school board. The district also benefitted from subsidies and the use of government buildings. But local grammar schools remained segregated, and as a result the number of Nez Perce high school students gradually decreased. Consequently, the government teachers taught mostly Anglo students in government buildings at the expense of the Indian Office.

The assimilation program, as envisioned by proponents of allotment, failed on the Nez Perce reservation. Many Nez Perce resisted the government's efforts, and those who did not usually met with other obstacles. By the 1920's the Nez Perce took matters into their own hands, realizing the futility of relying on the federal government to aid their situation. Forming the Nez Perce Home and Farm Association (NPHFA) in 1923, they attempted to help each other collectively—over a decade before the Indian Reorganization Act was passed to ameliorate reservation conditions.

The NPHFA could not give the Nez Perce direct self-government because of the federal government's custodianship policy. However, its formation expressed the tribe's desire for independence. The Indian office cooperated with their efforts and local newspapers and organizations also supported the venture. Corbett Lawyer drew up the NPHFA's five-year plan to improve Nez Perce education, health, and economy. Its goals met with limited success, but the Nez Perce had developed a prototype of Native American self-government.

In 1933, the United States Senate Subcommittee on Indian Affairs conducted hearings on the condition of Native Americans. The members visited almost every reservation in the country, including Lapwai. The investigation reflected the effects of the Great Depression by examining delinquent lease payments and the lack of available jobs. Notwithstanding the nation's economic problems, Chairman Burton K. Wheeler blamed

Native Americans' problems almost exclusively on alcohol. If only they would all stop drinking, he believed, they could utilize their education, have good homes, and build themselves up.

The problem of Native American economic conditions went much beyond alcohol. Agency physician C. H. Koentz told of overcrowded conditions that contributed to the spread of tuberculosis and other diseases; he had once visited a two-person home and found ten people sleeping in one room. Racism also played a role. Caleb Carter argued with Wheeler over the existence of prejudice. Wheeler claimed none occurred in the Northwest, but Carter pointed out that Anglos often refused to work with Nez Perce. He knew of one particular farm where stacks of grain had stood since World War I because Anglo farmers refused to thresh for the owner. He also told of Lewiston businesses that refused to deal with Nez Perce, posting signs proclaiming "White trade only" to prohibit them from entering. Caleb Whitman then told of a job in which he had been hired as a clerk. Whitman had attended high school and taken a civil-service examination. However, when he reported for work, the foreman told him he had no jobs for Indians. In the end, Whitman swept and washed dishes.

Struggling against racism, disease, and the Great Depression, Native Americans found it almost impossible to succeed in the vision of the Dawes Act. Myopic views such as those of Wheeler and Oscar Lipps discouraged any serious consideration of Indian affairs even after the Meriam Commission published its findings. The realities of reservation life in the form of trespassers, squatters, leasing, fractionated heirship, and BIA policies would by themselves have prevented the success of allotment, and Native Americans did not want to become Anglo-Americans. Reformers had envisioned the complete disintegration of tribal relations, but their utopian plan failed almost as quickly as it was implemented. All of these factors made any attempt to farm a formidable undertaking.

Despite the failure of the specific goals of reformers and missionaries, the assimilation program did affect the Nez Perce. Albert Moore perhaps personified the amalgamation of Anglo-American and Nez Perce culture. Born in 1861, Moore lived until 1963—a member of one of the generations directly affected by the assimilation campaign. Moore became a Presbyterian minister in his younger years and remarked to missionary Mary Crawford how much he enjoyed teaching his people about Christ. He said it reminded him of *ipnu'tsililpt,* a native religious movement popular among the nontreaty Nez Perce. Crawford reprimanded him for comparing the two and told him his remark was "savage" and "foolishness." Moore quit the ministry at that moment and immediately moved away to another part of the reservation. A week later, Crawford apologized to him in a letter and asked him to return. Moore refused, and years later he said about the incident: "the missionaries never asked us how we believed. We believed in heaven, through dreams. We were Christians before the White man came."

Moore spoke of many changes that occurred on the Nez Perce reservation and lamented the fact that younger generations of Nez Perce no longer sought guardian spirits. He often thought of traditional practices in regard to the Anglo-American world around him. For instance, he enjoyed baseball, played the game himself, and regularly attended area minor-league and college games. Combining America's national pastime with his own cultural heritage, Moore suggested that baseball players take sweat baths for strength and endurance. The Nez Perce could not avoid exposure to Anglo-American institutions during the assimilation period. Albert Moore represents just one example of how many of them thought about and reacted to the changing world. Few either completely accepted or completely rejected the influence around them.

By the time John Collier became Commissioner of Indian Affairs and designed the Indian New Deal in 1934—signalling the end of the federal policy of allotment—the Nez Perce had developed a political system. They were organized enough to seriously consider, question, and debate the plan. A tribal business committee wrote to the Indian Department, presenting their specific questions and concerns. Upon receiving a reply, the Nez Perce held an election and voted to reject the Reorganization Act. They seemed already to be doing what Collier intended, so they did not believe it would particularly benefit them.

As one of the most important pieces of Indian legislation in United States history, the Dawes Act affected Native Americans across the country. With some slight adjustments, the policy remained in effect for over forty years. During that time, people of all backgrounds and philosophies touched the lives of Nez Perce. They ranged from pious missionaries to politicians to ruthless businessmen. Before the Indian Reorganization Act superseded the General Allotment Act, Native Americans faced a great deal of adversity in the form of incursions on their land and indifference to their welfare. The Dawes Act unfortunately gave these forces leverage to invade the Nez Perce reservation and take whatever personal profit was available. The Nez Perce collectively attempted to alleviate their difficulties through such methods as forming the NPHFA and presenting their concerns to Congress. Only years of work finally reestablished the Nez Perce Tribe politically and economically. Some problems, such as fractionated heirship and loss of large amounts of land, have continued into the present.

Readings for Elizabeth James-Stern:

Many tribal histories include a chapter on this topic. For a good general discussion see Janet A. McDonnell, *The Dispossession of the American Indian, 1883–1934* (Bloomington: Indiana University Press, 1991), and Wilcomb E. Washburn, *The Assault on Indian Tribalism: The General Allotment Law (Dawes Act) of 1887* (Philadelphia: J. P. Lippincott Company, 1975). For another tribe see Marcia Larsen Odell, *Divide and Conquer: Allotment Among the Cherokee* (New York: Arno Press, 1979), and Willard H. Rollings, *The Osage: An Ethno-Historical Study of Hegemony on the Prairie-Plains* (Columbia: University of Missouri Press, 1992). Leonard A. Carlson examines allotment and agriculture in *Bureaucrats and Land: The Dawes Act and the Decline of Indian Farming* (Westport, CT: Greenwood Press, 1981).

17

"RIGHT IN THE MIDST OF MY OWN PEOPLE": NATIVE AMERICAN WOMEN AND THE FIELD MATRON PROGRAM

LISA E. EMMERICH

By the late nineteenth century the federal government had pushed most Indian groups onto reservations. At that point American officials expected to complete the long-thwarted efforts to acculturate the tribal people. Many saw Indians as being the remnants of a dying race and assumed that the compassionate thing to do was to hurry them into the general society. Other readings in this collection look at earlier efforts at working through churches, schools, and farming programs to accomplish that task. By the 1890s it seemed that the acculturation program should be expanded.

Because Indian women were perceived as having a central role in family and cultural affairs, they became the target of a new effort, the Field Matron Program. Its goal was to send women into the Indian villages and homes to teach the Indians proper, middle-class household management. In this essay the author examines the goals, methods, personnel, and results of the Field Matron Program at the turn of the century. Mostly whites, these women had the duty of introducing what was considered to be the proper way to conduct each household, from food preparation to proper ways to dress the children, and from household cleaning to women's roles within the family. This essay examines the efforts of the Indian women who became field matrons. It shows that neither racial nor gender ties united the reservation women and their assigned field matrons. By analyzing the cooperation and conflict the program generated the author demonstrates the degree of autonomy and initiative many Indian women exercised when it came to their families and societies.

Lisa E. Emmerich is an associate professor of history at California State University at Chico.

Source: Lisa E. Emmerich, " 'Right in the Midst of My Own People': Native American Women in the Field Matron Program," pp. 201–16. Reprinted from *American Indian Quarterly,* volume 15, number 2 by permission of the University of Nebraska Press. Copyright © 1991 by the University of Nebraska Press.

In January 1892 Indian Agent Major George LeR. Brown asked the Office of Indian Affairs (OIA) for assistance with the Pine Ridge reservation population. Little more than a year after Sioux attempts to reclaim a fading tribal past ended tragically at Wounded Knee, he found precious little evidence of individual or community progress toward "civilization." The agent, arguing that "the pressing need [here] is for better homes and better cooking," requested the appointment of a field matron.

Implementing an innovative Indian Service program begun in 1890, field matrons promoted assimilation through intensive domestic work with Indian women. Brown believed that Julia Kocer was an ideal candidate for the post. Interested in introducing tribal women to the "ways of White Women," she appeared to personify the "certified civilizer" reformers and OIA policy makers hoped to attract to the program.

Major Brown saw Kocer as a potential catalyst for change at Pine Ridge. The OIA, however, did not share his enthusiasm. Neither impeccable qualifications nor genuine interest could alter the fact that Julia Kocer differed from other prospective field matrons. They were all Anglo-Americans. Educated, competent, and respectable, she was a mixed-blood Arikara Indian.

The first Native American field matron might have been Julia Kocer. Assimilated and concerned with the welfare of her Arikara peers, she clearly represented the "new" Indian woman the OIA hoped to create. Nonetheless, the field matron corps remained closed to women like her until 1895. Then, Indian women could join Anglo-American women in helping their tribal peers accept the "White Woman's [sic] road." From 1895 to 1905, they played an active and occasionally prominent role in civilization work. Neither their participation nor their visibility, though, could guarantee a permanent place in the program. While field matrons continued their work on reservations until the 1930s, Native American involvement declined rapidly after 1905.

The story of Native American field matrons is a special, albeit abbreviated, chapter in the larger history of the field matron program. Their experiences as members of the Indian Service reveal the public and private worlds of women whose positions compelled them to create identities consistent with the demands of professional duties, traditional heritage, and adopted culture. Examining their work as role models in this program makes these long invisible women full participants in this story.

These women and their experiences also offer students of the assimilationist era of Indian policy a window into the world of Native Americans who incorporated Anglo-American culture into their lives. Scholars have concentrated on identifying the "friends of the Indian" and delineating their programs for Indian advancement. The shadows cast by this historical spotlight have somewhat obscured those tribal people who became partners with the Anglo-Americans. Cases like the Native American field matrons reveal the practical, and personal, ramifications of assimilationist rhetoric and policies.

Julia Kocer sought entry to a program established at a moment when many Anglo-Americans believed the struggle to end tribalism had begun in earnest. Education and land in severalty could erase some, but not all, remnants of Native American traditionalism. Ethnocentric reformers, profoundly influenced by contemporary Victorian reverence for domesticity and the "woman's sphere," concluded that Indian home life exerted a powerful conservative force. Within the homes, they regarded Indian women as degraded captives of ignorance, custom, and superstition. Congress created the field matron program in 1890 to bring both the women and their domestic world the benefits of modernity and Anglo-American culture.

Field matrons, boasted one OIA official, stimulated ". . . a contagion of home-making on the reservations." This process incorporated lessons in cooking, cleaning, sewing, basic carpentry, animal husbandry, and health care. The women were also directed to lead religious activities and sponsor social events that would further the cause of assimilation. Few skills or tasks, in short, did *not* fall under the rubric of the field matron's job.

Cooking classes, religious services, and child care seminars all offered tribal women much more than practical help in adapting to sedentary reservation life. The agenda of these activities grew out of the field matron program's mission: helping Native American women adopt Victorian Anglo-American standards of womanhood. Field matrons used their lessons to establish cross-cultural personal bonds and to emphasize the superiority of Anglo-American models of femininity, wifehood, and motherhood.

While the official version of this program remained relatively static, a number of factors acted in concert to alter the composition of the field matron corps and shift the focus of their duties. The domestic ideology of "true womanhood" may have helped to create the field matrons but health care rapidly took precedence over domesticity. Simultaneously, an increasing number of Anglo-American women who would never have identified themselves as "certified civilizers" found the program an attractive employment opportunity. Four decades of substantial change separated the field matrons of the 1890s and the 1930s.

Ethnocentrism, gender role redefinition, redirection of duties, and changes in Anglo-American personnel made up the backdrop to Native American participation in the field matron program. From 1895 to 1927, 34 Indian women representing a wide range of tribes and levels of assimilation worked as field matrons. Proximity to reservation communities and familiarity with conditions there probably, as in the case of Julia Kocer, accounted for the appointment of some women. But, the absence of any discernible hiring pattern suggests that the OIA gave no preference to any one tribal group over another.

Native American women constituted roughly 13 percent of the total field matron corps and 8 percent of those employed between 1895 and 1927. Slightly more than half, some 52 percent of the 34 Indian women, participated in the program between 1895 and 1905. For five years during that peak period, they formed a significant minority within the total corps. In 1897, for example, Indian women made up 31 percent of the field matrons corps; that figure increased to 33 percent in 1899. The remaining 16 who entered and left the Indian Service before 1927 never regained that statistical parity. In 1910, the next highest year, Native American field matrons comprised only 12 percent of the total corps. (Figures 1 and 2)

The OIA hoped to attract young, well-educated, single women to the field matron program. Both Anglo-American and Native American appointees usually deviated from this personnel profile. Indian field matrons ranged in age from 20 to 67. The median age for this group was 42. Sixteen were the products of one branch of the OIA's assimilation framework, the Indian School system. Twelve attended institutions like the Haskell Institute, the Phoenix Indian School, and the Albuquerque Indian School. Four more matriculated at the more elite institutions, the Carlisle School and the Hampton Institute. About half of the 16 women whose marital status can be determined were single; three were widows. At least one married while a field matron, helping set a precedent for her peers.

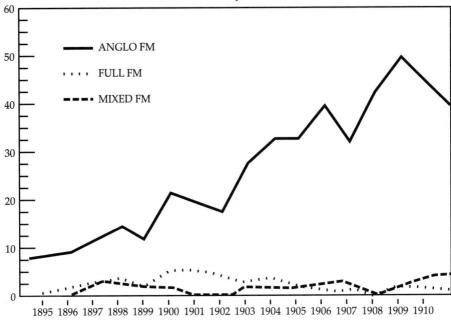

Figure 1
Field Matron Corps. 1895–1910

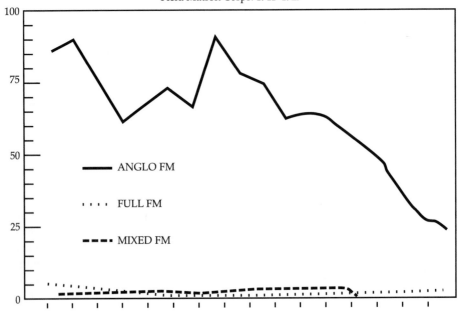

Figure 2
Field Matron Corps. 1911–1927

It is hardly surprising that racial differences superseded whatever commonalities these women shared with their Anglo-American peers. Yet, within the Native American group, there were also racial divisions. Blood quantum further segmented the group between full and mixed bloods. The total group was about evenly split between full and mixed bloods, the participation of the former women almost evenly matched by that of the latter. This factor was not initially an important consideration for tribal women interested in these positions. After 1897, though, mixed-blood women played an increasingly visible role in the program.

Native American women combined altruism and pragmatism in the field matron program by teaching skills defined as "civilized" to other Indian women in return for wages. Application letters sent to the Indian Office usually stressed the correspondent's desire to help other tribal women adjust to the new ways of life. Julia DeCora, a full-blood Winnebago graduate of the Hampton Institute, emphasized this theme in an 1899 letter. She explained her interest in the position by noting that "as a member of that tribe [Winnebago] I feel very anxious to do whatever is in my power [to help]. . . . " Mary Rice, a mixed-blood Pawnee woman looking for a position in 1903, echoed DeCora's letter. She felt the OIA should know that ". . . I am very anxious to see advancement among my people." Anna R. Dawson's plea in 1895 was heartfelt. The field matron position offered her a chance to work ". . . right in the midst of my own people . . . [teaching] them all I have been able to learn from the white[s]. . . ."

These women rarely mentioned salary as a factor motivating their employment search. This self-imposed reticence was in spite of the fact that the wages for a field matron, $600–$720 per year, and a $300 per year salary for assistant field matrons, were quite high by Indian Office standards. When it seemed clear that salary, not civilization, lay behind the interest in the job, women carefully couched that admission in language acceptable to OIA policy makers. Sadie Warren, a mixed-blood Ojibwa woman, tied her request for an appointment to salary because she was a widow. Emphasizing her wish to be self-supporting and help others, she explained "I am left a widow with two small children . . . I will in a very short time be in need."

Whatever their reasons for seeking employment, Indian field matrons shared with their Anglo-American counterparts the challenge of transforming the field matron position into a job that met the needs of the reservation population. This usually meant that immediately relevant lessons in sewing "citizens" dress or home sanitation took precedence over instruction in beekeeping or sidewalk construction. Field matrons spent much of their time working with tribal women on cooking, sewing, and housekeeping skills. These three subjects were the most useful and afforded the Native American field matrons their best chance for successful cultural transmission.

Pursuing this objective, many Indian women quickly became valued members of the OIA civilization team. In 1901, Omaha and Winnebago agent Charles P. Mathewson commended Maude Holt for her devotion and efficiency during four years of field matron work. He described Holt, a full-blood Winnebago herself, as an "exceptionally good employee." R. C. Preston, agent at the Seger Colony, was so impressed with the work of Mary C. Gillette, a full-blood Arikara, that he asked the OIA for additional field matrons. Two years of her work persuaded him that employees like her ". . . might do much toward advancing these Indian women in the ways of civilization."

Native American field matrons clearly equalled the efforts of their Anglo-American peers in the domestic education sphere. Yet, it was there that some subtle differences between these two groups became apparent. As a group, field matrons wanted to see tribal women adopt as many "civilized" skills as possible under their tutelage. Undoubtedly sensitized by their own experiences to the amount of effort this involved, the Indian field matrons seemed willing to take a longer view of change than their non-Indian peers.

In a variety of domestic areas where Anglo-American women would have criticized the practices of tribal women, Native American matrons often accepted and praised whatever degree of progress had been made. Maude Holt reported that the women of her tribe had a great difficulty in adopting civilized domestic practices like canning and sanitary food storage. Yet, she applauded them for their ready acceptance of "citizens" dress and their sewing skills. Marie McLaughlin, a mixed-blood Sioux woman stationed at Standing Rock, found much to criticize about tribal life but still saw noteworthy progress in the fact that "men are doing more of the chores." Howyer Senoia, a mixed-blood Pueblos woman working at Paguate, went so far as to append to her description of cooking lessons that the women there did well with traditional culinary techniques because "they are not so bad after all."

While this willingness to concede some value to traditional culture may initially seem rather innocuous, other Indian Service personnel may very well have interpreted it as damaging to assimilation efforts. Acceptance and praise of domestic traditions had especially frightening implications for this program when they came from women whose education supposedly freed them from that same world. Those Native American field matrons who, along with some of their Anglo-American counterparts, accorded a positive value to "uncivilized" domesticity challenged the very foundations of their position and duties. The great difference between the two groups was that there was no danger of Anglo-American field matrons "going back to the blanket." That was not the case for the Indian women.

Health care was a second area where these field matrons and the Indian Office seemed at odds. Part of a field matron's job was to campaign aggressively for better community sanitation and the prevention of the spread of disease. Women coming into the program, though, were not required to have any formal medical or public health training. Apparently relying on Florence Nightingale's assertion ("every woman is a nurse") that nursing, and other skills are learned through life experience, the OIA assigned them a demanding round of duties.

Education and individualized nursing formed the core of this attempt to make the Native American population less vulnerable to illness. Though health work did not start out at the center of the field matrons' activities, the appalling consequences of rampant tuberculosis and trachoma, high infant mortality, and a host of other diseases brought about a shift in priorities. Independent of the OIA, most field matrons took on greater responsibility for tribal health.

Native American field matrons generally responded to the demand for increased health care. They treated colds, nursed the critically ill, and delivered babies as part of their regular work. Yet, their involvement in medical affairs rarely ever reached the level that it did among the Anglo-American field matrons. These women left few reports or letters that directly address this issue. But some may have inadvertently spoken for the large group in reports that consistently ignored or under-emphasized health care. Marie L. Van Solen, a mixed-blood Sioux stationed at Standing Rock, summed up the attitude apparently shared by many Indian peers when she noted only that ". . . [health and medical] aid was given where it was possible to do so." Kiowa field matron Laura D. Pedrick echoed this sentiment in her reports when she stated that "I have taught and helped how they should care for their sick more properly." While assessing disinterest from medical reports is problematic, available information suggests that this may not have been one of the Indian field matrons' strong points. Perhaps here, more than in the realm of housework, they struggled to reconcile the conflicting demands of assimilation and traditional culture.

The reticence of Native American field matrons sometimes exhibited in connection with their health work was pronounced in their dealings with traditional healers and healing arts. Shamans, herbalists, sing doctors, and medicine men and women flourished on many reservations while the field matrons were trying to promote "civilized" medicine. Anglo-American field matrons regularly railed at the native healers for undercutting their efforts and allegedly endangering patients' lives. With two striking exceptions, Indian field matrons remained silent on this subject.

Mary C. Gillette and Anna Dawson Wilde were apparently the only Native American field matrons who directly challenged the authority and power of traditional healers in their respective communities. Gillette, assigned to the Cheyenne and Arapaho agency in 1909, reported a long siege of springtime illnesses. Exacerbating tribal bouts with the measles and influenza were the problems associated with the work of the native healers who, she believed, impeded her work. In an otherwise calm report, she confessed heatedly that "if the Indians are ever taught to care for the sick, the sick must be taken from the tent . . . and placed in a house near the school where the Indian medicine men would not be allowed to practice." Wilde, a full-blood Arikara from Fort Berthold in 1908, concurred with Gillette. Yet, she found some reason for optimism after confronting a local healer and discovering that "some of the most conservative class, even, have turned to us for succor when they have found their [the traditional healers] ways inadequate. . . ."

The cumulative effect of the Native American field matrons' seeming indifference to health care work was not good. As the OIA became more involved in promoting tribal health care after 1900, the agency demanded more from its field employees. Elsie E. Newton, Superintendent for Field Matrons, addressed this point directly in 1915 while assessing the efficiency of Ada Rice, a mixed-blood Kiowa woman stationed at the Klamath agency. Newton characterized Rice as only a "fair" matron and advocated her dismissal. An ardent supporter of professionalization within the field matron corps, the superintendent based her recommendation on Rice's "perfunctory" care of the sick. Newton's evaluation implied that Rice's failure to take on more health duties somehow suggested a faulty commitment to assimilation.

Tribal heritage sometimes played an important role for the Indian field matrons in a third area, where their relationships with the larger Native American community and the Anglo-American community intersected. Perhaps because of their genuinely sympathetic bonds with the other Indians they sought to serve, or perhaps because their authority as OIA employees carried with it the suggestion that the same power to help could be used for other, less beneficial purposes, few incidents of friction involving these women are documented. It was obviously to their advantage to disguise any unusual tensions that may have developed as they pursued their work. Nonetheless, the Indian Service informal network was usually quick to report any discord where field personnel, especially Native American employees, played a role.

Occasionally, these women did become entangled in tribal or community disputes. Factors like intraband factionalism, intergroup rivalry over land bases or Indian Office services, and intraband conflict over "conservative behavior" or religious rituals, either individually or in tandem, sometimes left them vulnerable to challenges from individuals and entire communities. These problems were not unusual in reservation settings: field service personnel sometimes found themselves involved in controversies whether or not they wished to be. These episodes were not happy events for any OIA employee; they proved especially dangerous for Native American field matrons. Such conflicts made it easier to single out these women, label them unreliable, and curtail their employment.

Conflict within an Indian group sometimes stemmed from factionalism born out of competition between family or clan members, or assimilated and traditional tribal segments. In 1905 Anna Dawson Wilde found herself at the center of a controversy that generated charges of dereliction of duty and land fraud. Married to one of the leading progressive men at Fort Berthold, Wilde aligned herself solidly alongside the other like-minded Indian residents. Because of the political affiliation, she found herself caught in a dispute that began with criticism of her treatment of a paralyzed woman who later died. Wilde was accused of deliberately neglecting the terminally ill woman, hastening her death through the resulting onset of gangrene. Agent Amzi Thomas reported the accusations to Washington, D.C., and agreed with Wilde's accuser that it was a "pitiful case." Next, the Indian field matron faced charges that she falsified her field matron reports and involved herself in a land fraud scheme.

As the accusations flew, the other Arikara field matron at Fort Berthold spoke out to defend her colleague. Mary W. Howard attested to the quality of Wilde's work and dismissed the charges by explaining that ". . . she [the accuser] has hated Mrs. Wilde . . . because she advised her to stop flirting with a certain married employee." Agent Thomas, apparently trying to keep his distance from the women involved to preserve his authority among the reservation residents, seemed unimpressed with Wilde's self-defense and Howard's corroboration. Reporting the details of the situation to the OIA, he alleged that the Native American woman who originally brought the charges against Wilde ". . . is likely to prove her case if given the opportunity." Though Dawson retained her position, the intraband animosity created by the quarrel made her work very difficult. Moreover, it tainted her relationship with the Anglo-American OIA personnel at Fort Berthold.

This same kind of tension was very much in evidence in a case involving Laura D. Pedrick, a full-blood Kiowa. In 1898 members of the Kiowa, Comanche, and Apache tribes living in Oklahoma petitioned the OIA for her appointment as field matron. More than two hundred signatures attested to her qualifications and their wish for her assistance as they learned ". . . the white man's road." In early 1899 she received her assignment.

Pedrick proved to be an energetic and competent field matron who pursued the standard housekeeping and health activities successfully. She also chastised members of the tribe who lived ". . . like the Lilies of the Valley or as if each day was to be their last." She criticized those who kept "useless" pony herds instead of raising cattle, pigs, and sheep. Participants in Ghost Dances and mescal feasts found themselves singled out in reports that alerted local OIA officials to those activities. This condemnation, it is worth noting, was not forthcoming from Anglo-American field matrons who probably did not have the language skills or the personal connections to learn about the dances and the feasts. Pedrick could, and apparently did, use her Kiowa heritage and personal ties to gather information possibly inaccessible to Anglo-American personnel.

Those same relationships proved problematic in 1900, when the opening of the Kiowa, Comanche, and Apache reservation looked imminent. Because her brother Apiatan opposed fellow Kiowa Delos Lone Wolf's attempt to keep the land base intact, Pedrick found her position in jeopardy. Ostensibly, her remarks about stock-raising and her exposure of the Ghost Dances and mescal feasts were to blame for the erosion of support that brought her to the field in 1899. In fact, tribal politics and family ties very nearly caused her downfall.

In 1901 the Anadarko area agent tersely informed the Indian Office that "the Kiowa and Comanche Indians . . . have requested me to inform you that Mrs. Laura Padrick [sic] . . . is objectionable. . . ." Members of the three groups who originally called for her appointment, apparently angered by her brother's position on the issue of tribal lands, asked that a special investigator examine her work and evaluate her conduct. Though Pedrick remained in her position, the incident irrevocably chanced her relationship with the reservation population.

Intertribal hostility and animosity were clearly forces, as Pedrick's case illustrates, that proved dangerous to the Native American field matrons. Such tension frequently caught them between Anglo-American Indian Service personnel and other tribal people in an unenviable tug of war. Assistant field matrons Rosalie M. Nejo and Juanita LaChappa found themselves in such a situation in 1909 while they worked with some of the Mission Indians of California. Members of the Guyapipa and Mesa Grande bands respectively, these young mixed-blood women entered the Indian Service in 1904 after graduation from the Sherman Institute. Nejo and LaChappa quickly won the affection and respect of Indian Service personnel and tribal people through their hard work and compassion. Less than a year after their arrival in the field Superintendent Charles Shell informed Mamie Robinson, the field matron supervising their work, that he was more than pleased with their efforts. Sending his regards to Nejo and LaChappa, he noted:

> each . . . fill[s] a different niche. If I should say what I real [sic] think, I fear each of you would think I was flattering and you know I am not given to that.

Five years after Nejo and LaChappa began their work they found themselves involved in an intertribal dispute that threatened their positions as it escalated. Tension between the Campo, Mesa Grande, Posta, and Guyapipa bands in 1909 resulted in complaints about their work habits and willingness to assist Indians outside their own groups. Controversies among tribal people were not rare, and Nejo and LaChappa were not the first field matrons criticized for alleged favoritism. Anglo-American field matrons usually survived such episodes unscathed: the two mixed-blood women did not. Superintendent Philip Lonergan used the problems among the Indians to call for the replacement of the field matrons. Foreseeing a future challenge to OIA authority if the conflict continued with Nejo and LaChappa near the center, he informed Washington, D.C., that "what the Campo situation requires more than a Field Matron is a good Farmer and teacher." Shortly thereafter, the positions were abolished.

For field matrons who needed the trust and respect of the tribal people and Indian Service personnel they worked among, confrontations like these could prove devastating.

Heightened visibility made them vulnerable to challenges that did not go unnoticed by the OIA hierarchy. Conflict inspired lasting animosity in Indian communities, rendering subsequent efforts at health care and domestic civilization all but useless. Such disputes also damaged professional reputations by creating a context for suspicions that these field matrons used their language skills and family ties to undermine Indian Service authority. Any one of those results could have been enough to justify the dismissal of a Native American woman from her post as "certified civilizer."

Studying the experiences of Native American field matrons allows us to assess the history of assimilation policy in the late nineteenth century. From Julia Kocer onward, Indian women presented themselves to the OIA as success stories anxious to impart their knowledge of Anglo-American culture to tribal peers. Their reports and correspondence reveal a number of important details about work within an environment that daily tested their commitment to assimilation.

Indian field matrons entered the program in 1895 confident of their ability to assist other tribal women in the assimilation process. Overcoming initial bureaucratic resistance, most pursued their work with competence and compassion. By offering other Native American women accessible role models, they materially contributed to the OIA's effort to end tribalism and replace traditional culture with Anglo-American culture. For this, their efforts frequently won them praise from the Indian Service hierarchy.

The assimilated personas these women projected in their work were not, however, totally seamless. In several areas, their experiences differed from those of their Anglo-American peers. Because they understood that the process of adopting civilized domestic techniques was a long one, they sometimes chose to be more tolerant of the habits Indian women had and were more willing to praise those adaptations already made. Native American field matrons did not always engage as fully as some Anglo-American peers in health care. They particularly did not try to challenge the status of native health care practitioners or ridicule those who accepted their help. And, the Indian field matrons sometimes became more visible than they might have wished because of involvement in tribal disputes. These field matrons often found that their personal identity gave them a political identity that could not be escaped on the reservation or in the Indian Service. Education and assimilation notwithstanding, the Native American field matrons were always Native Americans first, OIA employees second. The uncertainty perceived by Anglo-Americans to be inherent in that first identity ultimately helped curtail opportunities to adopt the second.

Stella Bear learned this in 1911. One of four Native Americans in the program that year, she asked the OIA for reassignment to Fort Berthold. A mixed-blood Arikara woman, Bear echoed many of the Indian field matrons employed before her in her hope to live and work with members of her own tribe. The OIA rejected her request for a transfer, not because of funding or staffing problems, or Bear's lack of qualifications. Stella Bear could not go home to live and work with other Arikara women because ". . . it is not the policy of this Office (OIA) to appoint Indians to positions of this character among their own people."

Readings for Lisa E. Emmerich:

The author's dissertation " 'To Respect and Love and Seek the Ways of White Women': Field Matrons, the Office of Indian Affairs, and Civilization Policy, 1890–1938" (University of Maryland, 1987) and the related work *"True Womanhood" on the Reservation: Field Matrons in the United States Indian Service* (Tucson, AZ:

Southwestern Institute for Research on Women, 1984) are the only works directly related to this topic. For examples of other Indian women who worked among their people see Jerry E. Clark and Martha Ellen Webb, "Susette and Susan La Flesche: Reformer and Missionary," chapter 6 in James A. Clifton, ed., *Being and Becoming Indian: Biographical Studies of North American Frontiers* (Chicago, IL: Dorsey Press, 1989) and Dorthy Clarke Wilson, *Bright Eyes: The Story of Susette La Flesche, An Omaha Indian* (New York: McGraw-Hill, 1974).

Appendix I
Field Matron Corps, 1895–1927

Year	Total N=	Full Blood N=	Mixed Blood N=	Percent
1895	10	1		10.00
1896	12	2		16.60
1897	19	3	3	31.57
1898	22	4	3	31.81
1899	18	3	3	33.33
1900	30	6	2	26.66
1901	26	6		23.07
1902	22	4		18.18
1903	34	3	2	14.70
1904	39	4	2	15.38
1905	38	3	2	13.15
1906	45	2	3	11.11
1907	37	2	3	13.51
1908	43	1		2.32
1909	53	2	1	5.66
1910	50	2	4	12.00
1911	89	3	1	4.49
1912	92	1	2	3.26
1913	77	1	1	2.59
1914	62	1	1	3.22
1915	69	1	2	4.34
1916	74		2	2.77
1917	66		1	1.51
1918	90		1	1.11
1919	78		1	1.28
1920	76	1	1	2.63
1921	63	1	2	4.76
1922	65	1	1	3.07
1923	63	1	1	3.17
1924	55	1		1.81
1925	49	1		2.04
1926	35	1		2.85
1927	29	1		3.44

Sources: *Annual Reports of the Commissioner of Indian Affairs,* Miscellaneous Salary Records, Employee Records, Efficiency Reports, and General Correspondence Files, RG 75, BIA.

18

RESERVATION LEADERSHIP AND THE PROGRESSIVE-TRADITIONAL DICHOTOMY: WILLIAM WASH AND THE NORTHERN UTES, 1865–1928

DAVID RICH LEWIS

For most tribes the late nineteenth-century reservation experience proved disruptive and traumatic. They lost mobility, saw their hunting and other lands greatly reduced and now had to face the dictates of white officials who came to implement government programs across the West. Once confined to specific reservations, Indians seemed to become contentious and divided into what scholars now call factions. What actually happened was that often two or more bands of related people came to live together, perhaps for the first time. That led to disputes that divided local communities. Much of the scholarship that examines reservation life focuses on the intra-tribal difficulties that emerged by the end of the nineteenth century.

The author presents the actions of William Wash, showing how this seldom-mentioned man became influential among the Uintah Utes although he never held a formal political position on the reservation. This narrative demonstrates clearly how Indians shaped their own lives while facing pressures from whites surrounding the reservation, directives from Indian Office employees on it, and divisions within their own society. Here the reader gets a close-up look at the workings of tribal politics and help in understanding the motivations of individual leaders during the early decades of the reservation era.

David Rich Lewis is an associate professor of history at Utah State University.

Abstract. In the early twentieth century, Indian Bureau officials noted an increasing incidence of tribal factionalism parallel to changes in Indian reservation leadership. They described this factionalism in terms of a progressive-traditional dichotomy. Modern scholars have unintentionally fallen into this semantic trap. This article explores the

Source: David Rich Lewis, "Reservation Leadership and the Progressive-Traditional Dichotomy: William Wash and the Northern Utes, 1865–1928," *Ethnohistory,* 28:2 (Spring 1991), pp. 124–42. Copyright © 1991, Society for Ethnohistory. Reprinted by permission of Duke University Press.

complexity of individual motivations and factional politics among the Northern Utes through the life of William Wash and suggests that such cultural middlemen offer a more complete picture of reservation politics.

In June 1865 leaders from the Tumpanuwac, San Pitch, and Pahvant bands of Ute (*Núćiu*) Indians gathered at Spanish Fork to relinquish their lands. In return, O. H. Irish, superintendent of Indian affairs for Utah Territory, promised them a permanent reservation in the isolated Uintah Basin of eastern Utah, where they could hunt and gather until such time as the government saw fit to transform them into settled and self-sufficient agriculturalists. These Ute leaders realized they had few options. They themselves were leaders of recent status—men like Tabby who rallied group consensus away from the Ute war leaders Wakara and Black Hawk. Since the Mormon invasion in 1847, they had watched their people succumb to epidemic disease, starvation, and warfare. In 1865 Ute leaders accepted the Spanish Fork Treaty as a tactical retreat and began moving toward their new homeland.

In that year of change—change in leadership, location, and future—a Uintah Ute child was born. Named Na-am-quitch, he was the eldest son of Zowoff and Nunanumquitch. In later years he became known as Wash's Son and finally as William Wash. Wash was both ordinary and extraordinary. He never became a formal political leader of his people, yet his success as a rancher gained him the recognition and respect of both Utes and whites at the Uintah-Ouray Reservation. Agency officials called him one of the more "progressive" full-blood individuals of the Uintah band, one of three Northern Ute bands to share the four-million-acre reservation. Yet Wash frequently frustrated these same agents by rejecting the progressive and acting in what they considered to be very "traditional" ways. Until his death in April 1928, he moved between two cultural worlds on the reservation. He was what Loretta Fowler calls an "intermediary" or a "middleman," one of the new or transitional types of leader to arise during the early reservation years.

The importance of people like William Wash lies not only in their own unique experiences but in their shared experiences and the larger themes which emerge from study of their lives. Nearly two decades ago Robert Berkhofer, Jr., told ethnohistorians that they must emphasize Indians in their histories, particularly "the uniqueness of the stories of specific individuals." From works on more famous or infamous individuals, the study of Indian biography has begun to focus on "culturally marginal personages," those less-known "bicultural" individuals who spent their lives on the borders between ethnic groups, mastering the knowledge of two cultures without being immobilized by the process.

Berkhofer also suggests that this individualized focus will aid scholars in untangling the web of inter- and intragroup factionalism. Existing models of tribal factionalism generalize "group" traits without getting "bogged down" in individual motivation and variation. Without paying close attention over time to individual actors (who are difficult to find and trace in most records), scholars tend to perpetuate the static emic categories of "traditional" and "progressive," an unrealistically neat dichotomy or unilinear continuum created by nineteenth- and twentieth-century observers and frequently used to generalize about the social, economic, and political nature of reservation factionalism. Reliance on these sources, particularly by historians who perhaps have been more susceptible to the generalization, produces a two-dimensional, dichotomous picture of native people, issues, and factionalism.

While anthropologists and ethnohistorians eschew the progressive-traditional dichotomy as ethnocentric and value-laden, the terms and their variants still appear all too frequently. Often qualified with quotation marks, they have become a kind of professional shorthand for describing individuals, factionalism, and the process of acculturation. The unspoken understanding is that we are simplifying a complex, dynamic situation out of necessity, trusting that colleagues will recognize our dilemma and hoping that others will not read overly static meanings into these useful, if somewhat misleading, terms. We deny the dichotomy but we fall back on it, perhaps because in our histories we do not understand or cannot fully untangle the temporal threads of personal motive and behavior which guide individuals and draw them into factions or groups.

The weakness of this progressive-traditional dichotomy becomes most apparent in attempts to categorize complex individuals, particularly the intermediaries, the middlemen, the cultural brokers, the "150% men" who operate on the cultural margins. William Wash became such a figure among the Northern Utes. Not a recognized "headman" yet vocal in councils, Wash represents the substratum of reservation politics, the influential individuals who worked the margins of tribal leadership and white acceptance. His experience mirrors that of perhaps a majority of early twentieth-century Native Americans struggling to come to terms with their own culture and with American society.

William Wash was born into a world of both change and persistence as his people moved toward the Uintah Basin. We know little about his early life other than what we can assume given the history of the Uintah Reservation. There the different Utah Ute bands coalesced into a single band called the Uintah. The federal government encouraged Utes to settle near the agency and begin farming. Most, however, continued their seasonal subsistence pursuits and drew rations in order to avoid starvation on the agency farms. Some, like Zowoff and Wash, tried their hand at farming, braving the ridicule of other Ute males for gathering vegetal material and digging in the earth, the subsistence province of women. Raising cattle or hauling freight for the agency came much more easily for Ute men seeking to reproduce male work and subsistence spheres. Wash and his father received special gratuity payments from the Indian Bureau for their farming efforts. By 1891, Wash owned a number of cattle and worked part-time for the agency as a herder. Agents viewed him as a progressive Indian.

According to Ute agents, the definition of "progressive" revolved around two elements, economic and historical. First, agents identified progressive Utes by their subsistence activities, particularly by their commitment to a settled and self-sufficient agrarian lifestyle. This lifestyle was defined in part by their willingness to dress, act, and speak like whites, live in houses, and send their children to school. Second, this designation devolved to a comparison of Ute bands and their reservation histories, particularly after the 1881 forced removal of White River and Uncompahgre Utes from their Colorado homelands to the Uintah and Ouray reservations. The consolidation of the Uintah, White River, and Uncompahgre bands created a number of problems, including a series of inter- and intraband factional disputes over leadership, past treaty negotiations, and the distribution of natural resources and annuity payments.

Out of these disputes Ute agents identified "progressive" and "traditional" factions. The Uintah Utes, because of their long contact history and exposure to reservation agriculture, were the most progressive of the Northern Ute bands. The Uncompahgre band suffered the most internal divisions between the progressive Indians (led by Shavanaux and Alhandra) who settled on river-bottom farms and those (led by Sowawick) who preferred to maintain a more nomadic, up-country, herding and hunting lifestyle. Finally, there were the White Rivers, whom agents classed as wild and rebellious traditionalists, adamantly opposed to any effort to change their way of life. This growing factionalism, based on what agents perceived as a progressive-traditional dichotomy running along band lines, was in fact individualistic, fluid, and issue- and economics-oriented.

William Wash played some role in these factional divisions by virtue of his Uintah band affiliation and his three marriages, particularly the last, to Lucy Alhandra, daughter of the progressive Uncompahgre leader "Charley" Alhandra. More important factors, however, were his economic activities as a farmer, rancher, and agency herder, as well as his familiar relations with the white agents. As agency herder, Wash came under fire from Tim Johnson, spokesman for the White River traditionalists. Johnson claimed that Wash was in league with agency attempts to lease Ute grazing lands in the Strawberry Valley to white Mormon ranchers. Johnson criticized Wash because "he does all kind of work" and asked that Wash and the agency farmer, men who symbolized progressive agriculture, both be "sent away."

In 1903, the White River and Uintah bands faced a common threat, the prospect of allotment. Despite widespread Ute opposition, 75 Uintah and 7 White River Utes out of 280 eligible males signed the allotment article. These, Special Agent James McLaughlin acknowledged, signed mainly to show their goodwill in the face of what they understood to be an inevitable process. Yet by signing the allotment agreement, these individuals reaffirmed a perceived division between "progressive" Uintah and "conservative" White River Utes and created a further division within the Uintah band. William Wash, aged thirty-eight, was one of these progressive Uintah signatories. Dissenting White River leaders threatened to leave the reservation if allotment proceeded; indeed, they carried out that threat in 1906–8, leading nearly four hundred Utes to South Dakota.

With this "tribal" division into two apparently distinct factions, Wash began to consolidate his social and economic position as a progressive spokesman. In 1903, he sold 25,530 pounds of loose hay to the troops at Fort Duchesne, and in 1905 he received his eighty-acre allotment on the southeastern end of Indian Bench above Fort Duchesne. That year he raised ten bushels of potatoes, fourteen hundred bushels of oats, and one hundred bushels of wheat and harvested three hundred tons of alfalfa. His 640 rods of fencing and his log cabin attest to his industry but probably more so to substantial assistance from agency personnel. At the same time, Wash ran a sizable cattle herd in the Dry Gulch region southwest of Fort Duchesne.

In a 1907 council with Uintah Utes, Agent C. G. Hall tried to quiet rumors that "Mormons" were going to take over both the opened reservation and allotted lands. In this council, with the absence of so many Utes in South Dakota, William Wash emerged as a Uintah spokesman. He told the assembly:

> I hear about the way Secretary of the Interior talk to us. I always take Washington's advice. About farming, about everything. I never say no any time. This land that is allotted to me is mine. That make my heart [feel good]. I can't wait to go work my land. I have been working the way Washington want me to. I have a fence around eighty acres. I am putting in some crops. I got hands to work with like everybody. I lost a good deal of money in some way by white men renting my farm. This leasing of land to the whites is a

swindle. If I work it myself I get the money that comes from the farming. The Indians do not know how to make money off their land. They don't know whether the white man is handling it right or not.

Beneath his own espousal of white economic values, Wash was apparently concerned about the vacant allotments of those White River Utes in South Dakota, fearing the land would be leased or sold—lost in either case from Ute control. He continued: "About the White Rivers. Washington never told them to go to another country. They are getting themselves poor. Losing everything. This is their home. . . . I want everything to be right. Don't want little children starving. It makes me feel sorry when people move around and let little children get hurt. They are pretty hard up I think. Maybe they come back now to raise something."

The White River Utes did return to the allotted reservation in 1908, under military guard, physically defeated, and with little means of support. Many had no idea where their allotments were, had nothing to work their land with if they wanted to, and were reluctant to work for wages on the ongoing Uintah Irrigation Project. Many ultimately leased their lands to white settlers, hoping to earn some money and protect their water rights against usufruct Utah water laws. Wash's hopes seemed dim.

At this juncture we get a glimpse of another side of William Wash, one that casts a different light on his economic activities and social aspirations. Inspector Harwood Hall visited the reservation shortly after the White Rivers returned and reported that all the Northern Utes "are quite poor, and were it not for rations issued by the government and assistance given many of them by an Indian by name of Wash, who is fairly well off, it is difficult to see how they would secure sufficient food to subsist." From this and other evidence, it appears not only that Wash was accumulating wealth in a white-approved manner (ranching and farming) but that he was using the proceeds (particularly his cattle) to help feed needy members of all three Ute bands. Instead of observing market economy values, he reproduced in part the individualistic role of local Ute leaders by distributing goods in return for sociopolitical recognition. Wash used his position as a cultural intermediary in order to help his people, to gain traditional respect, and to attempt to fill a growing vacuum in Northern Ute leadership.

Between 1912 and 1914, Wash's visibility in tribal affairs increased. He was not considered a "chief" in general Ute councils with the federal government, but he was actively involved in reservation politics, particularly over issues of ranching and land use. Once we discern some of the cultural values and motives behind his actions, it becomes clear that Wash's activities are more complex than can be explained with a static model of factionalism based on a simple progressive-traditional dichotomy.

In 1912, Uintah-Ouray agency stockmen expressed concern with the number of "wild ponies" roaming the 250,000-acre Ute Grazing Reserve. The issue of Ute horses had been a constant source of conflict between Utes and agency personnel. Agents argued that horses gave the Utes too much mobility, perpetuated racing and gambling customs, and grazed ranges more profitably reserved for cattle and sheep. Utes, on the other hand, valued horses as prestige items, traditional forms of wealth, status, and security. They felt (and still feel) an attachment to the horse out of proportion to its market value. The destruction of horses in 1879 precipitated the White River attack on the Utes' Colorado agency. Agents in Utah came to realize that horses, not cattle, defined the social and economic status of Ute men.

In 1912, Wash was one of these men, wealthy both by Ute standards (he owned about fifty horses) and by white (two hundred cattle and forty sheep). He headed an affinal and kin-based cattle association which controlled 395 cattle, 115 sheep, and one of the four bands of "wild" horses roaming the grazing reserve. His position gave him a great say in Indian Bureau plans to clear the range. At a gathering of seventeen leading Ute stockmen, Wash initiated a plan to periodically round up unbranded horses and divide them among members of the roundup crew. He offered to supply both mounted men and extra saddle horses for the roundup and agreed to the construction of corrals on his land. Wash may have been interested in rounding up wild horses, but it seems likely that he was interested in doing so not to preserve the range for additional cattle and sheep, as desired by the white officials, but to obtain or retain more horses, thereby adding to his source of traditional wealth and status.

In 1913, Ute livestock owners met in council to oppose leasing the Ute Grazing Reserve to James S. Murdock, a white sheepman. Once again Wash spoke for his people, summarizing Ute opposition to the proposed lease:

> When we used to talk about this reservation a long time ago, way back in Washington, we leased some land. That is past now. . . . Now the way it is about this land, it is different than before we were allotted. All these Indians understand what you told them to do and now we have talked about it. Now we have some horses, and we know about how to take care of them now and make use of them on this land. The Indian has always held it, they do not want to lease it at all. As we have horses, cattle, and stock there is no place for Murdock to lease, as all the Indians on the grazing land clear up to Lake Fork have stock and we do not want it leased at all. I have the right to depend on that country, I have some cattle of my own.

Superintendent Jewell D. Martin thanked him: "I am glad to hear what Wash has said because he has more stock than any other Indian on the reservation and knows more about the livestock industry here and I am glad he has expressed his judgment."

Two points of interest emerge from this exchange. First, by his words before his assembled peers, Wash indicated his continuing commitment to horses, even his commitment to horses *over* cattle and sheep. He came to this point of view as Ute agents attempted to reduce the number of Ute horses by emphasizing improved livestock and range management. Even progressive Ute stockmen like Wash resisted agency efforts to castrate their "ponie stallions," preferring a culturally derived balance between quantity and quality. Wash emphasized the continuity of the horse, as both symbol and reality, in Northern Ute culture.

Second, Wash opposed leasing the tribally controlled grazing reserve. In council meetings later that year Wash and other progressive ranchers clashed with a group of White River traditionalists over the creation of a tribal herd. The cattlemen argued that a herd would benefit the tribe economically, provide a market for surplus hay, and keep land-grabbing whites from getting a foothold on the reserve through leasing. The White Rivers also feared the threat of white homesteaders, but they desired cash, not cattle—an equitable distribution of benefits from the grazing reserve in the form of lease monies rather than its use by a select few Ute cattlemen.

Although the council approved the proposed tribal herd when the White Rivers walked out, Superintendent Martin killed the plan, which smacked of "tribal interest rather than individual interest." In his haste to stamp out collectivism, Martin missed the point. These progressive cattlemen intended to partition the herd, "allowing each family to take its share of the cattle and take care of them." In effect, these Utes understood better than Martin that the government would spend tribal funds only for tribal (as opposed to individual) economic development plans, that such communalism clashed with their individualistic subsistence traditions, and that in the past, communalistic policies and agency herds had failed. This proposal by Wash and the progressive cattlemen was both a way to get tribal funds over to individuals and a conservative plan to protect the integrity of the Ute Grazing Reserve. Ultimately, it promised to benefit each Ute household in more ways than the simple lease fees desired by the White Rivers—progressive-sounding means securing an essentially conservative outcome.

In 1914, Wash appeared in the middle of another reservation power struggle, between an overly enthusiastic superintendent and commissioner and the Ute followers of the Sun Dance religion. As early as 1905, Ute agents had complained that the annual Ute Bear Dance and Sun Dance were morally and economically counterproductive, that they destroyed health and morals and took people away from their farms at critical times in the growing season. In 1913, Martin failed to convince Ute leaders to hold the Bear and Sun dances together at midsummer agricultural fairs as a sort of commercial sideshow. Unable to co-opt or halt them, Commissioner Cato Sells officially prohibited both dances, which were "incompatible with industrial development and altogether out of harmony with a higher civilization."

While the Bear Dance was one of the oldest of Ute rituals, the Sun Dance religion was a recent innovation. Introduced in the 1890s by Grant Bullethead, a Uintah Ute who learned the ceremony at the Wind River Shoshone Reservation, the Sun Dance filled a void for people struggling with the unrest and dislocation associated with allotment. The dance echoed the individualistic tenor of Ute beliefs while offering group strength through communal participation. The Ute people seized the model, reinterpreted it in terms of their own cultural categories, and reproduced their own religious system, with its emphasis on curing, within the framework of that single dance. The Sun Dance religion offered the Northern Utes an active option for binding themselves together and dealing with the directed changes of an allotted agrarian lifestyle.

Despite the Indian Bureau ban, a number of White River and Uintah Utes proceeded with the 1914 Sun Dance. Upset and uncertain what to do, William Wash telegraphed Interior Secretary Franklin K. Lane: "Indians will hold annual harvest dance about June twenty fifth to thirtieth / ancient custom / supervisor objects / wire reply." Cloaking the Sun Dance in harvest imagery to make it more palatable to white officials was an old Ute tactic, but the reply shot back that the Sun Dance, "or dance of a similar nature, such as usually held at this season of year," was prohibited. Superintendent Martin assured the commissioner that after informing a "bunch of the influential ones" who had sent the telegram, the "better class" of Indians agreed not to dance. Still, two Sun Dances went on as scheduled that summer. Martin reported that about 150 "retrogressive White River Indians" insisted on the dance, which was attended by over three hundred Utes—what he dismissed as a "minor fraction." Martin asked for additional assistance to suppress the dance, for, as they often did, his Indian policemen protected their own people by selectively enforcing Indian Bureau orders.

Was William Wash, the leader of the "bunch of the influential ones" who sent the telegram, also one of the "better class" who agreed not to hold the dance? Or did this group concede defeat to Martin and then participate in the dance anyway? After investigating the dance, U.S. Marshall Aquilla Nebeker reported that Martin "believes that the best Indians, and a majority over all, are supporters of his and are in harmony with his ideas; but I am forced to the opinion that in this he is mistaken; and I could recite many circumstances and conversations which I think are withheld from the Agent, but such recitals would burden this communication and probably would not be considered competent." Nebeker heard and saw what Martin and the Indian Bureau ignored, and he probably heard some of it from Martin's own progressive Utes.

Nebeker reported that the dance took place on the grazing reserve around Lake Fork, thirty-five miles northwest of Myton, Utah. Other records indicate that William Wash "controlled" that particular area of the grazing reserve and thus that he probably knew about and approved of the dance location. It is possible that Wash was there, supporting the dancers and participating in the group event by his very presence. He was a prominent sponsor of other Sun Dances during this period of suppression. In describing the dances in his youth, Conner Chapoose noted that Ute individuals would sponsor dancers or contribute to the feast following the dance: "They'd either donate a beef if they had any cattle, like for instance Mr. Wash. He would make a statement at the time that he would furnish a beef for the food, and that was supporting the program as they was putting it on." In this and in other instances, Wash actively supported a ceremony deemed retrogressive and traditional by the very white officials who dubbed him the leading progressive Ute stockman.

Superintendent Albert Kneale, who replaced Martin in January 1915, was not particularly concerned about the Sun Dance. He considered it to be a fairly benign, rather commercialized celebration put on to attract tourist dollars. Kneale was more concerned about the appearance of peyote at Uintah-Ouray and the threat it posed to the welfare and advancement of the Ute people.

In 1914, Sam Lone Bear, an Oglala Sioux, introduced the peyote Cross Fire ritual to the Northern Utes. Working out of Dragon, Utah, an isolated narrow-gauge railroad terminal seventy-five miles from Fort Duchesne, Lone Bear held services and spread word of the benefits of peyote, particularly its curative properties. By 1916, half of the nearly twelve hundred Northern Utes participated in the peyote religion. Once again, Utes integrated the individualistic, power-seeking, and therapeutic elements of a new ritual into their own belief system. In later years, the Tipi Way became more popular among Northern Ute peyotists, perhaps because Lone Bear's unsavory business dealings and sexual reputation discredited the Cross Fire ritual.

Ute peyotism came under attack between 1916 and 1918 when both Congress and the state of Utah considered bills to outlaw peyote. Witnesses before a House subcommittee testified that peyote roadmen targeted "prosperous" Ute Indians, those with cattle, in order to addict them and "control their funds." They told of once prosperous Ute farms now "neglected" because of peyote addiction and claimed that Lone Bear counselled Ute stockmen to stay at home and pray to Peyote to look after their cattle. Other experts testified to the deaths and other detrimental physical as well as economic effects of the drug on progressive Indian farmers. Superintendent Kneale informed his superiors that "40 to 50 percent of the Indians on this reservation are, or have been, partakers of this drug." Lone Bear, Kneale reported, deliberately set out to interest "some of our very best men, particularly McCook, Witchits, Monk Shavanaux, Captain Jenks, Grant, Corass, and William Wash. These men were all leaders among their people."

As it turned out, Wash, the progressive Uintah Ute farmer, rancher, and emerging leader, was indeed an active and vocal peyotist. In 1917 Kneale called in U.S. marshalls to control the liquor and peyote traffic around Dragon. He advised Utes to abandon peyotism because it would kill them. Once again, Wash took his people's problems to the commissioner of Indian affairs. On 12 May 1917, Wash dictated the following letter, signing it with his thumbprint:

> My Dear Commissioner:
>   We want to know why these United States Marshalls come in here and try to get us to stop church. We like Church. We want to meet every Sunday and have Church and pray and be good. We don't want to steal, nor drink whiskey, nor play cards nor gamble nor lie and we want to rest on Sunday and then on Monday we want to work and farm. . . . Sometimes sick people sometimes die and sometimes we eat Peote and it make us better. Sometimes people die and no eat Peote. They die. Maybe eat Peote, no die. Horses die, cows die, sheep die. They no eat Peote. You can't stop them dieing. Anything die. Long time live maybe so eat Peote. We want to be good and we want you to let us have Church and not send Police from Washington to make us stop. You tell us why you do this. We don't know.
>   I have been here a long time and all the Indians like me and they ask me to write and ask you what is the matter. Randlett Indians maybe so they eat Peote. Pretty good, I guess. The White Rocks Indians no eat Peote. No like it and they like Whiskey and they play cards and fight, maybe so kill 'em. We don't like that, we want to be good.

Assistant Commissioner E. B. Meritt answered Wash's letter, explaining that he opposed the use of peyote because attending and recovering from peyote meetings took too much time, and because "it is bad medicine making many Indians sick, some crazy and killing others." Meritt noted that Utah state law prohibited the sale and use of peyote. He closed in typically paternal fashion by telling Wash, "If you and your people want to be good you should do what we think is right and best for you and what the laws of the State and the United States require that you should do."

Wash and his friends were not satisfied with this reply or with the suggestion that they talk to Kneale. On 3 July Wash responded to Meritt's objections, stressing the positive aspects of peyote use and pointing out that it was no more disruptive than Christian Sunday services:

> You say for me to talk the matter over with my superintendent but he won't talk to me cause I eat peyote. He won't shake hands with me. When I have my Superintendent to write for me I don't get any answer for it. . . . He don't like to write letters for Indians. The Superintendent's Indians at White Rocks play cards. He lets them play cards and he don't stop them.
>   I don't drink any more and I don't play cards nor swear. I go to meeting and eat peyote and that made me throw away drinking, playing cards and swearing. Church makes us good people. We are good when we go to Church. We farm all week and just have church on Sunday, just one day. We all work hard all week and go to church on Sunday after week's work is done. I raise all my own garden, all the food to eat myself and have good garden and just go to Church on Sunday. The Bible say that we should go to church on Sunday and rest. The Missionaries say to go to Church on Sunday too.

Meritt answered quickly this time, apparently aware that he was dealing with an influential and persistent individual. He assured Wash that he would write Kneale and have him explain the laws. He applauded Wash's "progress" and admonished him to give up peyotism. "If you are anxious to do what is right I hope you will stop using peyote and advise the other Indians to do likewise. Peyote will not make Indians live longer but instead will shorten their lives." Meritt advised Kneale that "by taking this Indian into your confidence it is possible that he can be induced to give up the peyote habit and use his influence in persuading others to do likewise." Kneale replied that he had held "many conversations with Mr. Wash relative to the peyote situation," and that Wash had discussed it with "many other employees in this jurisdiction," but to no avail.

Wash refused to accept the paternal advice of these two men. His own experiences led him to very different conclusions regarding peyote. He wrote Meritt a final note:

> I received your letter of July 18th and will say that I do not wish to hear from you any more. Do not write to me any more and I will not write to you. Indian no eat peyote, he die anyhow. Sometime he die young and sometime live long time. I will die anyhow. I will die if I eat peyote and I will die if I don't. White people die no eat peyote.
>
> I have a good home and have a good farm. I stay home all the time and watch cattle and sheep. I herd them in the mountain now. I send my boy to white school to learn and be good. I like to have my boy be good and learn to talk and read and write. They don't learn them to be bad and swear and steal, they teach them to be good all the time. I die sometime and my boy will have my house and farm and cattle and sheep. He stay there and live.

With that, Wash ended his correspondence, but not his involvement with the peyote religion.

Who was Wash defending and why? From the available evidence it appears that Northern Ute peyotists were mostly older full-blood Utes, frequently the people Kneale deemed progressive, the "very best men," the "leaders among their people." Peyote use was centered in the communities of Dragon and Randlett and occurred along the Indian Bench all the way to Myton—areas of predominantly Uintah and Uncompahgre Ute settlement (bands always considered the more progressive and economically self-sufficient among the Utes). Some argue that these progressive full-bloods were seeking a way to maintain particularly "Indian" cultural values in the face of directed culture change, to achieve group solidarity as Utes and as pan-Indians. Contemporaries observed that individuals, particularly young educated Indians, adopted peyotism to gain social prominence and leadership status otherwise denied them under existing tribal structures. Wash's active participation can be seen as an attempt both to revitalize or perpetuate elements he believed valuable in Ute culture and, despite his age, to gain social leadership status in addition to his economic prominence.

While many Northern Utes accepted peyotism, there remained a significant faction adamantly opposed to its use, deeming it dangerous, expensive, or simply an intrusive cultural element. The White River Utes living around Whiterocks, long considered conservative traditionalists, apparently rejected peyotism. Wash exposed them by playing off the "virtues" of peyote against their "vices" of gambling and drinking and thus claimed the moral high ground. Other peyote opponents included mixed-blood and younger boarding school–educated Utes from all three bands. In 1924, forty-six White River Utes petitioned the Interior Department and Congress to "prevent the traffic of peyote and remove it from the Indian reservations of the United States." Indian Bureau suppression and factional opposition within the tribe drove peyotism underground in the 1920s and 1930s. In the 1930s the issue merged with an increasing antagonism between full- and mixed-blood Utes over mixed-blood control of the tribal business committee.

The resulting social and political factionalism ultimately contributed to the termination of mixed-blood Utes in 1954.

It is unclear whether William Wash became a peyote leader, yet his open defense of it and his defiance surely increased his influence among segments of the Ute people. Peyote did not physically or financially ruin Wash. Kneale recalled that Wash, "a well-to-do and patriotic Ute," purchased one thousand dollars' worth of coupon bonds during World War I. In 1923, Wash owned six hundred head of sheep, which he leased to the care of white herders, as well as several hundred cattle, which he personally supervised. "He also controls a large acreage of farming land and this is leased to white men," wrote Superintendent Fred A. Gross. "He is one of the most progressive Indians we have and is successful in his various activities." While it is possible that Wash's "lapse" into leasing was a result of his peyote use, it is more probable that, since Wash was getting old and his son was in school, he could not personally manage his considerable estate. Leasing then became a viable short-term option that he could supervise to make sure the land was not lost to white ranchers.

Wash's wealth and political recognition increased dramatically in his later years. He was a leading member of the council which chose R. T. Bonnin as the Ute tribal attorney in 1926, and he represented the Uintah band in council meetings designed to form a tribal business committee in 1927. His age, wealth, peyotism, and outspokenness are probably what kept him off the final business committee, yet they gained him the recognition of both Utes and whites as a spokesman for the full-blood and Uintah Utes.

Wash spoke with particular authority on issues affecting Ute lands and land use. In 1925, Uintah Utes included Wash in a delegation bound for Washington, DC. While other members focused on "missing" annuity payments, siphoned off to pay for the Uintah Irrigation Project, Wash articulated the fears of his people that whites were scheming to gain control of the grazing reserve. Wash told bureau officials that he ran about 570 cattle, 800 sheep, and 70 horses on the grazing reserve, and that "we do not want any white men to come and take that piece of land away from us again because it is very small." He complained of having trouble with trespassing white ranchers and with forest rangers who restricted his access to former Ute grazing lands within the Uinta National Forest, "so that it makes it pretty hard for me to get along with these fellows." And in particular he complained that white homesteaders and irrigation companies took water properly belonging to Ute allottees.

In the second half of his speech, Wash moved from issues affecting Ute ranchers to the desires of those who were not so economically progressive—those without cattle or allotments. In an apparent ideological flip-flop, he suggested that unused portions of the grazing reserve be leased "so all Indians could get a little benefit of it, those that don't own any stock." He also suggested that arable areas of the grazing reserve be allotted to Ute children. He told the commissioner: "I am making this statement because I am old, I may not live long but I would like to have these children allotted because by and by white men might take it away and the children would be homeless. We would like to have the children allotted so that they will have something when they grow up." Wash, the "progressive" farmer and cattleman, recognized both the needs and rights of those Utes without cattle or land to share in the tribal estate. At the same time he reiterated his desire to preserve the integrity of what was left of the Ute land base, to leave enough land and water to sustain Ute identity and independence against the wave of white homesteaders.

Indian Bureau officials listened to Wash and the other Ute delegates and ultimately acted on Wash's recommendation, but they twisted his intent in the process. In 1927 the bureau levied grazing fees on ranchers running more than one hundred horses or head of cattle or five hundred sheep on the grazing reserve. Ostensibly, the point was to provide a more equitable distribution of tribal assets between those using the range and those without livestock, but in fact the fees promised to open more of the reserve to white stockmen who could afford to pay them. These fees posed a major problem for stock-rich but cash-poor Utes who found few outside markets and low prices for their livestock. The fees and regulations themselves posed a threat to Ute sovereignty. Wash, the premier stockman and cultural middleman, was the one individual most threatened by this fee system.

In January 1928 a number of older full-bloods from all three bands gathered in council to petition the Indian Bureau to lift the fees on livestock. Most owned no stock and had no vested interest in the outcome. Sampannies (Saponeis Cuch), a conservative White River leader, vigorously argued that Wash (and all full-bloods) should be allowed to run his stock on the grazing reserve without paying a fee. "We want his stock to be left alone. They have a right on our grazing land," Sampannies told the council. "We are doing this in order that Mr. Wash can hold our grazing land for us for some day some of us other Indians may have stock and want to run our stock on the grazing land." Sampannies, voicing full-blood Ute resentment toward the growing number and the political and economic influence of mixed-blood Utes, declared that anyone of less than one-half Ute blood had no right to use the tribal grazing reserve. Older full-blood leaders like John Duncan, Cesspooch, and Dick Wash and newer Business Committee leaders like John Yesto agreed. They defended Wash's right to use the grazing reserve, praised him as an example for the younger generation, and denied the mixed-bloods. Yet underpinning their support for Wash was an understanding that the real issue was sovereignty, the ultimate right to control their tribal resources. "Why," asked Cesspooch, "should we pay for our own land?"

Wash spoke at the end of the council, summing up the arguments of sovereignty by recapping his life experiences as a cultural intermediary, as one who tried to play by two sets of changing rules and expectations:

> When the agency was first established I was advised that stock raising was very profitable and I took that advice and I have found that it is so. Later on arrangements were made and the grazing land set aside for our use. It was then said that the grazing land was for the Indians['] own use and that they could increase their herds as much as they wanted as long as they had grazing land and were not to be charged any fee whatever. At the present time why should we be charged for our grazing land? I feel that I should be given a little consideration because I am the leading example of the whole tribe. I feel that I have been capable of holding the grazing land as a whole because I have more stock on the grazing land than any other Indian and the other Indians appreciate the fact that I have held the grazing land for them. That is why they have made their statements here today.

Wash played on his dual role, first in holding tribal land against outsiders and secondly in providing a progressive example of the benefits of work and self-sufficiency for Ute schoolchildren. In closing, he reiterated his long-standing objections to the alienation of Ute land and his hopes for an independent future for his people: "We have always been peaceable people and we intend to live here that way always. This is our home and we do not want to be disturbed. . . . We do not like for any white persons or anybody else to try to have our grazing land thrown open. We object to that very much. We feel that our younger people are beginning to realize the benefits derived from our grazing lands. We do not want to be discouraged by such hard regulations." Yet in the end the commissioner ignored the council and reaffirmed the new fee regulation. Shortly after word of the decision reached Uintah-Ouray, William Wash fell ill. Following a month-long struggle Wash, aged sixty-three, died on 30 April 1928 at his home on the Indian Bench near Fort Duchesne.

Wash's life illustrates some of the fundamental problems scholars face in defining individual Indians, or entire factions, for that matter, as progressive or traditional on the basis of narrow social or economic issues. Defining factions is difficult enough. What variables (kinship, residence, economics, religion, etc.) defined factional groups? Were they "floating coalitions of interests rather than of persons," and were the ends always disputed, or just the means to those ends? The activities of William Wash indicate that individuals frequently transcend the bounds of static factional categories; that these coalitions were informal, fluid, and issue-oriented as frequently as not; and that the means were perhaps more divisive than the ends. Wash plotted a course different from the traditionalist White Rivers, clashing with them over certain issues. Each undoubtedly suspected the other's methods and motives. Yet Wash and his White River opponents united on a number of other issues. Factionalism at Uintah-Ouray evolved from preexisting kinship and band differences, bloomed with economic and land use disputes from the 1880s through the 1930s, and played itself out under the guise of mixed-blood–full-blood politics in the 1950s.

The problem with dichotomizing factions into progressive and traditional elements is, as Fred Hoxie points out, that "there were usually more than two sides to most questions, and no single side coincided with the cause of resistance for the survival of tribal culture." Indian communities contained "a variety of interest groups which took a variety of positions on public issues," and accounting for community or cultural survivals by praising one group as traditional against all others "flattens history and distorts the complexity of reservation life." Equating *progressive* with change and *traditional* with resistance sacrifices individually complex behavior, diminishing our understanding of Native Americans' rationales and responses.

Defining traditional and progressive elements or actions is equally difficult because what passes for tradition changes over time. When innovations can be and are interpreted as cultural continuities, the category *traditional* becomes little more than a temporal indicator. Institutions today regarded as conservative among the Northern Utes (the Sun Dance and peyotism, for example) were revitalized or innovative features in Wash's time. The most conservative elements of Ute society opposed peyote, while so-called progressives embraced the pan-Indian religion. Today at Uintah-Ouray, that group definition would be reversed. Wash's actions, which appeared progressive to agents and other Utes, in time manifested rather conservative intents or results.

Then there is the jockeying for semantic position or advantage. Different sides in a dispute might claim to be traditional in order to gain the moral high ground and discredit the others. Each side usually has some legitimate claims to tradition, and yet each is equally untraditional. The opposite strategy, claiming progressive attitudes and actions for moral or political advantage, is also possible. As Loretta Fowler points out. "Indians have often . . . tried to influence federal policy by presenting themselves and their constituents as 'progressive,' " to preserve or protect certain cultural elements. But this strategy is double-edged. The real problem begins when modern readers see this dichotomy and unwittingly read in a whole set of values and traits which may not be present, allowing no leeway for individual and qualitative distinctions. Given the modern predisposition towards cultural pluralism and the emergence of "pan-traditionalists," progressives have become politically suspect and are not considered particularly "authentic." The result: simplifying or discrediting through semantics alone.

A final problem with the progressive-traditional dichotomy is that it too frequently implies *either* that one is progressive and committed to change *or* that one is traditional and resists attempts to alter cultural features. It also suggests a zero-sum equation, a "cultural replacement" in which one discards Indian ways in proportion to the assimilation of white goods or ways. There appears to be no middle ground in the dichotomy, no ambiguity in individual thought, action, or value, no notion of differential as opposed to unilinear (or unidirectional) change. And yet we acknowledge the presence and importance of certain individuals who embody these ambiguities as cultural middlemen, intermediaries, bicultural brokers in search of balance. As middlemen, they exemplify the coexistence of oppositions. They frequently work both sides (or multiple sides) and run the danger of alienating both reservation officials and various Indian factions. Ambivalence appears more frequently than a progressive-traditional dichotomy among established and emerging leaders and, I would argue, among the more numerous and less visible individuals like William Wash.

These terms are not inherently problematical; indeed, they have some descriptive merit, even if simply as academic shorthand for issue-specific situations. The problem lies in their misuse, in the simplification, the dichotomization, of complex issues, personalities, and relationships. Creating new sets of terms will not solve it. Dividing the progressive-traditional dichotomy into three or four categories—for example, "native-oriented," "transitionals," "lower- and upper-acculturated"—is perhaps better but still suggests overly static organization and a unilinear progression. Describing a group or faction demands a generalization, a search for the "common." But in that search we should never lose sight of individual complexity and variability over time. We must define and redefine circumstances and try to convey the ambiguity of human motive and action within the common. Nowhere are those complexities and ambiguities greater than in the changing nature of nineteenth- and twentieth-century reservation leadership and in the emergence of the intermediaries, the cultural brokers, the William Washes.

Readings for David Rich Lewis:

Indian leadership at the end of the nineteenth century has received considerable attention, but often in the context of broader studies. For example see Loretta Fowler, *Arapahoe Politics, 1851–1978: Symbols in Crises of Authority* (Lincoln: University of Nebraska Press, 1982) and two books by Frederick E. Hoxie, *A Final Promise: The Campaign to Assimilate the Indians, 1880–1920* (Lincoln: University of Nebraska Press, 1984) and *Parading Through History: The Making of the Crow Nation in America, 1805–1935* (New York: Cambridge University Press, 1995). David Rich Lewis himself has analyzed issues related to this essay in his *Neither Wolf Nor Dog: American Indians, Environment, and Agrarian Change* (New York: Oxford University Press, 1994).

19

URBAN INDIANS AND ETHNIC CHOICES: AMERICAN INDIAN ORGANIZATIONS IN MINNEAPOLIS, 1920–1950

NANCY SHOEMAKER

Few Americans realize the extent of Indian migration from the reservations to the cities during the twentieth century. According to the United States Census Bureau, by 1970 half of all Native Americans lived in the cities, and that number continues to grow. This reading discusses the pre-1950 organizational activities of Indian groups in Minneapolis–St. Paul. In doing so it focuses attention on a time that has come to be regarded as increasingly important for those trying to understand where Native Americans fit into the pattern of ethnic group strivings of the past several decades. The author places such post–World War II groups and movements as the American Indian Movement (AIM) and the demands for Red Power of the 1960s and 1970s into the context of Indian migration to the cities dating back at least into the 1920s. Her study examines fraternal, social, and political groups that laid the foundations for the post-1950s actions. Minneapolis attracted Native Americans from several reservations because of proximity and economic opportunity. Indians who lived there for more than a short time came to think of themselves as separate and distinct from those who remained on the reservations, and they worried about losing their ethnic identity and tribal rights. Having to deal with that and facing the usual urban pressures, Indians began to found groups for mutual support. Some developed with only members from a single reservation, while others included people from several tribes. This discussion shows how the groups established in the Twin Cities during the past several decades built on the experiences of the earlier groups.

Nancy Shoemaker is an assistant professor at the University of Wisconsin–Eau Claire.

Source: Copyright by Western History Association. Reprinted by permission. The article first appeared as "Urban Indians and Ethnic Choices: American Indian Organizations in Minneapolis, 1920–1950," *Western Historical Quarterly* 19 (November 1988): 431–47.

When Dennis Banks, an initial founder of the American Indian Movement (AIM), said in a 1976 interview that "urbanization was part of the downfall, part of the destruction of the Indian community," he articulated one of the most commonly held assumptions about American Indians' experiences in cities. Banks's statement is ironic, since AIM and other Indian organizations of the 1960s and 1970s emerged from Indian communities that urbanization had helped create. AIM began one evening in 1968 when several Indians met to try to prevent what they saw as discriminatory arrests of Indians in their south Minneapolis neighborhood. By organizing Indians living in specific communities to help each other, AIM members were acknowledging that Indians in cities belonged to ethnic as well as geographic communities. AIM's first meeting, its further development of Minneapolis-area projects in education and housing, and its proliferation nationwide suggest that urbanization has helped to reinforce American Indian identity.

Scholars studying recent American Indian history have exhibited a similar kind of historical shortsightedness. They generally share in Dennis Banks's assessment of the city as damaging to Indian communities. Because the federal government sponsored an urban relocation program for Indians in the 1950s, Indian urbanization is often treated as a by-product of misguided government policies. And the Red Power movement of the 1960s and 1970s is treated as a phenomenon of Indian ghettos, a response to poverty, unemployment, and alcoholism.

The experience of urban Indians before 1950 provides the necessary context for understanding post-1950 developments such as relocation, the growth of Indian ghettos, and the political activism of the 1960s and 1970s. In particular, Indian urban history before 1950 can offer insights on the twentieth-century emergence of an Indian ethnic identity. Scholars such as anthropologist Robert K. Thomas and historian Hazel Hertzberg have suggested that cities helped foster the development of a pan-Indian identity. To cope with social problems and discrimination, people who identified with a particular tribe or band came to identify themselves as Indian.

One way to express ethnic identity is to join an organization. While Indians living on reservations formed social and political organizations among members of the same tribe or band, urban Indians had many choices in determining the boundaries of their ethnic community. The Twin Cities—located between small Dakota communities in southern Minnesota and several large Ojibway reservations in northern Minnesota—offered opportunities for the Ojibway and Dakota, who had been enemies in the nineteenth century, to become allies in the twentieth.

While Indian urbanization resembles that of other ethnic and racial groups, especially the urban migration of blacks, there are important differences. Both blacks and Indians experienced a massive shift from rural to urban residence in the twentieth century, and discrimination forced both groups into ghettos. Members of both groups founded societies, clubs, leagues, and associations, but organizations founded by Indians reflected a different dynamic. Recent literature on the urbanization of blacks points to social class as an emerging dynamic among blacks in cities. Class distinctions also existed among urban Indians but were confounded by urban Indians' ambiguous relationship to reservations. For Indians, length of residence in the city greatly influenced such indicators of social class as occupation, income, and home ownership. Longtime residents of the Twin Cities distinguished themselves from newly arrived reservation emigrants by referring to the other Indians as "reservation Indians." And yet Indians with closer ties to the reservation had something urban Indians did not. Urban Indians found that living away from reservations threatened their rights to tribal membership as well as their ethnic identity.

From 1920 to 1950 Minneapolis Indians formed two kinds of organizations: political organizations for strengthening their tenuous tribal ties and social organizations for building urban communities. Members of these organizations identified strongly as Americans in their use of patriotic rhetoric and in their pleas for equal rights for Indians as American citizens. But they were more flexible in their ethnic identifications. Whether they referred to themselves as Ojibway (Chippewa) or as Indian depended on the organization's purpose. Political organizations seeking to maintain rights for members of tribes naturally needed to organize among members of the same tribe. Organizations with social or cultural goals organized multitribally and thus were pan-Indian. Membership between organizations overlapped, confirming that an organization's goals—and not the individual member's cultural attachments—determined the ethnic position of each organization.

Minneapolis Indians' detachment from reservation communities made the city itself an important influence on the goals and membership of organizations. Most 1920–1950 organizations emerged from the south Minneapolis neighborhood where AIM would later organize its first efforts. But the neighborhood itself offered a radically different urban environment for the first Minneapolis Indians. Before World War II living conditions for Minnesota's urban Indian population surpassed conditions on the reservations. The majority of reservation residents survived on some mixture of unskilled, seasonal labor and erratic welfare assistance. The city provided more stable employment and a wider variety of occupations; urban Indians had jobs as skilled workers, professionals, white-collar workers, and small business operators. The 1928 Meriam Report, a nationwide survey of conditions among American Indians, found that longtime Indian residents of Minneapolis and St. Paul lived comfortably in middle-class homes:

> The range in standards of living follows economic rather than racial lines. Indians newly arrived are found in cheaply furnished rooming houses with rents comparatively high, or scattered through low-rent neighborhoods in cheap flats of one, two, or three rooms in buildings where conditions are somewhat below a reasonable standard of living. Numbers of other well-established wage earners are rather attractively housed in pleasant one- or two-family dwellings in better sections. Some of the more successful have attractive homes in the less expensive suburbs.

In 1947 a Minnesota social worker specializing in Indian welfare similarly observed that some Twin Cities Indians enjoyed the best living conditions among Minnesota Indians, but Indians new to the city lived in cramped, inadequate housing in the poorer sections of town.

During World War II new arrivals rapidly began to outnumber long-time Indian residents. In the 1920s the Indian population in the Twin Cities numbered less than 1,000. By the end of World War II 6,000 Indians resided there. Plentiful jobs and high-paying defense work attracted Indians to the Twin Cities and other urban areas, but wartime and postwar housing shortages, combined with discrimination, forced Indians into substandard housing in what was fast becoming a slum area. A 1947 Minneapolis housing study uncovered stories of Indian families crowded into condemned buildings and of an apartment building where more than sixty-five people shared two bathrooms.

In her book *Night Flying Woman*, Ojibway author Ignatia Broker described how, when she moved to Minneapolis during the war, a landlord overcharged her for a room not legally listed with the War Price and Rationing Board. It was a dingy basement room without adequate washing or cooking facilities: "[H]e would have made the illegal offer only to an Indian because he knew of the desperate housing conditions we, the first Americans, faced."

The more than 4,000 Indians who moved to the Twin Cities during the war created new areas of concern for Minneapolis's public and private welfare agencies and for those Indians well settled in the cities. Juvenile delinquency, prostitution, and especially the crowded, unsanitary living conditions created serious social problems in the growing Indian neighborhoods. On the home front World War II had helped create the Twin Cities' first Indian ghettos.

Before the war, however, there were no special social problems plaguing Twin Cities Indians. Conditions were so good that local public officials expected that most of its urban Indian population was assimilating and becoming part of the mainstream. On the basis of hundreds of interviews, the Meriam Report observed that urban Indians had succeeded in "adjusting themselves to white civilization." They had homes, clothes, and forms of recreation that were no different from those of other people in their respective economic classes. In Minneapolis and St. Paul, in particular, there was a high rate of intermarriage (46 of the 120 Indians interviewed had married non-Indians), and "the majority of persons in these cities who claim to be Chippewas are persons whose Indian blood is so diluted that its presence would never be guessed from their personal appearance."

The report also noted that city Indians were resisting certain native traditions as befit workers competing in the industrial marketplace:

> In city life the "sponging" permitted by this traditional Indian hospitality in its most
> aggravated form is rapidly disappearing. An occasional relative or friend, however, still
> tries to secure a foothold during periods of voluntary idleness, but the steady working
> Indian who rents a home and tries to survive in the presence of white civilization is more
> and more resisting this pressure to furnish food and shelter to drones.

Although the Meriam Report advocated these changes and even advised that the government sponsor a small-scale urban relocation program, some of the report's other observations on urban Indians make clear that "adjustment to white civilization" is more complicated than linear models of assimilation would suggest. The report found, for instance, that "in a number of cases a claim of only one-sixteenth, one thirty-second, or one sixty-fourth Indian blood was made, yet great insistence was put upon the right to be designated 'Indian.'" It also found that urban Indians socialized mainly with other Indians. Even though Indians belonged to white clubs and churches or lived primarily in white neighborhoods, most of their friends remained Indian.

Members of Indian organizations in the 1920s reflected the ambivalence toward assimilation the Meriam Report captured. Many of them had intermarried with whites, had joined mainstream clubs and churches, and had become "steady working Indians." They advocated assimilation and were preoccupied with making Indians economically self-sufficient members of American society. But by organizing along ethnic lines, they inadvertently set up barriers to assimilation. As they strove to become more American, they still emphasized their ethnic differences.

The first Indian organization active in Minneapolis was apparently a local social club affiliated with the American Indian Association and Tepee Order, a national fraternal society. Two World War I veterans, George Peake, Ojibway, and Warren Cash, Dakota, organized the Minneapolis affiliate soon after the war. Along with sponsoring dances and other social functions for Twin Cities Indians, the Tepee Order Club established a fraternity house for Indian students attending Minneapolis schools. Club officers Cash and Peake also tried unsuccessfully to organize a national Indian veterans' association.

The American Indian Association and Tepee Order's national organization, which included Peake and Cash among its officers, directed its greatest effort toward achieving public recognition of the Indians' contributions to American life. Annually the organization distributed promotional letters to local government leaders, churches, schools, and other social fraternities, urging them to participate in American Indian Day. Initially conceived of by another national Indian organization, the Society of American Indians, American Indian Day was an accumulation of events including Indian speakers, music, and educational activities put together by local clubs in cities like Minneapolis, Denver, and Chicago. In 1923, when the national organization had its headquarters in Minneapolis, promotional letters for American Indian Day expressed hopes that "the day is not far when all our Indians will do away with their old mode of life, and accept the modern civilization, and we all be as one true American citizens." Club members seemed to celebrate their Indian heritage while anticipating a melting-pot demise of Indian cultural distinctiveness.

Other Minneapolis Indian leaders of the 1920s believed that Indians should be integrated into the American melting pot. Members of the Twin Cities Chippewa Council, the Minnesota Wigwam Indian Welfare Society (a local affiliate of a national organization), and the Twin Cities Indian Republican Club advocated assimilation while maintaining their own native identity by joining these ethnically based organizations. In the 1920s all three organizations had offices in one place, the home of Frederick W. Peake in south Minneapolis.

A graduate of Carlisle Indian School and a lawyer from White Earth Reservation, Peake moved to Minneapolis in 1915 and lived there until his death in 1934. While in Minneapolis, Peake continued to practice law and dabbled in real estate investment. Although Peake's organizations included members from Fond du Lac and Grand Portage Reservations, White Earth emigrants clearly dominated the membership. Some organization participants had probably known Peake at White Earth. And some, like Archie Libby, an officer of the Twin Cities Chippewa Council, probably had been a friend of Peake's at Carlisle Indian School.

There are other possible explanations for why Minneapolis Indian organizations attracted so many White Earth emigrants. White Earth's bitter factional politics, heightened by notorious land allotment frauds, may have provided some residents with experience in political lobbying and interest group organizing. Also, many political leaders, including Archie Libby, left the reservation shortly after World War I when a local economic depression set in at White Earth. However, the main reason for high White Earth participation may simply be that there were more Indians living in the Twin Cities with ties to White Earth than to other reservations. Because the federal government had tried to consolidate all Minnesota Ojibways, except the Red Lake Band, at White Earth in the late nineteenth century, it was the largest Indian reservation in Minnesota. By 1900

White Earth had a diverse population of about 3,000 Ojibways. A large proportion of them had acculturated to Christianity, wage earning, and pro-assimilation ideology. White Earth people predominated in Minneapolis Indian organizations probably because they were more likely to be city residents.

The Twin Cities Chippewa Council, a lobbying organization for Ojibway men dislocated from the reservation, was the most active of Frederick Peake's organizations. The council formed in response to 1924 congressional consideration of an Indian competency bill that would declare all Minnesota Ojibways legally "competent." The Indian Competency Bill proposed to release the Ojibways from government supervision and divide the tribal funds into individual payments to enrolled members of the tribe. Writing in support of the bill, Peake, acting as vice president of the Twin Cities Chippewa Council, suggested that government paternalism prevented Indian assimilation:

> [S]uch progressive measures as this [passing the competency bill] will be the means of getting the Indians to become a part of the melting pot, the same as other nations have been received by this Government and have become a part of it when they complied with the law provided for an emigrant to become a citizen.

The Indian Competency Bill never passed Congress, but the Council continued to lobby for per capita distribution of tribal funds as a solution to Indian dependency.

William Madison, another member of the Twin Cities Chippewa Council, would make similar pleas for "progressive" reforms ten years later to protest the Indian Reorganization Act. Like Peake, Madison had sold his White Earth land allotment shortly before World War I, moved to the city, and started a business. Before moving to Minneapolis, Madison lived in Missouri for about fifteen years. While there, he tried a variety of occupations, from working as a carpenter to owning his own cleaning and tailoring business. He may have moved away from White Earth for economic reasons, or he may have felt frustrated by a series of political disappointments at White Earth, where he tried several times to represent the tribe in its dealings with the federal government. Although Madison's grandfather was *me-zhuc-e-ge-shig*, a respected hereditary chief of the Mississippi Band of White Earth Ojibway, Madison's own efforts to influence political decisions at White Earth rarely succeeded. His political inclinations eventually met more success off the reservation, where he was a ubiquitous presence in local and national Indian organizations. Madison was one of the few Indians to participate in both the Tepee Order and the Society of American Indians. In the early 1920s he edited the Tepee Order's magazine and in 1923 served as an officer of the Society of American Indians.

In keeping with the progressive ideals of the Society of American Indians, Madison believed strongly in the ability of Indians to better themselves. Along with participating in national Indian organizations, he started a local, pan-Indian social club, The Indians of Greater Kansas City, which urged other Indians to follow its members' example and move to cities. Like Indian reformer Carlos Montezuma, whom he particularly admired, Madison viewed the Bureau of Indian Affairs as an insidious institution, intent on maintaining Indians as dependents of the federal government.

When Madison moved to Minneapolis in the late 1920s, he naturally joined his friends at the Twin Cities Chippewa Council as an advocate of progressive reform for Indians, in particular for the Minnesota Ojibways. In 1934 the Council sent Madison to

Washington to defeat what they saw as regressive legislation: the Indian Reorganization Act (IRA) and other Indian New Deal policies being formulated within Commissioner John Collier's administration.

Collier planned to reverse United States Indian policy's emphasis on the individual. By building up reservation land bases and economies and by emphasizing self-determination in reservation politics, Collier hoped Indians would achieve self-sufficiency as communities, not as individuals. The Twin Cities Chippewa Council attacked the proposed changes in tribal structure as just another attempt to deprive Indians of vital land and resources and predicted that the new policy would "reduce them to the old tribes and further prey upon them."

Collier's intentions to revitalize tribal authority on reservations also threatened the council's own ability to influence tribal affairs. As enrolled members of tribes, urban Indians had a personal stake in events and decisions occurring on their reservations, but their prime means of influencing tribal affairs was through the federal government since they could not participate first-hand in tribal politics. The council's vehement lobbying against the IRA resulted from an odd mix of progressive ideology, self-interest, and sincere concerns for reservation Indians. Progressive ideology helped shape their beliefs in individual success and influenced their rhetoric of assimilation, but self-interest dictated many of their actions.

The council's persistent attempts to influence both tribal enrollment guidelines and the distribution of tribal funds reflect its emphasis on pursuing the interests of non-reservation Ojibways. Tribal enrollment was an issue because urban Indians risked being removed from the tribal rolls. Before Collier's appointment as commissioner of Indian affairs, the Office of Indian Affairs had been trying to tidy up tribal rolls using reservation residence as one of the criteria for tribal membership. A series of court cases, culminating in the Patterson opinion in 1932, denied tribal enrollment to children born to Indians residing off the reservation. Consequently, many Ojibways moved back to their reservations in the 1930s.

Ojibways who stayed in the city tried to change enrollment requirements, but enrollment was a divisive issue. Members of the Twin Cities Chippewa Council agreed that Collier's focus on the reservation would reinforce the importance of reservation residence and undermine their rights as members of the Minnesota Chippewa Tribe. But they could not agree on how to change enrollment requirements. William Madison argued that the degree of Indian blood should be used as the primary standard. Such a decision would have benefited him and his family. He was listed as a full-blood on most government documents, but his children, those born after he left White Earth, were denied enrollment in the tribe. His children were half Ojibway since Madison's wife was white, but half was more than many reservation residents could claim. Other Minneapolis Indians could neither accept Madison's suggestions nor derive better ones since all proposed changes would exclude some of them.

The council, however, easily agreed on what to do with the tribal funds held in trust by the federal government. Throughout the 1920s it supported legislation that would distribute per capita payments of tribal funds to competent Indians. All the council members were "competent," some having proven their economic self-sufficiency by selling their land allotments and becoming wage earners in the city. As enrolled members of a tribe, council members periodically received interest from tribal funds, but funds continually dwindled because the government used that money to support reservation programs and facilities. Collier's plans promised to be even more expensive.

The council opposed the IRA, however, not just because it would delay a final per capita distribution of tribal money, but also because they had spent most of their lives believing that Indians should abandon the old way of life, assimilate, and seek individual success. In presenting the council's objections toward the IRA to the House Subcommittee on Indian Affairs, Madison argued that it would only prolong the Bureau of Indian Affairs' administration of reservations and would consequently encourage the Indians' dependence on the federal government:

> So far as I am personally concerned, I can make a livelihood in competition with others. They [the Bureau of Indian Affairs] are keeping the Indian down and that is un-American. They should be free like any other men. They should exercise their rights of citizenship like anybody else.

Because Madison and his fellow council members had achieved some success as individuals—as house painters, barbers, bankers, and lawyers—they thought individual success could and should be achieved by other Indians.

The Twin Cities Chippewa Council had organized to serve the particular interests of a few dislocated Ojibways, but members devoted some effort to purely charitable causes. Both Peake and Madison lobbied for more welfare relief for reservation residents (so long as tribal funds were not used) and organized a benefit dance in 1932 to raise relief money. Also in 1932, they lobbied the state for an exchange of state-owned land and Ojibway lands to give Minnesota Ojibways access to more of the lakes where wild rice grew. Wild rice was an important source of food and income for several Ojibway reservations. However, since they considered their organization primarily a tribal council with a political agenda, council members pursued welfare issues only occasionally.

One Indian woman, Amabel Bulin, initiated most of the Indian welfare programs that originated in Minneapolis before 1950. An enrolled Sioux and a graduate of the Bureau of Indian Affairs school at Tomah, Wisconsin, she later graduated from New York University, married a Scandinavian from Brooklyn, and settled into middle-class life in Minneapolis. In a 1954 newspaper interview Bulin described herself as a housewife, a member of women's clubs, and a faithful Catholic. She also bowled twice a week. She easily fit the Meriam Report's description of the assimilated Indians in Minneapolis who insisted on "the right to be designated 'Indian.' "

Beginning in the 1920s Bulin worked as a self-appointed, volunteer social worker. She located boarding homes for Indian children and temporary housing for reservation Indians taking advantage of the city's hospitals and schools. Young women from Minnesota, North and South Dakota, Wisconsin, and even Montana reservations used her as a connection for finding homes and jobs in the Twin Cities. During World War II she unsuccessfully tried to establish a boarding home for Indian women defense workers.

Amabel Bulin undertook some of these services at the request of several Indian Affairs agents in the upper Midwest, but her concern for young Indian women developed from her involvement in the General Federation of Women's Clubs. First, as a member of the Pathfinder Club, she helped provide educational scholarships to young women. In the late 1930s she formed her own affiliate to the General Federation of

Women's Clubs, *Sah-Kah-Tay* (*Sunshine* in Ojibway). *Sah-Kah-Tay* was an all-Indian women's club that sponsored young Indian women who wanted to go to school or work in the city. Bulin later became the director of Minnesota's General Federation of Women's Clubs, Indian Division, where she carried out the division's usual programs of collecting clothing and food for distribution on Minnesota's Indian reservations.

Before World War II Amabel Bulin's social-welfare programs, like Madison's and Peake's occasional welfare activities, aimed to help reservation Indians. During the war she helped Indian women move from reservations to Minneapolis to take up defense work, but gradually she directed her efforts at meeting the needs of the Indians already living in the city. Before the war she served as a link between the reservation and the city; after the war she became a link between urban Indians and public institutions: courts, welfare offices, employers, and the Fair Employment Practices Commission.

Speaking in 1944 before the House Committee Investigating Indian Affairs, Amabel Bulin pointed to an alarming rate of juvenile arrests among Indians. She told stories of juvenile drinking and prostitution, which were increasing in the Indian neighborhoods of both St. Paul and Minneapolis. Although concerned that Indians were "forced to live in unwholesome surroundings or in a dirty, filthy city," the committee would ultimately propose abandoning Collier's policies in favor of reservation termination and urban relocation.

Public and private welfare organizations in the Twin Cities, similarly ignoring the growth of an Indian ghetto, also established urban relocation programs for Indians after the war. Hitler's anti-Semitism had created a heightened sensitivity about racism at home, and state and local governments sponsored labor and housing studies, educational brochures, and lecture tours about Minnesota's black, Hispanic, Asian, and Indian residents. Members of the newly formed Minnesota Interracial Commission perceived urban relocation to be the solution to the state's so-called Indian problem. In 1950 the commission also sponsored an Indian social club, American Indians, Inc., and recruited several Minneapolis Indians to help new arrivals from reservations find homes and jobs in the city.

At the same time, private charities like the St. Paul Resettlement Committee, which formed in 1943 to help resettle Japanese-Americans interned during the war, decided to fund the Twin Cities relocation of Turtle Mountain Ojibways from North Dakota. Public and private administrators of welfare programs believed that Indians were ready to move to the cities. Many Indians had already left their reservations to participate in the war effort as part of the military and as workers in defense plants. But administrators did not ask whether cities were ready for Indians. They showed remarkably bad timing in promoting urban relocation to cities already crowded by wartime migrations.

The changing city provided opportunities as well as hardships, however. Social organizations emerged from Indian neighborhoods. Before World War II Minneapolis organizations with pan-Indian membership developed out of other networks: Warren Cash and George Peake were World War I veterans, and Amabel Bulin maintained numerous contacts with Indian Affairs agents and women's clubs. It was not until World War II that pan-Indian groups coalesced in urban neighborhoods.

The Ojibway-Dakota Research Society was one such pan-Indian group. It grew out of an urban neighborhood where Indians from different tribes and reservations came to know each other. William Madison founded the Ojibway Research Society in 1942 with White Earth friends who were also members of the Twin Cities Chippewa Council. They wanted to preserve the Ojibway language and gain some public recognition of Minnesota's Indian heritage. The society met periodically to prepare brief papers on the Ojibway origins of Minnesota place-names. The society soon expanded to allow Ojibway women, and in 1944, members from other Indian tribes. Although they renamed the organization the Ojibway-Dakota Research Society, membership included some Crees and Iroquois. Meeting attendance averaged fewer than twenty participants, but membership lists show that more people were involved than could regularly attend.

The research society's changing composition during World War II shows how the urban environment was beginning to contribute to pan-Indian organizing. Early membership lists show a majority of people with White Earth backgrounds and even some people who still lived at White Earth, but almost half of the 1945 members were not Ojibway. Most members lived in the same south Minneapolis neighborhood. Madison, Peake, and other Ojibway organizers had lived in this particular south Minneapolis neighborhood since the 1920s. They originally located in this area, and wartime migrations concentrated more Indians there.

The development of pan-Indian organizations in the Twin Cities did not replace tribal organizations. As in the 1920s, pan-Indian organizations existed simultaneously with tribal organizations, and despite their different ethnic label, both types of organizations attracted some of the same people.

In the late 1940s Madison and some of the Ojibway members of the Ojibway-Dakota Research Society formed another organization, the Ojibway Tomahawk Band. This organization's principal activity seems to have been the publication of a monthly, sometimes bimonthly, newsletter, *The New Tomahawk*. Madison named the newsletter after *The Tomahawk*, the White Earth newspaper published forty years earlier by a friend of his, Gus Beaulieu, a proassimilation political leader at White Earth. The newsletter published information and opinion on current Indian-related legislation and pushed for rights guaranteed Indians as American citizens and rights guaranteed Indians by treaties. Minnesota Ojibways as far away as Washington and California received the newsletter, as did several of the Ojibway Tomahawk Band's friends and relatives still living on the Ojibway reservations in northern Minnesota.

The Ojibway Tomahawk Band pursued some familiar political goals but abandoned other issues. The old issue of tribal funds was no longer pertinent. By 1943 the fund contained only $32,424. Although Collier intended tribal funds for capital improvements, most of the Minnesota Chippewa Tribe's funds went toward daily expenses, education, and relief. Passage of the Indian Claims Act in 1946 made tribal enrollment requirements still an important issue for urban Indians, however. The Indian Claims Act declared that the federal government would settle all Indian claims once and for all. The Ojibway Tomahawk Band may have formed to take advantage of this federal initiative. If the government was planning to resolve all claims, the urban Ojibways wanted to ensure that their interests as members of the tribe would be considered. The Ojibway Tomahawk Band's newsletter persistently argued that urban Indians, although living off the reservation, still had "rights to tribal representation at least until the final settlement."

The possibility of a final solution to the tribal-federal relationship encouraged urban Indians to maintain their tribal identities. Of the Minneapolis Indian organizations that formed before 1950, the Twin Cities Chippewa Council and the Ojibway Tomahawk Band organized among Ojibways because they wanted to pursue issues relevant to Minnesota Ojibways. Consistently, the politically active urban Indians tried to secure what they considered to be their share of federal obligations to Indians. Because most federal obligations were based on earlier treaties and agreements with tribes or bands, urban Indians' unresolved relationship to the federal government gave tribal ethnicity a legal and political imperative.

Minneapolis Indians organizing for cultural or social purposes seem to have readily identified with other Indians from very different cultural and social backgrounds. Although their previous experiences were different, their experiences in the city were similar: they shared the same needs and the same grievances about their relationship to the larger society. Thus Minneapolis organizations without political goals tended to be pan-Indian. The local Tepee Order affiliate, *Sah-Kay-Tay* and Amabel Bulin's other welfare activities, and the Ojibway-Dakota Research Society all had Ojibway, Dakota, and other tribal groups represented among their members.

The effects of pan-Indianism on tribal identity were ambiguous. Because members of pan-Indian organizations had different cultural backgrounds, those organizations seeking to make the American public more appreciative of Indian contributions encountered problems. The American Indian Association and Tepee Order relied on romanticized Indian stereotypes. The Tepee Order used a pseudo-Indian dating system on correspondence, consisting of suns and moons, and gave officers titles such as "Junior Guide of the Forest" and "Great Sentinel." The Ojibway-Dakota Research Society aimed at historical accuracy, but William Madison ventured into such schemes as selling "Madison's Indian Medicine" and publishing an Indian wild rice cookbook with native recipes, including "Spanish *Mah-no-min*" (rice in Ojibway). Tribal heritages had to find some common ground if Indian organizers were to promote the impact of Indian cultures on American life. That common ground often consisted of popularized images of Indian cultures.

Although symbols used by pan-Indian organizers had this synthetic quality, overall pan-Indian organizing probably reinforced tribal ethnic identities. Members of pan-Indian organizations always identified individual members by tribe, even though the organization labeled itself as Indian. One could not be Indian without belonging to a tribe or tribes.

Urban life presented a new environment, with new problems but also new solutions. As Indians residing away from reservations, urban Indians risked losing their ethnic identity. Legally, they risked being removed from tribal rolls, and emotionally, they risked losing the security and fellowship of their communities. Establishing Indian organizations in the city helped reservation emigrants maintain their tribal identities while expanding their ethnic identity to include a larger circle of people. Ignatia Broker described the positive side of urbanization when she eloquently observed that:

> [M]aybe it was a good thing, the migration of our people to the urban areas during the war years, because there, amongst the millions of people, we were brought to a brotherhood. We Indian people who worked in the war plants started a social group not only for the Ojibway but for the Dakota, the Arikara, the Menominee, the Gros Ventres, the Cree, the Oneida, and all those from other tribes and other states who had made the trek to something new. And because we, all, were isolated in this dominant society, we became an island from which a revival of spirit began.

The experience of Minneapolis Indians challenges most historical accounts of Indian urbanization. First, prerelocation urban Indian migration is important for explaining later migrations. As historian Kenneth Philp has argued, the federal government initiated its urban relocation program in part because many Indians on their own initiative had successfully settled in cities. Second, the activities and goals of these early organizations show that AIM and other Red Power movements were part of a continuous process. The first generation of Minneapolis Indian reformers—Frederick Peake, William Madison, and Amabel Bulin—had a progressive faith in legislative reform's potential to ameliorate the social and political situation of American Indians. Another generation of reformers would emerge in the 1950s and 1960s: social workers and other college graduates. This younger generation formed professional alliances with private and public institutions such as settlement houses, state and city social-welfare agencies, and church groups. Then, in 1967, a third generation of urban Indians founded AIM and rapidly began to utilize the radical reform methods that the civil rights movement had helped shape. Although the reform methods varied, urban Indian organizations have persistently addressed issues of education and welfare, treaty rights and federal Indian obligations, and what it means to be Indian.

Readings for Nancy Shoemaker:

Urban Indian actions have received considerable attention. One should begin with Jack O. Waddell and Michael Watson, eds., *The American Indian in Urban Society* (Boston: Little Brown, 1971). Jeanne E. Guillemin looks at strategies used by some Indians in her *Urban Renegades: The Cultural Strategy of American Indians* (New York: Columbia University Press, 1973). For an analysis of Indians in a single city see Elaine M. Neils, *Reservation to City: Indian Migration and Federal Relocation* (Chicago: University of Chicago Press, 1971). In *Termination and Relocation: Federal Indian Policy, 1945–1960* (Albuquerque: University of New Mexico Press, 1986) Donald L. Fixico considers what happened to urban Indian people during the decades immediately following those considered by Shoemaker.

20

INCONSTANT ADVOCACY: THE EROSION OF INDIAN FISHING RIGHTS IN THE PACIFIC NORTHWEST, 1933–1956

DONALD L. PARMAN

Native American people living in the coastal regions of the Pacific Northwest appear to differ widely from popular notions of what Indians are like. Instead of tepees, earth lodges, or hogans, they erected large plank houses, put to sea in immense canoes, and erected totem poles near their villages. They depended heavily on the sea and coastal rivers for their subsistence. Yet upon close examination it is clear that they faced the same issues as other tribes when facing the Europeans in North America. Disease swept through their ranks, invading whites took choice village and fishing sites, and gradually the Indians fell under the control of the United States. During the period of treaty negotiations and the establishment of reservations in the region, many tribes retained at least some of their fishing rights. Once the salmon-canning industry became well established in Washington and Oregon, however, both those states began a pattern of discriminatory legislation aimed at forcing the Indians out of the fishing business. This essay traces the emergence of that pattern and notes that not until objections were raised to the blatantly anti-Indian Initiative 77 passed in 1935 by the Washington legislature did BIA officials bestir themselves on behalf of the tribes. The narrative traces the halting steps that federal officials took during the next thirty years to protect or regain Indian fishing rights. It shows that greed and economic discrimination marched alongside the continuing efforts to destroy the tribal cultures through much of American history.
    Donald L. Parman is a professor of history at Purdue University.

Source: Donald L. Parman, "Inconstant Advocacy: The Erosion of Indian Fishing Rights in the Pacific Northwest, 1933–1956," *Pacific Historical Review,* 53 (May 1984), pp. 163–189. © 1984 by the Pacific Coast Branch, American Historical Association. Reprinted by permission of the Branch.

The issue of Indian fishing rights in the Pacific Northwest has aroused national attention since the "fish-ins" of the 1960s and Judge George Boldt's controversial decision in *United States* v. *Washington* in 1974. Though that decision was favorable to the Indians, it represented only one development in a conflict that has ranged from the territorial period of Oregon and Washington to the present. The more recent controversies have been essentially a fight over remnants since Indians lost many of the most valuable fisheries in previous decades. Although Indian fishing rights have exerted an important influence on the development of the Pacific Northwest and have been (and are) a significant determinant in race relations, the topic has received little attention from historians. The present study will focus primarily on the New Deal and immediate postwar eras when changes in the Bureau of Indian Affairs, state-federal relations, and the national economy modified but did not appreciably alter the erosion of Indian fishing rights, an erosion that had been going on for decades and which wreaked havoc on traditional Indian lifestyles and violated the spirit and often the letter of earlier treaties.

Coastal Indians prior to white settlement had since time immemorial fished for both anadromous (fish which ascend rivers from the sea to spawn) and nonanadromous species, collected various types of shellfish, and hunted seals and whales. Groups living inland mainly caught anadromous fish. By the twentieth century, Indian fishing was largely restricted to migrating salmon and steelhead in three principal fisheries. The first of these encompassed the streams which entered Puget Sound, the second included those rivers which flowed directly into the Pacific Ocean, and the third and largest involved the Columbia River and its many tributaries. The latter can be considered as a separate category because the Columbia and its tributaries, most notably the Snake River, permitted salmon and steelhead to reach spawning grounds hundreds of miles in the interior. The Cascade Mountains, which traverse Washington and Oregon north and south, have also significantly affected Indian fishing. This range divides the Pacific Northwest into two climatic zones. The area to the west of the mountains has heavy rainfall, lush forests, and high humidity. The opposite conditions prevail to the east because the Cascades prevent moisture from reaching the interior. Precontact Indians west of the mountains were called "fisheaters" because the thick forests prevented them from doing much hunting and forced them to depend almost solely on the rich fisheries in the streams, Puget Sound, and the Pacific. Salmon caught west of the Cascades were difficult to cure because of their high oil content and the damp climate, and they could only be preserved by smoking. The much drier climate in the eastern interior created a more open country, which permitted precontact groups to achieve a balance among hunting, gathering, and catching salmon migrating upstream on the Columbia and its tributaries. The same aridity led the interior tribes to filet and dry their fish on racks without smoking.

It would be difficult to overemphasize the dependence of the coastal Indians on fishing and the taking of whales and seals both before and after white settlement. Bureau of Indian Affairs (BIA) field workers in the region during the late nineteenth century attempted to force the "fish-eaters" to become farmers and frequently complained about their charges' unwillingness to abandon aquatic subsistence for agriculture. Indeed, the agents' reports bear a striking resemblance to those emanating from the Great Plains reservations in the same period. While the agents in the Plains states condemned the Indians for an unwillingness to abandon hunting, those in the Northwest criticized their groups for refusing to give up fishing and hunting seals and whales.

The Cascades continued to influence Indian fishing practices in the present century. Salmon caught on the Columbia east of the mountains were considered inferior in taste and sold for a lower commercial price than those taken downstream or at sea. Indians who lived west of the mountains in the 1930s used very little of their catch for subsistence and sold nearly all of their fish on the commercial market. Indians east of the Cascades, however, continued to use a sizable portion of their catch for subsistence because of the ease of curing.

The special fishing rights of Indians in Oregon and Washington derive from a series of treaties negotiated in 1854–55 mainly by Isaac I. Stevens, governor of the newly formed territory of Washington. The treaties reflected the prevailing philosophy at the beginning of the reservation era by requiring the Indian groups to cede their large holdings to the government and to relocate on smaller reservations. Stevens pushed the negotiations with unusual speed because of the burgeoning white settlement in Washington Territory and, more importantly, because he hoped that Congress would authorize a transcontinental railroad terminating at Puget Sound. His desire for haste and his awareness of the Indians' attitudes about the importance of fishing and hunting, prompted him to include provisions in the treaties similar to the following:

> The right of taking fish, at all usual and accustomed grounds and stations, is further secured to said Indians in common with all citizens of the Territory, and of erecting temporary houses for the purpose of curing, together with privilege of hunting, gathering roots and berries, and pasturing their horses on open and unclaimed lands.

The rapid white settlement in the Pacific Northwest after the treaties increasingly interfered with Indian attempts to fish at off-reservation sites. Because salmon and steelhead runs took place in every stream in the region, Indians no doubt originally fished at hundreds of sites of varying importance. Many of these were lost when white farmers and ranchers occupied lands along streams and denied access to Indians trying to reach traditional fishing grounds. Lumbering had somewhat the same effect, as that industry grew rapidly to meet both local needs and those of California settlements. The practice of floating logs down streams sometimes created jams which blocked fish from reaching their spawning areas. White settlement seems to have forced the Indians to give up their less important fishing places and to concentrate at the more productive points.

The advent of commercial salmon canning in the Pacific Northwest threatened even the best Indian fisheries. The first cannery on the Columbia opened in 1866, and that river soon became the largest source of canned salmon in the world. Annual catches rose dramatically, reaching a peak of 40,000,000 pounds in 1883–84. Only Chinook, the largest and best flavored of the five salmon species, was processed up to that time. Even though other species were taken afterward, the catch on the Columbia gradually declined from the early twentieth century until 1937, when it seemed to stabilize at approximately half of the catch of the mid 1880s. The developments on the Columbia were not unique. Numerous canneries followed a similar pattern in the rich fishing areas of Puget Sound and on many of the smaller streams which flowed directly into the Pacific.

Canneries brought some economic advantages to Indian fishermen, but their long-range effect was negative. Since Indians had always engaged in the barter of fish, they readily caught salmon for sale to the canneries, some even using their traditional equipment at first instead of adopting the fishing gear of whites. Other Indians found employment in the canneries. The superior capital, large-scale methods, and aggressiveness of whites, however, quickly led to their domination of the prime fisheries of the region. The Yakima agent, for example, reported in 1894 that "the disputed fishery rights of the Indians along the Columbia has given me a vast amount of trouble." He went on to describe how canneries located at the prime fisheries had "inch by inch" forced the Yakimas from their best sites. The scene was repeated elsewhere. The Tulalip agent complained in 1897 that large firms had appropriated nearly all the best fishing areas at Point Roberts and Village Point on Puget Sound, where the Lummi Indians traditionally fished. By 1905 conditions had worsened. "The tremendous development of fisheries by traps and by trust methods of consolidation, concentration, and large local development," reported the Tulalip agent, "are seriously depleting the natural larders of our Indians and cutting down on their main reliance for support and subsistence. Living for them is becoming more precarious year by year."

As public fears arose about the decline of salmon and steelhead runs, Washington and Oregon reacted by passing laws to regulate the length of fishing seasons, size of catches, and types of equipment. The Washington territorial legislature in 1871 banned nets or traps which entirely blocked rivers so some of the fish could escape upstream. The same measure demanded that all dams must provide a passage for fish. Six years later the legislature began fixing seasons and established a fish commissioner to enforce the law. Oregon followed a similar pattern in 1877 by banning fishing during part of the season and creating a three-man regulatory board in 1887. Until well into the twentieth century state legislation lacked any scientific rationale but, according to a careful study, was based on an "intuitive feeling" that the fish runs were declining and certain types of equipment were responsible.

State regulation of Indian fishing and hunting started in a lenient manner but increasingly discriminated against Indian rights. The legislature of Washington in 1891 acknowledged the proviso in the Stevens treaties by exempting Indians from a new fishing law, and early game wardens in the Puget Sound area overlooked violations of state laws if Indians fished or hunted for subsistence. By the second decade of the twentieth century the attitude toward Indians had toughened. In 1915 Charles M. Buchanan, the Tulalip agent, appeared before the Washington legislature and detailed the Indians' recent legal problems. The state insisted that the Indians buy licenses to hunt or fish off their reservations, but officials refused to sell the necessary permits on the grounds that the Indians were not citizens of the state. At the same time, whites, claiming state authority because they possessed licenses, seized control of ancient Indian fishing sites on the shores of reservations. Indians, Buchanan complained, were arrested not only when they left reservations to hunt, but also often while securing game within their own reservations. Although state courts released those arrested, the Indians had still faced humiliation, time in jail, and legal expenses.

The operation of state fishing laws and enforcement policies reflected the struggles of various interest groups (sportsmen, net fishermen, trap operators, canneries) to gain an advantage over each other. Unfortunately the competition often adversely affected Indian fishing as well. A notable example involved Washington state's practice of licensing fish wheels at prime spots for favored large canneries and simultaneously excluding Indians from traditional fishing grounds. Because of their small population, lack of political influence, and the hostility of whites, the Indians clearly did not figure in the design of state laws or their enforcement by officials.

Although the effects of state regulation must have been traumatic for Indians who were almost solely dependent on fishing, only glimpses of their reactions appear in agency reports. When the Washington legislature in 1897 imposed a tax on all nets used in state waters and banned such gear from within 240 feet of any fish trap, the Lummi complained bitterly that the measure and recent court decisions were aimed specifically at them. Their agent confessed that "no amount of explanation on my part" would change the Indians' opinion.

While it is clear from agents' reports and court cases at the turn of the century that Indians were encountering numerous and severe difficulties in having their fishing rights accepted by state officials and by private citizens, their problems did not cause BIA officials at Washington to take any major protective action. The first indication in central office correspondence of a response to Indian complaints was in 1914 when Samuel Eliot, a member of the Board of Indian Commissioners visiting the Northwest, reported that Indian fishing rights on the Quinault River and Quinault Lake needed protection. State regulations on commercial fishing should apply to citizen Indians, he stated, but not to the Quilleute who were still noncitizens. Except for the normal practice of referring Eliot's letter to the local superintendent, nothing evidently was done to meet his concerns. Nine years later the Quinault Indians complained that a weir installed by the Bureau of Fisheries to count fish had disrupted the fish run, and the BIA intervened to close the obstacle.

The event which brought Indian fishing rights into sharp focus was the implementation of Initiative 77 in Washington in 1935. This measure banned all fixed gear such as fish wheels, traps, and set nets from the entire state; established a line inside Puget Sound which severely limited commercial fishing in the southern portion of that body of water; and redefined legal fishing gear and closed areas for fishing. Initiative 77 was the handiwork of numerous sports groups, and perhaps small commercial fishing firms owned or associated with canneries. The effects of the new law were significant both immediately and in the long run as large-scale operators concentrated more on trolling and purse seining outside the restricted area, leaving the waters inside the line and the rivers to small commercial fishing interests and white sportsmen. The new regulations caused a sharp rise in the expenses of commercial fishermen, who could no longer use fixed gear in rivers, and they negated potentially simple and effective conservation practices that could have been used to preserve the runs. More importantly, the new legislation handicapped Indian commercial fishermen who lacked the capital necessary to buy the larger boats and equipment required for trolling and purse seining outside the restricted zone.

The Indians' attempts to adjust to the new situation caused the first serious conflict between Northwestern fishing interests and the BIA during the New Deal. At the start of the 1935 season Ken McLeod, secretary of the Salmon Conservation League, wrote the Indian Office complaining strongly that the Swinomish of Puget Sound had established two fish traps on their reservation for commercial purposes. State officials then arrested three Swinomish on the grounds that the traps were located off-reservation. Both a lower court and the Washington state supreme court denied that the traps were outside reservation boundaries and ordered the Indians released. Although the Swinomish emerged victorious, the arrests and suits created considerable public controversy. The local superintendent complained that sportsmen's groups had agitated so much about Indians' preferential fishing rights during the period that state officials had persecuted the Indians and threatened "their only means of independent subsistence."

The attitudes of state officials of Washington and Oregon about Indian fishing in the 1930s contrasted. Washington made few concessions for off-reservation fishing at the "usual and accustomed places." The Washington attorney general in 1937 speciously argued that the Indian Citizenship Act of 1924 had abrogated any special rights Indians had enjoyed earlier. Oregon, by contrast, did not demand full compliance with its regulations and permitted some out-of-season fishing if the Indians used the catch for subsistence. These differences apparently reflected the existence in Washington of a major fishing industry, and close cooperation between sportsmen's groups and state fish and game officials against a relatively large number of Indian fishermen. The population of Indians in Oregon was much smaller, and their fishing was mainly confined to the Columbia River.

When Commissioner of Indian Affairs John Collier took office in 1933, he vowed to defend Indian rights, but his reactions and those of his staff toward Washington state's attempts to regulate Indian fishing were surprisingly moderate. To McLeod's complaints about the Swinomish fish traps, Collier stated that they were located on reservation land and the superintendent would see that no violations of state laws took place off the reservation. Assistant Commissioner William Zimmerman, Jr., was even more candid about his position: "the state can make such laws and rulings it desires governing fishing within its borders" so long as such regulations applied equally to both races and were not enforced inside reservations.

The conciliatory attitudes of the Indian Office conformed with legal precedents established by state and federal courts. The U.S. Supreme Court, in *Ward* v. *Race Horse* (1896) and *Kennedy* v. *Becker* (1916), had dealt with Indians arrested while attempting to exercise treaty rights to hunt or fish on ceded land in violation of state laws. The Ward case involved a Bannock arrested in Wyoming for killing elk away from the Fort Hall Reservation. Although the Bannock treaty of 1869 guaranteed the tribe the right to hunt on "unoccupied lands" off the reservation, the court ruled that the 1895 federal act which admitted Wyoming as a state had failed to reserve any special hunting rights to the Bannocks. The Kennedy decision dealt with Seneca Indians arrested on ceded land while fishing in violation of New York laws. Since New York was one of the original states, the decision could not turn on admission legislation. Nevertheless, the court held that the Senecas' treaty rights to hunt and fish on ceded lands were not exclusive but included the individual to whom the land was ceded, subsequent grantees, and all others entitled to hunt and fish. More importantly, all such rights were subject to state authority.

In rulings on attempts of whites to exclude the Northwest Indians from fishing at the "usual and accustomed places," the court adopted a more favorable attitude toward the Indians. This was in keeping with past federal court decisions which had held that Indian treaties which dealt with fishing or hunting must be interpreted as the Indians understood the provisions at the time of their negotiations. The most important ruling for the Northwest tribes was *United States* v. *Winans* in 1905. The case grew out of the Yakimas' long-standing problem of being excluded from fishing sites on the Columbia River. Winans Brothers, a cannery, had purchased land along the stream at a fishing site, obtained state licenses to operate fish wheels, and built a fence to keep the Indians from the area. The firm's attorney argued that his client's ownership of the land and the licenses gave it the right to exclude the Yakimas because the latter possessed no greater rights than a white person. The U.S. Supreme Court disagreed, endorsing strongly the Indians' right of access to the fishing site. Ingress to fishing areas, observed the court, "was a part of the larger rights possessed by Indians" at the time of the treaty negotiations. Thus the federal government had not given them a right of access to fishing sites, because they already possessed that right. The court noted, however, that Indian ingress was not exclusive because the treaty permitted whites to fish in common with the Indians. Since the latter had never abandoned their right of access, the federal government must protect their entry, a responsibility not altered by the admission of Washington as a state. In 1919 the U.S. Supreme Court affirmed and broadened the Winans decision when it ruled in *Seufert Brothers* v. *United States*. This time the plaintiff was an Oregon cannery which argued that the Yakima treaty extended only to the Washington side of the Columbia, and therefore the Seufert Brothers' attempts to close a Yakima's fish wheel on the Oregon side were legal. The court sustained a lower court's ruling in favor of the Indians on the grounds that before and after signing treaties the Yakimas freely crossed from one bank of the Columbia to the other to fish and had associated and intermarried with Oregon tribes along the river.

Although the case law of Indian fishing was often contradictory, certain general principles were accepted by the 1930s. Past decisions had affirmed the sole jurisdiction of the federal government over all reservation fishing on trust lands. The tribes had an unqualified right of ingress and egress across private lands to reach traditional fishing sites, as well as the right to camp and build temporary drying sheds at such locations. Their fishing activities at off-reservation sites, however, came under state authority. The states could not prevent Indians from fishing on an equal basis with whites.

From the perspective of the Indians, state regulation anywhere was unacceptable. The Indians also challenged statements in the Stevens treaties indicating that access to the "usual and accustomed places" off the reservations was guaranteed to whites as well as to Indians. As one observer noted in 1941, "the Indians have always contended that when fishing at the usual and accustomed grounds they are (a) free from state regulation and (b) entitled to the exclusive use of such places."

Although the BIA under Collier denied the Indians exclusive use of off-reservation sites, it did uphold their freedom from state regulation on the reservations. This position received sharp criticism from state officials and sportsmen's groups which accused the Indians of fishing for commercial purposes rather than for subsistence. Particularly outspoken was Ken McLeod, secretary-treasurer of the powerful Washington State Sportsmen's Council. In 1939 he complained to Interior Secretary Harold Ickes that the amount of fish sold commercially in Washington by Indians from 1935 through 1938 totaled over 17 million pounds with a value of $1,127,015. Moreover, he noted, the Indians had fished out of season and then shipped their catch to out-of-state buyers. Also disturbing were the Nisqually, Swinomish, and Quilleute, who had recently gotten temporary court injunctions permitting them to fish off-reservation without state regulation.

While McLeod's statistics may have been exaggerated, the influence of his and other sportsmen's groups helped force the Indian Office into action. Pressures also came from the Bureau of Fisheries, recently transferred from Commerce to Interior, which supported Washington sports groups and urged Ickes to acknowledge the problems created by Indian fishing practices in the Northwest. At first Collier found himself stymied by lack of statutory authority to regulate hunting and fishing on reservations. He feared that sportsmen's groups might pressure Congress into filling this legal vacuum by enacting a stringent conservation law for all Indians which would be badly suited for an individual tribe's needs. Although Congress never approved such a measure, Collier nevertheless asked superintendents to report on what tribal councils had done in recent years to regulate hunting and fishing. With few exceptions the responses indicated that conservation regulations were woefully inadequate.

Collier's approach to the problem was to embark on a policy of education and to encourage tribes to establish their own codes. Always short on technical personnel, he enlisted the cooperation of the Bureau of Fisheries and the Biological Survey to study wildlife conditions on reservations and to assist in drafting the local game codes. He also instructed superintendents in Oregon and Washington to make accurate tallies of fish catches because of the large disparities between their past estimates and those of the state officials.

Collier, in addition, sampled field workers' views on the appropriateness of Indian fishing rights. In 1940 he dispatched his assistant, John Herrick, to preside over a regional conference of Northwest superintendents as well as officials from the Indian Service and several other federal agencies. The central question, observed Herrick at the inaugural session, was whether the Indian Service should maintain Indian treaty rights or modify "some of those rights where they do not accord with conservation practices." Those in attendance expressed a greater willingness to accept a fish and game law imposed on the Indians by Congress. They also indicated concern about the Indians' subsistence needs and the effects of industrial pollution on fishing. Collier responded by ordering a major study of Indian fishing rights in the Pacific Northwest. In March 1941 he dispatched Edward G. Swindell, Jr., an Indian Service attorney in Los Angeles, to Oregon and Washington, instructing him to identify the "usual and accustomed places" through interviews and to review pertinent treaties, statutes, and judicial decisions.

Swindell completed his voluminous report (483 pages) in 1942. He organized the material into three sections, with the first being a careful historical and legal survey of Indian treaty rights. Part two contained copies of the many affidavits he had collected in interviews, and the final section presented the minutes of Stevens's treaty negotiations and a digest of the treaties.

Swindell's findings were quite balanced. His legal analysis confirmed the prevailing view that Indians had no special rights on ancient fishing sites except for ingress and egress and freedom from paying state fees. On the other hand, his investigation of Indian fishing practices disputed the claims of sportsmen's groups and state officials. Indian commercial fishing, he stated, centered in three areas: Puget Sound, Gray's Harbor, and the mid-Columbia. Using an analysis by the Fish and Wildlife Service of fishing statistics supplied by Washington and Oregon, Swindell maintained that Indian commercial fishermen in Puget Sound had taken only 2.4 percent of the total catch in 1938, 2.8 percent in 1939, and 6.7 percent in 1940. The percentages were much higher in the Gray's Harbor area, where Indian commercial operators caught 49.4 percent of the fish in 1938, 26 percent in 1939, and 54.8 percent in 1940. The percentages were higher there because the Quinault and Queets rivers flowed through the Quinault Reservation, where the Indians caught and sold sockeye salmon free of state controls. Outside the reservation, state regulations prohibited the possession and sale of this species. Swindell estimated that Indian commercial fishing on the Columbia ranged from 8.6 percent in

1938–39 to 7.6 percent in 1939–40. Indian fishing, he concluded, was an important means of livelihood for many tribesmen, but it made up a very small proportion of the total catch in the Pacific Northwest.

Swindell admitted that unregulated Indian commercial and subsistence fishing had contributed to the reduced fish population, but he believed that other causes were far more important. Especially significant were numerous violations of state regulations by whites, the destruction of spawning grounds by erosion and flooding, the obstructions of runs in upper streams by irrigation dams, and young salmon swimming into un-screened irrigation canals. To Swindell the recent public furor over the Indians' damage to fishing was unwarranted and whites had made them scapegoats.

Despite the thoroughness of Swindell's report, it had no impact on the adminis-tration of Indian affairs. Evidently preoccupied with the war and resulting dislocations in his office, Collier thanked Swindell for his "careful research" and "painstaking work" but did little more than note that the "report will be filed for future reference purposes." It remained undistributed until a decade later.

Shortly before Swindell filed his report, the U.S. Supreme Court ruled in early 1942 on *Tulee* v. *Washington*, an important test of the Indians' treaty rights to fish in their "usual and accustomed places" without state regulation. The Tulee case grew out of a comprehensive new law passed in 1937 by the Washington legislature to control licens-ing of commercial fishermen. Included in the act was a license fee of five dollars for op-erating a dip bag net, the most common fishing apparatus used by Indians along the Co-lumbia. State officials insisted that the new measure applied to Indians fishing at their traditional sites and, despite considerable resistance, forced them to secure licenses for the 1937 season. Sampson Tulee was arrested on May 6, 1939, for taking and selling fish without a license at Spearfish, Washington, and placed in the Klickitat County jail. As a member of the Yakima tribe, Tulee held treaty rights to fish where he was arrested, and federal attorneys quickly entered the case on his behalf. They first petitioned for a writ of *habeas corpus* before the U.S. District Court in Yakima on the grounds that the state could not force Indians to purchase licenses. Judge J. Stanley Webster denied their peti-tion on the grounds that requiring a license did not violate the Yakimas' treaty rights. Tulee's attorneys then appealed to the U.S. Circuit Court of Appeals in San Francisco. That court ruled on April 3, 1940, that it would not act on the *habeas corpus* petition un-til the state courts had judged the case and Tulee had exhausted possible remedies at that level. The following month Tulee was tried before a jury in the Klickitat Superior Court, found guilty, and given a minor fine. The Washington Supreme Court heard the case in January 1941 and by a vote of five to three upheld the lower court's opinion.

The correspondence between the federal attorneys and the Washington attorney general's office indicates that both sides hoped that a judgment on the Tulee case by the U.S. Supreme Court would not only determine the legality of the Indians' payment of fees but define state authority at off-reservation locations. The ruling was not a total vic-tory for either side. The high court noted that the "treaty takes precedence over state law and state conservation laws are void and ineffective insofar as their application would infringe on rights secured by treaty." The court limited itself only to the question of whether Tulee had to pay state fees. The remainder of the opinion was dicta, or non-binding. The court noted that the state fees were both revenue producing and regulatory, but the latter function could be achieved by other means. Imposing fees on Tulee was deemed illegal because the state was charging him for exercising a right his ancestors had reserved. The practical effect of the ruling was that a state could not charge fees to Indians fishing on traditional sites, but the states could still regulate by such means as limiting seasons, prescribing types of fishing equipment, and imposing catch limits.

In addition to Collier's policies and the Tulee decision, another important development of the period that affected Indian fishing rights was the construction of large dams on the Columbia River that destroyed some of the best "usual and accustomed places." Unlike the numerous small dams built before 1930 on the upper tributaries and mainly used for irrigation, the Rock Island, Grand Coulee, and Bonneville projects spanned the Columbia itself and were aimed primarily at harnessing the enormous hydroelectric potential of the river. Cheap electricity was widely proclaimed as the key to the economic development of the Pacific Northwest, especially for future growth in such areas as metal refining, chemicals, and synthetic fabrics.

Interest in the huge new dams on the Columbia predated the New Deal by several decades. Numerous studies of individual dam sites had been made by federal agencies in the past, but the Rivers and Harbors Act of 1925 authorized surveys of all navigable rivers of the United States, except the Colorado, to determine the potential for hydroelectricity, navigation, flood control, and irrigation. The following year the estimates were presented in House Document 308, and the surveys of the Columbia River and its tributaries were published in 1933. The so-called 308 Reports laid the foundation for the vast construction program of dams in the Pacific Northwest during the New Deal and postwar eras. The Calvin Coolidge and Herbert Hoover administrations had initiated the surveys, but Franklin D. Roosevelt immediately sensed their political importance and used a promise to start construction to good advantage in his 1932 presidential campaign.

Of the three major dams built on the Columbia before World War II, only the Rock Island was privately constructed. Located in central Washington, a few miles below Wenatchee, the site was purchased in early 1929 by the Puget Sound Light and Power Company, which by the end of 1931 had completed the $28 million project. Fish ladders installed at both ends of the dam permitted salmon and steelhead to pass over the fairly low obstacle.

Unlike the Rock Island, which was built solely for power generation, the two government dams started in 1933 were multipurpose in nature. Grand Coulee Dam, built in northeastern Washington as a PWA project under the Bureau of Reclamation, began to produce electricity in 1942 and after the mid 1950s supplied water for vast reclamation projects in the state. Bonneville Dam, near Vancouver, Washington, was a PWA project under the Corps of Engineers and completed in 1938. In addition to power generators, Bonneville included a set of locks that permitted large vessels to go upstream as far as The Dalles.

Although the issue of "fish vs. power" became especially keen in the postwar period, the construction of Grand Coulee and Bonneville dams gave an unsettling preview of future threats to the Indian fisheries on the Columbia. The damages of Grand Coulee to the Colville and Spokane Indians were twofold: First, the dam was so high that fish ladders could not be employed to permit fish to surmount the obstacle and reach the extensive spawning areas upstream; and second, the huge Franklin D. Roosevelt Lake created by Grand Coulee flooded Kettle Falls, one of the largest and most productive Indian fishing areas on the Columbia. The impact of Bonneville was less serious. Although the Bonneville reservoir flooded Cascade Falls, another major Indian fishing site, ladders at the dam permitted passage of salmon and steelhead upstream. The largest and most important Indian fishing area at Celilo Falls remained available for the Yakima, Warm Springs, Umatilla, and other groups.

The Indian Office initially did not protest the loss of Indian fishing sites on the Columbia. Collier apparently did not consider compensation for the Indians until the Solicitor's Office notified him in 1936 that the Indians might be entitled to damages caused by Bonneville Dam. There is no evidence that the commissioner sought monetary rewards or took any special interest in the Indians' plight. In 1939 the Corps of Engineers reached agreement with the Yakima, Warm Springs, and Umatilla tribes on six substitute fishing sites on the Bonneville reservoir. The Corps included $50,000 in its 1941 appropriation bill to acquire the sites and build such facilities as drying sheds, toilets, and access roads, but the money was lost when President Roosevelt vetoed all new construction because of national defense needs. Funds for the "in-lieu sites" finally won approval in 1945, but hampered by other duties and difficulties in finding suitable locations, the Corps five years later had only purchased one site. The delays embittered the Indians, whose disappointment continued even when sites were allegedly completed. Access remained difficult and facilities inadequate. In one case a fishing site was on a cliff above the shoreline. The record of the Bureau of Reclamation at Grand Coulee was similar. That agency delayed compensation for flooding Kettle Springs until after World War II, when the Colville and Spokane Indians received "paramount use" of a fourth of the area of Franklin D. Roosevelt Lake for hunting, fishing, and boating.

With the close of World War II the drive to complete the system of dams on the main stem of the Columbia and on the lower Snake threatened Indian fishing rights anew. The postwar plans envisioned eight new dams on the Columbia and four to six on the lower Snake to meet the Pacific Northwest's burgeoning demand for hydroelectric power. The need for electricity in 1947 was twenty-five percent greater than during the peak wartime years, while population in Washington and Oregon had grown forty percent between 1940 and 1947, compared to a national average of only eleven percent. Pressure for the dams also came from advocates of improved navigation. The four new dams projected above Bonneville and those planned for the lower Snake would permit barge traffic from The Dalles to Lewiston, Idaho. The prospect of a cheap transportation link between Lewiston and the Pacific Ocean proved highly attractive to agricultural and industrial interests of eastern Washington and western Idaho.

The major impact of postwar construction on Indian fishing rights would be the dam at The Dalles, which would flood Celilo Falls, the only remaining Indian fishing site of importance on the Columbia. The estimated annual commercial catch by Indians at Celilo from 1936 to 1943 was valued at $250,000, while the annual value of subsistence fishing during the same period was $134,000.

Changed leadership of Indian affairs in the postwar years produced considerable concern about Indian fishing rights. Collier had been replaced by William Brophy, who was preoccupied with decentralizing Indian administration and frequently absent from office because of illness. Moreover, mounting congressional hostility toward the BIA signaled the beginning of the termination policy and greater indifference for Indian welfare. Still, the record of the BIA in protecting Indian interests during the "fish vs. power" conflict reflected improvement over that of Collier's administration in the 1930s.

The BIA found new allies in its efforts to preserve Celilo Falls by forestalling construction of new dams. Some of the private interest groups which had been most inimical to Indian fishing rights in the 1930s now joined with the BIA because the new dams threatened to eradicate salmon on the Columbia. The private groups included the Columbia Basin Fisheries Development Association, the Oregon Wildlife Federation, the Columbia River Fishermen's Protective Union, and the Izaak Walton League. Within the Interior Department, similar realignments occurred. The Indian Office joined forces with the Fish and Wildlife Service, successor to the Bureau of Fisheries. Both agencies contended that the proposed fish ladders, turbines, and spillways associated with the new dams might destroy the Columbia fisheries. The agencies also enlisted the support of the National Park Service, which was concerned about damage to public recreation if sport fishing was harmed.

In opposition to the BIA and its allies were the Bureau of Reclamation and the Corps of Engineers. The Reclamation Bureau, then in the midst of completing the vast irrigation works made possible by Grand Coulee, endorsed the new dams for their electrical output but saw no pressing need for additional irrigated land during the next ten to fifteen years. The Corps of Engineers wanted the navigation link from The Dalles to Lewiston completed as rapidly as possible. The resulting interagency battle reached a decisive stage in early 1947, when both the Fish and Wildlife Service and the BIA recognized the futility of defeating the comprehensive plan and sought instead to reschedule the construction of the proposed dams. They asked that the McNary and The Dalles dams and those on the lower Snake River be delayed for at least ten years. Regional power needs, they argued, could be met by increasing the generating capacity at existing dams and by building new dams on the headwaters rather than on the lower Columbia and Snake. The rescheduling would permit the Fish and Wildlife Service to work out a possible solution for preserving a portion of the fish run above Bonneville and to revive or reestablish runs on the tributaries below that point.

The policy statement issued in March 1947 by Assistant Secretary of Interior Warner W. Gardner accepted most of the proposals of the Fish and Wildlife Service and the BIA. He rejected attempts to stop construction of McNary Dam, since Congress had authorized the project and appropriated some construction funds, but he endorsed rescheduling the other projects. Gardner's later statements indicated that he was unwilling to establish a moratorium of any fixed time. Gardner also recommended compensating the Indians for the eventual loss of Celilo Falls. Monetary payments would never be entirely satisfactory to the tribes affected, he acknowledged, but he proposed that the Indians be given exclusive fishing rights at sites on the lower Columbia and use of fish carcasses at hatcheries. Gardner also urged the tribes to develop alternative economic programs for members displaced from fishing. The federal government, he insisted, must pay a just amount for the loss of Celilo Falls with that amount determined either by negotiation with the Indians or by court decision. The expense of the settlement should be charged to construction costs and not to a special appropriation. "There is no difference in principle," he stressed, "between flooding out a white man's factory and an Indian's fishery."

The outcome of the fish vs. power struggle in succeeding years did not fulfill all of Gardner's expectations or entirely satisfy the Indians, but it followed the principle of just compensation. Hopes of a moratorium were lost when Congress authorized The Dalles Dam in 1950 and made the first appropriation for construction the following year.

A four-year study of the Indian catch at Celilo Falls by the Oregon Fish Commission, the Washington Department of Fisheries, and the Fish and Wildlife Service led the Corps of Engineers in 1951 to calculate the value of Indian fishing rights at $23 million. In 1953 the Corps negotiated settlements awarding the Warm Springs and Umatilla tribes over $4 million each. The Yakimas rejected the offer made to them and attempted unsuccessfully to block construction of the dam. They accepted a settlement of $15 million in 1954. All three tribes were represented by their own attorneys and aided by BIA officials during the negotiations. The receipt of the money was made contingent on the tribes devising economic programs to offset the loss of fishing revenues due to flooding of Celilo Falls. Later the Corps also negotiated a settlement with the Nez Perces, who belatedly claimed treaty rights, and paid the relocation costs of some Indians living at Celilo Falls. Unlike the endless delays and confusion of earlier settlements, the government acted promptly and offered reasonable compensation. The total award amounted to slightly under $27 million.

Typical of most claims settlements, the awards themselves created new difficulties. Some Indians later maintained that they had been promised in-lieu fishing sites on the lower Columbia, but the Corps of Engineers denied that such promises had been made or could have been made since it was impossible to secure new fishing areas downstream. Tribesmen who had moved to urban areas thought that using the settlement money to create economic programs on the reservations was unfair, and they demanded a per capita payment. The Indians who had actually fished at Celilo Falls complained that their settlements did not adequately compensate them for the loss of the fishing rights. Almost instinctively they sensed that the money would eventually be gone, although the fishing could have continued forever.

What sort of conclusions can be reached about Indian fishing rights in the New Deal and postwar period? Clearly Collier's record was lackadaisical. In contrast to his autobiographical accounts and the initial assessments by historians who depicted him as an aggressive defender of Indian rights and a reformer of major dimensions, more recent studies indicate that some New Deal Indian policies offered improvements but others were arbitrary and badly flawed. This view seems applicable to Collier's handling of Indian fishing rights. Despite the potential for improving the Indians' situation, Collier did not aggressively pursue a protective role but seemed content to respond in piecemeal fashion to problems.

Explaining these inadequacies presents difficulties because the records do not reveal a clear picture of Collier or his administration's motives. A partial explanation for Collier's weak role was his lack of familiarity with the complexities of Indian fishing rights. He apparently had never dealt with the problem extensively in the years before he became commissioner in 1933. An examination of his regular weekly (and later biweekly) reports to Interior Secretary Harold Ickes from 1934 to 1939 shows that Collier visited the Pacific Northwest only twice during the five years. Neither visit prompted him to comment on Indian fishing rights in subsequent reports. Collier did not broach the subject until July 1936, when the Solicitor's Office advised him that the Indians might be entitled to compensation because of flooding of fishing sites by Bonneville Dam. In sharp contrast, Collier's reports contain detailed information on the programs involving the Navajos and Pueblos. There may be more than passing validity to observations that Collier's inordinate interest in Southwestern Indians caused him to neglect Native Americans elsewhere.

On the other hand, Collier may have viewed the Indians of the Pacific Northwest as a kind of "cultural lost cause." In comparison to the Navajos, Pueblos, and other groups who had retained much of their cultural heritage, most Indians of Washington and Oregon had assimilated in dress, language, religion, economics, and psychology. While Collier expressed sympathy with Indians who caught and cured fish for subsistence, he seemed less interested in those who fished for commercial reasons. Moreover, given his strong interest in conservation, he may also have viewed state regulation of Indian commercial fishing as appropriate.

In Collier's defense, it must be noted that he lacked vital information needed to understand the situation in the Northwest. Reliable scientific data on salmon and steelhead runs did not exist until the late 1930s and the 1940s. Hatchery management was still quite crude, particularly in nutrition and disease control, while artificial propagation was widely regarded as a cure-all for decreased runs. Collier was unaware of recent technical findings, and until Swindell's study he lacked even general information on the destruction of spawning grounds by irrigation projects, the severe problems of stream pollution, the minor role of Indians in fish depletion, and the tendency of whites to blame all problems on Indians. Moreover, even Swindell was not fully cognizant of the severity of ecological disturbances caused by industrial pollution and the release by cities of raw sewage into rivers.

Collier became concerned about fishing rights only after 1939, when Congress threatened to impose stringent fish and game regulations on all reservations. Such restrictions violated his belief in Indian self-government and might have worked a serious hardship on Indians. To thwart the congressional threat, he encouraged tribal councils to regulate the taking of fish and game, supported the Tulee test case, and ordered Swindell's study. With the exception of the Tulee case, the dislocations of World War II halted even these modest efforts.

Different reasons explain Collier's failure to react to the threats to Indian fishing rights posed by Grand Coulee and Bonneville dams. The overwhelming importance of hydroelectric power to the Pacific Northwest during the 1920s and 1930s evidently convinced him that construction of the dams and destruction of Indian fishing sites were inevitable. The demand for electricity transcended partisan politics, and any attempt by Collier to block construction on behalf of preserving the Indian fishing sites would have been futile. Several legal peculiarities additionally hampered a defense of Indian fishing rights. The Indians did not hold title to the "usual and accustomed places" but rather enjoyed treaty rights to gain access to those "places" and to take fish. Thus this was not a situation where reservation lands were threatened by confiscation. Moreover, Indian tribes prior to passage of the Indian Claims Commission Act of 1946 could not file claims for damages against the federal government without special legislation, and Congress rarely gave such authorizations. Both these circumstances may help explain Collier's failure to seek damages for the loss of prime fishing sites on the Columbia. Certainly the war paralyzed efforts by the BIA to gain compensation, just as it stymied efforts to gain additional protection of Indian fishing rights against state regulation.

In the postwar drive to build dams, the situation changed rather dramatically. The creation of the Indian Claims Commission in 1946 doubtlessly made the BIA and other agencies aware that failure to indemnify the Indians for the loss of Celilo Falls would result in later claims cases. Moveover, the size of the $27 million settlement demonstrated that the BIA was fairly effective in meeting its trust responsibilities when the stakes were high, but less diligent and capable when handling the more mundane and day-to-day duties. In other words, the BIA previously had not always defended Indian fishermen from unfair treatment by state officials and private individuals because such episodes were commonplace and did not arouse wide public attention, but the postwar negotiations over the loss of Celilo Falls were reported widely in the national press and aired in congressional hearings. Such publicity and the importance of the issue motivated the BIA and the Corps of Engineers to act fairly and promptly in negotiating the rewards. Thus the Indian Office's traditional lack of strong constituency and a major voice in government was temporarily offset after 1945. The money awarded for the flooding of the last major Indian fishery on the Columbia may not have satisfied many tribesmen whose way of life centered around fishing, but the government rarely had met its responsibility as well.

Readings for Donald L. Parman:

Discussions of Indians' loss of natural resources abound. For fishing rights one of the most useful is Robert Doherty, *Disputed Waters: Native Americans and the Great Lakes Fishery* (Lexington: University Press of Kentucky, 1990). See also Michael Lawson, *Damned Indians: The Pick-Sloan Plan and the Missouri River Sioux, 1944–1980* (Norman: University of Oklahoma Press, 1982), and Jerry Krammer, *The Second Long Walk: The Navajo-Hopi Land Dispute* (Albuquerque: University of New Mexico Press, 1980). Donald L. Parman, *Indians and the American West in the Twentieth Century* (Bloomington: Indiana University Press, 1994) examines resource issues in the context of modern developments. Daniel L. Boxberger, *To Fish in Common: The Ethnohistory of Lummi Indian Salmon Fishing* (Lincoln: University of Nebraska Press, 1989) and Janet A. McDonnell, *The Dispossession of the American Indian, 1887–1934* (Bloomington: Indiana University Press, 1991) give other insights on related topics.

21

BUILDING TOWARD SELF-DETERMINATION: PLAINS AND SOUTHWESTERN INDIANS IN THE 1940s AND 1950s

PETER IVERSON

During the 1980s students of Native American history began to pay serious attention to the Indian experiences of the twentieth century. Such trends as population growth, urban migration, the development of pan-Indian groups and thought, and increasing success in dealing with the federal and state governments now receive careful attention. As tribal leaders and multitribal organizations strive for more authority over programs and funds earmarked for use in Indian communities, they call increasingly for self-determination—that is, for the right to decide their future. This selection examines the decades during and after World War II, when actions taken laid the groundwork for the more recent demands of self-determination. The text demonstrates how the process of rapid change worked when groups such as the National Council of American Indians and the later National Indian Youth Council mobilized opinion and directed attention to issues. Native American spokesmen and organizations lost several major battles, including the crucial fight over termination. Nevertheless, the discussion traces the development of a growing Indian self-awareness as tribes succeeded in developing or expanding local economic and cultural activities. At the same time, the author shows how tribal and pan-Indian groups increased Indian influence over policy creation and implementation. The narrative ties the developments of the 1940–60 era clearly to events of more recent decades.

Peter Iverson is a professor of history at Arizona State University.

Within the past decade more students of Indian history have turned their attention to the twentieth century. Until very recently the topical focus of this work has been primarily

Source: Copyright by Western History Association. Reprinted by permission. The article first appeared as "Building Toward Self-Determination: Plains and Southwestern Indians in the 1940s and 1950s," *Western Historical Quarterly* 16 (April 1985): 161–73.

in the area of federal Indian policy, and the chronological focus, for the most part, has been on the years before World War II. This article represents a change in both topic and time. It attempts to analyze the period from World War II until the beginning of the 1960s, with specific consideration given to Indians of the Plains and the Southwest.

This era is often referred to in the literature as the era of termination. During this time many members of Congress and the Truman and Eisenhower administrations made sporadic but persistent efforts to reduce or eliminate federal services and protection for American Indians. The public rhetoric spoke of liberating the Indians by reducing governmental interference. Termination sought to immerse Indians in the mainstreams of their counties and states. This crusade resulted in significant hardship for many Indians. Tribes such as Menominees in Wisconsin or the Klamaths in Oregon saw their reservation status ended. Indians who relocated to cities, with or without federal sponsorship, confronted many dilemmas. State and local agencies proved unwilling or unable to shoulder responsibilities previously bestowed upon the federal government. Economic development programs on reservations usually did not markedly improve unemployment, housing, and other critical problems.

Yet to label these years as the termination era and to emphasize so exclusively the negative aspects of this generation is to present an incomplete picture. We cannot ignore federal policy in our consideration of any period, for it always has an important effect. But the 1940s and 1950s are more than a time of troubles. Just as new research is starting to reveal the late nineteenth and early twentieth centuries as a time when Indians in many areas made important and necessary adjustments to continue their lives as Indians, so, too, a closer examination of this more recent era shows it to be a period in which tribalism and Indian nationalism were reinforced. Indeed, to a significant degree the threat and the enactment of terminationist policy often strengthened rather than weakened Indian institutions and associations. In addition, the attitudes of state and local officials, as well as the perspectives of urban residents, encouraged Indians throughout the nation to recognize increasingly their common bonds and needs.

During the 1940s and 1950s, then, Indians in growing numbers tried to identify and take advantage of their own economic resources and tried to affirm their identities as members of tribes and as Indians. They rejected the conventional wisdom that they would be "less Indian" if they gained more education, acquired new jobs, or moved to a new residence. Actually, greater contact with the larger American society promoted greater awareness that the English language, new technological skills, and other elements of the American culture could be used to promote a continuing, if changing, Indian America.

A review of Indian actions in two important regions—the Plains and the Southwest—reveals a vital maturation in Indian leadership and a reaffirmation of Indian identity in the 1940s and 1950s. Far from vanishing, Indians emerged from this generation more determined than ever to be recognized on their own terms. The more publicized activism of the late 1960s and 1970s thus may trace its origins to these ostensibly more quiet years.

World War II marks a critical turning point in modern American Indian history. Indians took great pride in their involvement in the war effort. For example, Cecil Horse, a Kiowa, remembered his son John winning a bronze star and a purple heart and in turn receiving from his people a war bonnet and a giveaway ceremony in his honor. Navajos celebrated their Codetalkers' role in the Pacific. In a publication of November 1945 the Office of Indian Affairs recorded the military honors earned by Indians and the investment by Indians in more than $17 million of restricted funds in war bonds. It quoted the instructions of Private Clarence Spotted Wolf, a Gros Ventre killed on December 21, 1944, in Luxembourg:

> If I should be killed, I want you to bury me on one of the hills east of the place where my grandparents and brothers and sisters and other relatives are buried. If you have a memorial service, I want the soldiers to go ahead with the American flag. I want cowboys to follow, all on horseback. I want one of the cowboys to lead one of the wildest of the T over X horses with saddle and bridle on. I will be riding that horse.

The war generated more than memories and emotions. It meant that Indians had become more a part of the larger world in which they lived. As Ella Deloria, the Dakota linguist, wrote in 1944: "The war has indeed wrought an overnight change in the outlook, horizon, and even the habits of the Indian people—a change that might not have come for many years yet." Through the service, through off-reservation experiences, and through wage work, Indian perspectives and Indian economies began to change. Returning veterans and other participants in the war effort recognized the significance of better educational opportunities. Navajo Scott Preston put it simply: "We have to change and we have to be educated."

Change also demanded organization. Indian delegates from fifty tribes, hailing from twenty-seven states, met November 15–18, 1944, in Denver to organize the National Congress of American Indians (NCAI). In the words of one of the congress' first presidents, N. B. Johnson, the delegates set "an example for speed, diplomacy and harmony." Within four days they "adopted a constitution and formally launched the organization in an effort to bring all Indians together for the purpose of enlightening the public, preserving Indian cultural values, seeking an equitable adjustment of tribal affairs, securing and preserving their rights under treaties with the United States, and streamlining the administration of Indian affairs." In subsequent meetings in Browning, Montana, in 1945 and Oklahoma City in 1946, those in attendance proved to be, according to Johnson, "a cross-section of Indian population: old and young, full-bloods, mixed-bloods, educated and uneducated Indians from allotted areas and others from reservations," all of whom "were dissatisfied with many phases of the government's administration of Indian affairs." Improved health care and educational opportunities, protection of Indian land rights, and increased Indian veterans' benefits were advocated. The National Congress of American Indians urged the U.S. Congress and the current administration "not to enact legislation or promulgate rules and regulations thereunder affecting the Indians without first consulting the Tribes affected."

Such, of course, would not be the case. In both the Truman and Eisenhower administrations the federal government proceeded to pass legislation and carry out policies contrary to the will of the vast majority of American Indians. For many Americans the Indian war record had prompted concern that Indians be treated fairly. O. K. Armstrong's influential article in the August 1945 *Reader's Digest* urged America to "Set the American Indians Free!" House of Representatives Majority Leader John W. McCormack read Armstrong's piece advocating the removal of "restrictions" from Indians and wrote to his colleague W. G. Stigler that he was "interested in seeing justice done for all—and this applies with great force to our fine American Indians." Cherokee/Creek historian Tom Holm has properly summarized what happened: "In the end, fighting the White man's war gained sympathy for American Indians but it also fueled a fire that they did not want and eventually found difficult to extinguish."

While they were not without effective allies, Indians had to lead the fight against Public Law 280, House Concurrent Resolution 108, and other features of termination. Protests against such measures soon resounded throughout the West. Through a variety of means, Indians attempted to ward off the implementation of a policy they realized could bring them great harm. In the early years voices from tribal councils and business committees rang out against a specific action in a particular locale. For example, Richard Boynton, Sr., and George Levi of the Cheyenne-Arapaho business committee telegrammed Oklahoma congressman Toby Morris to protest against the impending closing of the Cheyenne-Arapaho school in El Reno. Kiowa leader Robert Goombi argued that abolishing the Concho Indian School would be counterproductive. Yet as the wider pattern of the era emerged, multitribal associations were strengthened as a more effective means of presenting a more powerful Indian voice.

The National Congress of American Indians therefore continued to expand in its influence in the years that followed its establishment in 1944. Plains and Southwestern Indian peoples remained active in the executive ranks of the organization throughout the 1940s and 1950s. In the mid 1950s over half the elected members of the executive council would come from regional tribes, including the Osages, Gros Ventres, Gila River Pimas, Taos Pueblos, Blackfeet, Oglala Sioux, and Cheyenne-Arapahoes. Colorado River tribes, Hualapais, Omahas, and the San Carlos Apaches appointed additional representatives. Oglala Sioux Helen Peterson served as executive director; Papago Thomas Segundo was regional representative.

The NCAI filled two critical functions. It helped Indians speak out against termination, but it also advocated programs that would contribute to Indian social, political, and economic revitalization. Through publicity releases from its Washington office, specially called tribal forums, and other means, the congress directly confronted the forces favoring termination. John Rainer from Taos Pueblo thus in 1950 attacked Commissioner of Indian Affairs Dillon Myer for imposing "drum head justice" upon Indians by denying tribes the power to choose their own attorneys.

The organization did more than criticize. It manifested a maturing capacity to articulate counterproposals when it offered suggestions to reduce Indian poverty, improvements for health care and educational facilities, and provisions to use reservation resources more effectively. A specific example—the Point Nine Program—was formulated and adopted by the congress in November 1954. It addressed critical questions relating to such matters as land and water resources, planning, credit, land purchase, and job training. Pointing to the assistance provided by the United States to underdeveloped countries around the world, Helen Peterson and other leaders demanded that this country apply the same principles within its borders.

Indians addressed the issues of the day through other forums as well. The Association on American Indian Affairs (AAIA), under the direction of Oliver La Farge, helped publicize both the dangers of federal policy and Indian moves to oppose it. Thus when the NCAI mobilized Indian representatives from twenty-one states and Alaska to come to Washington, D.C., on February 25–28, 1954, to protest impending legislation, *Indian*

Affairs, the newsletter of AAIA, not only gave extensive coverage but also proper credit to NCAI for its actions. Other institutions and organizations put together symposia for the examination of contemporary Indian well-being. Tribal spokesmen from the Plains and the Southwest participated vigorously in such gatherings, be it the annual meeting of the American Anthropological Association in Tucson in 1954 or the annual conference on Indian affairs at the University of South Dakota's Institute of Indian Studies.

By the end of the era new forums had been sought for the expression of Indian views. In 1961 representatives from sixty-four tribes, totaling approximately seven hundred delegates, met in Chicago to create the Declaration of Indian Purpose. They did not all agree with one another, but the so-called Chicago Conference was an important landmark in modern Indian affairs because of its size and its impact upon many of the participants.

Another example is the National Indian Youth Council (NIYC), which came into being soon thereafter. The NIYC had its roots in the annual conferences of the Southwest Association on Indian Affairs, beginning in 1956. This one-day session at the St. Francis Auditorium in Santa Fe brought Indian community people together with high school and college students, with the latter speaking to the former about their studies and the applicability of these studies to the communities. From this local beginning, the conference became regional in its focus in 1957 and was called the Southwest Regional Indian Youth Council. The council held annual conferences in the spring until April 1961, when the last meeting was held in Norman, Oklahoma. According to the Tewa anthropologist Alfonso Ortiz, "It was a core group from these youth councils, augmented later by alumni of D'Arcy McNickle's Indian Leadership Training Programs, who founded the NIYC in Gallup after the American Indian Chicago Conference was held in June."

Other experiences and associations prompted heightened pan-Indian feelings. Relocation programs to American cities brought Indians into contact with non-Indians indifferent to tribal distinctions. Prejudice sometimes spurred pan-Indian identification. The formation of Indian communities and intertribal marriages in the cities also could foster such sentiments.

The Cherokee anthropologist Robert K. Thomas and other observers have noted that this movement frequently had a pan-Plains quality to it. Thomas also suggested that within the Southwest something of a pan-Puebloism could be perceived. Pan-Indianism, as it continued to evolve during this time, could be "very productive, as nationalist movements often are, in literature and the arts," but it also developed institutions dealing with non-Indians. One such development was the growth of powwows—a source of pleasure and pride for participants and enjoyment and education for spectators.

A final example of the pan-Indian movement in the 1940s and 1950s that should be cited is the Native American Church. It found significant support within the Plains and the Southwest, and leaders for the organization frequently hailed from these regions. At the tribal level, the Native American Church increased its membership during this period. Many Indians looked to participation within the peyote religion as a way of accommodating the various demands of modern life and reaffirming their identities as Indians. In Montana perhaps half the Crows and many Cheyennes embraced the church. Adherents included prominent tribal leaders such as Robert Yellowtail, Crow, and Johnnie Woodenlegs, Northern Cheyenne. Frank Takes Gun also emerged as an important, if controversial, church leader.

Attitudes toward the practice of the faith varied considerably, to be sure, from one Indian community to another and within communities. In the Navajo nation the peyote religion grew considerably in its membership during the 1950s, despite an antagonistic stance taken against it by the tribal chairman, Paul Jones. Raymond Nakai gained the chairmanship in 1963 in part because he pledged to stop harassing the Native American Church. On the Wind River reservation in Wyoming, Northern Arapaho political and traditional leaders became more conciliatory toward the well-established practice. As was true in many tribes, the Arapahoes often added the Native American Church to prior participation in other religious ceremonies, be they Christian or traditional.

The reservation continued in the 1940s and 1950s as a centrally important place for religious observances, but for other reasons as well. The guiding philosophy of federal policy dictated that reservations were economic dead ends. After all, people were supposed to relocate because there were not enough jobs being generated at home. Since the land, families, familiarity, and, indeed, everything that went into the definition of home continued to be valued so deeply, Indian communities within the Plains and the Southwest endeavored to keep more of their citizens at home. While organizations such as the NCAI could advocate local development of resources, such development had to be prompted and managed.

Navajo economic and political development has been described elsewhere in some detail. In the face of termination Navajos who distrusted state governments and desired to maintain a working ethnic boundary between themselves and whites had little choice during the era but to pursue a more nationalistic approach. With large sums newly available to the tribal treasury from mineral revenues, the Navajo tribal government became far more ambitious. Federal assistance through the long-range rehabilitation program also assisted internal Navajo development. While the 1960s and 1970s would bring more fully to fruition some of these plans and programs, the 1940s and 1950s were crucial in the reinforcement of a working tribal identity and a commitment to a revitalized tribal economy.

Arts and crafts came to command a more important place in many tribal economies in the Southwest. For the Navajos, silversmithing and weaving continued to be vital sources of income. Pottery also gained widening acclaim, particularly at San Ildefonso, but also in other Pueblo communities along the Rio Grande and at some of the Hopi villages. Silverwork at the Hopi and Zuni pueblos, basket weaving especially among the Papagos and Walapais, the paintings of such artists as Fred Kabotie, Hopi, and Harrison Begay, Navajo, and the sculpture of Alan Hauser, Apache, also found appreciative audiences. Though the boom in Indian art had yet to arrive, a foundation had been established.

Cattle ranching represented another important element in economic development. On the San Carlos Apache reservation the cattle industry underwent significant alteration. The tribal council in October 1956 approved Ordinance 5–56 to reorganize and consolidate existing associations and implement various reforms in grazing regulations and practices. Improved range management could be combined with maintenance of cooperative efforts among the people of San Carlos. Cattle sales created some income for most families in the tribe. The quality of the Apaches' Herefords consistently attracted cattle buyers from throughout the West and generated a positive image of the Apaches to the non-Indian residents of Arizona.

Similarly, the Northern Arapahos gained greater control over their tribal ranch established during the Indian New Deal. With the assistance of an attorney, the tribe eventually was able to hire a ranch manager and to have the ranch's trustees be Arapahos appointed by the Arapaho business council. This sizeable operation returned a consistent profit to each Arapaho. As with the San Carlos Apaches, the ranching enterprise contributed to tribal self-esteem, the status of the tribal government, and an enhanced view of the Arapahos among outsiders, including the Shoshones who shared the Wind River reservation.

In 1950 the tribal council of the Pine Ridge reservation in South Dakota passed a tax of three cents per acre for grazing privileges on tribal lands. The tax met with strenuous objections by white cattle ranchers. In the face of such opposition the Department of the Interior quickly assigned responsibility of collecting the tax to the Sioux. By 1956 white ranchers had challenged the tax in court, but in the following year the U.S. District Court judge ruled against them, contending that Indian tribes were "sovereign powers and as sovereign powers can levy taxes."

Greater assertion of Sioux power was not limited to Pine Ridge. Under the leadership of Chairman Frank Ducheneaux, the Cheyenne River tribal council approved a firm resolution against Public Law 280. Both on Rosebud and on Pine Ridge, tribal voters in 1957 overwhelmingly defeated the assumption of state jurisdiction in South Dakota on Indian reservations. Opposition to repeated efforts to institute state jurisdiction led in 1963 to the formal organization of the United Sioux Tribes.

By 1959 the Rosebud Sioux tribal chairman, Robert Burnette, had filed complaints of discrimination under the Civil Rights Act of 1957 before the Civil Rights Commission. Burnette contended that Indians in South Dakota had been excluded from juries, had been beaten and chained in prisons, and generally had been greeted as people without equal rights in the state. While the commission was not very responsive to Burnette's allegations, the very act of publicly challenging local conditions indicated that a more activist stance would be assumed in the 1960s.

In the Dakotas, Wyoming, Arizona, and elsewhere, then, the growing importance of attorneys could be observed. For many tribes the establishment of the Indian Claims Commission in 1945 had prompted their first acquisition of some form of legal counsel. While the Bureau of Indian Affairs in the 1950s had often discouraged tribal use of attorneys or tried to dictate the choice of a specific firm, by decade's end it was clear that legal assistance would play a vital role in many realms of tribal life.

Williams v. *Lee* is a useful example of this evolution. Called by Chemehuevi attorney Fred Ragsdale "the first modern Indian law case," *Williams* v. *Lee* involved a non-Indian trader on the Navajo reservation who sued a Navajo in the state court to collect for goods sold on credit. While the Arizona Supreme Court ruled in favor of the trader, the U.S. Supreme Court reversed this decision. Justice Hugo Black, on behalf of the Court, stated: "There can be no doubt that to allow the exercise of state jurisdiction here would undermine the authority of the tribal courts over Reservation affairs and hence would infringe on the right of the Indians to govern themselves." This landmark decision served as a crucial statement in support of tribal sovereignty, presaging additional legal battles to be waged in the years to come.

In any reappraisal of the 1940s and 1950s, it is important to not overstate the case. The negative aspects of the period remain, even with the vital developments outlined above. And in a treatment of this length, some events of magnitude must be slighted. For example, the damming of the Missouri River created great hardship for the Indian peoples of that area. Scholars have correctly underlined the problems that seemed to exist everywhere, from the most isolated reservations to the largest city.

Nonetheless, a more careful examination yields a more balanced picture. In overdramatizing the difficulties of the time, we may not give sufficient credit to the enduring nature of Indians in this country. By the end of the 1950s tribal resources were more studied and better understood; tribal council leadership was often more effective. The Salish scholar and writer D'Arcy McNickle appreciated the transition that had taken place. He spoke in 1960 of the growing Indian movement toward self-determination. Indians in the future, he suggested, would "probably use the white man's technical skills for Indian purposes." McNickle affirmed that "Indians are going to remain Indian . . . a way of looking at things and a way of acting which will be original, which will be a compound of these different influences."

The 1940s and 1950s not only witnessed a change in Indian policy and a resurgence of pressures to assimilate Indians into the larger society, but they also saw maturation and growth of Indian leadership at the local and national levels and efforts to develop tribal institutions, as well as a reaffirmation of identity and a willingness to adapt and change in the face of new conditions. In the immediate future seemingly new demands would resound for self-determination. Yet these demands were firmly based upon a foundation gradually constructed in the previous generation.

Readings for Peter Iverson:

Twentieth-century issues get particular attention in Iverson's own *The Plains Indians of the Twentieth Century* (Norman: University of Oklahoma Press, 1985) and *When Indians Became Cowboys: Native Peoples and Cattle Ranching in the American West* (Norman: University of Oklahoma Press, 1994). Kenneth L. Philp has edited *Indian Self Rule: First-Hand Accounts of Indian-White Relations from Roosevelt to Reagan* (Salt Lake City, UT: Howe Brothers, 1986) which contains first person accounts of Indians describing their experiences with federal policies and helps to humanize some of the issues. Graham D. Taylor, *The New Deal and American Indian Tribalism* (Lincoln: University of Nebraska Press, 1980) gives background for Iverson's ideas.

22

LISTENING TO THE NATIVE VOICE

MARGARET CONNELL SZASZ

American Indian Schooling in the Twentieth Century

Throughout American history the government, educators, and church officials sought to acculturate Indians. This effort, beginning with the earliest Spanish activities in North America, persisted to the near present. As the United States expanded its control over the tribes, efforts to force them to send their children to the white man's schools intensified, and by the late nineteenth century increasing numbers of Indian children spent years living at off-reservation boarding schools. These institutions did their best to strip the children of their language, religion, and cultural practices, and to replace those with English and work skills.

This essay examines the changes that have taken place in the Indian educational system during the twentieth century. In it the author presents three basic shifts or developments that led to today's system for educating the children of reservation dwellers. These began during the 1930s and have continued to the present as the tribes moved from their status as administered people to groups now enjoying a measure of self-determination. It is necessary to remember, however, that government schools did not replace tribal efforts to pass on language and culture that occurred in the reservation homes and villages. Rather, Indians saw the schools as adding to their existing knowledge and not taking the place of traditional knowledge, something usually overlooked by white teachers and government officials.

Margaret Connell Szasz is a professor of history at the University of New Mexico.

In her poem, "Leaves Like Fish," Pacific Northwest poet Gladys Cardiff, who is of Cherokee descent, writes of an enduring form of schooling:

Source: Margaret Connell Szasz, "Listening to the Native Voice: American Indian Schooling in the Twentieth Century," *Montana: The Magazine of Western History* (Vol. 39, Summer 1989), 42–53.

267

Cottonwood, willow, and briar,
Night air billows in the dark grove,
Hauls the alders over, their leaves

Jumping, spilling silver bellied on the lawn;
The lighted wind is running with a flood
Of green fish, phosphorescent and wild

On the winter grass, breaking like struck matches
Without warmth or place, random as green
    minnows.
Above the cloud the sky waits, one-celled,

Expanded over tides and winds, loving
The south wind as much as the north,
Schooling the planets in discretion and form.

For centuries, Native Americans have educated their children in "discretion and form," and most of them were still engaged in this ancient task as the twentieth century opened. Those Indian children who did not attend a white-run school were well-educated in skills for maturity, and even those who did go to school experienced the early stages of this native training before leaving their homes.

Historically, whites have underestimated or ignored the wisdom of Native American child rearing. As diverse as other aspects of native culture, native education nonetheless shared some common characteristics that transcended cultural boundaries. Whether native children were reared beneath the shadow of the Rocky Mountains, along the upper Missouri River, or among the redwoods of northern California, they were expected to learn specific skills for maturity. They were taught endurance and patience, and they committed stories and other knowledge to memory. They also learned that it helped to cultivate a lively sense of humor, which provided a partial reprieve if a "joking cousin" ridiculed foolish behavior, such as stumbling into a bee's nest. Autobiographies of American Indians and Alaska Natives, studies by anthropologists, and accounts by missionaries and others who have had the privilege of observing native child rearing attest to the complexity and holistic nature of this form of education.

From the earliest post-contact times, the strength of this traditional education led American Indians and Alaska Natives to view EuroAmerican schooling as an overlay to their own diverse educational systems. During the 1600s, Franciscan priests taught Rio Grande Puebloans to read Spanish; the Puebloans added this to their native oral tradition. During the 1700s, tutors at the College of William and Mary taught eastern Algonquians to read and write English; some of these Algonquians became translators. During the 1800s, Methodist missionary "Father" James Wilbur thrust the "Bible and the plow" upon the Yakimas in the Columbia River Plateau: the schooled Yakimas added literacy to their skills in fishing, hunting, and gathering. By 1900, Euro-American schooling had provided an additional educational option for thousands of Indian youth. Missionaries, Indian and white schoolmasters, traders, educational leaders among the Five Civilized Tribes, and, finally, the federal government had gotten into the act.

At the turn of the century, most Native Americans still did not perceive this Euro-American schooling as a substitute for their native education. It had not become a replacement in the same sense that iron pots had replaced basket or clay pots or rifles had replaced bows and arrows. Most American Indians saw Euro-American schooling as an *addition* to their own child-rearing traditions. Moreover, as with other aspects of Euro-American culture, they approached it selectively, gauging their adaptation according to their own experience—individually, culturally, and historically.

A young Hopi illustrated this selectivity. During the early 1900s, after Talayesva had returned from Sherman Institute, a Bureau of Indian Affairs boarding school in California, he asked his uncles and fathers how to make a living. They replied: "Talayesva, you must stay home and work hard like the rest of us. Modern ways help a little; but the Whites come and go, while we in Hopi stay on forever."

Hopi perseverance in the twentieth century has brought them their own school. Although Hopi children began to attend boarding school at nearby Keams Canyon during the late nineteenth century, they waited almost one hundred years until the federal government built a junior-senior high school for them in Polacca. When "Hopi Dunawakni" opened its doors for five hundred students in 1986, one Hopi wrote:

> Our school is for us
> It is for our community, ourselves
> It is also for all our people
> It is a beginning.
> Look.
> Look what Hopi has done.
> Look what Hopi has.
> Teach us Hopi.
> It is so.

The Hopi achievements symbolize the direction of change for Indian schooling. The Hopi Tribe and its counterparts, some four hundred diverse tribal groups around the nation, have been urging the federal government to listen to their needs and to their wishes, and in recent decades the government has finally begun to open its ears to the many voices of Indian people. The story of twentieth century Indian schooling, therefore, is largely the story of when and how this listening has come into being.

When the twentieth century opened, only a fragment of the Native American population had survived the devastating effects of disease, warfare, and removal. In 1900, the Bureau of the Census reported that fewer than 250,000 Americans claimed to be American Indian, and Seattle photographer Edward S. Curtis had already committed himself to documenting what he and many contemporary Americans perceived as the "vanishing race." About half of the children of these erroneously labeled "vanishing Americans"— about 21,500 children— attended school. The responsibility had shifted from Catholic and Protestant mission schools to federal BIA schools.

The Five Civilized Tribes proved to be the major exception to this trend; they continued to direct their own widely acclaimed schools until the Curtis Act brought an end to this lively tradition shortly after the turn of the century. In 1900, those Indian children who were enrolled in school attended BIA day schools and BIA boarding schools both on and off the reservations. The twenty-five off-reservation BIA boarding schools had already attracted the public eye through the shrewd publicity campaigns of Captain Richard Henry Pratt, who founded the famous Carlisle Indian School in 1879. The school's highly visible profile had led to a rapid proliferation of off-reservation boarding schools in the West, in locations such as Chemawa, Albuquerque, Chilocco, Haskell, Santa Fe, Phoenix, Pierre, and Flandreau. In 1900, therefore, outside of the Five Civilized Tribes, BIA schools dominated Indian education: one percent of the Indian children who were enrolled in school attended public school; 15 percent were in mission schools; and over 80 percent were in BIA schools.

This was the statistical picture in formal Indian schooling at the turn of the century. Some nine decades later, the portrait had turned upside down. During the 1980s, the Indian population in the United States has hovered at about 1.4 million people; over 95 per cent of all Indian children, or almost 400,000, are enrolled in school. The BIA's responsibility for education has declined dramatically, and the number of Indian children in BIA schools has dropped accordingly. Less than 10 percent of all Indian children enrolled in school attend a BIA school, and most of them on reservations. More importantly, of the 168 BIA schools, 65 are contract schools, responsible to and directed by Indian tribes. These contract schools educate 39 percent of all children in BIA-funded institutions. Only a handful of the off-reservation boarding schools remain, including those at Sherman, Flandreau, Ft. Wingate, Riverside, Chemawa, and Sante Fe (Phoenix Indian School was scheduled to close in 1990). Today, public schooling dominates Indian education. About 5 percent of Indian children enrolled in school attend mission or private schools; almost 10 percent attend BIA-directed or contract schools; and about 85 percent are enrolled in public schools.

Post-secondary education has also undergone a tremendous growth during the late twentieth century. Currently, some ninety thousand Indians are attending colleges and universities. Of this number, about four thousand are enrolled in Indian-controlled colleges and other post-secondary institutions; about five thousand are enrolled in graduate schools; and about one thousand are enrolled in professional schools. In 1988, the BIA operated two post-secondary institutions: Haskell Indian Junior College in Lawrence, Kansas, and Southwestern Indian Polytechnic Institute in Albuquerque. In 1988, the Institute for American Indian Arts in Santa Fe made a dramatic change: it became a congressionally chartered institution, acquiring a status similar to that held by the Smithsonian Institution.

Indian schooling during the twentieth century has undergone three upheavals: an increase of Indians enrolled in school, a shift to the public school, and a transfer of school leadership and direction from the federal government to the Indians. Contrary to popular perception, these changes did not emerge spontaneously amidst the turmoil of the 1960s and 1970s. The roots of the schooling innovations of those tumultuous decades reach back to the 1930s and to World War II.

From 1900 to 1928, federal decisions on Indian education emanated largely from outside the Indian world. Indian families could hide their children when outsiders attempted to take them away to boarding school, or they could accept schooling as an opportunity. But once their children were in school, families and communities generally lost their voice. During those early years, most Indian parents had not attended school themselves, and they did not understand those foreign institutions.

The first glimmer of change came in the late 1920s. In 1928, the federal government published a severe critique of the BIA in a study that became known as the Meriam Report. In its censure of Indian education, the Meriam Report lambasted the BIA boarding schools for their gross inadequacies and their insensitivity to the needs of Indian children. A strongly worded government response to the Indian reform movement in the 1920s, the Meriam Report was a watershed in twentieth century Indian education, but its importance lies not in its immediate accomplishments in BIA schooling. In fact, the changes recommended by W. Carson Ryan, Jr., who was largely responsible for the education section and who later directed BIA education, were only partially implemented. The Meriam Report signaled the end of an era. It suggested to the Indian people that the federal government might become responsive to their needs, and it recommended a program for change. The report's credibility was partly due to the presence on the staff of educator Henry Roe Cloud (Winnebago), a prominent Indian leader.

At the same time, another change in Indian schooling was gaining momentum. By the end of the 1920s, Indian children had begun to enroll in public schools in such numbers that the scales weighing public versus BIA schools were already tipping in favor of public schools. The federal government had reimbursed public schools for the enrollment of Indian students since 1891, but during the early years the financial incentive for the schools—ten dollars per student—did not result in rapid growth. By 1930, however, the prevailing pattern of the twentieth century was established: more than half of all Indian children who were enrolled in school were attending public schools.

During the 1930s, Carson Ryan, who directed BIA education from 1930 to 1935, simplified the procedures for getting federal funds to those public schools that enrolled Indians. Following the pattern adopted by Oklahoma, Ryan urged state departments of education to contract directly with the Secretary of the Interior for the funding rather than having the Department reimburse individual school districts as it had been. In 1934, Congress legalized the new arrangement in the Johnson O'Malley Act, soon shortened to "J-O'M."

J-O'M simplified public school funding by allowing for direct contracting with the states, but for many decades the program was not held accountable to the Indian people. J-O'M enabled the states to create independent enclaves of control over the funding procedure, and state departments of education eventually began to use these monies as all-purpose slush funds. Although Indian children enrolled in public schools had special needs that J-O'M should have addressed, such as school lunches and bilingual instruction, most of the departments turned a deaf ear to their Indian constituents from the 1930s through the 1960s.

The BIA directors for education during the 1930s and 1940s also struggled to improve the fossilized federal Indian school system. Under the guidance of Ryan and his successor, Willard Walcott Beatty, BIA schooling began to move in new, largely positive directions, although the changes continued to emanate from largely outside the Indian community. The educational reforms of these two prominent leaders were an integral part of John Collier's Indian New Deal.

Transferring his aggressive leadership of the 1920s reform movement to his equally aggressive leadership as commissioner of Indian affairs between 1933 and 1945, Collier provoked such controversy that he has seldom been out of the limelight since. Responsible for dramatic, although sometimes oppressive, policy changes, including the passage of the Indian Reorganization Act (sometimes known as the Wheeler-Howard Act) in 1934, Collier also created a favorable milieu for education directors Ryan and Beatty. Collier's long-term interest in the concept of community gave encouragement to the directors' not always successful efforts to establish community day schools.

Throughout the 1930s, Ryan and Beatty sought to follow the recommendations that Ryan had made in the Meriam Report. Against strong local opposition, they closed a number of boarding schools and improved physical conditions in those that remained. They broadened boarding school curricula and added courses that examined the richness of Indian cultures, such as the art programs at the Santa Fe Indian School and a course in Indian history at Chilocco. Beatty's sensitivity to cultural diversity led him to introduce two innovations: summer in-service training sessions that instructed BIA teachers in some of the unique dimensions of their specialized work, and a bilingual publishing project that relied on Indian artists such as Andrew Tsihnajinnie (Navajo) and Andrew Standing Soldier (Sioux) to illustrate stories written for Sioux, Pueblo, and Navajo children.

Beatty was moving in new directions, and his innovations were often responsive to the needs of Indian children. But as the 1930s drew to a close the momentum of educational change engendered by the Meriam Report and the Indian New Deal slowed. During World War II, it ceased altogether. In the area of Indian education, World War II was a watershed. If the Meriam Report and the Ryan-Beatty innovations provided the backdrop for the educational breakthroughs of the 1960s and 1970s, the Second World War and its aftermath of termination and relocation offered the grist for change.

Statistics tell part of the story. Indians were in the forefront of volunteers for the armed services during the war. Months before the bombing of Pearl Harbor, Indians began leaving the boarding schools to enlist. By the end of the war, over twenty-four thousand Indians had served in the armed forces, and the effects of the war had reached deep into the reservations. Over fifty thousand Indians found work in war-related jobs, some of them located near the reservations but others, such as those at aircraft factories and shipyards on the Pacific Coast, in frenetic urban centers. Probably the most famous group of Indians from those years was the Navajo Code Talkers, whose unique communication skills were vital for American victory in the Pacific.

Assessing the impact of the war on individual Indians and on tribes and education, however, is more difficult than compiling statistics. Most Americans have heard of Ira Hayes (Pima), the private first class marine who helped raise the U.S. flag at Iwo Jima, but few have encountered N. Scott Momaday's *House Made of Dawn* or Leslie Marmon Silko's *Ceremony,* which probe the inner struggles of Indian veterans in the post-war world. Nor are many Americans aware of the revolutionary role played by those Indian veterans from World War II, Korea, and Vietnam who moved into leadership positions in their tribes and in the pan-Indian organizations that have multiplied since the National Congress of American Indians was founded in 1944. Those Indian veterans would not acquiesce to the BIA bureaucrats who tried to dominate tribal-government relations, but they were not able to deny the need for schooling.

During the first months of World War II, Indian students at Chilocco claimed that Indians "do not know the value of an education." But that attitude soon began to change. The war had a direct effect on Indian education: partially schooled Navajos saw their non-English-speaking friends rejected for the service, Indian veterans were able to continue their education with the aid of the GI Bill of Rights or the Vocational Rehabilitation Bill, and tribes began to set aside funds for educational scholarships and to pass tribal laws for compulsory schooling. In addition, personal war-time experiences broadened Indians' perceptions of the significance of schooling in ways that few could have foreseen in the 1930s.

After the war, Willard Beatty led BIA schooling in directions that responded to what he perceived as changing tribal needs. During the early years of the century, BIA Superintendent Estelle Reel and others had designed curricula that theoretically trained Indian youth for life on the reservations. But BIA schools at that time were geared neither to reservation nor to mainstream, urban life; beyond training in basic literacy and arithmetic, students learned vocational skills, such as carpentry, shoemaking, and baking, which often contributed to the schools' maintenance. Teachers and staff at the schools gave little or no recognition to the cultures from which the students had come and to which they would likely return. During the 1930s, Ryan and Beatty responded to changing tribal needs. They had tried to move Indian education away from the drudgery of institutional maintenance toward practical vocational training and from the denigration of native cultures toward a celebration of their diversity and uniqueness.

After World War II, however, the cross-cultural focus of the 1930s seemed hopelessly out of date. Thousands of Indians had lived away from their reservations, and even those who had remained had moved toward a cash economy. A new mood took hold: Indians and tribes wanted not only more education, they also wanted education that would help them survive in the non-Indian world. Beatty responded most dramatically to these changes when he created the Navajo Special Program, which established five-year programs offering basic education, vocational training, and practical skills for survival in mainstream culture to thousands of "overage" Navajo youth ranging in age from twelve to eighteen years.

After Beatty left the BIA in 1952, Hildegard Thompson, his successor, struggled to realize one of Beatty's goals: providing schooling for all native children. By creating yet another program for Navajo children (fourteen thousand of whom were still not in school) and programs for Mississippi Choctaws and Alaska Natives, Thompson was able to provide schooling for most of the nineteen thousand Indian children who were not enrolled in school in 1952. In keeping with the post-war congressional mood of mainstreaming American Indians, Thompson was a strong advocate of public schooling for Indians, and the number of Indian children attending public school continued to grow during her years as director of BIA education.

Thompson's flexibility enabled her to survive some of the most traumatic years for Indians. From 1946 until the end of the 1950s, Congress attempted to dismantle the legal relationship between Indian tribes and the federal government and to provide material incentives through the relocation program for Indians to move into cities. Thompson remained at the BIA well into the 1960s as an important transitional figure. But it was the end of an era. By 1965, when Thompson left the BIA, the world of Indian education had begun to respond to Lyndon Johnson's idea of a Great Society. In the spring of 1966, the nomination of Robert L. Bennett (Oneida) as Indian commissioner sent a deliberate message to Indian country, in essence acknowledging the spirit of reform engendered by the Kennedy and Johnson administrations.

The Indian educational reforms of the 1960s and 1970s were partly a product of a political climate that led to "rising expectations" for American Indians, blacks, and Hispanics. Centered in the programs directed by the Office of Economic Opportunity, this experiment operated under the principle of "maximum feasible participation," that is, allowing for local control as far as it is feasible. During the 1960s, a liberal Congress and an aggressive president offered the nation an opportunity to disseminate the traditional reins of power by including groups that had always been powerless. Until Johnson's obsession with the war in Vietnam corroded his presidency, Indians and other low-priority groups captured a rare moment in the national limelight.

For the Indians, there had been some preparation. Change had begun slowly during the 1930s, with the growth of tribal self-government under the IRA, the acquisition of economic skills under programs such as the Indian Civilian Conservation Corps, and the recognition of cultural heritage in the BIA schools. World War II had accelerated the pace of change, especially for tribes that lived far from urban centers. In 1930, only one in ten Indians lived in an urban area; by the end of the war the number had jumped to one in four; and by 1980 it was one in two. During the 1960s, therefore, many Indians no longer lived in rural areas and they no longer sent their children to BIA schools. There were also more Indian children attending school. Before World War II, most Indian parents had not gone to school themselves. But by the 1960s, Indian school enrollment was almost universal, and increasing numbers of Indian parents had had some experience in school, experience that gave them confidence when their children began school.

Another change had also prepared Indians for the Great Society's idea of "maximum feasible participation." In 1946, the Indian Claims Commission was established, a long-postponed measure to reimburse Indian tribes for loss of land and other damages incurred by the federal government. Anticipating the need for a cooperative tribal response to the process of reimbursement, D'Arcy McNickle, a prominent BIA leader of mixed-Indian descent from Montana, helped bring together Indian tribal leaders to form the National Congress of American Indians. The first pan-Indian group to organize since the Society of American Indians disintegrated in the 1920s, NCAI could not have made a more timely entrance onto the stage. No sooner was it organized than it was faced with the threat of the termination movement. In 1945, an NCAI executive committeeman declared: "It is time for Indians everywhere to begin facing certain propositions which will determine the future of Indians. . . . It is important that a consideration of these matters should be entirely from the Indian point of view rather than from the angle of administrative expediency and government interest." During the 1950s, NCAI leaders who were fighting to retain tribes' legal rights acquired invaluable experience that would serve them well during the 1960s and 1970s. One of the most important successes of astute Indian leaders and liberal members of Congress during these two decades was in Indian education.

All of these threads came together during Lyndon Johnson's presidency. The federal government began to listen to the Indian voice, and Indian education moved to the forefront of the new reform movement known as self-determination. As the reform movement got underway, it affected many kinds of schools and educational programs: both BIA and public schools; government bureaucrats, teachers and counselors, tribal leaders, and Indian community educational leaders; Indian parents and Indian youth, from students attending Head Start through those in community colleges and universities.

The initiative for self-determination in BIA schooling came from several directions: from members of Congress, such as Senator Robert F. Kennedy (D, New York) and Congressman Lloyd Meeds (D, Washington), who sought to break the conservative grip of the Senate and House committees on insular affairs; from the Office of Economic

Opportunity; from prominent Indian leaders, such as William Demmert (Tlingit/Sioux); and from newly formed Indian organizations, such as the National Indian Education Association, which first met in Minneapolis in 1969. There were also national studies and reports that had been commissioned by both President Kennedy and President Johnson: the U.S. Office of Education completed its five-year report entitled *The National Study of American Indian Education: The Education of Indian Children and Youth* in 1971; and the U.S. Senate published its 1969 study, *Indian Education: A National Tragedy—A National Challenge,* which became known as the Kennedy Report. Although the Kennedy Report severely criticized BIA education, it contained sixty recommendations for change. Reminiscent of the Ryan-Beatty initiatives of the 1930s, the Kennedy Report emphasized the need to include cross-cultural curricula and encouraged the involvement of Indian parents in BIA schools.

Stung by this barrage of well-publicized attacks, BIA educational leaders began to respond. At first, the response was agonizingly slow. When the BIA founded the Rough Rock Demonstration School on the Navajo Reservation in 1966, the agency's first major commitment to Indian-controlled schools, it provided the building but relied on the OEO for funding. Rough Rock remained a solitary experiment for several years. By 1973, eleven additional schools had contracted with the BIA in Arizona, New Mexico, Montana, Wyoming, and North and South Dakota, but most of them opened between 1970 and 1973.

Rough Rock helped to change the perceptions of BIA educational leaders toward contract schooling. When the Navajos proposed to charter a tribally controlled community college in 1968, the BIA was more receptive than it had been in 1966. The Navajo Tribe provided funding and donated land for the college, the OEO made a three-year financial commitment to the project, and private sources picked up the rest of the tab. The BIA supported the final product and Navajo Community College was founded in 1969. Like Rough Rock, NCC established a precedent. In 1969, it was the only tribally controlled community college in the nation; by 1988, it was part of a network of twenty institutions located in the Southwest, the Northern Plains, and the Pacific Northwest.

In another major concession to Indian self-determination during the 1960s, the BIA established Indian advisory boards for all BIA-directed boarding schools, a measure that met mixed reactions from Indian country. By 1970, the BIA had provided more words than actions toward fulfilling the concept of Indian self-determination. But the studies and reports of the 1960s had served a purpose. As Robert A. Roessel, first director of Rough Rock and first president of NCC, pointed out in 1970: "The Bureau has finally learned to listen to Indians."

If the 1960s, like the 1920s, was a decade of investigation, the 1970s, like the 1930s, was a decade of legislation. As the Meriam Report had helped to create a climate for the IRA, the Kennedy Report and the *National Study of Indian Education* helped to create a climate for the Indian Education Act of 1972, the Indian Self-Determination and Education Assistance Act of 1975, Title XI of the Education Amendments of 1978, and the Tribally Controlled Community College Assistance Act of 1978. But the 1970s were also different from the 1930s. Between 1972 and 1978, more reform legislation was passed on Indian education than at any other time in American history. Moreover, the legislation passed during the 1970s stands apart from all previous congressional Indian educational reform because it reflected the needs and wishes of the Indian world. In fact, that part of the Indian Self-Determination and Educational Assistance Act that shifted control of J-O'M programs from state departments of education to Indians was designed independently by Indian educational leaders meeting in Albuquerque and was then drafted is legislation by Congress. In acknowledgment, these regulations were soon dubbed the "Red Regs."

The new Indian education laws were a triumph for the Indian people. Collectively, they provided for Indian participation in and direction of all federally funded programs for Indian children in public schools; for contracting of BIA-funded schools (and other ventures) by Indian tribes or groups; for local control of BIA schools by Indian school boards; and for federal funding for tribally controlled community colleges. Assessing the significance of this legislation, the president of the Sequoyah High School Board of Education in Oklahoma said: "education is one of the key ingredients toward self-determination."

Title IV of the Indian Education Act established the Office of Indian Education (later changed to Indian Education Programs) under the U.S. Office of Education (later the Department of Education). William Demmert, first Deputy Commissioner for Indian Education at OIE, directed the Title IV programs that affected thousands of Indian children who attended public schools and who had been outside of BIA jurisdiction since the 1930s. Through this measure Congress had established a separate Indian power base at the federal level. And since 1975, despite strong reactionary measures under Ronald Reagan's presidency, Indians have continued to direct and maintain these programs.

The differences between Indian self-determination in the 1960s and the 1980s can be seen in the changes that have taken place at the Santa Fe Indian School. In 1962, BIA educators under Hildegard Thompson transformed the school into the Institute of American Indian Arts. With this distinct change, the BIA acknowledged the importance of native art, but it also ignored the needs of many Pueblos who remained loyal to the old school and its traditions. In 1981, an emotional struggle among several contending forces—the All Indian Pueblo Council, the BIA, and the supporters of the Institute—was resolved by moving the Institute to the College of Santa Fe and shifting the students and staff of the Albuquerque Indian School to the old Santa Fe Indian School. This victory for the Pueblos, which resulted in Santa Fe Indian School becoming a contract school responsible to the AIPC, could not have occurred in the early 1960s. In 1987, Joseph Abeyta (Santa Clara), the school's superintendent, pinpointed the importance of the change: "The difference today is that this is an Indian school run by Indian people. . . . The community is coming to believe it is *their* school—that's what's making it work."

When Congress shifted control of Indian education to the Indians, it acknowledged a condition that Native Americans had known about long before the United States came into existence; hundreds of different Indian cultures had maintained different traditions and different needs. As scholar Dave Warren (Santa Clara) recently observed: "American Indian life will continue to harbor traditions that were born well before the fifteenth century." Indian direction of Indian education meant that these needs could be met locally and that tribes, Indian school boards, and Indian parents could determine the best policies for their children—and what was best depended on who they were and where they lived. Education suitable for Sioux children at Standing Rock was not suitable for Navajo children at Rock Point; schooling appropriate for Chippewa and Cree children at Rocky Boy in Montana might not be appropriate for Ojibwa youth at Ojibway School in Minnesota. Even with the spread of pan-Indianism, Indian groups still retain unique qualities. "Tribal identity is strong," declared one Comanche educator, and the core of that identity remains the education of Indian children, whether in public, contract, or BIA-directed schools. By recognizing the importance of local control, the federal government had begun to listen to the Indian voice.

The challenge for Indian education during the 1980s has been to retain the rights gained during the 1970s, but the years under Reagan have taken their toll. Although Indian educational leaders have generally been able to maintain overall funding levels, they have had to work with declining federal education budgets. They have also been forced to counter strong efforts to remove the BIA from education altogether. During Reagan's first term of office, the BIA attempted to prove that Indian education was not a "trust responsibility" and, hence, not a federal responsibility. Toward the end of Reagan's second term, Assistant Secretary of the Interior for Indian Affairs Ross Swimmer (Cherokee) led an aggressive campaign to transfer responsibility for BIA schooling to the tribes and then, by default, to the states. In both instances, Indians fought back and, with the aid of allies in Congress, defeated the proposals. When the Joint Economic Committee held a hearing in Santa Fe to discuss Swimmer's proposal, Senator Daniel Inouye (D, Hawaii), chairman of the Senate Select Committee on Indian Affairs, said that he "viewed the proposal as a diminution of responsibility by the federal government." Indian leaders at the hearings concurred. Leonard Atole, president of the Jicarilla Apache Tribe, warned: "The mere transference of the responsibility from one education agency to another will not improve education"; and Peter MacDonald, chairman of the Navajo Nation, announced that the Navajo tribal council was "unequivocally completely opposed to such a proposal."

Undaunted by Indian criticism, the Reagan administration curtailed the Indian voice in education in yet another way. Using its right to control administrative appointments, Reagan appointed acting education directors in the BIA and the Department of Education's Indian Education Programs (which, incidentally, was downgraded from the 1970s Office of Education). Through these temporary appointments, the administration sought to inhibit effective Indian leadership at the federal level. For Indians, the 1980s has been a decade of federal opposition, but there is one major difference between the 1980s and the 1950s. By the 1980s, Indians had gained solid legal support for self-determination in education.

Despite the severe challenges of the 1980s, the Indian voice in Indian schooling can no longer go unrecognized. When Swimmer's plan was announced, the reaction of Suzan Shown Harjo (Cheyenne/Creek), executive director of NCAI, reflected the Indians' uncompromising attitude toward education. The plan to transfer Indian schools to the states, Harjo charged, "ignores tribal wishes . . . it proposes to turn over our most precious assets, our children, to the states, which the Supreme Court has called the deadliest enemies of the Indians." By reiterating the necessity of Indian control, Harjo and other Indian leaders have demonstrated that the Indian voice in Indian schooling cannot be silenced. Since World War II, that voice has gained power, and during the last quarter of the century it has come into its own.

Readings for Margaret Connell Szasz:

Indian education has gotten a lot of attention since Szasz wrote *Education and the American Indian: The Road to Self-Determination, 1928–1973* (Albuquerque: University of New Mexico Press, 1974). For the decades immediately preceeding those examined in her book see David Wallace Adams, *Education for Extinction: American Indians and the Boarding School Experience, 1875–1928* (Lawrence: University Press of Kansas, 1995). Studies of individual Indian boarding schools include Robert A. Trennert, Jr., *The Phoenix Indian School: Forced Assimilation in Arizona, 1881–1935* (Norman: University of Oklahoma Press, 1988); K. Tsiania Lowawaima, *They Called It Prairie Light: The Story of Chilocco Indian School* (Lincoln: University of Nebraska Press, 1994); and Donal F. Lindsey, *Indians at Hampton Institute, 1887–1923* (Urbana: University of Illinois Press, 1995).

23

TERMINATION AND THE EASTERN BAND OF CHEROKEES

JOHN R. FINGER

The bold changes in American Indian policies ushered in by John Collier during the 1930s lost broad support by the time World War II had ended. Following that conflict many Americans wanted to cut the size and scope of the federal government. As a result the Bureau of Indian Affairs came under intense scrutiny and by the early 1950s Congress proposed a new policy. Called termination, this program strove to get the government out of the Indian business by freeing Indians from what was seen as the heavy-handed bureaucrats then thought to be repressing reservation dwellers.

Tribes that had made noticeable economic progress and others that seemed to have a solid resource base were to have their relationship with the federal government severed. The Eastern Band of Cherokee was one of the first groups suggested for this fate, but they successfully avoided that result. Like other Indian groups the Eastern Cherokee split sharply over the new program, but leaders with a clear understanding of what was at stake worked to avoid being terminated. They enlisted local support from legislators and business groups who saw these Indians as a major tourist attraction in a region of little wealth. In this case study the author explains how termination worked and he shows that while the experience of the Eastern Cherokee was far from universal, it demonstrated how tribal initiatives did bring desired results.

John R. Finger is a professor of history at the University of Tennessee.

Immediately following World War II, political pressures mounted to get the federal government "out of the Indian business" by terminating trust responsibilities to tribes and "emancipating" them from the stifling paternalism of the Bureau of Indian Affairs (BIA). The call for termination was both a repudiation of former Indian Commissioner John Collier's New Deal programs and a reaffirmation of earlier assimilationist assumptions and

Source: John R. Finger, "Termination and the Eastern Band of Cherokees," pp. 153–70. Reprinted from *American Indian Quarterly,* volume 15, number 2 by permission of the University of Nebraska Press. Copyright © 1991 by the University of Nebraska Press.

policies regarding Native Americans. As many terminationists noted, Indians had served well in the war and deserved something better than second-class citizenship. Surely people who had adjusted to military service and a world war were capable of looking after themselves. Surely they would want to enjoy that freedom and share its prerogatives. It was time for Indians to become part of mainstream American society.

Indian policy also reflected some of the postwar paranoia concerning the Soviet Union and the specter of communism. Critics had long decried Collier's programs as socialistic and even communistic and now, amid the tensions of the Cold War, many Americans idealized an individualistic society standing in dramatic counterpoint to the collectivism of our perceived enemies. Tribalism and the maintenance of a number of separate cultures within American society seemed unpatriotic as well as expensive. Many saw the BIA as a collection of entrenched bureaucrats wedded to un-American programs and determined to protect their own jobs.

At one time or another during the postwar period, almost every tribe had to confront the possibility of termination. The Eastern Band of Cherokee Indians, with more than 4,000 members, was no exception. Occupying a reservation of some 56,000 acres scattered over several counties in the mountains of western North Carolina, the Eastern Cherokees claimed descent from a small number of Indians who, through curious and complicated circumstances, remained in the Southeast after the Cherokee Nation was removed to present-day Oklahoma in 1838. They enjoyed federal recognition as a tribe and also operated under an 1889 state charter of incorporation. The Band's precise legal status had been a source of endless dispute, with both the state and federal governments exercising an undefined mixed (or concurrent) jurisdiction. Isolated from most Native Americans, the Eastern Cherokees suffered from a sometimes inattentive BIA and a state government with little knowledge of Indian problems. Thus the Band's experiences amid the termination controversy, while similar in some respects to those of other tribes, more often reflected its unique historical, physical, and economic circumstances. Especially important were the tribe's location next to the Great Smoky Mountains National Park and the remarkable growth of tourism, which gave both Cherokees and many local whites a vested interest in maintaining an Indian identity.

For the Eastern Cherokees, the battle over termination began in January 1947, following a call by Senator Dennis Chavez of New Mexico for abolition of the BIA. A small faction of acculturated tribal members immediately echoed Chavez's sentiments. Their leader was Fred Bauer, former vice chief of the Band, who during the 1930s had been active in the American Indian Federation, a rabidly anti-Collier and pro-assimilationist organization. Bauer had moved to the reservation too late to prevent Cherokee ratification of Collier's Indian Reorganization ACT (IRA) in December 1934, but the following year he successfully blocked efforts at drawing up a new tribal constitution under that act. And early in 1939, while at the height of his influence, he even persuaded the council to ask for a reconsideration of the Reorganization Act as it applied to the Eastern Band. In a scenario worthy of a Greek tragedy, Bauer's cousin and adoptive brother, Principal Chief Jarrett Blythe, staunchly supported both John Collier and the Indian Reorganization Act.

By 1940 Bauer had lost his influence, and the House of Representatives failed to pass a Senate-approved bill which would have ended the IRA's application to the Eastern Band and several other tribes. But Bauer was not to remain silent, and he heard the postwar clamor for termination as a clarion call to renew his holy war against the BIA and tribalism. His wife, Catherine, a former teacher on the reservation, was equally vehement as was W. P. ("Pearson") McCoy, a former member of the tribal council.

McCoy was a "white Indian" whose family had been included on the tribal roll—the Baker Roll—despite having only minimal Cherokee ancestry. As proprietor of a gift shop and other tourist-related enterprises on the reservation, he viewed the BIA as an obstacle to his pursuit of private enterprise. Without its meddling, he believed, the Cherokee reservation would be able to compete successfully for tourists with the town of Gatlinburg, Tennessee, on the opposite side of the national park. He succinctly expressed his sentiments in a letter to North Carolina's Senator Clyde R. Hoey:

> We wish the Indian Beaureau Abolished as far as the Cherokee Indians of N.C. are concerned. We wish to injoy our oppertunities that our fine roads, and the Great Smokey Mt. National Park, has made possible for us[.] We wish to lease and develop our Tourist Trade, we want Tourist Courts, Hotells, and everything a free enterprise[.] We in other words Senator would like for Congress to transfer the Indian Bureau over to Gatlinburg, Tenn. And keep it there till we could catch up with those people. . . .

McCoy said the Cherokees were not wards but citizens, and he believed the BIA was denying them their constitutional rights. He also reiterated a view developed by Fred Bauer that the Eastern Band was not a tribe but a corporation and that its lands were not a reservation because the Indians themselves had purchased them during the preceding century. In 1925 the Band, acting as a corporation, had transferred those properties in trust to the United States so the government could distribute them as individual allotments to each member. But distribution never occurred—first, because the Cherokees resisted it as long as the Baker Roll, compiled during the late 1920s, included so many white Indians; and second, because Congress finally discontinued all allotments with passage of the IRA in 1934. In the eyes of the Bauers and McCoys, the federal Government exercised illegal control over the Band, and its failure to proceed with allotment constituted a breach of contract. (Indeed, Bauer forcefully argued these views right up to his death in 1971, despite numerous court decisions refuting his contentions.)

In February 1947, soon after Senator Chavez's call for abolishing the BIA, Acting Commissioner of Indian Affairs William Zimmerman issued a report assessing the readiness of various tribes for termination. In it he cited four major criteria for making such a decision: the tribe's degree of acculturation; its economic resources and condition; the tribe's willingness to be relieved of federal control; and the willingness of the state government to assume responsibility. His report listed three categories, the first being those tribes ready for immediate termination, the second including those which should be ready within two to ten years, and the third consisting of tribes that would not be prepared until some indefinite time in the future.

Zimmerman placed the Eastern Band in group two—mostly, it appears, on the basis of its acculturation. Using questionable tables based on census data from 1930, the Indian Bureau, in its magisterial wisdom, concluded that the Band retained 31.28 percent of its Indian culture. Each state with federal Indian populations was listed in this acculturation index. North Carolina, with only the Eastern Cherokees, ranked tenth out of 23 in terms of acculturation levels of its Indians. Kansas ranked first, with its several small groups supposedly retaining only 16.22 percent of their Indian culture. New Mexico ranked last, with its Indians retaining 69.30 percent of their traditional ways. It appears from the listing of various tribes in the three categories of readiness that if the North Carolina Cherokees had retained a few percentage points less of their Indian culture they might well have been placed in group one, those supposedly ready for immediate termination.

Despite Zimmerman's assessment of Cherokee readiness, the Bauer-McCoy faction had already convinced some North Carolina politicians that the Eastern Cherokees were indeed prepared for emancipation. In January 1947 Dan Tompkins, the state representative for Jackson County, which included much of the reservation, introduced a bill to memorialize Congress to abolish Indian Bureau control over the Eastern Band. He argued that such a step was "simple justice to a great people" and denounced the BIA's "dictatorship." About the only Cherokee political leader echoing those sentiments was councilman John C. McCoy, Pearson McCoy's kinsman. Tompkins's bill passed the North Carolina House unanimously, prompting officials to invite Cherokees to hearings in Raleigh before the senate education committee, which was considering the bill. Some hardliners like the McCoys refused because they already denied any jurisdiction by the BIA and expressed confidence in their state representatives.

Ten defenders of the Indian Bureau, including Principal Chief Jarrett Blythe, had no such qualms about attending. Wisely avoiding an ideological stance, the wily chief first thanked Tompkins for his interest in the tribe but then pointed out that the federal Government spent about $300,000 a year to provide health care and education for the Eastern Cherokees. His tribe would have no objection to Tompkins's bill if North Carolina was willing to provide the same quality of services. In testimony that must have made federal officials blink with surprise, another Cherokee praised the United States government and claimed that without its protection local discrimination against Indians would become even worse. The hearings in Raleigh appear to have been orchestrated by senate committee member Frank Parker of Asheville who had already performed legal services for the Band and would later become its full-time attorney. Parker was primarily responsible for killing Tompkins's bill in committee.

This setback merely encouraged Fred Bauer to redouble his attacks on the BIA and its connections with the Eastern Band. Early in March 1947 he protested to the chairman of the U.S. House Appropriations Committee about the BIA's alleged wrongdoings. Shrewdly, he also introduced a little Cold War rhetoric:

> Bureau policies for the past thirteen years have been communistic, and their schemes have seriously curtailed private enterprise, and will eventually make it non-existent at Cherokee. We are denied hundreds of thousands of dollars annual revenue through the Bureau's refusal to permit enterprises that are begging to be allowed here at the Park entrance.

Bauer also attacked the Band's plans to create, with BIA backing, a tribally-owned complex of tourist facilities on the Boundary Tree tract adjacent to the national park. He labelled it "a Government controlled cooperative" and then returned to the Cold War by claiming that it was inconsistent to spend millions of dollars under the Truman Doctrine to fight communism abroad while spending money at home to promote communism "among a helpless minority of First Americans." He called for an end to all appropriations for the Cherokees' BIA agency.

This letter no doubt was the main reason work on Boundary Tree was held up that spring while Joe Jennings, the superintendent of the BIA's Cherokee Agency attempted to explain the situation to acting Indian commissioner Zimmerman. After attacking Bauer and Pearson McCoy by name, Jennings noted that most opponents of Boundary Tree were white Indians who had gained inclusion on the Baker Roll over tribal protests. Under the Band's unique system of landholding, which permitted nearly unlimited acquisition of possessory claims on tribal lands, these relatively acculturated individuals had earned control of some of the most attractive tourist sites. Jennings said the white Indians felt insecure and favored abolition of the Indian Bureau because they hoped to receive titles in fee simple. He also pointed to a residue of ill will among local whites who favored termination so they could tax Indian lands. Predatory real estate speculators were likewise lurking about, eager to pounce on choice Cherokee business sites when government trusteeship ended.

When told that Cherokees had signed petitions against the BIA, Jennings replied that the names of some had been used without their knowledge. Others, he alleged, had been swayed by promises of receiving $3,000 each if the reservation were divided following federal withdrawal, while a few had been told they would be deported to Oklahoma or lose certain business rights on the reservation if they did not sign. Although work on the Boundary Tree facilities soon resumed, Jennings was clearly on the defensive.

The Cherokee council was not a passive spectator to these maneuverings. The most striking evidence of how threatening it found any radical alteration of federal ties came in October 1947 at its first regular meeting following the latest Bauer-McCoy crusade against the Indian Bureau. Although Bauer's Cherokee ancestry was sufficient for enrollment, the council noted the disputed status of many of his followers, who were "continually stirring up trouble," denouncing federal actions, and asserting their desire for "freedom" from the BIA. The council therefore resolved to ask Congress to enact legislation allowing the Band to revise its roll in order to eliminate such individuals and asked the government to use non-tribal funds to pay each challenged person a sum equal to the value of one share of tribal assets. The council agreed to pay each for any improvements on reservation lands. A major proviso was that no challenged member would receive such compensation if he had not recently lived on tribal property.

The council was even more forthright a little more than a week later when it resolved that a majority of the Eastern Band wanted "to continue under the bureau." It asked Congress to pass legislation allowing any bona fide members of the Band with less than one-fourth Eastern Cherokee blood to withdraw and sever their relationship with the Band any time they wished. Clearly the council preferred to maintain a tribal identity within the existing federal network and to encourage discontented members of minimal Cherokee ancestry to withdraw. That was probably the major consideration, but no doubt some councilmen also perceived the status quo as a means of retaining political influence and jobs within the BIA. To this extent, at least, Bauer and other critics were probably correct. Whatever the reasons, by the end of 1947 it was apparent that at least two of acting Indian commissioner Zimmerman's four criteria for termination were lacking in the case of the Eastern Band: consent of both the tribe and its state of residence.

Another facet of Indian "emancipation" was the creation by Congress in 1946 of the Indian Claims Commission. For many years various tribes had been arguing that the United States should compensate them for past injustices, but the only way they could obtain redress was through direct congressional intervention. Under the new legislation, a three-person claims commission would review legal briefs and other evidence presented by tribes and make binding judgment on the merits of each case. Congressional sponsors believed the claims commission would streamline tribal litigation, pay off federal obligations in an honorable fashion, and, perhaps, "financially liberate Native Americans from dependency on federal programs implemented during the Collier years." The Indian Claims Commission was thus seen as a necessary step by those politicians who favored termination of federal services to tribes. In effect, supporters believed creation of the commission meant the final reckoning of federal responsibilities to American Indians. Judgment Day was at hand.

Like many tribes, the Eastern Cherokees saw establishment of the claims commission not as a prelude to termination but as a long-needed means of satisfying old grievances. In 1951 the Band filed three claims seeking compensation for some 40 million acres taken from the Cherokees by the United States. These claims were in addition to similar ones filed by the Oklahoma Cherokees. Both groups also argued that various subsequent accounting and procedural errors by the government had cost the Indians millions of dollars. The Band found that dealing with the claims commission was an exasperating, time-consuming process. The volume of tribal claims was so great that Congress several times extended the life of the commission and expanded its membership to five. Not until 1972, long after the threat of termination had passed, did the United States finally award the Band more than $1.8 million.

Prospects for termination brightened considerably in 1950 with President Harry S. Truman's appointment of Dillon S. Myer as Commissioner of Indian Affairs. By the time of his appointment, there was a general consensus among policy makers in favor of Indian "self-determination" which, for Myer at least, meant ending wardship and regulation of Indian lives by the federal government. He had been given a "free hand to put the Indian Bureau 'out of business as quickly as possible' " and wanted to integrate Native Americans into the cultural mainstream. Many Indian leaders also supported self-determination but, it soon became apparent, defined this as greater Indian freedom of action without complete withdrawal of federal assistance.

One of Myer's most ambitious termination-related programs was the voluntary relocation of young Indians into urban centers as a means of offering more opportunities for employment than were available on reservations. The government would provide transportation for Indian families, their first month's living expenses, counseling, and even training. Later the program also included job placement. While many Indians saw relocation as a means of escaping tribal poverty, others viewed it as simply another effort to break up the reservations, abrogate federal responsibilities, and destroy Native American culture. Relocation among the Eastern Cherokees is difficult to assess. Anthropologists pronounced it a failure, while the tribal relocation officer called it a success. This disagreement may reflect different outcomes for those relocated under the aegis of the federal government and those who left the reservation on their own. Certainly by the 1950s more and more Eastern Cherokees were taking outside jobs or entering military service; many periodically returned to the reservation or chose to retire there after satisfying careers elsewhere.

Besides advocating relocation, Commissioner Myer was systematically taking other steps toward termination. In 1952, at the request of the House of Representatives, he collected voluminous information pertaining to the functions of the BIA and tribal readiness for withdrawal of federal services. Joe Jennings reported that many Eastern

Cherokees were fearful of being left to the mercy of local whites. Resentment against Indians was especially high in Swain County, he said, because Cherokee lands had been withdrawn from the tax rolls when the federal government assumed trusteeship in 1925, and thousands more acres had been withdrawn when the national park was created a few years later. Cherokees had additional objections to termination, including distribution of tribal assets on the basis of the hated Baker Roll and loss of federal funding for education and health care.

Education was a particularly troublesome issue. Both Swain and Jackson counties, where most Indians resided, were among the poorest in the state, and public schools there did not offer the same opportunities that Cherokees enjoyed on the reservation. Because of federal support, the expenditure per Cherokee student in 1951–52 was almost three times that for students enrolled in North Carolina public schools. Likewise, health services for Cherokees were "at a far higher standard in terms of quantity and probably of quality than those available to the general population of the area." State officials had already informed Joe Jennings that even under the best of circumstances it would be at least six years before North Carolina could assume educational responsibilities for the Indians. But first the federal government would have to agree to construct modern school facilities on the reservation so the counties would not have to incur added financial burdens.

Jennings also said that individual Cherokees held possessory rights to all but about 8,000 of the more than 36,000 acres on the reservation. In his opinion at least 80 percent of the entire reservation should be left in forest, and this obviously required considerable advance planning and cooperation among both Indians and federal agencies. After noting the lack of good agricultural land, Jennings sounded what was to be a recurrent theme in arguments against precipitous termination: "If the tourist business is properly exploited the possibilities are such that it should provide nearly all of the Cherokees with a good living. These same possibilities make the Cherokees very vulnerable if withdrawal should come without proper safeguards set up by the State and Federal Governments." Many whites realized the reservation was a major economic attraction and were therefore interested "in working out a plan whereby the Indian can retain the reservation intact in Indian ownership," but in the meantime federal services should continue while Cherokees developed an ability to handle their own affairs.

Jennings' assessment figured prominently in the subsequent recommendations of the BIA's Minneapolis Area Office, which supervised the Cherokee agency. It placed each tribe in its jurisdiction in one of four groups, the first being those most prepared for termination. The Eastern Cherokee, along with the Menominee of Wisconsin and the Red Lake Chippewa of Minnesota, were in group four, the least prepared. These were not final assessments, however, and the Menominee were soon adjudged ready for termination. As for the Cherokees, the opinion was that their valuable timber resources, complicated system of landholding, and valuable tourist-related real estate necessitated special precautions before ending trust responsibilities. The office believed the Cherokees were still unable to administer their resources because they lacked tribal leadership, and the necessary infrastructure. The report concluded with a call for a thorough study by specialists of the "entire complicated and complex Cherokee situation."

For those Indians fearing termination, the change of national administrations early in 1953 offered little solace. There seemed to be a groundswell of political sentiment to "emancipate" as many tribes as possible. President Dwight D. Eisenhower's

Commissioner of Indian Affairs, Glenn L. Emmons, was a prominent businessman who intended to continue Myer's policies. Congress was similarly inclined and in July 1953 passed House Concurrent Resolution 108, calling for abolition of several Indian offices and termination of trust responsibilities for certain specified tribes. Emmons enthusiastically supported HCR 108 and suggested a number of additional suitable tribes. During the next decade Indian Office cooperation with politicians like Senator Arthur V. Watkins (Utah) led Congress to pass termination laws for more than 100 Indian groups, ranging from small communities and rancherias to large tribes. For several, notably the Klamaths of Oregon and Menominees of Wisconsin, termination proved disastrous.

The North Carolina Cherokees, while not included among tribes listed in HCR 108, were also affected by the rising terminationist sentiment. In August 1953 Congress passed Public Law 280, which transferred civil and criminal jurisdiction over most tribes in five states to the respective local governments and allowed any other states to assume similar jurisdiction over their own Indian reservations. Assistant Secretary of Interior Orme Lewis sent a copy of PL 280 to North Carolina's Governor William B. Umstead and noted the provision allowing state assumption of jurisdiction. When Umstead requested a legal opinion, state Assistant Attorney General Ralph Moody argued that North Carolina did not need to follow up on PL 280 because it already exercised such authority over the Eastern Band. While the Band had received federal recognition as a tribe, Moody said its otherwise unique status had resulted in North Carolina's criminal laws applying "to all offenses committed within the Indian Reservation"—a statement inaccurate both in law and historical experience.

Perhaps the foremost factor working against termination of the Eastern Band was the burgeoning tourist industry, which both whites and Indians saw as the most viable cure for western North Carolina's economic ills. Amid the postwar prosperity, millions of Americans were buying new automobiles and taking to the highways, many to visit the Great Smoky Mountains National Park. The opportunity to see a "real" Indian on the nearby Cherokee reservation was a bonus. By the late 1940s Western North Carolina Associated Communities (WNCAC), a consortium of 11 counties, had created the Cherokee Historical Association (CHA), a non-profit organization ostensibly dedicated to preserving and promoting Cherokee history and culture. Though established in cooperation with the tribal council and including some Cherokee members, it was clearly a white-dominated organization hoping to attract tourists to the region. In 1950 the CHA first staged its outdoor drama "Unto These Hills," an instant success which became a fixture of every subsequent tourist season and has drawn more than four and a half million paid spectators. The drama and other new tourist attractions on the reservation gave local whites as well as Indians a vested interest in preserving the Cherokee tribal identity—or at least a generic "Indian" identity—and the CHA, with Joe Jenning's enthusiastic support, became a powerful force to that end. Tourism had mixed effects. On the one hand, it brought sorely needed revenue to the reservation; on the other, it created antagonisms between tribal haves and have-nots and brought a dependency on the CHA's business expertise. In the opinion of many whites and the BIA, the Indians themselves lacked sufficient skills to manage their tourist industry or tribal resources.

This pessimism regarding Cherokee competency did not prevent the BIA from beginning negotiations with state, local, and even tribal officials about assuming responsibility for providing specific services to the Eastern Band. The government promised to continue federal operation of the reservation hospital while current Principal Chief Osley Saunooke attempted to find a private, non-profit sponsor to take it over. Saunooke was also instrumental in establishing a three-percent tribal sales tax, enabling the Band to assume more responsibility for sanitation and police and fire protection. Officials of the Cherokee Historical Association also participated in the planning and suggested a 25-year program of tourist-related development, which, much to the disgust of Fred Bauer, would attempt to preserve the "unique quality" of Cherokee life.

Despite these modest gains in tribal self-sufficiency, there remained the troublesome matter of Cherokee education. In July 1954 the BIA reduced the status of the main reservation school from a boarding to a day facility and then attempted to persuade state and local authorities to assume total responsibility for Indian education. The major problem was access to public schools in Swain County. Officials in Bryson City, the county seat, admitted that a few Indian children were already enrolled, but these were predominantly white individuals from acculturated families. There was considerable opposition to accepting phenotypical Cherokees because of racism, past frictions, and resentment over the recent landmark Supreme Court decision of *Brown v. Board of Education,* which declared segregated public schools unconstitutional. State officials were even more nervous about *Brown* because of widespread southern opposition to integration of Blacks. Federal efforts to get Indians into the schools appeared to be one more case of outside meddling in racial matters. Another concern over the Cherokee situation was its possible implication for the state's Lumbee Indians, a heterogeneous group of uncertain origins who had long been segregated from white society.

Hildegard Thompson, Chief of the BIA's Education Branch, thought the volatile racial atmosphere in North Carolina dictated that the government proceed gingerly with efforts to integrate Cherokees into public schools. The BIA should continue to provide education on the reservation and meanwhile work on public relations to change white attitudes in Bryson City, emphasizing the economic benefits of the Band to the area, directing as much business as possible to the town, and also quietly attempting to enroll more Indians there.

Thompson's recommendations basically determined the course of action taken, and the BIA tiptoed diplomatically around the school desegregation issue. Southern race relations and the simmering impact of the *Brown* decision, while perhaps not decisive, certainly delayed prospects for full termination of federal services. Meanwhile, without undue publicity, Cherokee enrollment in public schools began to climb. During fiscal year 1955 Indian enrollment in Swain County schools totaled 54, half of whom had at least three-fourths Cherokee blood, while 38 attended school in Jackson County. Four more were enrolled in Graham County. However, the overwhelming majority of Cherokee children—798—still attended federal day schools. The state of North Carolina, moreover, failed to allot enough money for about 50 Cherokees to attend the Whittier public school because it argued they were strictly a federal responsibility.

The BIA's caution on the educational front was offset by an administrative blunder that attracted considerable negative publicity. On November 12, 1954, the *Asheville Citizen* announced in a front-page headline that the government had notified Joe Jennings that, effective December 1, his office would be eliminated and he would be transferred. In an editorial entitled "Another Trail of Tears?", the paper attacked the removal, which came "in the midst of an orderly and well-timed liquidation of the Indian agency's responsibilities at Cherokee." Certainly the paper did not quarrel with an eventual transfer of responsibilities to the state, but argued that it should be done slowly and rationally. The editorial stated Swain County was unable to bear the costs associated with termination and pronounced the situation to be is "unalterably dark."

A storm of protest followed Jennings's removal. Editorial comment from other cities echoed that of the Asheville newspaper, while tribal councilmen, choosing their words carefully, denounced the action. Harry Buchanan, chairman of the Cherokee Historical Association, and Bill Sharpe, publisher of a Raleigh magazine, expressed outrage and lobbied with politicians and BIA officials alike. Sharpe complained to Senator W. Kerr Scott that the action would harm the Indians, western North Carolina, and the entire state. He made it clear he feared economic dislocations attending a likely reduction in the role of the Cherokee Historical Association and believed the Indians were incapable of managing "Unto These Hills" themselves. The whites of western North Carolina and the historical association, he believed, "have done more for the Indians' independence than all the efforts of the federal government in 100 years." He concluded by saying:

> Realizing that sooner or later the Cherokees must be cut loose and must stand on their feet, yet I believe this move now is like towing a drowning man half way to the bank and then going off and leaving him in deep water. The move should be delayed, and study given to a situation which I am sure is unique among the tribes.
>
> All of North Carolina has a deep interest in and stake in the Indians, both economically and morally.

This barrage of criticism forced Indian commissioner Glenn Emmons into a partial retreat. Joe Jennings would still be transferred, but Emmons insisted the BIA never intended to abolish the Cherokee agency. It was merely withdrawing the agency from the Minneapolis area office and bringing it directly under supervision from Washington. The commissioner agreed that any termination of the agency must be "on a gradual, planned and orderly basis," and insisted that for the present no such program was envisioned. Richard D. Butts, the new Cherokee agent appointed in March 1955, likewise reassured the tribe on this point.

In the meantime the Cherokee Historical Association was mending its fences with certain disgruntled Indians, including Chief Saunooke, and late in December 1954 announced a comprehensive program of protecting Cherokee lands, health benefits, and educational facilities. Chairman Harry Buchanan said his association's objective was "to represent the thinking of the Cherokee and to help the Cherokee get all that they deserve. If federal policies are to be put into effect that the Cherokee don't want," he continued, "we will go to bat for the Cherokee and fight for you." The CHA's program called for continued corporate land ownership by the Indians; an effort to find a suitable non-profit organization to operate the hospital; federal construction and state operation of a consolidated regional school; continued maintenance of reservation roads by the state after the federal Government brought them up to standards; assistance in maintaining extension, soil conservation, and forestry services after transferring those responsibilities to state agencies; and continued cooperation in working toward Cherokee community objectives. The tribal council's own program, adopted in March 1953, incorporated most of the CHA's objectives. In addition, it stressed revision of the tribal roll, registration of all possessory claims, and improvement of tribal housing.

Revising the roll was a crucial part of the tribal blueprint for confronting possible termination because of the large number of contested white Indians on the old Baker Roll. Frank W. Swan, a white and longtime Cherokee friend, said that practically everyone except white Indians wanted a new roll requiring at least one-sixteenth Cherokee blood. Dewey Tahquette, an acculturated fuller-blood who favored termination, also insisted on eliminating many of the contested names or else "our 'real Indians', as before would be *losers again.—*"

In September 1955 Representative James A. Haley (Florida), chairman of the House Subcommittee on Indian Affairs, held a congressional hearing in Cherokee which probed Indian attitudes toward tribal affairs and, especially, termination. Fred Bauer and a few others predictably called for ending the federal relationship and granting fee simple titles, but many other Cherokees at all levels of acculturation, including Chief Saunooke, were opposed. Haley's call for a show of hands revealed that 45 to 50 Indians wanted to maintain the present trust status while nine favored its abrogation. A few Bryson City whites were also present and testified that Swain County could not afford to take over Cherokee education without considerable federal assistance.

Termination gradually assumed less urgency during the next few years as the BIA, facing mounting national opposition, began to emphasize Indian economic development on and off the reservation as a necessary prelude to *voluntary* termination in the *indefinite* future. Thanks to a continuing expansion of tourism and success in attracting small year-round businesses to its reservation, the Eastern Band was increasingly able to steer a middle course between dependency and tribal autonomy. Indeed, the Eastern Band anticipated future official policy by embarking on a program of self-determination without abrogation of federal trust responsibilities. It had already gone a long ways in that direction by 1962, when Representative Wayne N. Aspinall (Colorado), chair of the House Committee on Interior and Insular Affairs, formally laid to rest the threat of Cherokee termination. Speaking on the reservation at the annual convention of the National Congress of American Indians, Aspinall prompted cheers from delegates by declaring, "As long as I am chairman of the committee no Indian tribe in the United States will be terminated until it is ready for termination."

And so the threat passed. Like Indians elsewhere, many Eastern Cherokees had opposed termination simply because it meant the loss of benefits supposedly guaranteed by treaties and federal guardianship. Local circumstances, however, were even more decisive in safeguarding the Band against possible termination. While tourist-oriented Indians took both sides of the issue, most believed tourism required preservation of their reservation and a Cherokee tribal identity. They had powerful allies among concerned whites, especially those in the Cherokee Historical Association, who also saw a continuing Indian identity as essential for developing the regional economy. Other factors included the inability of Swain and Jackson counties to provide required services to the Indians, the Band's complex legal status and system of possessory landholdings, the unwillingness of most Cherokees to include white Indians in any dissolution of tribal assets, and the volatile racial atmosphere of the mid-1950s. These local considerations merged with a growing national opposition to termination and a conviction that it was possible to be both a modern American and a tribal Indian.

Readings for John Finger:

Finger elaborates on ideas presented in his *Cherokee Americans: The Eastern Band of Cherokees in the Twentieth Century* (Lincoln: University of Nebraska Press, 1991). Other analyses of southern Indians include Sharlotte Neely, *Snowbird Cherokees: People of Persistence* (Athens: University of Georgia Press, 1991) and Harry A. Kersey, *An Assumption of Sovereignty: Social and Political Transformation among the Florida Seminoles, 1953–1979* (Lincoln: University of Nebraska Press, 1996) For a solid discussion of termination see Donald L. Fixico, *Termination and Relocation, 1945–1960* (Albuquerque: University of New Mexico Press, 1986).

24

THE PAWNEE OF NEBRASKA: TWICE REMOVED

ORLAN J. SVINGEN

In the 1870s the Pawnee people of Nebraska moved south into Indian Territory, present Oklahoma. Once the tribe left its home region, amateur archaeologists looted the Indians' graves repeatedly, and many of the remains found their way into the holdings of museums and private collectors. Almost 120 years later, in 1990, Congress enacted the Native American Graves Protection and Repatriation Act to deal with questions raised by Native Americans over the practice of gathering funerary materials. Aimed primarily at research institutions and museums, the law called for an inventory of religious items, other funerary objects and human remains found in their collections.

This essay examines the issues stemming from the debate over the acquisition and retention of Indian burial materials. When enacted the new law pushed professional researchers and Native Americans into opposing camps as the scholars defended their disciplines and the Indians demanded that the sacred objects and bones of their ancestors be returned for reburial. The often bitter debate that followed passage of the law raised many basic questions. Should scholars be allowed to continue excavating Indian gravesites? Should human and cultural remains be put on display? Under what circumstances should museums and universities return these materials, and if so to whom? What is to be done with materials not clearly identified with a particular tribe? The author uses the Pawnee experience as an example to illustrate the approaches used in the often angry debates over this subject.

Orlan J. Svingen is an associate professor of history at Washington State University.

The policy of removing American Indian people from their traditional homelands to other locations considered by non-Indians to be more suitable forms a long and painful chapter in the history of Indian-white relations. The word itself—*removal*—is a negative term

Source: Orlan J. Svingen, "The Pawnee of Nebraska: Twice Removed," *American Indian Culture and Research Journal,* 16:2 (1992), pp. 121–37. Reprinted with the permission of the author.

describing a volatile situation between the haves and the have-nots, the powerful and the powerless, between the "removers" and the "removed."

For the Pawnee, removal from Nebraska to Oklahoma created tremendous stress and dislocation. As the years passed, they adapted to their new home; ultimately, however, removal came to have another, even more dreadful meaning for the Pawnee than any of them could have imagined. Once they had departed Nebraska, non-Indians began removing the contents of Pawnee cemeteries, looting graves of Pawnee remains and funerary goods. Grave robbers and trophy hunters sought out abandoned Pawnee villages and included their cemeteries in their "treasure hunt" for what remained of Pawnee life in Nebraska. Amateur archaeologists continued the cultural plundering in the 1920s, systematizing their searches—even purchasing parcels of land believed to contain the remnants of Pawnee villages. In the 1930s and 1940s, Work Projects Administration personnel joined with the Nebraska State Historical Society to professionalize the activity, labeling their work *archaeological excavation.* By the 1950s, the Nebraska State Historical Society in Lincoln had in its possession between five hundred and one thousand Pawnee bodies and thousands of funerary goods taken from their graves. In this sense, the Pawnee of Nebraska were "twice removed" from their homeland.

Prior to removal, the Pawnee ranged over a wide territory on the Great Plains, extending from the Niobrara River in the north to the Arkansas River to the south, and from the mouth of the Platte west beyond the confluence of the North and South Platte rivers in western Nebraska. By the nineteenth century, their earthlodge villages stood along the Platte River in central and eastern Nebraska and on many of that river's tributaries, such as the Loup River. Pawnee population numbers vary somewhat, but during the 1830s they totaled at least ten thousand and possibly as many as 12,500.

Treaties between the four confederated bands of the Pawnee (the Chaui, the Pirahawirata, the Kitkahahki, and the Skidi) and the United States began in 1818. With the treaty of 1833, the Pawnee lost their lands south of the Platte River. In 1848, they ceded a narrow strip along the Platte River. By 1857, Pawnee holdings had been reduced to a small 285,440-acre reservation on the Loup River north of the Platte in present-day Nance County, Nebraska. As Pawnee land holdings diminished, non-Indian settlement and government organization grew, with Nebraska Territory established in 1854 and statehood declared in 1867.

By the mid-1870s, the Pawnee had departed Nebraska for a small reservation in Indian Territory in present-day Oklahoma. Numerous scholars have argued that intertribal warfare between the Sioux and the Pawnee persuaded the Pawnee to abandon Nebraska for a more peaceful location in Indian Territory. These scholars cite, in particular, an encounter in August 1873 between a Pawnee hunting party and enemy Sioux. Oglala and Brulé warriors killed the Pawnee leader, Sky Chief, together with another one hundred Pawnee at what became known as Massacre Canyon near present-day Trenton, Nebraska. "The massacre . . . ," historian James C. Olson concluded, "convinced many of the Pawnee that it was useless to try to remain in Nebraska."

Other scholars have suggested that more complex factors played a role in addition to the "flight from the Sioux" argument. David J. Wishart argues that the Pawnee agreed to move to Indian Territory as a means for preserving their cultural traditions in a less hostile setting. Richard White contends that a host of factors persuaded the Pawnee to remove to Indian Territory, including social, demographic, and ecological considerations.

More, perhaps, than any other non-Indian scholar, White acknowledges non-Indian intolerance toward the Pawnee in Nebraska, although his work focuses on centuries of warfare on the Plains that concluded with Sioux predominance.

A recent work by Martha Royce Blaine accepts many aspects of earlier scholarship on Pawnee removal but addresses more squarely the deleterious effects that non-Indians had on Pawnee culture. Pawnee leaders, poised to respond to the government's plan to remove them to Indian Territory, drafted a "supplemental list of resolutions," which followed six previous resolutions signed by tribal leaders, superintendent Barclay White, and agent William Burgess. In particular, the second of the supplemental resolutions offers important insight into Pawnee perceptions of non-Indians. It states that

> outside traders and other white persons, near our present reservation having taken advantage of our necessities and received by purchase, in trade, or pawn, our government wagons, gov't plows, and poles of our winter lodges, we have by request that none of these parasites, or any white squaw men, be permitted to remove, or settle among us there. We have suffered from them in the past, we desire to be rid of them in the future.

Blaine cites chronically unresolved problems such as starvation, reservation confinement, and non-Indian harassment as conditions that the government might have allowed or even encouraged so as to erode the determination of the Pawnee people to remain in Nebraska. "Perhaps the government did not force the Pawnee to leave," Blaine postulates, " but it programmed the outcome by allowing devastating conditions to exist."

Still another important study examining Pawnee removal was conducted by James Riding In, an historian and an enrolled member of the Pawnee tribe of Oklahoma. Riding In criticizes the "Sioux theory" as a one-sided and incomplete explanation that ignores the tribal perspective regarding removal. From a Pawnee position, Riding In argues that a pervasive hatred toward Indians by non-Indians was the most important factor in Pawnee removal. "Racial hatred, rather than an insatiable hunger for Indian land," he argues, "was the primary motivating force behind the state-wide movement for Pawnee removal." Stripped of legal protection, stereotypically depicted as lazy and worthless, denied access to their traditional livelihood, the Pawnee had no alternative but to accept removal.

The conclusion reached by Olson and others oversimplifies a complex concern and clouds the issue by seemingly absolving non-Indians of responsibility in the matter of Pawnee removal. More to the point, the Sioux theory holds other tribal people—the Oglala and Brulé—largely responsible for Pawnee removal and might suggest to some that abandoning Nebraska for Indian Territory was actually a plan hatched by the Pawnee people themselves. Hostilities between the Sioux and the Pawnee had existed for years, but the latter had never before chosen to relocate to avoid conflict with the Sioux. Some scholars may regard Riding In's analysis as presentistic, but it underscores the attitudes of Americans in the nineteenth century who embraced scientific racism and the notion of greater and lesser "breeds" of people. That the Pawnee were *removed* to Indian Territory is crucial to the Pawnee's interpretation of their history, because any other definition suggests that they abandoned their homeland and forsook the graves of their ancestors who remained in Nebraska.

The removal of living Pawnee from Nebraska to Oklahoma was, however, followed by another form of removal: the removal of dead Pawnee from their graves. From early American contact in present-day Nebraska, Indian skeletal remains—Indian bodies—have been regarded as "fair game" for the curious, including scientists, soldiers, and pothunters. The Long expedition of 1820, a government-sponsored exploration into the Rocky Mountains, passed through Nebraska. En route, the expedition obtained the skull of a Pawnee who had been killed in 1818, and, according to Edwin James, a botanist who chronicled the journey, "we thought it no sacrilege to compliment [the skull] with a place upon one of our pack-horses." The skull appears to have been used later by the craniologist Dr. Samuel George Morton—one of the founders of American physical anthropology—in his 1839 *Crania Americana,* as one of the 144 Native American skulls that he examined and measured. Morton's studies scientifically "proved" the intellectual inferiority of Indians and African-Americans.

The business of removing and collecting Pawnee body parts continued. Orders issued by the United States surgeon general in 1867 and 1868 directed army personnel to send Indian skulls to the Army Medical Museum for scientific study. Accordingly, in 1869 the post surgeon at Fort Harker, Kansas, sent the skulls of six Pawnee killed by the army to the Army Medical Museum. The surgeon described problems he encountered collecting the skulls:

> I had already obtained for the Museum the skull of one of the Pawnee, killed in the fight you speak of, & would have had all had it not been that immediately after the engagement, the Indians lurked about their dead & watched them so closely, that the guide I sent out was unable to secure but the one.

In 1898, Harry Coons, a Pawnee visiting Nebraska from his home in Oklahoma, stopped at Wild Licorice Creek, a former Pawnee town, to visit the graves of his two sisters. He observed that a cornfield stood at the site of their burial and that the graves had been opened and their contents looted.

Graphic evidence of Indian grave robbing appeared in a photograph on a Nebraska postcard in 1907. The photograph shows the remains of an individual removed from the vicinity of the 1873 Massacre Canyon site. A wooden Bromo Seltzer box had been placed on a sidewalk, with two large bones propped against it, and a skull placed in the middle of the box, presumably atop additional human bones. Handwriting on the postcard dubbed the remains "Pawnee Jim."

These examples of disturbance of sepulcher pale, however, in comparison to the systematic procedures introduced by Asa T. Hill. In 1906, Hill had visited the unveiling of a monument in Kansas commemorating what was believed to be the site of the Pike-Pawnee village where the American explorer Zebulon Pike met with the Pawnee in 1806 and replaced a Spanish flag with the American flag. A long-time resident of Nebraska who was well traveled throughout the region, Hill questioned the accuracy of the Kansas claim.

In November 1923, Hill obtained information indicating that a Pawnee town had been found on the George DeWitt farm near Red Cloud, Nebraska, in Webster County. The next week, accompanied by A. L. Dougherty and Dewitt, Hill visited the site, opened a grave, and uncovered the remains of an adult Indian. After removing the remains and funeral goods, Hill contacted superintendent Addison E. Sheldon of the Nebraska State Historical Society (NSHS) and described the village site and the contents of the grave.

The next spring, Hill "excavated" several more burials and concluded that the earthlodge rings and numerous burials indicated that the settlement had been occupied for many years. After examining and comparing the Webster County site with the Kansas Monument location, he and Sheldon concluded that the Webster County site was the actual location visited in 1806 by Zebulon Pike. To reserve the Pawnee Indian village for his personal use, Hill purchased the 320-acre parcel from the landowners.

In addition to Hill, early residents of Nebraska freely indulged their curiosity regarding the contents of Pawnee graves. In a 1925 letter written by Hill concerning Pawnee cemeteries on his recently acquired property, he acknowledged that "settlers have been digging into these graves for the last 50 years." His estimation corroborates reports that indicate that the looting of Pawnee graves began almost immediately after the tribe's removal to Indian Territory.

Over the years, Hill, who became the curator of the museum and field archaeologist for the Nebraska State Historical Society, in conjunction with the federally sponsored Work Projects Administration, dug up the Pike-Pawnee village cemeteries, recovering scores of Pawnee bodies. In a 14 March 1941 letter, Hill informed Waldo Wedel (one of Hill's field assistants and later an authority on Pawnee archaeology) that his farm near Red Cloud, Nebraska, was "covered with Pawnee burials." To date, approximately sixty-five bodies have been removed from graves on what has become known as the Hill site. Hill and his assistant recovered thousands of grave goods from the site.

The Genoa site, which was located farther north in Nance County and was the place from which the Pawnee people were removed to Indian Territory, is an example of a location visited by a variety of individuals over the years. The National Register of Historic Places nomination form for the Genoa site indicates that the only excavations at the location were "salvage work done in State Roads Department barrow pits in 1960 and 1966." Evidence suggests, however, that other excavations were conducted. For example, on a Nebraska State Historical Society Archeological Survey form dated 24 October 1938, Waldo Wedel observed that "large Pawnee cemeteries to west and north on bluffs have been extensively looted with several hundred graves said to have been opened."

More recent activity continued there when, on 14 September 1966, the State Department of Roads informed archaeologist Wendell Frantz that it planned to conduct road repairs on highway N-39 south of Genoa that would require ground leveling on the Genoa site. Frantz traveled to Genoa, where he found and exposed five burials. Three Pawnee bodies and associated mortuary offerings were removed. Another, "an infant burial with two military buttons," was "not excavated, some bone saved." The fifth individual was in poor condition, with "no artifacts, not excavated."

On 10 September 1970, archaeologist Carl Hugh Jones learned from landowner Allen Atkins that he and others had been "land leveling on the Greek site [same land as Genoa site] and were hitting burials." Jones and three others (Curt Peacock, Ron Kivett, and Kevin Leitch) arrived at Genoa and found "six or eight pothunters gathered around a couple of burials trying to dig out the bones before the other guy could." As with other excavations, the Genoa site received many visitors. "A rural school showed up and kept us company much of the morning," Jones noted. "Some of these kids," he continued, "collected bones from the area where they had been scraped and dumped."

The Genoa site is an example of a place where local landowners found opportunities to acquire "trophies." As Carl Jones explained, one of the landowners "brought us a skull that his boys had gotten from the site." Jones then added that other landowners had "some material" and that "sometimes the pothunters get all the good stuff."

The Hill and Genoa sites are particular examples of non-Indian interest in the Pawnee dead, but numerous other instances portray cases of grave robbing, desecration, and disrespect. Archaeologists frequently recorded grave disturbances by landowners and private individuals throughout Nebraska. For example, at burial hill site 25HM2, which was excavated on 31 October 1940, archaeologists noted that extensive looting had occurred. Of the seven burial pits excavated at the site, only two retained burials. Archaeologist Robert B. Cumming observed that field burial number 7 lacked a skull and stated that "the region had been potted before and the owner of the land remembers digging up skulls here 55 years ago."

In addition to accounts of looting, examples abound of disrespectful treatment of skeletal remains seemingly "in the way" or tossed aside as unimportant. While excavating the Larson site (25PT1) in 1936, George Lamb reported that a power canal had been built several years before, and project workmen "claimed that human bones were thrown out in a number of instances." Furthermore, Webster County's first settlers discovered many Indian burial grounds during house and fence construction. Settlers frequently showed callous disregard for the graves. In his "Early History of Webster County," Emanual Peters described how a neighbor built a dugout and in the process "several skulls were thrown out." The same neighbor later fenced in a hog lot. "The hogs soon rooted out so many skulls," Peter claimed, "[that they] would roll down and form a drift against the fence."

In a site description on a National Register of Historic Places nomination form, the recorder explained that at the time of excavation in 1941, the Hill-Rupp site (25PT13) had been cultivated "for some 30 years and hunted over by collectors." Webster County residents reported that pothunters optimized their visits to burial sites by arriving just after rain showers.

The callous disregard evidenced by looters, grave robbers, and pothunters is paralleled by the attitudes of archaeologists who depicted grave goods as "treasures" in publications, reports, and correspondence. In a 1 September 1928 letter to A. T. Hill, Charles Bertrand Schultz remarked that "Webster County is getting up a little collection of relics . . . [and] they would like to have the products or contents of one of the graves on your farm." Schultz also claimed that he had "been out collecting bones ever since the first of June." Likewise, Hill boasted, "I don't play golf. . . . [M]y only recreation is this Indian investigation. I come out here Sundays and dig up Indians. . . . [T]his hill is my golf course."

It also appears that some excavations took on a sporting event atmosphere. Site files, photographs, and newspaper accounts record the presence of visitors to the sites during the excavations. Hill, for instance, invited people through newspaper notices to visit his farm and to "join in the further hunt for 'finds.' " On one occasion, one hundred people responded and spent the afternoon digging, with two graves located and opened that day. A note by Hill indicated that sightseers were common: "We are having good luck finding skeletons. Have lots of visitors."

In the 1970s, former NSHS director Marvin Kivett related a story involving Dr. L. M. Kunkel from Weeping Water, Nebraska. Reportedly, in the 1920s Dr. Kunkel accepted items unearthed from Indian villages located on his land as payment for medical services he provided.

Another example of insensitivity and an unscientific and unprofessional attitude toward human remains appeared in photographs taken in 1940 at the Burkett site

(25NC1). Two separate photographs illustrate non-Indian WPA personnel reclining inside a burial pit next to a partially exposed human skeleton, presumably Pawnee. Climbing into a burial pit, holding one's own head with one hand, placing the other hand on an exposed skull, and then being photographed while others look on is inconsistent with professional and scientific behavior at an archaeological excavation. It is, however, consistent with a mocking attitude, "trophyesque" posture, and grave desecration. The question begs to be asked: Would the pictured non-Indians have found it appropriate to display this type of behavior in a non-Indian cemetery?

Once the skeletal remains and burial offerings came into the possession of the historical society, archaeologists and WPA workers handled these items in a variety of ways. They began by photographing and bagging the burial goods. In some instances, site files reveal conservation measures that included applying shellac to the remains. Next they numbered and catalogued the remains and burial goods according to the site location. By this point, archaeologists had separated the deceased Pawnee from their burial possessions. The funerary goods became "artifacts" that were identified and placed in an ethnographic collection, and NSHS personnel routinely incorporated selected grave goods into a variety of museum exhibits over the years. Rarely, if ever, were any of the hundreds—maybe thousands—of funerary articles used in historical exhibits identified as Pawnee grave goods; rather they simply were referred to as artifacts. In regard to the human remains, physical anthropologists have studied the Pawnee skeletal "material"—as it was commonly termed—for information on dental pathology, craniometrics, mortuary practices, and subsistence patterns.

Pawnee removal continued well into the 1980s, for on 18 July 1984, Douglas Owsley, a member of the Department of Anthropology at Louisiana State University, concluded a loan agreement with NSHS. The society agreed to lend its entire Pawnee skeletal collection to Owsley for a period of five years. Owsley rented a moving van to transport the boxed Pawnee remains from Lincoln, Nebraska, to Baton Rouge, Louisiana. When Owsley was hired by the Smithsonian Institution three years later, he arranged for another specially equipped moving van to convey the remains from LSU to Washington, D.C.

As the revelations regarding the second removal of Pawnee deceased became known to the general public and to the Pawnee people in the late 1980s, questions emerged over who held title to the Pawnee remains and whether permits had been required to exhume them. Despite clear and indisputable statutory law in Nebraska that protected the remains of the dead, the only documentation relating to the "ownership" of Pawnee human skeletons and funerary goods was a bill of sale from Asa T. Hill to the Nebraska State Historical Society dated 17 April 1942. The document plainly illustrates that Hill regarded the contents of Pawnee graves on his land as his personal property, to dispense with as he saw fit. Hill sold the entire collection to the society for one dollar. In addition to thousands of mortuary offerings, the Hill Collection included the bodies of approximately thirty Pawnee men, women, and children.

Throughout his career as an amateur archaeologist, Hill represented himself in one way to Indian people and in another to non-Indians on the subject of grave excavation. In discussions with non-Indians concerning graves and grave goods, he spoke openly about bones, skulls, and "relics" such as spoons, mirrors, beads, and trinkets. In a letter to Waldo Wedel, Hill boastfully declared himself "the champion pothunter of Nebraska." Likewise, in a letter to Hill, Wedel referred to him as "The King of Pothunters." In another instance, Charles Bertrand Schultz of Red Cloud informed Hill that he had "been out collecting bones since the first of June." He then asked Hill's permission to hunt artifacts on Hill's farm in Webster County. Hill agreed, with the proviso that he would retain certain items such as medals. "Beads and the ordinary Indian trinkets that you find in the grave," Hill added, "you are welcome to keep."

To Indian people, however, Hill's correspondence presented a very different attitude toward graves and their contents. For example, he never invited Pawnee to his farm to hunt for bones or artifacts. He never reported to them that he was having good luck finding skeletons or that the digs attracted many visitors. Nor did his correspondence with Indian people ever include references to himself as a pothunter. Instead of inviting Pawnee out for one of his Sunday afternoon digs, he informed them that he had "stopped the promiscuous digging." Although he described to Stacy Matlock, a Pawnee from Oklahoma, the removal of a "few of the contents" of the graves for the Nebraska State Historical Society's use, he failed to explain the extent of the grave disturbances and what he meant by the *society's use*. In the 5 June 1926 letter to Matlock in which he discussed his activities at the site, Hill never used the words *skeletons* or *dead bodies*. More to the point, Hill's vague and ambiguous language with Matlock contrasts with his actual activities, which can be described as exhuming Pawnee bodies and removing grave goods.

Hill's correspondence gave Matlock no hint that thousands of mortuary offerings and scores of deceased Pawnee were "free for the taking" or intended for permanent curation, preservation, scientific study, and display. Moreover, because of the generally poor condition of the graveyards, Hill declared his intention to "fill up all the old holes that had been dug previously, and place little markers at each grave," clearly implying that Pawnee remains were still interred in their resting places. Regarding a skeleton removed from a grave near Clarks, Nebraska, alleged to be Petalashero's, Hill claimed that "it is my intention to place this skull and the other stuff back in the grave and place a monument over it."

The two sides of Asa T. Hill, regarded by some as the "father of archaeology in Nebraska," makes it clear that the man represented himself differently to Indian and non-Indian people. His actions and words to non-Indians reveal a man who spoke and behaved unprofessionally and insensitively toward Indian burials. To non-Indians, he compared excavating Pawnee to playing golf. In correspondence to Pawnee people, the same man cast himself as an advocate of reburial and a protector of Pawnee grave sites and cemeteries. The disparity between Hill's correspondence with Indians and his letters to non-Indians reveals an individual who used deception and misrepresentation in his relations with the Pawnee people.

Research uncovered no evidence of documentation establishing an NSHS right to exhume Pawnee remains and maintain them under perpetual curation. Although Nebraska state statutes require permits for the exhumation of human bodies, records reveal no court orders sanctioning exhumation, no permits by the Smithsonian Institution, and no Pawnee Tribal Council resolutions authorizing the disentombment of Pawnee Indian remains. Against the historic backdrop of unrestrained looting and pothunting, the state of Nebraska appears to have looked the other way in regard to Native American graves and cemeteries. The remains of Indian bodies were made available in the academic marketplace of scientific inquiry (e.g., the NSHS loan to Louisiana State University and the

Smithsonian), where careers were established, furthered, and pursued over the bodies of dead Pawnee people without the consent of living tribal members.

Disturbances of Pawnee cemeteries by non-Indians prompted an outcry from Nebraska's tribal people and the Pawnee of Oklahoma, who saw the skeletal excavations as a desecration of their spiritual tradition. Lawrence Goodfox, former Pawnee Tribal Council chairman, described his people as distraught over the "indignant, insulting, and sacrilegious treatment" of their ancestors. Similarly, Reba White Shirt, former director of the Nebraska Indian Commission, observed that Indian people "want the graves of our ancestors to be treated with the same dignity and respect as anyone else's grave."

Ethnologists acknowledge that Pawnee mortuary practices included formalized ritual treatment of the deceased. An individual would be painted, dressed, anointed, and then enveloped in a robe or blanket in preparation for interment. One observer, Father Peter DeSmet, witnessed a Pawnee burial in 1858. Members of the funeral party, DeSmet related, placed the young man's body into the grave "amid the acclamations and lamentations of the whole tribe." A wide range of personal effects might be placed into an individual's grave, including such items as a bow and arrow, a pipe, and beads. Frequently, sacred medicine bundles were also entombed with the deceased. Ethnologists Dorsey and Murie explain that "the people believe that when they die they take all their belongings with them to Spirit Land." The aforementioned objects were considered to belong to the grave's occupant. Only in rare and unusual circumstances did the Pawnee sanction grave disturbances. Such acts were undertaken only for compelling religious purposes and only with the permission of the family of the dead.

Pawnee earthlodge towns characteristically had cemeteries located in their vicinity, situated on hilltops and ridges near the towns. Subsequent to their departure to Oklahoma in the mid-1870s, the Pawnee continued to bury their dead in cemeteries in the same fashion they had followed in Nebraska. When deceased Pawnee were buried, it was understood that their graves would be a permanent resting place and that the sacred possessions of the dead would remain with them for their use in the afterlife. Leaving Nebraska for Oklahoma did not mean, however, that the remains left behind were abandoned to looters, grave robbers, or archaeologists. The sanctity of the grave was intended to be perpetual.

A 1971 statement adopted by the American Anthropological Association makes it clear that the "anthropologists' paramount responsibility is to those they study." In other words, scientific study should not be considered more important than the dignity of human beings, living or dead. Because archaeologists are responsible to the people they study, they must make it their business to understand when their techniques are offensive to their subjects. Failure to do this will continue to expose archaeologists and the scientific community to charges of scientific ethnocentrism and scientific racism. They will be seen as guilty of objectifying tribal culture by coldly severing remains and funerary objects from Native American mortuary traditions. They could, moreover, be seen as practitioners of a form of conquest scholarship wherein they sanction and promote academic and scientific investigations of indigenous cultures solely through the use of Euro-American standards and oblivious to the objections of the subjects. The persistent demand by non-Indian scientists and scholars for continued scientific activity against the wishes of protected minorities courts danger for all involved and endorses the undignified treatment of certain members of a society.

In June 1989, the Nebraska Unicameral passed the Unmarked Human Burial Sites and Skeletal Remains Protection Act, which set in motion a series of legal remedies that have begun to reverse the injustices suffered by the Pawnee and their deceased ancestors. Slightly more than one year later, on 10 September 1990, the Pawnee people reclaimed the remains of more than four hundred of their ancestors from the Nebraska State Historical Society in Lincoln, Nebraska. (In November 1990, President Bush signed into law H. R. 5237, which established the Native American Grave Protection and Repatriation Act.) The return took place at the State Museum, where representatives of NSHS and the Pawnee tribe signed papers finalizing the process. Later that day, Pawnee representatives loaded more than four hundred small wooden coffins into a vehicle and transported them to Genoa, Nebraska, for reburial in the municipal cemetery there. Genoa was the site of the Pawnee Reservation before their removal to Oklahoma.

Louie LaRose, from the Winnebago Indian Reservation in Winnebago, Nebraska, attended the repatriation as a representative of his tribe and observed the transfer. During the exchange, LaRose spoke with John Ludwickson, a salvage archaeologist for the state of Nebraska. Throughout the repatriation debate, Ludwickson had remained a staunch opponent of returning skeletal remains and the attendant funerary goods. At one point in their conversation, LaRose commented to Ludwickson that the return of the Pawnee remains in the wooden coffins was a reason for celebration. Ludwickson countered that "those aren't coffins; they are storage boxes."

Ludwickson's remark came after more than two years of intense controversy between the Pawnee and the Nebraska State Historical Society over the disposition of Pawnee remains held in the State Museum collection and lent to other institutions. It illustrates deep, fundamental, and abiding cultural differences that made the dispute such a painful ordeal for both sides in this issue. LaRose could not have used any other term than *coffin* to describe the $1' \times 1' \times 2'$ wooden boxes, but Ludwickson stubbornly clung to the scientific, dehumanizing term *storage boxes*. LaRose's and Ludwickson's attitudes depict cultural polarization. At what should be a time of reconciliation and understanding, the John Ludwicksons of the world refuse to make allowances for the rightful claims of minorities to their traditional expressions of spirituality. These scholars have internalized their scientific training to such an extent that they no longer conduct themselves in a respectful manner when dealing with the contemporary culture of the people they study.

Readings for Orlan J. Svingen:

The repatriation of artifacts, funerary, and skeletal remains continues to be a hotly contested and much discussed issue, but little solid historical scholarship on these questions has been produced. One entire issue of the *American Indian Quarterly* 20:2 (Spring 1996) is devoted to the questions that Svingen has raised. Of most significance is the essay in that issue by James Riding In, "Repatriation: A Pawnee's Perspective." For a recent discussion of earlier treatment of the Nebraska Indians see David J. Wishart, *An Unspeakable Sadness: The Dispossession of the Nebraska Indians.*

25

THE POLITICS OF INDIAN GAMING: TRIBE/STATE RELATIONS AND AMERICAN FEDERALISM

ANNE MERLINE MCCULLOCH

For most of the last century Indian reservations have been isolated poverty pockets. Since the 1960s that has changed slowly. In fact, the passage of the 1989 Indian Gaming Regulatory Act brought dramatic changes in the situation of some tribes. That legislation allowed Indians to negotiate agreements with the states that enabled the tribes to build and operate gambling facilities on their reservations. Casinos opened quickly across the country as tribal leaders foresaw possible wealth and security for their people. By 1994 Indian gambling operations functioned in at least twenty-five states, creating a vast new industry that grossed $1.5 billion for the Indians that year.

This has changed the lives of people from groups fortunate enough to have successful gaming operations. Some tribal governments now can fund improved health-care facilities, public schools and better housing, while their casinos offer good paying jobs to formerly unemployed people. This essay examines the process of federal establishment of the system, the relations between tribes and the states surrounding their reservations as they negotiated over gaming compacts, and of the reduction in Indian autonomy because of federal regulation and the need for state approval for the Indians' actions. Numerous contentious issues have arisen over Indian gambling and the author provides a background for understanding them.

Anne Merline McCulloch is a professor in the department of history and political science at Columbia College, Columbia, South Carolina.

In 1988, the Congress passed the Indian Gaming Regulatory Act (IGRA). The act recognizes the right of Indian tribes in the United States to establish gambling and gaming facilities on their reservations, providing the states in which they are located have some form of legalized gambling. High-stakes gambling has now become a leading industry

Source: Anne Merline McCulloch, "The Politics of Gaming: Tribe/State Relations and American Federalism," *Publius* 24:3 (summer 1994): (99–112). © 1994 by CSF Associates.

301

for many tribal economies. As of 1994, the Bureau of Indian Affairs reported that seventy-four tribes in eighteen states had signed 100 tribe/state compacts concerning reservation gambling. Numerous other tribes and states were involved in compact negotiations. Seventy-two tribes had operating gaming facilities in twenty-five states, and it is estimated by *Gaming and Wagering Business* magazine that the Indian gaming industry grosses over $1.5 billion per year.

The Indian Gaming Regulatory Act is having a major impact on intergovernmental relationships among Indian tribes, states, and the federal government. First, the revenues generated by the gaming and gambling industry have helped to spur economic development in Indian country, which in turn is supporting the dual goals of tribal sovereignty and economic self-sufficiency. Second, IGRA has generated intergovernmental conflicts between the tribes and the states over issues involving state sovereignty, criminal jurisdiction, and gambling revenues. Third, while the tribes and states contend over issues of sovereignty and jurisdiction, IGRA ensures that the federal government maintains its position of supremacy over tribes and tribe/state relations.

The Indian Gaming Regulatory Act of 1988

Although traditional Indian games and the gambling associated with them have long been played on reservations, it was not until the Seminole tribe opened the first high-stakes bingo parlor in 1979 that gambling became a major industry in Indian country. When Florida tried to close the operation, the U.S. 5th Circuit Court of Appeals ruled in *Seminole Tribe of Florida* v. *Butterworth,* that bingo fell under statutes classed as regulatory rather than prohibitory.

> Bingo appears to fall in a category of gambling that the state has chosen to regulate by imposing certain limitations to avoid abuses. Where the state regulates the operation of bingo halls to prevent the game of bingo from becoming a money-making business, the Seminole Indian tribe is not subject to that regulation and cannot be prosecuted for violating the limitations imposed.

The regulatory/prohibitory distinction made by the court meant that gambling fell outside the criminal provisions of Public Law 280 and could not be prohibited by the state. The *Seminole* case opened the doors to high-stakes bingo on reservations across the country, and similar cases were soon decided by other federal courts. Finally, in *California* v. *Cabazon Band of Mission Indians,* the U.S. Supreme Court declared that once a state has legalized any form of gambling, Indian tribes within that state can offer the same game on trust land without any state interference or restrictions.

The *Cabazon* decision provoked dissimilar responses from the tribes and the states. Generally, the tribes saw the decision as an affirmation of their sovereign right to govern their lands and people. Tribes that previously had been willing to discuss the possibility of federal regulation of gambling were now unwilling or much less willing to support any outside regulation. However, states, particularly those with non-Indian gaming, opposed Indian-regulated gaming. In testifying before the Congress on 25 June 1987, Governor Richard H. Bryan of Nevada advocated "a comprehensive system of strict gaming regulation [over Indian gambling]." It was his view that the "Nevada Gaming Control Act provides the comprehensive regulatory structure necessary to protect our citizens and tourists from the dangers otherwise associated with unregulated and uncontrolled gambling." Bryan maintained that because of the cost of regulatory control ($13 million for Nevada in 1986), it was in the best interests of the tribes and the federal government to let the state bear the financial burden of regulating gaming. G. Michael Brown, former director of the New Jersey Division of Gaming Enforcement and, at the time, counsel to a number of foreign and domestic casino interests, testified in a similar manner.

Gambling interests in Nevada and New Jersey were not the only ones concerned about tribal regulation of Indian gaming. The National Association of Attorneys General (NAAG) passed a resolution in 1985 calling for state regulation of Indian gaming. After *Cabazon,* NAAG switched its support to federal regulation. Following NAAG, the National Sheriffs' Association came out in support of federal regulation as well.

In response to demands by all sides, the Congress hurriedly passed the Indian Gaming Regulatory Act (IGRA), which went into effect on 17 October 1988. The act is intended to (1) promote tribal economic development, self-sufficiency, and strong tribal government; (2) provide for a regulatory base to protect Indian gaming from organized crime; and (3) establish the National Indian Gaming Commission.

The act defines three classes of gambling and gaming:

Class I: Social games solely for prizes of minimal value or traditional forms of Indian gaming engaged in by individuals as a part of, or in connection with, tribal ceremonies or celebrations.

Class II: All forms of bingo, and other games similar to bingo such as pull tabs, lotto, etc. and card games that are explicitly authorized by state law, not including blackjack, baccarat, or chemin de fer.

Class III: All forms of gaming that are not Class I gaming or Class II gaming.

Class I gaming is wholly within the exclusive jurisdiction of the tribe. Class II gaming is allowed if the state within which the tribe is located allows it by anyone or under any conditions. A tribe is allowed to license and regulate Class II gaming on Indian lands. Class III gaming requires a negotiated tribe-state compact. The National Indian Gaming Commission (NIGC) was established to approve the compacts and to become the watchdog agency to prevent abuses. The final set of regulations concerning NIGC was published in January 1993, and the commission began operating in late February 1993. The federal district courts are given jurisdiction by the act over cases in which a state does not negotiate in "good faith." According to the act, if the district court finds that a state has not negotiated in "good faith," it can direct a mandatory sixty-day negotiating period, and if a compact cannot be concluded by the end of that period, a federal mediator will select one based on the plans offered by both sides.

Tribal Sovereignty and Gaming Casinos

The Indian Gaming Regulatory Act has been heralded by many tribal leaders as a key ingredient in achieving tribal sovereignty. In his seminal work on federal Indian law, Felix Cohen defined tribal sovereignty as *those powers which are lawfully vested in an Indian tribe [and] are not, in general, delegated powers granted by express acts of Congress, but rather inherent powers of a limited sovereignty which has never been extinguished. . . .* The powers of sovereignty have been limited from time to time by special treaties and laws designed to take from the Indian tribes control of matters which, in the judgment of Congress, these tribes could no longer be safely permitted to handle (italics in original).

Three views on tribal sovereignty are extant today. The first view argues that Indian tribes are aboriginal sovereign nations with full rights under international law. This view is supported by the U.N. Working Group on Indigenous Populations. At the other extreme is the view that tribal sovereignty has been extinguished and that Indians hold no more special rights than any other American citizens. This view is held by a few Indians, and by a number of non-Indians who object to special Indian treaty rights. It is the intermediate position, though, which has been adopted by the Congress and the courts. Stated first by Chief Justice John Marshall, this view recognizes that Indian tribes have inherent, retained powers as "domestic, dependent nations" under the umbrella of U.S. government protection.

Although there was a period of time when tribal sovereignty was ignored and Indians were considered to be "wards of the government," beginning with *Williams* v. *Lee* in 1959 the U.S. Supreme Court again acknowledged the right of tribes to govern themselves free from state "infringement." This position was reaffirmed in several subsequent cases, including *McClanahan* v. *Arizona State Tax Commission, U.S.* v. *Mazurie, U.S.* v. *Wheeler,* and *Merrion* v. *Jicarilla Apache Tribe.* The U.S. 10th Circuit Court of Appeals at one point even declared that Indian tribes held a status higher than states, a position which has never been supported by the Supreme Court.

Congressional support of tribal sovereignty and self-government began in 1934 with the Indian Reorganization (Wheeler Howard) Act (IRA), which provided for the establishment of tribal constitutional governments. However, lack of funding, paternalistic treatment by the Bureau of Indian Affairs (BIA), and House Concurrent Resolution 108 (termination), and P.L. 280 prevented much progress toward self-government until the Indian Self-Determination and Education Assistance Act of 1975. This act, first sponsored by President Richard M. Nixon, provided for tribal programs to be funded by the federal government, but to be planned and administered by the tribes. In 1988, this act was strengthened when the Congress provided for Self-Determination Demonstration Projects. These were to be funded by federal block grants, but administered by the tribe. The demonstration projects were successful enough to lead the Congress to make them permanent for selected tribes.

Further strides toward autonomy were made when the Congress passed the Indian Child Welfare Act, the Alaska Native Claims Settlement Act, and the Indian Tribal Government Tax Status Act of 1982. Together, these acts have helped to make tribal sovereignty an economic and political reality.

The major roadblock for Indian tribes in achieving autonomy has been lack of economic independence. It is widely known that Indians living on reservations have the highest unemployment rate in the nation and the lowest life expectancy rate. Reservations are often compared to Third World nations. No other type of government in the United States is so dependent on intergovernmental transfers for its existence.

The prime structural hindrance to economic development on reservations has been trust land. Trust land is reserved for and owned by Indians but held "in trust" by the federal government for the benefit of the Indian owners. Trust land can either be owned by the tribe as a whole or by individual Indians (allotment or heirship lands). Congress' intention in creating trust land was to prevent it from being usurped by states or by private individuals. The Congress must consent to any sale of trust land.

While trust lands have helped tribes retain a land base and some cultural integrity, trust lands also make it difficult to attract industry and commercial enterprises to the reservation. Industries can only lease trust land, and banks are often unwilling to lend money for construction on the reservation because they may be unable to repossess in case of default. Even where the land on the reservation is owned in fee-simple title, non-Indian entrepreneurs may be reluctant to risk subjecting themselves to the authority of governments in which they can have no authoritative voice. Only when the potential gain is so great as to offset the risk and uncertainty of doing business on the reservation will companies take the risk.

The few large-scale enterprises on reservations have been the multinational resource-extraction companies experienced in taking risks in unstable economies. Unfortunately, oil and mineral leases often led to cycles of boom and bust, accentuating the instability of reservation economies. What economic stability there was often came from a system of leasing tribal and heirship lands in large quantities to non-Indian farmers or ranchers, providing only a minimal income for the reservation residents and resulting in an inefficient use of the land.

Tribes were caught in a vicious paradox where the system that ensured their cultural identity through preserving their land base also promoted poverty by limiting the use of that land. Gambling provided an alternative industry which, because it was not resource dependent, would maintain tribal control over the land while still creating jobs and bringing in outside revenues. In order to ensure that gambling, as an industry, supported tribal independence, rather than leading to further erosion of tribal resources by non-Indians, IGRA requires that the gaming facilities be owned by the tribes and be operated on trust land.

The Economic Impact of Gaming on Indian Tribes

American Indian tribes have looked to gambling as a means to achieve the economic autonomy requisite for tribal sovereignty, and to improve the lives and the health of their members through employment. The immediate effect of Indian gaming seems to have done just that.

The economic benefits of gambling for the tribes are most evident in the labor market. Casinos have hired large numbers of resident and non-resident Indians for both skilled and unskilled jobs, thus lowering the tribal unemployment and welfare rates. According to the Midwest Hospitality Advisors report on Indian gaming in Minnesota,

> [t]he 13 Indian gaming operations in the State of Minnesota currently employ approximately 5,700 people. Four casinos have become the largest employer for their nearest city, four others are among the top five employers for their communities, and one other is in the top ten. Current employment includes 1,350 Native Americans, or approximately 24 percent of total employees.

The report notes that between 1990 and 1992, the percent of Indian AFDC (Aid to Families with Dependent Children) recipients residing in counties with Indian casinos decreased by 3.2 percent, while in the same period recipients in non-casino counties increased by 14.6 percent. The Flandreau Santee Sioux in neighboring South Dakota turned a 30 percent unemployment rate into almost nothing while virtually eliminating unemployment for the whole county. The Grand Casino in Mille Lacs, Minnesota, has reduced unemployment for the Mille Lacs Ojibwe from a high of 45 percent to zero.

The best example of what gambling can mean to a tribe is found in Connecticut. The tiny reservation of the Mashantucket Pequot Tribe is located about halfway between New York City and Boston on I-95 in Ledyard, Connecticut. Their gaming facility, Foxwoods High Stakes Bingo and Casino, has 234 gaming tables and 3,108 slot machines, and is the second largest casino in the world. Since its opening on 15 February 1992, estimates place the daily gross at $1.6 million (approximately $584 million a year). The tribe recently expanded its facilities to include a 312-room hotel/casino, and it has plans to add retail shops, restaurants, a health club, theaters, two golf courses, campgrounds, and lakeside entertainment to the complex.

While few tribes have the locational advantage of the Mashantucket Pequot, the gaming industry is having positive economic benefits for all. With the millions of dollars that the tribes are receiving in profits, they are building schools and community centers, setting up education trust funds, underwriting the cost of tribal government, financing new business enterprises, and putting in water and sewer systems on the reservations. For instance, the Fort Randall Casino in Wagner, South Dakota, employs 654 people, 66 percent of whom are Native American. It has an annual payroll of more than $7.3 million and generates more than $600,000 in federal taxes. Profits from the casino have been used to fund a state-certified day-care facility, build a culturally based addiction-treatment center, construct a new Bureau of Indian Affairs building, and establish an intern program for young tribal members. Over $50,000 was contributed to local charities.

Gambling and gaming do present the opportunity for tribes to develop an industry that has the potential of solving, in the short run, their economic problems and of promoting tribal government. The outlook in the long run is more doubtful. Indian gaming facilities have entered a market where, at this time, they have little or no competition. The greater the number of tribes that enter the market, however, the smaller the share for each. The Grand Casinos of the Ojibwe are being challenged in Minnesota by the Mystic Lake Casino operated by the Shakopee Mdewakanton Sioux and the Shooting Star Casino, which opened in May 1992, operated by the White Earth Band of Chippewa Indians.

However, Indian competition is not the real threat. As Nelson Rose, law professor and expert on gaming, noted, "Gambling begets gambling." Indian gaming has led to pressures on lawmakers to open gambling to all. Already, riverboat gambling is legal in four Mississippi River states. Small-scale casinos are run in resort towns in Colorado and South Dakota. Chicago's mayor, Richard Daley, was approached in March 1992 by a consortium composed of Circus Circus Enterprises, Hilton Hotels, and Caesars World to design, develop, and operate a $2 billion casino/entertainment center in the heart of Chicago. A large casino complex has been approved for New Orleans, Louisiana. Supply and demand dictate economic success. If casinos open within major population centers, there will be no reason for gamblers to travel to Indian reservations. The market could become oversupplied, and the tribes may be left with empty casinos and high unemployment rates again.

State Responses to Indian Gaming

State government responses to Indian gaming involve several issues, including protection of state sovereignty as provided for in the Tenth and Eleventh amendments, criminal jurisdiction over non-Indians involved in Indian gaming, and questions relating to IGRA terminology regarding what constitutes Class II and Class III gaming.

The most common defense by the states against Indian gaming has been the Eleventh Amendment. The amendment reads: "The Judicial power of the United States shall not be construed to extend to any suit in law or equity, commenced or prosecuted against one of the United States by Citizens of another State, or by Citizens or Subjects of any Foreign State." The amendment was ratified in 1795 as a result of *Chisolm* v. *Georgia* in which the U.S. Supreme Court allowed a citizen from South Carolina to sue the State of Georgia in federal court. The decision caused a great uproar among the states, who feared a rash of lawsuits. In order to protect state sovereign immunity, the Eleventh Amendment was rushed through the Congress and then quickly ratified. The Supreme Court has ruled that the Congress has the power to make exceptions to the amendment. According to Edward Corwin and Jack Peltason, "Congress in exercising its delegated powers may make state participation in some activities conditional on the willingness of a state to waive immunity."

In recent years, the Supreme Court has begun to question just how explicit the language of the congressional statute must be in order to abrogate state immunity. In 1991, the Court extended that issue to Indian tribes when it ruled in *Blatchford, Commissioner, Department of Community and Regional Affairs of Alaska* v. *Native Village of Noatak* that the Eleventh Amendment bars suits by Indian tribes against states without their consent unless the statute in question reflects an "unmistakably clear intent to abrogate immunity." Subsequently, three U.S. District Court cases brought by tribes against states when compact negotiations broke down were dismissed on the basis of the Eleventh Amendment. This happened despite rather explicit language within IGRA allowing for suits by tribes in federal court against states that do not bargain in "good faith." The impact of these rulings seems to have slowed tribal litigation and placed a greater premium on compromise and concession by both parties.

The Tenth Amendment has also been used by non-Indian casino operators to oppose the competition posed by Indian gaming. In April 1993, Donald Trump, Atlantic City casino owner, filed suit in federal district court against Secretary of the Interior Bruce Babbitt, claiming that IGRA violates the Tenth Amendment. Trump argued that IGRA gives Indians preferential treatment by not making them subject to the same regulations that govern other gambling establishments and as such discriminate against him. Trump's interest was spurred by competition from the Foxwoods casino of the Mashantucket Pequot in Connecticut and the push by the Ramapough Indians of New Jersey to gain federal recognition so that they can open a casino.

The second field of concern for state government is the impact gambling may have on state criminal justice systems. State officials have expressed concern over problems in two areas: infiltration of Indian gaming by organized crime and enforcement of IGRA by the federal government. The experience of Nevada and New Jersey officials with organized crime and gambling was enough to make many state officials uneasy with any form of non-state regulated gambling. As if to confirm their fears, on 2 February 1992, *The*

Sacramento Bee reported that "Chicago crime bosses, John 'No Nose' DiFronzo and Samuel Carlisi, along with eight of their allegedly criminal associates, [were arrested by federal agents] on charges of racketeering, extortion, and fraud in connection with an aborted attempt to take over gambling on the Rincon Indian reservation near San Diego."

The tribes argue that the states are overreacting to rumors of organized crime. Gaiashkibos, president of the National Congress of American Indians and chairman of the Lac Courte Band of Lake Superior Chippewa, believes that rather than increasing crime, Indian gaming will reduce crime.

State officials have also expressed concern over federal enforcement of IGRA. In the words of Charles B. Hoslet, general counsel to the governor of Wisconsin, "Quite frankly, our experience to date indicates that Federal enforcement is sparse at best. . . . In fact, the United States Justice Department's apparent policy of nonenforcement of illegal Indian gaming is so widely understood that a tribal attorney has referred to it as such in arguments to the court in litigation over Wisconsin's criminal jurisdiction." The lack of federal enforcement is particularly troubling to the states because tribal police lack jurisdiction over non-Indians, and IGRA prevents state regulation. Lack of effective regulation has led to several instances of Indians and non-Indians establishing gambling facilities without either tribal or state approval.

The problem with unauthorized gaming facilities is in large part a result of vague language in IGRA's definition of Class II or Class III, particularly regarding electronic video gambling devices. In order to eliminate as many disputes as possible between tribal and state governments, the National Association of Attorneys General adopted a resolution at its 1991 winter meeting requesting a number of specific changes to IGRA's language that would better define Class II and Class III gambling devices.

There have also been conflicts between tribes and states concerning state legislation regarding gambling. For example, after a very fierce battle, Idaho voters approved a constitutional amendment to allow a state-run lottery. During the 1988 debate, some Idahoans forecast that approval of a state lottery might lead to Indian casino gaming. At the time, it was seen as a scare tactic by anti-gambling forces. However, the issue was brought up again in 1992 when the Nez Perce, Coeur d'Alene, Kootenai, and Shoshone-Bannock tribes began pressing for tribe-state compacts to allow gaming. Governor Cecil Andrus (secretary of the interior under President Jimmy Carter) and Attorney General Larry EchoHawk (former tribal counsel for the Shoshone-Bannock tribes) found themselves in the unlikely position of opposing the tribes on this issue. Andrus and EchoHawk sponsored a successful state constitutional amendment that year prohibiting casino gaming. The Nez Perce tribe immediately filed suit in federal court challenging the vote by claiming that the language misled the voters. Later, they filed a second suit charging that Idaho was illegally selling state lottery tickets on the reservation. Since that time, however, two other tribes (Coeur d'Alene and Kootenai) have signed tribe-state compacts with Idaho.

A similar situation exists in Arizona where, two years ago, the legislature passed and Governor Fife Symington signed into law a bill banning statewide gambling. The bill was targeted at reducing the kinds of gaming in which Arizona tribes could engage, not at eliminating Indian gaming altogether. Since the ban, the governor has signed thirteen limited tribe-state compacts. Nevertheless, the issue remains a bone of contention for the tribes and, as of this writing, the Arizona legislature was attempting to craft an agreement that would lift the earlier ban and be satisfactory to all parties.

The Idaho and Arizona governors were joined by forty-seven other governors (only Governor Joan Finney of Kansas opposed the resolution) when the National Governors' Association passed a resolution on 2 February 1993 expressing concern about IGRA. The resolution stated that, despite support for tribal economic opportunities, "some Governors find themselves in the position of being expected to negotiate Indian gaming compacts that would be in conflict with the laws of their states." This is not to say that all interactions have been negative. In March 1994, the California Legislative Black Caucus, the California Latino Legislative Caucus, and the California Asian Legislative Caucus sponsored a resolution that reaffirmed their "recognition of the status of California's Indian Nations as sovereign governmental entities" through IGRA.

The issue of Indian gaming may be less one of jurisdiction than of money. Casinos located on trust land and run by the tribes are not subject to state taxation. The inability to control or profit directly from gambling facilities located within state borders, especially in a time of fiscal constraint, may increase state opposition to Indian gaming. The State of Connecticut, initially opposed to the Mashantucket Pequot Foxwoods casino, reversed its position after the U.S. Supreme Court denied *certiorari* in the state's appeal of a lower court's approval of the casino, and after the Mashantucket Pequot agreed to pay the state $30 million for FY 1993 and $113 million for FY 1994 out of its slot-machine revenues. In return for a cut of the profits, Connecticut promised the Pequot the sole right to operate slot machines in Connecticut, much to the consternation of some non-Indians.

State government helped to bring the problem of Indian gaming and gambling on itself. States that adopted lotteries as a means of raising revenue conveyed a mixed message. The message said it was acceptable to gamble in order to refurbish the coffers of state government but not for other reasons, particularly to benefit Indian tribes. The moral ambivalence of Idaho, Arizona, and Connecticut weakens their arguments against gaming. As the appeals court noted in *Seminole* v. *Butterworth,* the state cannot have it both ways, gambling is either prohibited or regulated. If it is regulated, then it falls under federal, not state, jurisdiction.

The Federal Government and IGRA

The position of tribes in the federal system is still unclear, despite 205 years of U.S. history. Unlike states, Indian tribes are not part of the constitutional construction of the United States. Other than referring to "Indians not taxed" in Article I and the Fourteenth Amendment for purposes of enumeration for apportionment, the only reference to tribes is in the commerce clause: Congress shall have power "to regulate commerce with foreign nations, and among the several states, and with the Indian tribes." The ambiguity of the meaning of the Indian commerce clause as to what position Indian tribes held in relation to the federal system led to federal Indian policy that fluctuated widely through the centuries.

Indian tribes started out equivalent to the national government when treaties were made between sovereign nations. In 1831, the tribes dropped to "domestic, dependent nations." By 1886, the tribes were ignored as political institutions, and Indians became individual wards of the federal government. Tribes were again acknowledged in 1934 through the Indian Reorganization Act, which gave tribes powers similar to those of city councils. Today, the Congress and the courts are equating tribal power with state power. Tribes have thus run nearly the full gamut of possible relations to the federal government. If there is one constant in terms of federal Indian policy, it is that the Congress has claimed plenary power over the Indians.

IGRA does not change that pattern. The Congress had the option of leaving the gambling issue solely within the purview of the tribes after *Cabazon,* or of giving it to the states through legislation similar to P.L. 280; instead, the Congress chose to determine what forms of gambling would be regulated by which governments and then placed the federal government (in the form of the district courts and the commission) as the official arbiter in all matters of controversy. That preemption of regulatory responsibility has, as previously mentioned, led to enforcement problems and controversies among all parties over what constitutes Class II and Class III gaming. Enforcement has also been slowed because it took several years for the National Indian Gaming Commission to issue its regulations and begin operating. The issue of enforcement was critical for the Justice Department because the provisions of IGRA were "much less restrictive than the Department had originally recommended."

Federal control over Indian gaming has been a mixed blessing for the tribes. On the one hand, it prevented state restrictions and control over tribal economies, thus allowing economic gains otherwise unlikely. On the other hand, tribes still depend on the discretionary will of the Congress for the future of Indian gaming. Senator Daniel Inouye (D-HI), chairman of the Senate Select Committee on Indian Affairs and a longtime friend of Indian tribes, held hearings in 1993 on revisions to IGRA. In November of that year, he announced that all sides were close to compromise; however, the agreement has not yet been reached. As long as the issue is still under consideration by the Congress, the tribes are apprehensive.

Russell Barsh has argued that the recent trend in the Congress of returning power to the tribes is based less on recognition of tribal sovereignty and more on fiscal cost-shifting in order to relieve some of the federal budget deficit. He asserts that by giving tribes the power of self-determination over economic matters (e.g., Indian gaming or self-governance legislation), the Congress saves money. "It is clear that Congress is not prepared to yield any real power to tribal councils, except in exchange for budgetary relief. In other words, Congress is willing to allow tribes to make more decisions for themselves as long as they are prepared to pay for them."

One should not assume that federal power in this case is directed only toward the Indian tribes. Federal preemption probably has caused even more frustration for state governments, which have lost nearly all jurisdictional and decisionmaking control over Indian gaming within their borders. It is significant that the Tenth and Eleventh amendments have been used by the states in opposition to Indian gaming; both of these amendments were originally intended to protect the states from federal intrusion.

Conclusion

Gambling under the Indian Regulatory Gaming Act has become a most unlikely issue on which questions of federalism and intergovernmental relations are debated. For tribes, gambling has become the "new buffalo" (i.e., a way of exercising tribal sovereignty through economic autonomy). State governments also see Indian gaming as a sovereignty issue—state sovereignty (i.e., the right of a state government to have a say in the forms of domestic policy enacted within its borders). Conflict has arisen between the tribes and states as each party has tried to define and delineate its legitimate jurisdiction over this issue. Only the federal government seemingly remains sure in its ability to control the future jurisdictional boundaries of tribal and state government over gaming.

Readings for Anne Merline McCulloch:

Not only does this reading focus on contemporary issues, but Indian gaming enterprises have become highly controversial in many parts of the country. As a result, scholars have little access to the data needed for careful analysis most of the time. One local study of the role of gaming in present Arizona is Shelby Jo-Anne Tisaale, *Cocopah Identity and Cultural Survival: Indian Gaming and Political Ecology of the Lower Colorado River Delta, 1850–1996* (Tucson: University of Arizona Press, 1996).